TAKI

TAKI

The Spectator Columns 2001–9

TAKI THEODORACOPULOS

Edited by
CHARLES GLASS

Foreword by
CHARLES MOORE

QUARTET BOOKS

First published in 2010 by
Quartet Books Limited
A member of the Namara Group
27 Goodge Street, London WIT 2LD

ISBN   978 0 7043 7192 7

Typeset by Antony Gray
Printed and bound in Great Britain by
T J International Ltd, Padstow, Cornwall

Contents

Foreword

Whenever a new editor of *The Spectator* is appointed, the first question he is asked is, 'Are you going to sack Taki?' But Taki is now on his seventh editor, and has been in post for nearly thirty-five years. How can this be?

There are, after all, many apparently good reasons for sacking the self-described 'poor little Greek boy'. People say that he is a racist, a snob, a vulgarian, a sex-maniac, a cad, a fascist and a drunk. When I was Taki's (second) editor, he went to prison for bringing cocaine into the country, and I was assailed with letters from readers telling me to get rid of him. I replied that he was our *High Life* correspondent, and so one could not really complain if, now and again, he got high.

It was a flip answer, but I was trying to make a real point. You don't read Taki as you read a sermon (in the unlikely event that you do read a sermon). Taki writes about all those things which men often secretly feel but rarely dare to say. He expresses the childish desire for attention, yachts, champagne, parties, gambling, women; and he has always found ways of getting what he wanted (see, for example, *Taki's Ten Rules for Playing Away*, p. 240). He knows intimately the places where these pleasures are to be found and the people that provide or enjoy them. He is an expert in his chosen field, with more than half a century of experience: he is to the high life what Henry Kissinger is to foreign policy. As the years pass, he has never given up. Instead of becoming bitter or monastic, he has pursued his chosen career as a playboy with relentless dedication. Some of his best columns are about the difficulties of doing this when you are over seventy. They are very poignant. As George Galloway once said to Saddam Hussein, 'Sir, I salute your courage, your indefatigability'. Unlike Saddam, Taki is honest too.

One way you can tell a writer is worth reading is that he produces sentences which no one else could have written. This anthology is full of them. Here is Taki on Juan Peron, whom he regards as a dreadful Leftist: 'Franco should have suicided him, but he was too decent a man to do it.' Here he is on a car journey to Italy with Lord Lambton, throughout which, while telling Taki how handsome he is, Lambton is making surreptitious attempts on Mrs Taki's thighs. 'A cheap feel took precedence over friendship,' exclaims Taki, before adding, 'and why not?'

It may surprise people to know that Taki is the most conscientious of all *The Spectator's* columnists. Except when his jail-term prevented him, he has filed every week throughout his time. The single occasion when a column did not appear was when it was libelous from beginning to end. He clearly believes that he has a duty to his readers, and many of them respond with fervent devotion. It is a foolish editor who gets in the way of a relationship like that.

Critics say that Taki is indefensible. In our cowardly, legalistic and hypocritical culture, I say that it is precisely because Taki is indefensible that he should be defended.

Charles Moore

2001

Rich Rewards

Saturday, 24 February 2001
Rougemont

The jet-set is in mourning and, like Electra, it becomes it. Marc Rich has called off his Las Vegas-theme party in St Moritz this weekend, which will force a few Englishmen in the Engadine to commit an unnatural act and pay their own bill. The reason given was the bad publicity and the hounding of the host by the press. The last time Marc Rich called off a party was in Spain, about five or six years ago. His Mossad-trained bodyguards were tipped off that his private jet would be forced down the moment it left Swiss airspace by Yankee F-16s, so he stayed put. No reason was offered back then. Although the US government was out to grab him, Rich had the proverbial ace up his sleeve. By giving lotsa moolah to Israel, he was being fed information by Mossad that even the top brass of the Pentagon weren't getting. Mossad knew that the snatch was on by listening in on the Americans. They tipped off the fugitive fraudster, a move that eventually made Bill Clinton rich, pun intended.

Last week I wrote in my own 'Taki's Top Drawer' that, as America was not as yet Israel-occupied territory, the 200 million Rich gave to those nice guys, who attack rock-throwing youth with armour-piercing missiles, should not count as philanthropy where America is concerned. To my great annoyance the sentence never appeared. When I rang in an Orlando Furioso mood, I was told by a very polite flunky that 'we were trying to protect you, this is New York.'

Well, there you have it. Marc Rich I have never met and hope never to. I once went out to dinner following a Norman Mailer book party with a Greek called Olga and Norman's son, my buddy Michael Mailer, the boxer and film producer, who happened to have an Estée Lauder blonde (common but not too bad) in tow. The blonde thought my girl was from the lower classes because she (Olga) stood up to shake hands with her. She snubbed her throughout the evening. (Actually, she's a Greek royal.) We went to Elaine's, and after lotsa boozing, I asked the blonde her name. 'Daniella Rich,' came the answer. Being well oiled, I told her it was not her fault her father was a Christian-basher who had caused more harm to Broadway and the theatre in general than Bomber Harris had to Dresden. She looked nonplussed. 'My father hates the theatre, never goes' – or words to that effect. Then the penny dropped. Papa was not fat Frank Rich of the *New York Times*. Papa was the crook who was to pull off the impossible: drag the whore Bill Clinton down to his level. But back to the party which never was.

A pretty American girl called Serena Boardman was coming all the way from Noo Yawk for it. When I asked her whether she would go to a party given, say, by John Gotti, the dapper Don, as the Big Bagel tabloids refer to him, she told me it was not the same thing. 'Yes,' I said. 'Gotti is dumb and in jail; Rich, the far bigger criminal and traitor, is in St Moritz.' That's the way it goes, sports fans. The truly big crooks get away with it and go to St Moritz and Gstaad; the little guys go to the big house up the river. And if any of you believe that Rich has not passed money under the table to Bill Clinton, then you should also believe that I'm Monica Lewinsky's mother.

Marc Rich, however, has done us a favour. By bribing everyone and sundry, he managed to expose the side of Clinton so many leftists and liberals refused to see. He also proved what we, *soi-disant* anti-Semites for daring to protest about soldiers shooting at kids, always knew. The way to Uncle Sam's heart runs through Tel Aviv and Israeli-occupied territory. Rich and Clinton deserve each other. Both make everyone around them seem bigger.

No Justice

Saturday, 10 March 2001
Rougemont

This is by far the saddest column I've written in twenty-four years, and certainly the most frustrating. It has to do with a judicial decision that mocks justice, a ruling that renders null and void the *cri de coeur* of a young woman from beyond the grave.

Let's take it from the start. Four years ago, an incredibly beautiful girl killed herself aged twenty, leaving a note naming the man she claimed had sexually abused her from the age of twelve to fourteen. She was Philippine Lambert, daughter of Baron Philippe Lambert and his wife Marion. The Lamberts are an old and aristocratic Belgian banking family. The accused is Vincent Meyer, president and benefactor of the Philharmonia Orchestra. The extremely rich Meyer is the grandson of André Meyer, of the Lazard Frères banking dynasty; a man who befriended the Lamberts, and who 'was in our house almost daily over a period of three years, was glued to us, in fact, speaking highly of the way we lived and how well we were bringing up our children . . . '

Meyer was accused of rape and sexual misconduct towards a minor and arrested by the Swiss authorities shortly after Philippine's suicide. He has always denied any wrongdoing but was remanded in custody for three months and was eventually released on £2.5 million bail, one of the largest ever demanded by a Swiss court.

Earlier this year, however, the Swiss court ruled that he will not stand trial, despite the public prosecutor's statement that the charges against Meyer 'were not inconsiderable'. The case was a difficult one from the start. The court was anxious to have 'witnesses of the acts' of abuse. Child molestation does not take place in public and in front of witnesses. What was most important, in my opinion, was that the facts reached the statute of limitations – everything that took place before September 1992 was not permitted in court. The horror of it is that had Philippine died two days earlier, things may have been a lot different. She died on 28 August, and the Swiss law was changed on 1 September. The case was filed on 2 September. A less lenient law would have applied had the case been filed forty-eight hours earlier.

Space prohibits me from writing about Philippine and her family in depth. They don't come any better, as far as I'm concerned. Philippine was a hauntingly beautiful child, with rare looks that I've never before encountered. Henry, her brother, is working with refugees in Bosnia, and is a very good-looking and well-rounded young man. Philippe and Marion I've known always and I am immensely fond of them.

Soon after the case began all sorts of rumours went around, mostly about Marion. This was Geneva society at its most vicious. Friends of Meyer were said to be spreading the rumours, although I have suspicions of my own where they started. As my friend Dominic Dunne wrote in Vanity Fair, 'Marion has been known to be difficult.' (Dunne is himself a grieving father of a murdered daughter.) That she is, but since when is a mother trying to win justice for her daughter judged to be difficult?

When I first broke the story as Atticus in the *Sunday Times* four years ago, I received letters from old and decent friends of mine vouching for Meyer. I tried to be open-minded. Meyer was, after all, vigorously denying all charges. But it is not up to us to judge innocence or guilt in such situations. That is what our legal systems should do. Meyer may be innocent, but when he is accused in a dying girl's last words and has admitted having a physical and sensual (though not sexual) relationship with Philippine when she was fourteen years old, he must at least be tried. What the Lambert family have experienced in Switzerland is not justice.

The Bagel Beckons

Saturday, 31 March 2001
New York

Just before I left for the Big Bagel, Charlie Glass (known as the London Lothario since his appearance with Goldie Hawn and her daughter at the BAFTA awards) came to stay with me in Rougemont. After a couple of days I noticed the Swiss farmers had changed. No more ruddy looks and mud-splattered boots, no leather plus-fours, green alpine hats, traditional pipe and gruff manners. Some of them even looked scared of their cows. Well, not to worry.

The so-called Swiss peasants who hung around my place for days turned out to be paparazzi and hacks sent over by august publications such as the *Globe* and the *National Enquirer*. They were looking to catch Goldie and her daughter Kate Hudson in *flagrante delicto* with the London Lothario, but all they got was Taki and Charlie going on long romantic walks as the snow had done a Lucky Lucan.

How wonderful the hacks are. They simply never get it right. As the great Yogi Berra said, 'It's *déjà vu* all over again.' Charlie Glass is a childhood friend of Goldie's, having grown up with her in El Lay. There is as much hanky-panky going on between them as there are virgins in Hollywood, and Goldie, as nice a woman as one can encounter, called Charlie to apologise for the inconvenience. When the hacks could have had a story, they were literally out to lunch – or perhaps too busy filing phoney expenses to notice.

Some time ago the London Lothario was cautiously stepping out with Rachel Weisz, the star of Enemy at the Gates, in which she shoots and kills hundreds of terrified Wehrmacht soldiers. The romance fizzled out because Charlie has a terrible habit, which he got from me, of seeing carnal beauty as visible evidence of spiritual beauty. But that's not always the case where his girls are concerned, ergo the problem with Charlie, although I have yet to find one of mine lacking in both – and if you believe that you'll believe . . .

Mind you, the Bagel is fun to come back to after three months of staring at cows wondering if they're mad or not. There are a few parties lined up already, starting with a Henry Kissinger and Oscar de la Renta blast to celebrate Ahmet and Mica Ertegun's fortieth anniversary. Of marriage, that is. Ahmet is the greatest Turk since Ataturk, and a friend of very long standing. I don't suppose Marc Rich will be attending, nor Bill Clinton, both gents being rather busy nowadays with splitting up the loot.

And speaking of loot, those who are campaigning for a cut in the death tax are not impressed with the worries of Bill Gates, George Soros and Warren Buffett. The three, as well as Paul Newman, are scared stiff that repealing the death tax might discourage rich people from giving money to charitable foundations. But as with most things George Soros says and does, he is being disingenuous.

The foundations in America are mostly private slush funds that the super-rich use to promote liberal causes and to enhance their own political influence. For example: Bill Gates put $25 billion into his private foundation, which is run by his old man, and when the billionaire dork dies, the $25 billion will be exempt from the estate tax. The same estate plan applies to Buffett, the Fords, the Rockefellers, and Soros. Billions and billions have escaped death taxes through the foundation scam, foundations that are notorious for promoting left-wing causes.

Oh yes, I almost forgot. Bill Clinton is also working the foundation scam, with his Little Rock library (which incidentally does not contain any books), raising tax-deductible money from ladies who lunch like Denise Rich and I'd hate to think who else. These tax-deductible funds allow crooks like the Clintons to live and travel in the style that even I have not been accustomed to, at taxpayers' expense. So, next time you read about a death tax being a tax cut for the rich, don't be fooled yet again by scam artists like Soros. Ninety per cent of federal estate tax returns filed are for estates of $2.5 million or less. These are the mugs that aren't rich enough to escape death taxes through private foundations, so their small businesses or farms are sold to pay up to 55 per cent rates.

It was a good try Paul, Bill, George and Warren (I'm amazed at the company the last name keeps; I thought he was a good guy) and you did manage to fool most of the people, but the poor little Greek boy has got your number.

Generation Game

Saturday, 14 April 2001
New York

His other talents aside, the great Talleyrand was known for having seduced three generations of the Duchesse of Dino, granny first, then her daughter, finally granny's granddaughter. I only know of one other, an American, who has managed this feat, but I'm certainly not going to name him as he's a gent and quite elderly.

Although it may shock some of you, I find absolutely nothing wrong with seducing different generations. After all, what's good for a mother is surely good for the daughter, too. Needless to say, in the natural progression of things, a mother should precede a daughter, but sometimes the opposite happens. Well, actually, in my case it didn't happen, although the Kissinger, Santo-Domingo and de la Renta party for the Erteguns was by far the best bash I've been to in a hell of a long while, despite my lack of success with a lady called Pauline. But first a few words about the party.

They say a good mix, good music and young people make a party, but this one lacked the latter and was a far greater success as a result. The dance floor was packed throughout the evening because people my age know how to dance the samba and the rumba and the fox-trot and the merengue, and do not sit around on their arses staring at the ceiling as juventus tends to do. The music was to die for, the real thing, not those Zulu ululations we're used to hearing in sweaty nightclubs. Mind you, if one fails under such perfect conditions, one should hang up one's jock, which I'm seriously thinking of doing.

Alas, Pauline said thanks but no thanks, despite tripping the light fantastic on the dance floor. In order to gain her confidence I told her I was a cross-dresser and gay, but I never got to first base. Having stepped out with her daughter for a while in the past may have put her off, but I doubt it. Oh well, you know how these upper-class Americans are, puritanical and all that. Perhaps I should stick to Europeans. From past experience, mothers almost never mind when I go after their daughters, and daughters certainly don't care if I chase their mothers.

Failing to seduce, of course, is a fate worse than death, especially for a Greek. As a child, while learning the myths, I was taught in no uncertain terms that Helen of Sparta, the greatest beauty ever, became Helen of Troy because she was abducted, not seduced by Paris. It was rubbish, of course. In the Iliad she is treated tenderly by Homer, and there is a touching episode in Book Three where the old men of Troy agree that it was worth fighting a war to keep her in Troy. In the *Odyssey* she is reconciled with Menelaus and domesticated as a housewife. The first person who admitted that Helen had voluntary hanky-panky with Paris was my German nanny, who had obviously read Euripides. Old Euripides was as hostile to Helen as Aeschylus is in Agamemnon, blaming her for the disaster she caused. The Romans were just as bad. Virgil, Ovid and Seneca thought her morally weak, and Dante put her among the lustful in the swirling storm of his Second Circle.

Being seduced, in other words, was considered not cricket by the Ancients, but I suppose only because Helen was married, something Pauline is not. (She's a widow.) Zeus, however, was allowed free rein to seduce to his heart's content. Accounts of his quarrels with the jealous Hera, who was his wife and also his sister (both being children of Kronos), were legendary. Zeus seduced everyone, and if occasionally rebuffed à la Taki, he would turn himself into

Ganymede – the male equivalent of Helen of Troy in looks – and then score freely. Hera got so pissed off with Ganymede, she abducted him to Olympus and turned him into a butler serving the gods. Poor Ganymede. Not only didn't he do anything wrong, someone else got laid by impersonating him.

Ironically, I tried this once myself. I spotted this beautiful girl in a nightclub while talking to a friend of mine who is as good-looking a man as I've seen. I asked him to go and chat her up and tell her his name was Taki. 'What do you hope to gain by this?' he asked. 'Just get her telephone number and I'll do the rest,' I told him.

My plan was simple. After a while, over the telephone or in a letter, I would admit to her my deception, declare undying love and ask her to meet the real Taki. The plan didn't work. As soon as my friend said his name was Taki she said: 'No it isn't, you're Julio Mario and you are thirty years younger than Taki.'

Now to find somebody Pauline doesn't know, preferably a modern Ganymede.

Roman Holiday

Saturday, 2 June 2001
Rome

Throughout history, visitors to the Eternal City have always found more or less what they deserved to find. To romantic sensualists like myself, it's Roman fever, the sentimental dangers Edith Wharton warned our great-grandmothers about. To stuffed shirts like Henry James, Rome was an awakening of the senses. 'At last – for the first time I live! For the first time I know what the picturesque is.' Byron, the man who gave his life in the cause of Greek liberty, went one better. 'As a whole, ancient and modern, it beats Greece, Constantinople, everything.' And a young Edward Gibbon wrote to his father that 'I am really almost in a dream.' (He then went on to write that he hoped for the happiness of mankind there would never be another state such as Rome again.) Henry Wadsworth Longfellow was rendered delirious, whereas Tennessee Williams was 'downright embarrassed' over the abundance of young men eager to service him.

Where does one start? The Forum, the Capitol, Piazza della Rotonda, Piazza Navona, the Campo de'Fiori, Piazza di Spagna, St Peter's? The Borghese Gardens, the various palazzos, the great churches, the Villa Medici, the Colosseum, the fountains, obelisks, museums? Classical Rome, mediaeval Rome, Renaissance and Baroque Rome, even Mussolini's Rome? Like Tosca, *Vissi d'arte, vissi d'amore!*

Mind you, had a past Taki been crucified on the Appian Way like Spartacus, I might not be as effusive in my praises, but then I've never been a revolutionary. Gibbon's strong emotions when he arrived in the Eternal City kept him from sleeping. He stood in the ruins of the forum where Romulus, Tully and Caesar had stood before him, and decided to write about the fall of the empire. As Chilton Williamson Jr wrote, 'In expressing hope that, for mankind's sake, no new Rome would ever arise, Gibbon expressed his ambivalence on the subject that became his life's work.' Poor Gibbon. He'd already swallowed all that nonsense of democracy and mother of parliament bullshit. In imperial Rome, the troops had more loyalty to the generals than to distant politicians, giving men like Sulla, Pompey and Caesar the muscle to seize political power. Give me MacArthur over Truman, Patton over Roosevelt, von Runstedt over Hitler any day. Democracy, after all, means only one thing, demagoguery, and anyone who tells you different must live in Switzerland.

Just look at what's happening in England and weep. Next week Blair and his gang of thieves and liars will be returned to power by a populace so zonked out by tabloids, bad football and downmarket TV that they could, Caligula-like, have appointed their cats or dogs to run in their place, and still win. But back to the splendour that is Rome and my four unforgettable nights there.

I arrived last Thursday, as dusk was falling. My friend Charles Price, son of the American ambassador to London during the Reagan years, was marrying Drusiana Sforza Cesarini, daughter of Ascanio Sforza, as grand a ducal name as one can find among Italian nobility. Ascanio and Monica Sforza have another attribute. They are as nice as they are noble, and for once nice guys finish first. The Sforzas are loaded because Ascanio has fought to keep his land from the crook politicians who have been trying to take it away from him for six hundred years or so.

As Americans tend to say, their house on Via Garibaldi is not to be believed. Overlooking all of Rome and surrounded by a large garden, we danced on one of the terraces, ate on another, and snuck into the bushes of yet a third one. I danced to wonderful old Italian tunes non-stop and with everyone brave enough to try it. No one has made me feel more at home than Ascanio and Monica, and – believe you me – I was at times out of line. I ran into my childhood friend Giovanni Volpi and reminisced into the night. Count Volpi is the son of Mussolini's finance minister, and his palazzo in Venice is famous for its balls. At the end of the most nostalgic evening ever, I felt like Prince Salina in the Gattopardo, watching the young and beautiful dancing, knowing that there is no more room in this crude world for civilised living, just master-of-the-universe glitzy showing-off.

Next day I gave a lunch for about twenty friends, ran in the Borghese gardens to get rid of some of the alcohol, and off I went to the Palazzo Taverna for Charles and Carol Price's formal dinner for the newlyweds. Another great night. Then came the big one. The ceremony took place in the Sforza summer house, an 1eighteenth-century marvel outside Rome in Porto, the Roman port where the victorious Caesar arrived from Egypt with a Greek queen in tow. The property is unsurpassed in beauty, full of wildlife, flowers, fish and fowl, and after the lunch we were taken by horse-drawn carriages to watch three falconers put on an unforgettable show on horseback. That night, Astrid Kohl, a friend of the couple, gave the Dolce Vita ball at Palazzo Lancellotti, lit in a manner that only a Renaissance artist could equal. I introduced my twenty-five-year-old daughter to sons of friends of mine, young and eligible bachelors like Paolo Borghese, Guido Torlonia and Alessandro Attolico. She'll probably end up a Roman princess, which beats living in Oldham any day. But then I flew from Rome to London, which was like going to bed with Ava Gardner and waking up next to Polly Toynbee.

Instant Happiness

Saturday, 14 July 2001
St Tropez

Happiness is getting it wrong last week in predicting Goran wouldn't make it. Happiness is seeing a big-time athlete crossing himself before the most important point of his life (and, alas, losing it three times in a row). Happiness is being in St Tropez, on board a 1930s classic sailing boat, on calm waters with strong winds.

And now I'll tell you about unhappiness. It's being anchored in a quiet bay and having ghastly people riding grotesque jet-skis all round one's boat. It's seeing nouveau-riche slobs relaxing on refrigerator-on-steroids type boats in the harbour and having to decide what's uglier – the human cargo or the carrier. It's going to the Byblos nightclub and seeing men and women my age sipping champagne, and not a young person within a mile except my son and his girlfriend. Last but not least, it's going to Club 55, the only game in town where lunch is concerned, and running into fat American financiers smoking large cigars and talking billions. But back to happiness.

Nigel Nicolson, writing in the *Sunday Telegraph,* asked hypothetically whether a player serving underhand on match point was half cheating. He made his point, but in real life the receiver would run up and put it away for a winner. In fact, the great Budge Patty did this twice on match point against Freddy Huber of Austria in the 1956 and 1957 Wimbledon first round, both times for fun, not profit, Huber winning both points.

Incidentally, this was one great review issue. I loved Gyles Brandreth's take on celebrity: 'You would like to be extraordinary, but you sense that, fundamentally, you aren't, so you try to associate with those who are.' Hear, hear! I have always hated groupies, especially since the Sixties and Beatlemania, as opposed to hero-worship of the military. I can understand genuflecting in front of Patton, but Eminem? The mind reels. I know a man who inherited millions whose knees tremble whenever he finds himself within a mile of a celebrity. Some think it's because he is extremely obese, and the knees can't take it, but I know better. According to Brandreth, celebrities make groupies seem more important, and it certainly makes sense. When was the last time you saw a good-looking or talented person sucking up to some zombie celebrity?

Mind you, this is where a boat comes in handy. One fills it up with beautiful girls, a few male friends like Charlie (Casanova) Glass and, if one's Greek, also the family, and, presto, instant happiness in St Tropez. I must have been a fool all these years to stay in Greece and Gstaad. This is where the action is. For sixty-four years I've suffered horrible deprivations, but no longer. For my big sixty-fifth next month I've decided enough is enough. I'm giving myself a great head-turner of a boat, the first time I've done this – pay for it, that is. My first three boats were paid for by Daddy, the last one inherited from him. The next Bushido will be Bushido number V, but for reasons known only to myself, the Roman numeral will not appear.

Needless to say, it takes getting used to. This is why I'm on a charter right now. In Gstaad and in Greece one hides behind tall hedges and private islands. On a boat, even going to the loo is a semi-private function, especially on a sailer. Never mind. The other day, with the poor little Greek boy as skipper, we were running good, as Papa Hemingway would have said, with a steady hand on the tiller, as some pompous politician would use as the title to his memoirs. Twelve to fourteen knots windward, we sailed by a Maxi lying low in the water and her owner told me afterwards we were moving like a train. (The doghouse and all that, as compared to flush decks in modern races.)

Cell Mates

Mercifully, the worst is over for Jeffrey Archer by now. He's been inside for a week, and the first week in jail is by far the worst. When I went down for cocaine possession, I had the bad luck to be the first case of the day, thus I had about eight hours to while away in a tiny six by four cell. Seventeen years later, I still remember the feeling of disgust that came over me once I was taken down from the courtroom. How could I have been such a fool, so recklessly stupid, and so on?

The second-worst part is also behind Lord Archer. The first night in the nick one does not sleep a wink, except just before dawn, and then suddenly the bell jars one back to reality. The processing phase – at least back in 1984 – goes as follows. The prisoner is fingerprinted and ritually divested of his outer self except for a watch and a small radio with one frequency. Then comes the cold shower and the issuing of two pairs of blue jeans, two blue-striped cotton shirts, two pairs of grey socks, one sweater, one denim jacket, one toothbrush, a small mirror, one pair of plastic black shoes, one towel, two blankets (soiled and dirty), two sheets and one pillowcase. (Again, this is how it was in Pentonville, yours truly never having made it to Belmarsh.)

Lord Archer's one great advantage inside will be the same as one great advantage outside: his intelligence. Judging from the types I met in Pentonville, criminals are not very shifty upstairs; in fact they're downright dumb, predictable, cowardly and prone to whingeing. One of the great misconceptions about prison is that it is a place full of hard guys: they're hard all right, but only when they're three against one, just like in London's violent Belgravia and Mayfair streets.

Mind you, anyone who thinks that a multi-millionaire writer and lord to boot will be liable for more than the average ration of bullying and abuse has got it all wrong. Even his accent will not be a disadvantage. Prisoners are notorious social climbers. During my first week in Pentonville a small riot broke out when George Best arrived fresh from having beaten up a copper. Every thief and bank robber wanted to rub shoulders with George, the nick being a microcosm of outside, and a celebrity as sought after as in Hollywood. The warders will have versed themselves in the grand history of their new inmate. Even if they won't exactly love a lord, they will be extremely fair with him. In fact I'm certain Jeffrey Archer will do just fine. The first three months will be tough, then he'll settle into a routine and time will fly.

When I was doing bird, I was not allowed to write or keep a diary; I kept one by writing in between the lines of the hundreds of letters of support I received. One is searched on the way out, so I smuggled my diary out with an American lawyer who came from the Bagel for a visit. Not being allowed to write while in jail makes absolutely no sense. Unless rules have changed, that is. Reading is also a no-no in prison. The so-called library in the Ville was two cells knocked into one, with most of the books being cowboy westerns. The librarian was by tradition gay, and the books had all been masturbated in. The screws thought it quite funny.

Needless to say, I am on Lord Archer's side. My heart goes out to his family and to him, just as it did when my friend Jonathan Aitken went to jail. Back then, the scum at the Guardian ululated with delight, calling the fallen man every adjective they could think of. Unlike Jonathan, Jeffrey Archer I hardly know. I have never enjoyed his hospitality, and have spoken to him and Mary only twice, I believe. Yet what I find outrageous and anti-Christian is the vilification, demonization and public ignominy he is being put through by the very people whose talents lie mostly in entrapment, lies, filing false expenses and inventing – namely the Fourth Estate. Talk about duplicity. And who the hell is Robin Cook, an adulterer himself, to announce that Archer should not be allowed in the House of Lords?

The owner of the Star and Express became rich through porn, a far greater crime, as far as I'm concerned, than anything Archer did. Another clown bleats in a broadsheet how he knew all about Jeffrey's lies back in 1987 but was not allowed to proceed by his editors. Yeah, sure, and I would have won Wimbledon but for a bad call in the first round. In any other country Archer would have apologised to his wife, admitted having had nookie with a prostitute, and got on with his public life. In hypocritical Britain he had to lie, and now he has had to pay the price. An unfair one. Potts made a mockery of the law. Four years is a bad joke. Clinton perjured himself through-out and perverted the course of justice and is being feted around the world and getting paid millions. Archer's in jail, and the vultures are circling, but my prayers will be for Jeffrey and his family.

Age Concern

Saturday, 11 August 2001
Rougemont

Bob Hope defined old age as the time when the candles cost more than the cake. This Saturday I hit sixty-five, and I've cancelled the cake. In fact, like Henny Youngman's grandmother, I might be turning sixty-five but I still don't need glasses. I drink straight out of the bottle. This is the bad news. The good is that Carol Iannone, a writer for *Taki's Top Drawer*, had this to say in last week's *New York Press*: 'Ironically, the attraction of young women to older and often married men may actually be a misguided attempt to capture some degree of this male-female complementariness. Women have always had a tendency to be drawn to men significantly older than themselves, of course, as attested to by certain famous literary couples such as Emma and Mr Knightley, Kitty and Levin, Scarlett and Rhett.' (Whoa, Carol, the poor little Greek boy as Rhett? Why even the saintly Ashley would double over on that one.)

She goes on to say that the age gap is widening to an alarming degree. Young women now go out with men old enough to be their fathers and grandfathers. Which, as I said, is the best news since Bill Clinton caught the clap. 'What was once a joke in mediaeval literature is becoming more common in the late modern era.' Hooray for the modern era! For the last couple of decades boys have been brainwashed not to grow to become men, but to become women, ergo the need for the gentlemanly macho type. What self-respecting lady – and I do not include 'It' girls – would ever be seen dead with some man wearing a baseball cap backwards and looking androgynous at best? Take my word for it. Women do not like to be free and, always according to Carol Iannone, 'to engage in unimpeded self-definition.'

This is where I and others of my ilk come in. My purpose in life is to give a young woman a true sense of worth based on the fulfilment of her nature. The important part is not to play young. Take for example the recent marriage of Nixon Doorman, a man whose chief affairs are buying stocks and selling shares (with apologies to Hilaire Belloc) to Jackie Lane's little girl, thirty-three years younger than the arthritic groom. The age difference is a mere bagatelle. What's wrong is that Nixon Doorman dyes his hair, a sign of desperation if ever I came across one. My advice to oldies is: keep it white, keep it clean, keep it uncovered. Mix with her age group as well as your own. Do not buy a two-seater convertible, do not go for a honeymoon on the Riviera (the place is full of rich old men and poor young women, and they'll mistake her for a whore) and for God's sake do not get angry when people compliment you for having such a nice daughter, or granddaughter, as may be the case. Always act like the Sicilian widower who at ninety-eight married a twenty-one-year-old, and told his outraged grandchildren who warned him about death, 'If she dies, she dies.'

One month or so ago I went to a dinner party and ran into Georgina Rylance, twenty-five, beautiful, intelligent, extremely well-read, and with a tiny scar on her knee. My opening line was that it's the imperfections in a girl that make her attractive. We got along fine until I asked her to come up and see me sometime. 'I'll come right now,' she said, and my heart leaped. It was 2.30 in the morning. But can I bring my sister?' We had a platonic lunch a couple of days later, and I'm still pining. Georgie Rylance is a hell of a girl. No 'It' publicity-seeking dummy. She set up Palimpsest

Productions all on her own, is appearing in her company's first production of *Alpha Beta* at this year's Edinburgh Festival, and has a part in the new Nigel Havers series *Manchild* – 'Otherwise, I'd come on your boat and to your birthday party.'

Oh well, perhaps I'll take her with me to Cuba this autumn, when I go to interview Fidel about women, something the (Greek ambassador assures me is a done deal. But I don't trust that old lecher. He might just put her in his harem, and goodbye Taki. So, no cake on Saturday, lotsa booze but not too many loose women (my family is here and they tend to throw water and alcoholic drinks on pretty young things who befriend me) but good music and many old friends. Next week I will tell you all about it, and also about time. Did you know that had I been born one trillion seconds ago, I would now be 31,001 years old? Almost as old as Nixon Doorman.

What a Sorry Lot

Saturday, 18 August 2001
London

I'm in London on my way to Cowes for the jubilee of the America's Cup. I shall be staying with my old friend Gianni Agnelli, that most charismatic of tycoons – in fact, the last tycoon. It is a funny thing, but modern-day CEOs leave a lot to be desired where personality and charisma are concerned. When I think of Jimmy Goldsmith, Lord Hanson, Gianni Agnelli, Aristotle Onassis, Jock Whitney, Bill Paley, Guy de Rothschild and others of their ilk, and compare them with today's sorry lot I want to curse the day Marc Rich was born.

What a bunch of wankers. Bill Gates, Henry Kravis, Ron Perelman, Richard Branson . . . the list is long but without style or substance.

Mind you, it's not just the business world. Just look at Hollywood. Once upon a time there was Gary Cooper, tall, elegant, soft-spoken, lover of beautiful women, a real man. Now we have a midget like Tom Cruise: grungy, inarticulate and a control freak. In the literary world, ditto. Papa Hemingway, Norman Mailer, Robert Ruark, John O'Hara, Scott Fitzgerald, two-fisted drinkers, hell-raisers, womanisers and stylists, as opposed to, well, you know who I mean, those *soi-disant* magic realists whose names are very well known but whose books remain unread. Not to mention newspaper tycoons. The Northcliffes as opposed to a pornographer like that *Express* fellow.

Even playboys ain't what they used to be. Rubirosa, Aly Khan, Gunter Sachs, Dado Ruspoli, Juan Capuro, the list is endless. Now we have pillow-biters posing as walkers, posing as men. Which brings me to the point I wish to make. Style is as elusive as it is because it's the opposite of pretence. A characteristic of style is that it suggests depth of character and commands attention without soliciting it. Gianni Agnelli personifies style. He is a noble-looking man with a face deeply lined by what Balzac called private defeats.

Style is the most abused word in the English language. It is usually attributed to fashionable people by those not in the know. Style, however, is impossible to buy and unthinkable to learn. It is of an abstract nature. One either has it or doesn't. It is typical of the world without style in which we live that Tony Blair and his mentor, scumbag Bill Clinton, have to resort to taking orders from pollsters and image-makers in order to govern. Can you imagine Winston Churchill asking some broken-down hack whether the public would go for a landing in Normandy with the expected heavy casualties? Can you see my hero George Patton whining like that wimp Wesley Clark that he is being mistreated by the suits in Washington? Style is intense conviction. It is not having regard for spurious morality. Not respecting power. It is welcoming into one's house anyone who's likable, not anyone who's powerful or rich. Finally, any person who is authentic and does not make a conscious try at being authentic has style.

Having got that off my chest, London in August – a first for the poor little Greek, no longer a boy – is surprisingly pleasant. Restaurants are half full, traffic is light, people less stressed. I noticed very few European faces, however. On Sloane Street, in fact, Europeans were a distinct minority, the few I saw working putting up scaffolding. Perhaps it is not such a bad thing. Reading what European-looking people have done to the unfortunate Hamiltons is enough to make me go and live in Grozny for the duration. How low, cruel and malicious can the British media sink? The Hamiltons have lost everything: their job, their house, their good name, their fortune. Yet the police arrest them on a charge that wouldn't stand up if Lavrenti Beria's daughter made it against a Soviet dissident. What the hell is going on? The *Daily Express* even went as far as to highlight the phony charges and call the Hamiltons evil. I only hope that both the police and the gutter press pay through their you-know-what, and the quicker the better.

A loyal reader, Monte Vanton, writes to me from afar about rape. 'Imagine what would be the fate of *Gone with the Wind* if Rhett Butler had first approached Scarlett and, coughing politely, said, "Excuse me Miss Scarlett, ahem, er, may I – I don't want to offend you – but, may I make love to you? I mean – er – go all the way?"' In other words, permission to proceed must be obtained in writing before penetration. The Hamiltons were a mile or so away and dining with friends when the woman was supposedly raped . . . even a militant feminist must admit it's most unlikely. Still, mud sticks, and the Hamiltons are stained for ever unless a colossal amount of damages is paid to remind future mud-slingers and blackmailers that people are innocent until proved guilty. Next week I will tell you about my birthday party and Cowes because in my anger I've run out of space.

Prole Position

Saturday, 8 September 2001
Rougemont

'Why, when those of us who actually fought the Germans in 1939–45 have long buried the hatchet, must our tabloid newspapers incite British yobs to hate them?' asks Lord Deedes in the *Daily Telegraph*. Well, that's an easy one, dear Bill. Proletarian values, for one, which are the same as Murdochian standards and morals, championed by men and women of almost cartoonish crudeness and vulgarity, the so-called British tabloid journalists of today.

Ironically, just after the England–Germany football match, my friend Charlie Glass and I watched *The Blue Max*, a golden oldie about a German squadron during the First World War. In the film, a working-class German soldier manages to be sent to flying school after two years in the trenches and eventually joins up with lots of vons, aristocratic Prussian flyers who see jousting in the sky as a form of sport rather than combat. Eager for fame and glory – twenty confirmed kills earns one the Blue Max, the highest decoration the Fatherland can bestow – the prole shoots down a defenceless British pilot whose gunner is dead. His squadron leader is appalled. 'This is not warfare,' he tells the oik. 'It's murder.' 'Just like the yobs we saw fighting in the streets,' said Charlie.

I know it's only a film, but that's how I've always understood warfare, as well as sport, to be. A couple of days later, England's numero uno gossip columnist, Nigel Dempster, arrived at Rougemont from Baden-Baden. 'Were the Germans pissed off?' I asked him. 'Not only did I not hear a word against England,' he told me, 'four people came up and congratulated me for the English victory.' Yes, but Nigel was attending a race meeting in Baden-Baden, full of well born and gracious Germans. In fact, one of the British commentators said to him how surprised he was to see so many well-mannered people.

Par for the course. Society today, especially in Britain, is shaped by the lowest standards of decency and by the nastiest people. With the fall of socialism, the progressive forces have placed most of their chips on the undermining of morality, and woe to those who believe in such tired-out values as fair play and magnanimity in victory. This is the Murdoch era, a crazy, over-hyped celebrity culture, with our entertainment so debased we now regard beauty as offensive.

Mind you, what puzzles me is the jingoism of the scummy tabloids against Germany on one hand, and their willingness to go along with Blair's surrender to the new class of international bureaucrat – as in the EU – on the other. A fat rodent of a gossip columnist, a man so ugly he would be refused entrance to an Albanian whorehouse, criticised Jemima Khan for continuing her father's crusade against the Euro. The rodent went as far as to make fun of the Goldsmith family's looks. Now if there's one family whose looks do not exactly need improvement it's the Goldsmiths. The mind boggles. Yet Jemima's message was right on target. 'Only experts are qualified to decide the direction of public policy and that ordinary people, be they dustmen or dukes, cannot be expected to grasp the complexities of modern politics . . . '

The Democracy Movement, whose president is Annabel Goldsmith and whose director is Robin Birley, Jemima's mother and brother respectively, is a going concern which I support. We have 300,000 signed-up members and two hundred branches. Unlike the tabloid scum, we have nothing against the Germans – my favourite army and people – but for the fact that Democracy Movement members believe that having won two wars against the Fatherland they have the right to remain British and independent of Berlin. It's very simple, really, but how are the yobs and oiks who 'read' Murdoch tabloids and watch Murdoch TV expected to understand? Like the prole pilot in *The Blue Max*, they have not been imbued with aristocratic values rooted in Christianity, ancient Greece and Rome. And Prussia, for that matter.

Needless to say the man who got it absolutely spot on was Frederick Forsyth, writing in Bill Cash's *European Journal*. The novelist does not mince his words. 'Within three years (1995) it was plain that the majority of the Tory party's members, and even a majority of the population as a whole had no taste at all for abolition of their national currency.' But John Major and the coterie around him refused to admit it. Major had to be the worst Tory premier ever. Firmly in the grip of Michael Heseltine and Kenneth Clarke, he did not have the guts to throw out the bums, despite the fact that he was sorely tempted. Heseltine, a traitor in my book, is fortunately now out of politics and alongside people like that Levy chappie in the House Blair built. But we still have oik Clarke. He should take out a video of *The Blue Max*. Duncan-Smith is the squadron-leader, and he's the prole.

The Chaos Theory

Saturday, 22 September 2001
Rougemont

Very long ago, the age of the Gods was challenged by the rise of individual men. Kings and heroes came onto the scene and one of them, Alexander the Great, even believed himself divine (only towards the end). Kings created oligarchies in which patricians and heroes fought to be number two, until freedom-loving types left the old continent and established a great republic across the pond. All's well that ends well, but not quite. As Gore Vidal wrote in an essay on Giovanni Batista Vico, published in the *New York Review of Books*:

> Thanks to man's nature, the established republics tend to imperial acquisitiveness, and so, in due course, these empire republics meet their natural terminus in, let us say, the jungles of Vietnam.

Mind you, although Gore Vidal's scholarship is on a par with Vico's, he has been known to be rather hard on Uncle Sam, especially about Vietnam and where big, bad conglomerates are concerned. The jungles of Vietnam did not defeat America; Congress and a reluctance to use its real power did. Vidal wrote his essay on chaos two years ago, and it makes more sense today than it did back then. In fact, it is as apt as anything I've read since Tuesday's suicide bombing:

> A characteristic of our present chaos is the dramatic migration of tribes. They are on the move from east to west, from south to

north. Liberal tradition requires that borders must always be open for those in search of safety or even the pursuit of happiness. In the case of the United States the acquisition of new citizens from all the tribes on earth has always been thought to be a very good thing. But, eventually, with so many billions of people on the move, even the great-hearted may well become edgy once we have gobbled up all the computer-proficient immigrants.

Hear, hear. Some on this side of the globe have called the third millennium the Christian era, which brings to mind Hitler calling on phantom divisions to defend Berlin in April 1945. Most of the world is not Christian at all, and even the Christian Western societies now live in a secular world of greed and porn. Christianity and Hollywood are a lousy mix. One billion three hundred million Muslims the world over are looking at what Uncle Sam will do over the coming weeks and months, and the poor little Greek boy predicts chaos. Here's Vidal again, this time quoting John Jay Chapman, one of America's greatest essayists. Chapman, who died in 1933, on Plato:

It has thus become impossible for anyone to read Plato's dialogues or any other creation of the Greek brain with real sympathy, for those creations speak from a wonderful, cruel, remote, witty age, and represent the amusements of a wonderful, cruel, remote, witty people, who lived for amusement, and for this reason perished.

On one side we have religious fanatics leading the people to sacrifice in return for a heaven of milk and honey and virgins, while on the other there's a remote, witty and sometimes cruel people bent on making money and on amusing themselves. I wonder who will perish first? Will our technology prevail? Or will it become the new theocracy, one which will turn all of us into its prisoners? And what happens when the mediaeval mullah casually dumps a bag of bacteria in powdery spores out of an aeroplane, an aeroplane he hasn't even had to hijack? Bioterrorism is the future, one that could foment political instability and total chaos. Barbarians used to toss plague-infected corpses over the walls of besieged cities, spreading the deadly infection inside the walls. Next time it will be easier, and much more deadly.

So, what is to be done? Dunno, is the answer. Americans are rightly howling for revenge, but against whom? All the computers and state-of-the-art high-tech will not produce incontrovertible proof of guilt. As a moral and democratic state America cannot kill innocents, as it has in the past. Hiroshima, Nagasaki and Dresden saw hundreds of thousands of old men, women and children incinerated. I never bought the canard that it was in order to save lives. Why, then, did we bomb Serbia? In order to save Albanian Muslim drug-runners, and a hell of a lot of mujahedin to boot?

No. What I think America should do now is to wait. Waiting for the counter-strike can be more unsettling for the guilty than a rainfall of Cruise missiles. Wait, get some good intelligence, lean on Israel to stop the settlements and harsh treatment of the Palestinians, and, once it's ready, bring the guilty to justice. Uncle Sam was never meant to be Alexander the Great, or Napoleon for that matter.

The Right Stuff

Saturday, 20 October 2001
New York

Exactly one month before 11 September, Arnaud de Borchgrave, big chief of UPI and known as the last of the great foreign correspondents, came and addressed the Gstaad Symposium, the poor little Greek boy's contribution to international relations. Arnaud spoke about the coming terrorist threat, and in no uncertain terms informed us that biological and even nuclear terror was on its way. 'It is not a matter of if it happens, but when it will happen,' said Arnaud. Although everyone was fascinated, and the audience asked him to stay on after the dinner, one man's reaction sticks in my mind. He was an Egyptian unknown to most of us. 'Why did you come all this way just to scare us? Haven't you any good news?' Arnaud dismissed him outright, as well he should have. The man afterwards complained that both the speaker and I had been rude, which was only half true. Arnaud had been very polite in his dismissal; I had been rude over the stupidity of the question.

Well, we all know what happened one month later. It wasn't chemical, biological or nuclear, but it was almost as bad. Last week, during my stop-over in London, I picked up James H. Jackson's *The Reaper*, a novel which is as prescient as it is topical. Jackson is a postgraduate in military studies and a specialist in conflict analysis. He writes like a dream. The book begins with a spectacular outrage in St Peter's in Rome. Little do the millions watching realise how much more horror there is to come. For the perpetrators are no ordinary madmen. They are Satan's legions attempting to provoke the free world into a final confrontation that will usher in the apocalypse.

Does this remind you of something? While on the subject of books, my old Yom Kippur buddy Bill Tuohy, a double Pulitzer Prize winner, has written a non-fiction story about *The Bravest Man*, the story of a US submariner in the Pacific War. A wonderful story and also very topical. The men who will now do the fighting are those with the right stuff, just like Tuohy's hero.

Later, at Heathrow, a not so heroic Pakistani woman working in security managed to lose my cufflinks as she opened my carry-on bag. I had words with her and a United Airlines supervisor happened to be present. She informed the pilot that a passenger had been mistreated by United security personnel. The pilot, a tall and imposing black American, Captain Williams, came to my seat, apologised for the airline, gave me his card and told me that unless I got back my property he would make sure that heads would roll. I asked him if he had been in the military. It was a dumb question. Of course he had been. Which brings me to another point I wish to make.

Airline pilots are among the most highly trained and carefully screened professionals in the world. The majority are military-trained with previous firearms experience. They are level-headed and stable. The nature of their job requires them to make critical decisions in less than a split second, and they perform very well, day after day, in stressful and sometimes life-and-death circumstances. Ergo, they are uniquely qualified to carry firearms. Just think about it. Wouldn't you trust the man in the cockpit with a gun? Yet there are always knaves and fools who object to anything that makes sense and might be beneficial to mankind. They argue that arming pilots could make hijacking situations worse. Horse feathers. If a terrorist boards an aircraft with a weapon, and he is the only armed person on board, he is in charge. As long as a pilot is armed, and securely locked in, he is in charge.

Air marshals, incidentally, are a pipe-dream. In order to place one on each flight we'd need at least 50,000 of them, and disarming them in the cabin would be easier than getting a gun away from a well-trained pilot locked in the cockpit. I say give guns to pilots like Captain Williams and see hijacking go the way of well-dressed passengers.

And now for some good news. I had a wonderful time in London, a place I swore I'd never set foot in until those jokers in power go back to the bed-sits they came from. Two nights of drinking in San Lorenzo, followed by a great party given by an Italian friend of my daughter's, where I ran into my old cricket adversaries: Zac Goldsmith, Tom Parker-Bowles, his cousin Ben, Victoria Aitken, Kate Reardon, the beautiful Berangere (and future Mrs Taki), you get the picture. Lily Phipps, another future Mrs Taki, was also there, but my daughter cramps my style and every sweet young thing got away. Just as well. My oldest English buddy, Charles Benson, is in hospital and cheerfully announced that he was on his last legs, pun intended, as he can't walk. Time is catching up on my old crowd. Here's some invaluable advice to young *Spectator* readers. Don't get old.

Beyond Belief

Saturday, 10 November 2001
New York

Human nature being what it is, it was only a matter of time before thoughts of misfortune turned to thoughts of money. Last week, lobbyists for Larry Silverstein, the developer who holds the lease on the World Trade Center, helped ensure that a bill passed by the House protects him from claims by victims of the attack and their families. Nobody has sued, thousands of bodies are entombed, there are tens of funerals daily, the area is a disaster, and Larry Silverstein is trying to stay rich. The reason his sharks were successfully lobbying the crooks in Congress was that Silverstein is trying to maximise the obligation of insurers, while trying to limit his liabilities. Larry the louse insists that the insurers – Swiss Re – pay him for two buildings. Swiss Re insists that the WTC as a whole was insured for $3.2 billion. The louse wants 7.2 billion big ones.

Unfortunately, Silverstein has the least to lose financially and the most to gain. Taking a leaf from another American patriot, Marc Rich, Larry the louse has hired Jack Quinn, the lawyer who got the Draft Dodger to pardon the fugitive fraudster in his last day in office. The lawyer, in turn, lobbied his pals in Congress to limit how much money victims can obtain from Silverstein's real-estate companies. The louse wants to obtain $7.2 billion and to limit his liability to $1 billion. It's called having it both ways, à la Marc Rich, but in view of the enormous human tragedy, what Silverstein really should get is a bullet up the arse – from some cop who lost his buddy in the rubble.

What a grotesque bunch. A greedy developer tries to enrich himself with the help of a lawyer who made his name by getting a crooked American president to pardon a fugitive traitor/fraudster billionaire. A film scenario such as this would be considered unbelievable even in Hollywood. Now, with the help of pols, Silverstein wants to cash in.

But not to worry. It will get worse. Trial lawyers, those nice guys who extorted billions from tobacco and gun manufacturers while the Clinton gang was in power, will now go after airlines and other corporations, and then after the city's fire department, the police and the emergency and rescue services, many of whom lost their lives. Mark my words. Trial lawyers are America's cancer, and the cancer will stop at nothing in pursuit of a buck.

The problem, of course, is not the greed and utter loathsomeness of certain people, but of democracy. America calls itself a free society but it does not provide protection against people like trial lawyers, Jack Quinn or Larry Silverstein. Last week I attended the funeral of Christian Reganhard, a twenty-eight-year-old judo black belt friend of mine. (One of the three martial arts friends I've lost.) Christian was very tough on the mat, and very gentle off it. He left the Marine Corps in January this year to join the fire department. Assigned to ladder 131 in Brooklyn, he died the way he lived, heroically, while trying to save others. His father, a retired police detective, called me to thank me for what I had written in the New York press about his son. As if I had done something heroic. Christian was the prototype Hollywood villain. He was patriotic, respectful of the flag, a gentleman, a churchgoer, with all the attributes the freaks and conmen of Hollywood and the Left detest. In fact, he and the rest of the fire fighters and cops who gave their lives embodied what the Clintons and their friends hated and looked down on.

As I said, it will get worse. And I wonder how Christian's parents (his mother still makes the hospital rounds, unable to accept his death) will feel when one day soon Larry Silverstein rakes in seven billion big ones, while they get at best the minimum of compensation. Probably the same as William Buckley's (the CIA agent tortured to death in Lebanon) family did when Marc Rich, who traded with and made billions from the very people who ordered their son to be tortured to death, was pardoned by the Draft Dodger. But I am preaching to the converted. Thanks to the IRA, thousands of ghosts rise from their white crosses thundering the word justice, but their murderers are walking around free. This is a very evil world full of evil people.

Payback Time

Saturday, 8 December 2001
New York

The very first article, not column, I wrote for *The Spectator* was in 1977. And it was about Greek paranoia. Yes, you guessed it. It was about plane-spotters, back then arrested near Kalamata just like the present bunch, their actions just as incomprehensible to the Greek mind as today's Peloponnese Twelve. The then sainted one, Alexander Chancellor, thought it rather quaint to have an Hellene comment, so I called my dad. 'Of course they are spies,' said my father. When I protested, he hung up on me, telling me that I was naive as well as a fool. Be that as it may. Greek fathers are not exactly known for spending their time patiently explaining life's complexities to their children. They operate, instead, from a vantage point of experience mixed with knowledge. One is told how things stand in black and white. At least that is how it was in 1976.

Twenty-five years later, we're back to square one. At the time of writing, the plane-spotters are doing bird, The Speccie is furious, the Greeks are bullying and the British government is helpless. Here I must declare an interest. Although I feel sorry for the plane-spotters, I think sixteen months in jail would do nicely, thank you. This is divine payback time, and don't let anyone tell you differently. When the saviour of Chile and Britain's best friend, General Augusto Pinochet, was Strawed by a judicial European Union subterfuge, Tony Blair claimed he was helpless to act. If 'modern reality is being usurped by the implementation of an antiquated legal system' in the birthplace of selective democracy, well, too bad. An antiquated legal system, in my book, is a lot better than a European Union system that thrives on coercive bureaucracy which controls our behaviour as well as thought. Of course the twelve schmucks are innocent, but they did go to Turkey first and they did accept Turkish baklava. What are the Greeks supposed to think? After all, in Greece eccentricity means making love to one's own wife, not walking around taking down the registration numbers of some rusting choppers.

When gangsters blew up my boat in 1994, the Greek socialist state was reluctant to chase them out. Once I flushed them out with private help, I had to produce the evidence. The fuzz did absolutely f— all. The individual means as much to a socialist state as the fact that Bill Clinton has the clap means to me. The November 17 terrorist group has been murdering people since 1975. Not a single terrorist has been caught because the socialists not only refuse to catch them but they are actually protecting them. This is a fact. The N-17 Marxist–Leninist terror cell was begun by Andreas Papandreou in Canada during the seven-year rule of the Colonels, 1967–1974. The government obviously does not wish to be exposed as having played footsie with this scum, and I hate to think who among the present cabinet was involved with the killers at the start.

Yes, I agree with last week's leader that the Greeks must grow up. But so should the Brits. I didn't hear Robin Cook read the riot act to the Greeks when Brigadier Stephen Saunders was murdered in cold blood. The Brits used diplomatic language, which is as useless as the Draft Dodger's oath in a court of law. As they say down on the farm, the chickens have come home to roost. Mind you, a couple of weeks in the nick never hurt anyone. Greek jails are better than British ones: apparently one can have girls come in, not that this might interest any of the Brits. I just can't imagine someone who plane-spots being mad about nookie.

Oh well, it could be worse. I did three months in Pentonville, General Pinochet was kept under house arrest for sixteen, and the Peloponnese Twelve will most likely do three weeks. Next week I will write my twenty-fifth Christmas double-issue column – actually the twenty-fourth, because Christmas 1984 was spent in the pokey. And the Peloponnese Twelve will be home by Christmas, at least I hope so.

Rats and Heroes

Saturday, 15 December 2001
New York

Howard Lutnick, head of Cantor Fitzgerald, the firm that lost more than six hundred employees at the World Trade Center on 11 September, would have made the greatest Scrooge ever – and that includes Scrooge the original. Days after the tragedy, the notoriously hard-edged Lutnick wept and promised to take care of the families of his 657 dead employees. Then he stopped their payroll. But like the Dickensian Scrooge he has now changed his mind. (Having been spat upon concentrates a man's mind.) All's well that ends well, but I'll believe it when I see it.

They say that this is the time for counting our blessings. The trouble is that we now have so many blessings that previous generations could hardly have dreamed about, we take them all for granted. In fact, we are more likely to count our grievances and the ways that others have been unfair to us.

Take, for example, the hustlers who are crying murder over President Bush's decision to invoke his power to establish military commissions to try enemy belligerents who commit war crimes. This is a given. They spare American jurors and judges the grave risks associated with terrorist trials. The order covers only foreign enemy war criminals. Yet the hustlers are up in arms. It's as if the constitution had been abolished and Bush had declared himself a tyrant for life. This in a country that prosecuted thousands of dissenters during the First World War, detained 120,000 Japanese

Americans during the second, and used military tribunals to try to execute German saboteurs landing on these shores. However, military commissions during the Second World War acquitted some German and Japanese defendants. The suggestion that these military tribunals will afford only sham justice is like saying the Clintons don't lie. It's a canard, a ploy, an outrage – and politics as usual.

Although it doesn't sound very Christmassy, why should the masterminds of 11 September deserve constitutional protection? I'll try my luck in front of honourable soldiers than in front of a jury any day. We know all about juries here in America. O. J. Simpson murdered two white people in cold blood and walked free because his shyster lawyers packed the jury with blacks. It's called jury nullification for past wrongs. Does anyone in their right mind believe that if Osama Bouf Kaka was in the dock, Mohammed Ahmed and Abdul Hamid will vote for him to fry? If the towel doesn't fit, you must acquit – that's the name of the game. Anyway, if martial justice was good enough for Germans, it's also good enough for al-Qa'ida, and to hell with political correctness.

Civil libertarians should be worried about what is taking place in The Hague, where Serb nationalists are being railroaded by a Swiss woman who thinks she's Torquemada, and looks like him to boot. Or in Zimbabwe, where a maddening spiral into chaos and violence is taking place in order for that murderous thug Mugabe to continue living it up. What about the civil rights of the white farmers who made the country what it was before Mugabe stole it all? Not to forget the plight of the Palestinians, who are being pounded as I write and paying the price for the actions of the madmen of Hamas and war criminals like Sharon. Occupation, after all, and the taking away of one's dignity, is an act of violence.

But I digress. This is our Christmas double issue and I must be nice. Here in the Bagel, however, things are not so nice. The rats are coming on board quicker than one can say Bloomberg. There is a new crime wave (as well as a heat wave – I sunbathed bare-chested in Central Park on 7 December) because the presence of the fuzz has been cut back. Bloomberg may be a billionaire, but his first act was to reach out to race hustlers who will eat him up alive once installed as mayor. Pushy panhandlers are back, some quite combative, and as the greatest mayor ever rides off into the sunset, so the quality of life Bagelites got to enjoy these last eight years goes too. There is a 24.4 per cent rise in murders compared with the same period last year.

The good news is that the giant metaphorical velvet rope that separated cool downtown from uncool up has come all the way down, and one even gets a smile from the behemoths guarding downtown dives. Hollywood types blew it by taking the chicken-run to the Los Angeles hills after 9/11, and fire fighters and cops replaced them as instant celebrities. Alas, it will not last. I'm on my way to Gstaad via London, but in the meantime (and despite the fact the PC police might arrest me for mentioning the word) I wish every *Spectator* reader a very Happy Christmas.

2002

Warhol's Indiscretions

Saturday, 2 February 2002

Rougemont

I got to like Andy Warhol a lot, but only after his death. Reading about him in the *Sunday Telegraph* in connection with the Tate Modern upcoming exhibition brought back a lot of memories. Mostly of Studio 54, the ghastly smell of poppers and the 'toilet' man. The 't' man was an unfortunate soul who approached Andy one day and asked him if he could spend the rest of his life in the Factory's loo. 'Please, Andy, I'd like to make a statement . . . ' or words to that effect. I happened to be around and heard about it. 'You mean there's a guy who lives in the toilet?' I asked my buddy Bob Colacello, Warhol's Boswell. 'Oh, sure, in fact he never comes out, although he's looking awfully pale lately,' said Bob. Alas, I have to admit I never got to see the 't' man, despite the fact that I spent a hell of a lot of time in loos back then. It was simply too awful to contemplate, no less to look at the poor bastard. Apparently one day he simply keeled over and died, although very few people took any notice. I guess the toilet man was one reason I used to dislike Andy. Mind you, the whole story could have been made up.

Warhol's parents were from the Carpathian Mountains, but when I once asked him how they (the mountains) compared to, say, Gstaad, he said, 'Wow, that's amazing!' Bob Colacello aside, the one Warhol associate I really liked and got along with was the film-maker Paul Morrissey. Paul was talented and knew his way around, yet Andy managed to get him to film a man sleeping. For thirty hours. Fred Hughes, Warhol's Chief of Staff, was from Texas and pretended to be a cousin of Howard Hughes. (Actually he was trailer park who had developed an English accent while still back in the Lone Star State.) Fred was a dandy, although the *mauvaises langues* used to say he looked like a maitre d'. On a trip to Houston, Andy put a lot of pressure on Fred to produce members of his family. Colacello told me never in his life did he see a man squirm like poor Fred. And then there was Bianca Jagger. She was always around the Warhol crowd, sporting the dyspeptic demeanour of a duchess who has mistakenly found herself in a brothel. She fooled most of the press, but Andy had her measure. A caddy for the rich and famous. She's now an expert on American foreign policy, and a cheerleader for the Clinton gang.

I met the Warhol family when Andy decided to run a profile of me in his Interview magazine. Bruce Weber, the photographer, took a pic that made me look a cross between Paris of Troy and Gary Cooper. A famous actress saw it, and asked Andy about me. 'But he's totally gay,' said Andy. At a dinner to celebrate that month's issue, Andy had the actress next to him when I confronted him. 'Why you so and so, how dare you . . . ' He looked at me with those dead eyes and only said, 'Gee.'

In his posthumous diaries he could not have been more complimentary about me, although very, very indiscreet. In fact so indiscreet, he almost ruined a wedding. I once broke down a door thinking a girlfriend was cheating on me. But once inside – as Warhol wrote in his diary – I found the bride to be in bed with 'Mr Quaalude', Well, the bridegroom read it and rang me one day before the wedding. 'It's just Andy making trouble from the grave,' said I. He chose to believe me. Or pretended to.

The only proper conversation I ever had with Andy was when I quoted a sonnet by Harry Crosby, the infamous drug-taking nephew of J. P. Morgan who shot and killed Josephine Bigelow and himself at Stanley Mortimer's studio in New York while his wife and mother and Hart Crane were waiting for him at Morgan's house for dinner. 'I think I understand you, Baudelaire,/ With all your strangeness and perverted ways,/You whose fierce hatred of dull working days,/ Led you to seek your vision elsewhere . . . ' 'Gee whizz,' said Andy, 'some statement. I wonder what the banks thought of it.'

Why do I like Andy now? Dunno. I guess his lack of humbug, his cartoonish pursuit of publicity for his art, that twilight feel he carried around him like a cloak. Compared to shit like Damien Hirst, Andy was Matisse.

Teenage Rats

Saturday, 16 February 2002
Rougemont

I was going to write about the twenty-five year-old female teacher whom a jury judged not guilty of raping teenage boys, but then the sainted editor took the words right out of my typewriter. In his *Daily Telegraph* column, that is. Let's face it, Amy Gehring was no looker, but then she was no rapist either, simply because only men can rape, women cannot. Motivated by greed and coached by the tabloids, those guttersnipes committed the greatest of sins – they ratted on a fast girl, the proverbial lifesaver in the turbulent sea of a boy's adolescence.

When I was that age I would have given anything in the world to stop self-service and get laid with a woman ten years older than myself. And the uglier she was, the easier I knew it was going to be.

55

In the nine years of boarding school, there were some encounters with nurses and secretaries, but, alas, not before I had turned fifteen.

Those ridiculous female columnists who wailed what if those boys had been girls were just blowing smoke. England is full of male paedophiles and dangerous sex offenders and they're worried about some pimply ruffians who knew the price of ratting, but not the value of easy sex. Fifty-three years ago, at Lawrenceville Prep, next to Princeton, the fastest townie was 'racy Gracie', a pretty little thing who once let me kiss her but told me I was too young when I touched her breasts. (I was twelve.) By the time I had full town privileges, she was long gone. This is all well and good, and lotsa fun, but now I come to the serious part.

On 27 October 2001, in the *Daily Telegraph* magazine, Emma Soames, the editor, and Mick Brown, the writer, showed great courage in publishing the story of Philippine Lambert, daughter of Baron and Baroness Lambert, who at twenty years of age killed herself, leaving a note by her bed accusing a family friend of sexually abusing her from the age of twelve and demanding that he should pay for it.

I have written about this case before, and it's very close to my heart. The Lamberts have been good friends of mine since youth. Baron Lambert is the scion of a Jewish banking dynasty, related to the Rothschilds, upper class, and very, very low key. (Baron Lambert's grandfather financed King Leopold's Congolese takeover.) Philippine was probably the most hauntingly beautiful child, young girl, and teenager I'd ever seen. Her brother Henri is a beautiful young man. The tragedy of Philippine's suffering was encapsulated in her suicide note: 'I want Vincent Meyer to pay for having sexually abused me from the ages of twelve to fourteen. He kissed me everywhere – he put his sex in my mouth – he touched me everywhere. It happened in Capri, in Crete, in Geneva, in Aix-en-Provence, in Sicily . . . I want him to pay 40 million Swiss francs and go to jail for the rest of his life.'

Three months after Philippine's suicide, in December 1997, Vincent Meyer was arrested and charged with involuntary homicide, harm to the sexual development of a minor, and rape. He was held in a Swiss prison for three months before being released on bail of 6 million Swiss francs (£2 million).

Vincent Meyer is extremely rich, being the grandson of André Meyer, the Lazard-Freres wizard, and is president and principal benefactor of London's Philharmonia Orchestra. He is married to Elizabeth Stuart and has one child with her, three children from an earlier marriage, and one from another relationship.

When Meyer was arrested, all sorts of big shots from the British music world came forward attesting to his 'sensitivity, generosity and civilised nature'. I say: they would, wouldn't they? What does generosity have to do with child molestation? In fact, and here I will tread very lightly because of libel, one of my daughter's closest friends had an encounter with Meyer while in Gstaad a long time ago, and although nothing happened, her mother warned me not to let my daughter near this individual. (Her daughter was at the time very under age.)

Meyer walked free after an investigation lasting three years. The general prosecutor acknowledged that the evidence against him constituted 'serious charges', yet he ruled that because of a five-year statute of limitations they could not be considered. On the count of rape, he ruled the accusation not sufficiently proven. The Lamberts had dropped the involuntary homicide charge. Needless to say, the family was devastated. In my opinion, a very rich man who is guilty as hell is walking around free. But do me a favour. Look for the *Telegraph Magazine* of 27 October 2001. Look at the pictures of the divine Philippine and read the book-length article. There are also pictures of her with Meyer. Read it and make up your own mind.

Steer clear of idiots

Saturday, 23 February 2002

Rougemont

OK, sports fans, what do General William Tecumseh Sherman and Sir Jocelyn Stevens have in common? I warn you, it's a tricky one. General Sherman was the first Union general to use total war tactics in his March to the Sea. When asked to take it easy, the irascible Sherman announced, 'I'm here to win a war, not a popularity contest.' Before his victories, the newspapers had actually reported him as being insane. Sherman, who replaced Grant as commander-in-chief after the war, established the Command School at Fort Leavenworth, a most important contribution. He died on 14 February 1891.

Jocelyn Stevens was born on 14 February, forty-one years later. Where the similarity begins is in both men's absolute refusal to win popularity contests. After Jocelyn's successes at *Queen* and his rescue of the *Evening Standard* (where a real David versus Goliath situation existed, with the *Evening News* making 1 million per annum profit and the *Standard* losing the same amount), followed by his years at the *Express*, but before those at the Royal College of Art and English Heritage, there were scandal sheet reports that he was mad. Like Sherman, who had a low opinion of volunteers and called them idiots, Stevens said upon accepting the chairmanship of English Heritage that all he knew about the institution was that it was run by idiots. Neither Sherman nor Stevens ever used diplomatic language, which in a way explains why neither man ever became familiar with failure. (Mind you, Sherman failed as a banker and as a lawyer before he returned to the army.)

But enough of history and on with the party. Dame Vivien Duffield of opera fame has been Jocelyn's girlfriend for close to twenty-five years. (I refuse to use the term partner except in homosexual relationships, and even then it's a bummer, no pun intended.) Having thrown parties for his fiftieth and sixtieth birthdays, she pulled out all the stops for the big Seven O. Three parties, on three successive nights, left those of us who tend to take a drink now and then feeling like the Taliban. The Saturday night bash had a Thirties theme, and took place in a local school house that had been transformed into a Parisian cabaret, cancan girls included. (These girls were tall and beautiful, and made the Lido dancers look like Transylvanian midgets by comparison.)

Space being what it is, I cannot list all the swells, but the mix between old and young was perfect, and I admit this despite being assigned to a table of people my age. The best disguise by far was Sir Rocco Forte's – that of a Sicilian gangster, scars included – the worst that of the Duke of Marlborough, who came as himself. Royalty was represented by Princess Benedicte of Denmark and her husband Prince Richard Wittgenstein, Maria Gabriella of Savoy, and lotsa Serene Highnesses, including the mother of my children. Brains, not usually located in Gstaad and its environs, were also present, with William Buckley and William Shawcross leading the charge. The Rommel of fashion, Valentino, stayed until the end, as did the Rommel of ship owners, George Livanos. The Rommel of Christie's, Lord Hindlip, ditto. All in all, I can't remember having had as much fun throughout an evening.

Usually I am quickly bored and get drunk, then the fun begins. Not this time. I actually made sense – well, almost – until the bitter end. I danced with Charlene de Ganay, the only girl I know whose dancing makes foreign legionnaires blush. Around five in the morning I went to the Palace where all the Rosey girls were still dancing away, but my son John Taki had gone and done a Philby and given the game away. (I'd been posing as his older brother.) It was downhill after that, literally, and I've been in bed since then. The flu hit with a vengeance the very next afternoon.

As Dorothy Parker once said when in a word game she was asked to use 'horticulture' in a sentence, you can lead a horticulture, but you can't make her think. There are many new rich people in Gstaad looking for whores, but there are also a few who still can think. We lost the great Roger Moore to Crans Montana, but gained John Sutin, a wit to match la Parker, despite the fact he's Swiss. In other words, Gstaad is still a hell of a place where one can have a very good, old-fashioned time, but barriers are of the essence. Jocelyn Stevens shook up the Eagle Club when he joined the committee. (I nominated him during the general assembly by comparing him to Rommel: 'Couldn't you have used another name?' asked Vivien).

Now our hopes are riding with the Gstaad Yacht Club, with around sixty members, and three kings on the committee. We desperately need a Rommel to keep the barbarians out, and our commodore, George Nicholson, is starting to look a lot like good old Erwin.

Brave Little Island

Saturday, 9 March 2002
Valetta

To Malta, where St Paul was shipwrecked in AD 60 on his way to Rome, under arrest, to be judged before Caesar as was his right as a Roman citizen. Although a prisoner, the Apostle spread his message, performed many miraculous cures and converted the unbelievers. Three months were enough. The Maltese people are to this day overwhelmingly Christian, and devoutly so.

Unlike St Paul, I flew there of my own free will, by private jet, in the company of William Buckley, John Radziwill and Sebastian Taylor. The reason for the trip was to inspect a classic sailing boat, with Bill, an experienced and intrepid sailor, acting as adviser (I dreamed that Renée Zellweger would have me if I owned that particular boat, so off we went). But my old friend Bill let me down. 'You must be mad to buy this, you need a hurricane to do six knots . . . '

Valetta, of course, was a pleasant surprise (even without Renée). Especially the people. They're friendly, helpful and extremely polite. The dialect they speak is a cross between Italian and Arabic, and is pleasant to the ear. Malta's finest hour was in 1565, when 48,000 Turks attacked the island. Facing them were 540 Knights and 4,000 Maltese. Also some Spanish and Italian mercenaries. La Valette, the Grand Master, wisely chose not to meet the invaders on the beaches but to face them behind fortified positions. Against all odds and behind crumbling walls, the Christian forces kept the infidels at bay despite ferocious bombardments, losing only one fort, St Elmo. Demoralised by disease, fire and steel, the vastly superior Turkish forces withdrew, never again to attempt another invasion in that part of the Mediterranean. In saving themselves, the Knights, the mercenaries and the entire Maltese population had saved Europe from the dreaded Turk. Two hundred years after the event, Voltaire wrote that nothing was better known than the siege of Malta.

The walled city of Valetta resisted the corsairs and the Turks until the Turkish Crescent waned. The fall of the Order did not come about from attack, but from lack of it. As the might of the Ottoman Empire weakened, the fleet of the Order lay idly at anchor in the Grand Harbour and the Knights, especially the young ones, whiled away their time in activities far removed from their monastic vows. Let's face it, conflict and war keep people on their toes; peace makes them flabby, horny and lazy. Republican France did not help by taking over the possessions of the Order. Napoleon provided the *coup de grâce* by capturing the island in 1798 with a ruse, using a fifth column of French Knights. Then came the Brits, more or less holding the island until independence in 1964. But once again the Maltese people proved their mettle during the Second World War, when they resisted both the Italian and German bombardment from the air, and even a seaborne attack by Italian E-boats in 1941. The people of Malta were awarded the George Cross by King George VI for their bravery and efficiency.

But enough of history. I found the town nostalgic as hell, the buildings reminding me of Athens before the vulgarians took over. The tree-lined streets, the sidewalk cafes, the atmosphere – that of so many southern European cities of my youth that no longer exist. And the place is full of beautiful churches, starting with St John's Cathedral, which we visited early Friday morning before flying back to Belp.

And now a word about travel, with a private jet, that is. It is not as simple as you might think. First of all one must tell the pilot the approximate time of departure in order for him to get a slot (beats me, but that's what they call it). Which means you can't change your mind at the last second; in fact you must give two hours' notice. The other thing that bothers me is the fact that the company which hires out the aircraft needs to know how many you will be. As the citation has eight seats, I asked seven friends to come along. This meant we'd have to stop in Rome to refuel (fortunately all the women dropped out when the snowstorm hit, so we flew non-stop to our destination).

Last but not least, the pilot reserves the right to fly to a different location in case of bad weather, and private aircraft are more prone to bad weather conditions than commercial airlines. Oh, the problems of travelling by private jet. But here's a tip. I'd rather fly private in the company of, say, Jack Straw than commercial with Renée Zellweger next to me (just kidding, of course).

Natural Friendship

Saturday, 13 April 2002
New York

The first friend I made when I arrived in the then merry old England during the swinging Sixties was a cherubic, incredibly pink, forever laughing and joking Old Etonian called Charles Benson. Bendix, as we called him after his nom de plume as racing correspondent for a then major newspaper (now a downmarket porn sheet), was no hooray Henry. He commanded a position of respect among gamblers because he topped John Aspinall's suicide stakes list for three months running, an unheard of achievement. The suicide stakes were for real. Aspinall used to post the list every Friday, giving the odds. However, there was an inherent weakness in the whole business. Aspinall assumed that a man who lost everything, or was hopelessly in debt, would commit suicide. The trouble was that none of the people on the list minded being in debt. After a while people stopped betting. The heavy favourite, Benson, and the perennial runner-up, Daniel Meinertzhagen, I am happy to say, are still around.

When I look back, our friendship was as natural as that of Blair and that Levy fellow. (Both are hustlers and bullshit artists.) Benson loved gambling, women, food and booze. I loved women, gambling, booze and sport. We've never had an argument, still less a fight, in over forty years of comradeship.

Although pink and cherubic, Benson pulled some incredible looking birds, most of them titled, blonde and rich. (He was even named as co-respondent in the divorce of the Aga Khan, no small achievement). At present he is not feeling his best, lying semi-paralysed. But I'd rather tell you of the good times.

Benson's mother was a formidable lady who gave even more formidable lunches in her house on Cliveden Place every Sunday. She was quintessentially English, so much so, in fact, that she had never met a foreigner before yours truly. The first time I came to lunch, circa 1962, she greeted me rather suspiciously, and after a drink or two we sat down to lunch - roast beef and all that. She then addressed me for the first time. She pointed at her mouth and made a yummy sound, and said, 'Good lunch, you eat, yum, yum . . . ' Needless to say, I took it rather badly, and told her in no uncertain terms that I spoke perfect English and did not need her pantomime. 'What, he speaks English?' she spluttered.

Benson and I travelled the world gambling, whoring and playing tennis. He was a very good cricketer and useful in tennis. Although always broke, he was generous and an incredible spender. He drank only the best and dined only in the top establishments. In the famous South of France car accident with Jimmy Goldsmith, Mark Watney and Sally Crichton-Stuart (as the ex-Begum Aga Khan then was), Benson was the most seriously hurt but was totally ignored and left on the road by the French ambulance. When I asked him why, he matter of factly said it was because Jimmy was making all the noise, so they assumed the quiet one was all right. (Jimmy had a slightly cut little finger.)

His stag party at Langan's was a riotous affair, still talked about by those of us who attended. I provided the hookers, and Benson's jockey friends went berserk. (That is the night I met Jeffrey Bernard, a turf mate of Benson's.)

Then his life changed. His wife Carolyn's father was a friend of the royals – Nigel Dempster dubbed him polo-stick-in-waiting – and Charlie soon was hanging out in places such as Balmoral and Sandringham. I felt abandoned and wrote about it in these pages. In fact, I called him a social climber. Here is his answer, published in The Speccie on 24 January 1981:

The poor little Greek boy has got it wrong again. I must advise Taki that, more than 200 years ago, wicked Ralph Benson was gadding about with the Prince Regent and, indeed, married one of his girlfriends. At much the same time Captain Riou, another direct ancestor, was the hero of the Battle of Copenhagen, in which he was Nelson's right-hand man and was, sadly, killed. And my grandmother was a Cholmondeley (pronounced Chumley, Taki). Unfortunately wicked Ralph blew the family fortune on gambling and racehorses. No, Taki, it is Mick Jagger, Robert Sangster, Bryan Ferry, the Aga Khan and my wife who are the social climbers in cultivating my friendship; but I don't mind! My family tree was flowering when Taki's ancestors were swinging from an olive branch.

Charles Benson is a man straight out of a Simon Raven novel; in fact he's like the great cad, except for his love for women rather than boys. I love him like no one else, and am flying over to see him. If the worst comes to the worst, it will be people like Robert Sangster, Sam Vestey, Bryan Ferry, Nigel Dempster and myself who will be the losers.

To London with Dread

Saturday, 20 April 2002
New York

Nicky Haslam sure got it right a couple of weeks ago, when writing in the diary he remarked: 'There's a depressing drift across the Atlantic of rich, bored women who . . . are inflicting themselves on London. Their idea of a night out involves being with the same age-and-income group people at some recently invented obscure charity evening . . . ' Hear, hear! All I can say is something must be done about these American women. As Nicky pointed out, the whole point of London life is its varied content.

I remember walking down some street with Kate Reardon following a cocktail party, and trying to talk her into going to a hotel de passe, as a joke, of course. (First she wouldn't go, second there are no longer hotels de passe in London.) A taxi would have solved our problems but there were none around. Suddenly a car stopped and a friendly man asked if we needed a ride. Once inside he asked which way we were going. 'Harry's Bar, or anywhere near there would be fine.' 'Oh, my name's Tom Stoppard, nice to meet you,' came the reply. I asked Sir Tom, as he had just become, to join us for dinner but he refused. 'I have to baby-sit.' Which is Nicky's point: I don't know many playwrights in America who would offer a ride to two unknowns, then refuse dinner because they had to baby-sit.

Although I never set foot in grubby, dirty, disgusting, depressing (Simon Heffer's words in *The Speccie* three weeks ago) London any more, I do miss its varied content. Just before Christmas last year I missed the great party Ben Goldsmith gave because of some monkey business over here. When I got the reports I realised no monkey business was worth it. All my friends were there, starting with people older than me and ending with kids much younger than my children. Now that's what I call a good mix. Over in the Bagel, a good mix is what they call three billionaires mixing with some multimillionaires.

Last week I had dinner with twelve people at Swifty's, the in place for rich Bagelite ladies who lunch. Every one of the men had gone either to Yale or to Harvard, every one of the women to Vassar or Brown. They all had children of the same age, worked downtown in banking, had summer houses in the Hamptons and winter places in Palm Beach, and I spent most of the time sitting in the loo asking myself how could I possibly have been roped into such a ghastly dinner.

The evening got off to a bad start when my hostess placed me on her left. 'What do I owe this honour to?' I asked. Then for some strange reason – she is very proper – before she answered, I added, 'And by the way, who's the c— on your right?' Well, I never! There's something about shocking Americans that gives me a thrill.

Late last year a Greek friend asked me to lunch at a gold club near the Bagel. My friend had a Mr Aquaviva and a Mr Mezzacalsa lunching with him. I declined, telling him that having spent the summer with super Wop, Gianni Agnelli, the last thing I needed was to break bread with two ersatz dagoes. (They're Italian Americans, but affect Wasp mannerisms.) Again, I never! I don't know, perhaps it's little old me, but people get awfully touchy over here.

As Paul Johnson wrote two weeks ago, the collapse of Soviet communism and the decision of China to participate in the world market economy has left a huge vacuum in the Left's pantheon of hero-states. There is nothing that makes me laugh more than the anti-Americanism of those ludicrous, smelly, ugly Brits who pass for the Left nowadays. Their envy and hatred of Uncle Sam puts me in a wonderful mood, especially when I read their drivel in the British rags over here in the sunny Bagel. Sure, there's no varied content over here and not much sense of humour, but that's a very small price to pay for total freedom, terrific pussy and good weather to boot.

I'm on my way to London to see my buddy Benson, and I'm already dreading the rain, depressing atmosphere and 'the anodyne blandness of American money-matrons' living in London. But it could be worse. I could be living in Palm Beach, like that fat fool brother of mine.

Unacceptably Boring

Saturday, 4 May 2002
New York

Like many very, very rich men, Heini Thyssen was very much a bore. I first met him when I was still a teenager on the Riviera, where else? He was a good-looking man, but lugubrious and almost Dracula-like at times. And, like Dracula, he had good taste in women. Certainly in the beginning. His first wife, the present Princess Teresa von Furstenberg, is a grand lady of impeccable credentials and impeccable behaviour. I have never met her, but I hear from my father-in-law that they don't come any grander. (Except for himself, that is.) Due to a family feud over the root of all envy, Teresa's name was recently dragged through the mud, but it simply wasn't on. It was like saying Margaret Thatcher went to war against the Argies because her husband owned Falkland Islands stocks, which is what an Argentine professor of economics told me at the time of the war in Buenos Aires. Heini junior was certainly Heini's and Teresa's son, and he has lived an extremely quiet and useful life.

Then came Nina Dyer, an Anglo-Indian of exotic looks but Sapphic tastes. There were no children and Nina committed suicide later on. I put the moves on Nina, but got as far as Mussolini did against Greece. His third wife, Fiona, was the great beauty and still is, fifty years after he married her. (There were two children.) Denise, his fourth wife, whom I knew when we were both very young – she tried her damnedest to break up my first marriage and succeeded – turned out to be the most controversial. After some years of married bliss, Denise became awfully chummy with one Franco Rapetti, an extremely good-looking blond Italian adventurer from Genoa. Heini played possum while the two love birds frolicked. Then Denise gave birth to a son, Franco threw himself out of a window in the Bagel, and Heini paid to fly his body back to Italy on a private jet. 'Did he jump or was he pushed?' wrote yours truly twenty-five years ago. The last thing Rapetti told me – loudly and in public at Isabel Goldsmith's wedding – was, 'Go ahead, kill me if you like, I'm not paying.' He owed me and others lotsa moolah from a poker game that had got out of hand, and I had bailed him out at the time. Once he got connected with Denise I asked for it back. This was his answer.

Never mind. All I know is I didn't push him and nor did Heini, in fact, although he got the credit for it. Franco was living on coke and had a paranoiac coke fit. He was convinced people were trying to kill him, and maybe they were. So he jumped, and people began to fear Heini Thyssen. Despite his newly acquired reputation as a tough guy, Heini remained a terrific bore. When I had Bruern Abbey in Oxfordshire, he was nearby at Daylesford, the old Rothermere house, now owned by Sir Anthony Bamford. He used to drop round, a lonely man, sit in my drawing room, observe the high jinks, drink non-stop and say very little. This is why he always had trouble with women. A wife will accept anything – lovers, drinking, drugs – but never boredom. Bore your wife and soon there will be someone else in her bed, no ifs or buts about it: and Heini bored for Holland, where he was born; Switzerland, where he lived; Hungary, where he picked up a title; and Spain, where he ended his life.

And speaking of Hungary, Thyssen was known throughout his life as Baron Thyssen, somewhat a misnomer. Heini's grandfather, August Thyssen, was a man of peasant stock who built a chicken-wire business into a steel and armaments empire. Heini's father, Heinrich, settled in Hungary and married the daughter of the king's chamberlain, who passed on a baronial title to his son-in-law. Whether courtiers can pass on titles to their sons-in-law is at best questionable. It's as if I were to call myself Prince Taki because my father-in-law is a Serene Highness. In Heini's case, the guy was just a Hungarian baron, a dime a dozen in the land of goulash.

Again, never mind. As long as I can remember, the wrong people sucked up to Heini, mostly art dealers and hustlers. His great achievement was his art collection, a fabled one that rivals the Queen's. But he blew it at the end by choosing to sue Heini junior on the advice of his fifth wife, Tita, a one-time Miss Spain. Heini teased everyone, from Prince Charles to King Juan-Carlos to the President of Switzerland (whoever he or she is) as to which country would get to house his collection. Spain won out in the end, but at a price: Tita, the widow. All I can say is I'd hate to have been born a Thyssen and see it all go to Tita at the end. Even some of it.

Old-fashioned Charm

Saturday, 25 May 2002
New York

It was that rarest of occasions, an old-fashioned dinner-dance for 476 people given by a couple celebrating their fiftieth wedding anniversary without a corporate sponsor in sight and no PRs within ten miles of the place. Yes, dear readers, even in the Bagel there are still some folk – very few mind you – that actually give parties and invite only people they know. Such a couple gave probably the best party I've been to this year, at the Bronx Botanical Garden, as exotic a venue as one can hope to find in the asphalt jungle of Noo Yawk; in fact almost as exotic and as novel as a society marriage that has lasted fifty years.

Tommy Kempner is the chairman of Loeb Partners Corporation, grandson of Carl Loeb, the grand Jewish family patriarch. Nan Kempner is the globetrotting socialite and fashion victim, a lady who has attended more parties than Lester Lanin, Edmundo Ros and Xavier Cugat combined; the only person I know of who has breakfasted at the Beverly Hills hotel with Betsy Bloomingdale, lunched in New York with Brooke Astor and dined with Mark Birley at Harry's Bar – all on the same day.

Not surprisingly, the marriage has lasted fifty years because Tommy Kempner never goes out, and Nan never stays home. As I entered the magnificently decorated tent in the gardens, a *New York Times* friend of mine, Billy Norwich, cornered me for a quote. Already well-oiled, I told him that it was easy for anyone to stay married for half a century as long as the man could have mistresses, 'as happens to be my case'. The next day the mother of my children was not best pleased to read it while enjoying her breakfast. Oh well, it could have been worse. I coulda stood in bed.

What a great party it was. For lovers of nostalgia like myself, the ball had the allure of yesterday. For daydreaming youth – and there were plenty of those – the glorious clarinet glissandos expressed the exuberance of the young and hopeful. The special grace of old money and good manners, alas, is no longer imitated. We live in the time of Puff Daddy, a thug, and the Hilton sisters, two sub-moronic low-lifes. But not that night, thank God.

I've always insisted that the only way a party can succeed is by inviting only very good and old friends. The philistines who have taken over say that the mix is all-important. By mix they mean rock stars, movie people, politicians and society swells. Well, I got news for them. That's the reason good parties have gone the way of good sportsmanship in tennis. Film people are slobs, rock stars belong behind bars, and politicians are smiling wallet-lifters. Ladies and gentlemen do not belong in such vulgar company, which is why the 'mix' doesn't work. If one wants to go slumming, all one has to do is to go to a public place, and presto.

Needless to say, I was among the last to leave, with a feeling of distilled happiness but also of evanescence and loss. Oh, to be back when the rules of behaviour were rigid, and only gentlemen rogues had no intention of sticking to them. I then did go slumming, near Times Square, dancing yet again, but this time it was *à la The Wild Party*. 'And the party began to reek of sex, White arms encircled swollen necks . . . ' What was it that Moncure March had to say about love? 'Some love is fire, some love is rust. But the fiercest, cleanest love is lust.' Is it ever! And I sure got a fierce welcome when I came home at eight in the morning.

Never mind. New York is a hell of a place. It is now safer than London by far, although I don't know for how much longer. Manhattan has the lowest crime rate of the five boroughs, which led an essayist, Karl Zinsmeister, to attribute its non-violence to the fact that Manhattanites are terrific cowards. After the horrendous World Trade Center attack last September, huge numbers of them were not inspired to fight. According to recruitment data, the Big Bagel contributed members to the armed forces at only two thirds of the national rate, and Manhattan was by far at the lowest end. This is not surprising. Why fight when others will do it for you? Taking the chicken run became chic during the late Sixties, so chic, in fact, that it took 9/11 for the uniform to once again be looked up to. But, as Yogi Berra said, for a while last week it was déjà vu all over again!

Cracking up

Saturday, 15 June 2002

Three oiks ruined it for me on Concorde coming over. Modern day travel is bad enough as it is, but to pay through the nose and then have to sit and listen to swine who have paid ten pence in the pound is too much even for a man of the people like myself. My God! This proletarian brutalism has made the English loathed the world over, and even those terribly nice girls working the aircraft looked a bit shocked.

I told one of the slobs to keep his voice down as I was trying to read, and he looked at me in that cowardly way punks have – half smile in case I'm someone well connected, and half defiant because I am, after all, a pensioner – but nothing came of it. I know that BA is in trouble but punks should be told to behave or else before they get on. When I asked the stewardess exactly how much 'these gentlemen' had contributed to fly Mach 1, she smiled ruefully and said nothing. Enough said. I sat with the beautiful Princess Ferial of Jordan, talked about the Middle East, and in no time we had landed.

The first pleasant surprise was being met by Nigel Dempster, who drove me in pelting rain to see my oldest English buddy, Charles Benson, confined to his bed in hospital and giving it his best shot. Nigel went in first and told Benson that he had just been to Heathrow to pick me up but I had been arrested for drugs and gone straight to the cells. 'Oh no, that stupid Greek will never learn,' croaked Bens.

When I was arrested eighteen years ago, Charles and Nigel were the first to come to my rescue, Benson accompanied by a posh lawyer who supposedly could reduce a murder charge to a traffic violation. Like a fool, I chose a local Indian chap who convinced me that posh lawyers were the wrong mouthpieces for drug cases. I, of course, went down. Benson has never allowed me to forget, nor has his posh lawyer friend.

When it was my turn to enter, I told Charles that the fuzz had allowed me to go free because I was visiting the greatest man of the English turf. That got a laugh out of my old friend, but then it all became a bit too much for me. What a bummer. Without Benson there's no way I'm going to Ascot – it would be a bit like going to Windsor Castle and discovering the Blairs living there. Mind you, miracles do happen, and Benson has got out of trickier situations.

We once went to Paris together – he had a beautiful blonde in tow, who told us she couldn't stand the French because they were all perverts. As luck would have it, during dinner a small, elderly, extremely well-dressed man came in, stood before us, and exposed himself. Although I was in the middle of a steak poivre, I cracked up. As did Benson. My girl ditto. But Benson's woman was furious. 'I told you, didn't I?' she kept repeating. When the man saw us laughing he took heart and began to do what boys do in school. The whole place began to rock with laughter – even the waiters were holding their sides – until Benson's lady ran out in tears. '*Ah non, ça suffit*,' said le patron, and threw the masturbator out. I believe the restaurant was La Closserie des Lillas, Papa Hemingway's favourite haunt. The year was 1970.

The trouble was that Benson and I couldn't stop laughing because in all the time we've spent in locker rooms never had either of us seen such a miniature willy. 'I want to go back to England,' said the English lady. 'I told you they were all perverts, and you're just as bad.' But Benson finally had his way, explaining to her ladyship that the French had an instinct for first-time visitors, and tested them in extremis. She was dumb enough to believe him and I had to listen to her groans for the rest of the night as my room was connected to his. She certainly changed her mind about sex and perverts, that's for sure.

The whole scene was terribly funny. Two drunks, Benson and myself, a sophisticated Parisienne and an English girl who burst into tears when a funny little man showed her his funny little willy, but then turned into a tiger when Benson introduced her to his heavy artillery. The next day we went racing, Benson lost his shirt, and by the time we got back to England he, too, had gone Francophobic. Oh well, I wonder whatever happened to that little man, and so does Benson, who credits him with the victory he had later that night.

And, speaking of victories, the great Arletty was brought to trial for having slept with some awfully good-looking German officers during the occupation, but she got away with it by announcing that, 'Yes, I did, but, if you didn't want us to sleep with them, you shouldn't have let them in!' There's something about Paris that makes everyone horny as hell, and, although I love Benson much more than I love my brother, I think it's Paris that did it, not the funny little well-dressed wanker.

Next week I'll tell you about two royal parties I'll be attending this week, parties to which the funny little man I'm sure is not invited.

Trouble in Soho

Saturday, 22 June 2002

Where was I? It's been a rough week. Following Robert Miller's and King Constantine's bash at Annabel's – more about that later – I found myself somewhere in Soho, alone and facing a young man covered in blood. 'Good God, what happened?' said I. 'My girl's mad at me, Mr Taki, I need you to help me,' came the reply. 'How do you know me, and why's your girl mad at you?' 'I broke her jaw . . . ' 'Jesus H. Christ, why did you break her jaw?' 'My mate put his hands on her breasts . . . so I belted her one.' 'You hit your girl because your mate felt her up, and you want me to help you?' 'You're my friend, Mr Taki, please help me.'

One couldn't make this up, but it seems that, having broken his girl's jaw, he then tried it on his mate, who took a bottle and smashed it over my new best friend's head, ergo the bloody mess. Now, remember, this is late Thursday night outside a seedy Soho nightclub, where I've left two friends and gone looking for trouble on my own.

And it gets better. My NBF turns out to be a *Spectator* reader whom I once helped get into an after-hours club. How did he recognise me? Dunno, I guess I've got the kind of looks crooks and whores and people bleeding heavily don't forget easily. But I'm intruding on Jeremy Clarke's territory. This is, after all, supposed to be High life. And, boy, has it been high throughout!

Robert Miller is a billionaire whose daughter is married to Crown Prince Pavlos of Greece. Unlike most billionaires, Miller is friendly, totally unassuming and very generous with his hospitality. He owns possibly the best grouse-shooting estate in England, one that he doesn't use in order to meet English nobs, but to shoot with his buddies. He and his wife are among the very few people I have consistently mooched off (actually the only other one is Professor Yohannes Goulandris of Nuremberg University), a very upper-class English trait, but one I do not usually indulge in. Let's put it this way. The Millers have as much in common with those two ridiculous couples who went to court over who owed whom what after a holiday in Cannes as the beautiful Jessica de Rothschild has with that fat frump Monica Lewinsky.

I thought of them, the Millers, when I met the bloody one in the seedy Soho alley. Imagine if they had come along after their party, as I had asked them to. Well, it might have made a change. You don't see many people bleeding up in Gunnerside.

King Constantine, of course, is another who indulges me and turns a blind eye to my juvenile shenanigans. He seated me at his table and from this vantage point I could look down at the beautiful Caroline of Hanover's – aka of Monaco – poitrine, but I better leave it at that as Ernst, her husband and a friend of mine, is known to do a Rommel when men bother his wife.

And speaking of Jessica de Rothschild, it was her fault I ended up in Soho. Earlier on at Annabel's, I had put the moves on her and came up empty-handed, pun intended, so I proceeded to drink in order to forget my misery. Mind you, it wasn't hard, my system was already well oiled. Twenty-four hours earlier I was lying in my bed preparing for the big night when Sebastian Taylor rang inviting me out to dinner. Just a quiet little din-din with Jemima Khan and Kate Reardon is the way he put it. Then Ben Goldsmith happened. Ben-Ben arrived with his nineteen-year-old beauty, Kate Rothschild, to whom I jokingly proposed. 'Leave Benjamin for someone more

78

mature like yours truly.' Like his father Jimmy, Ben has no sense of humour where the fairer sex is concerned. He challenged me to go to Aspinall's, where I proceeded to finance the gorillas in Port Lympne for the next three hundred years.

The next night, upon entering Annabel's and greeting the Queen of Greece, she asked me to please behave and not get too drunk. 'As I've lost everything and no one is speaking to me any longer . . . ' I began, 'Oh good!' said the Queen, obviously not having heard a word I said.

Then it was time for deepest Dorset, to Wembury House, where Tim and Emma Hanbury hold their annual cricket match against Zac Goldsmith's young whippersnappers. It would not be cricket to show off, but show off I must. Last year I went out on a golden duck, and dropped four balls. This year I made no errors on the field, did not drop my bat while running and was not out at the end. Taki not out is like Tony telling the truth, unheard of.

That night I celebrated at Zac's among the nicest and best-looking young people since Brideshead. I somehow dragged my weary and aging carcass up at dawn, and was driven to Cirencester for the King Constantine Cup which benefits the Hellenic College Trust. Lotsa moolah was raised during the auction, and some of my guests even raised their hands, but it's hard for foreigners to have a winning bid when there are Greeks around. Even Prince Charles was impressed when someone bid 30 grand for a picture painted by him when he (Prince Charles) was two years old.

Playing the Game

Saturday, 6 July 2002

Let me quote you a passage from a book about a Second World War battle by Antony Beevor:

> The Greek garrisons on the Metaxas line fought with great tenacity. The German 5th Mountain Division, which later formed half the invasion force for Crete, 'was repulsed in the Rupel Pass despite strongest air support and sustained considerable casualties'. But the line was eventually broken by the 6th Mountain Division. One garrison fought so bravely that the Germans allowed the defenders to march out with their weapons and saluted them.

Pretty good, wouldn't you say? A bunch of under-armed, ill-equipped, badly clothed and hardly fed Greek boys holding out longer than the whole bloody French army had done the summer before. Not to mention the ludicrous Belgians and the fleet-footed Dutch. My mother's oldest brother, Evangelos Miropoulos, long-time Greek and Balkan champion in the 110 and 400 metre hurdles, and Olympic competitor in 1932 and 1936, marched out leading his platoon and ran into a German officer by the name of Trosbach, who had held the world record in the hurdles but had been beaten by Miropoulos in Athens. My uncle did not recognise him, but Trosbach did recognise my uncle.

According to my uncle – now running the hurdles up above – the German was visibly moved and almost in tears. Miropoulos was fighting alongside Otto Simitsek, a naturalised Greek who was the national track and field coach. They were offered a ride and provisions by Trosbach but had to refuse. They never saw him again.

I don't know why I bring this up, probably because of all the anti-German hysteria involving the unspeakable World Cup. Some German haters cast the kraut goalkeeper as a tank commander. I ask, what is wrong with being a tank commander? There are countless instances of British officers signalling to the enemy – especially in the desert – their appreciation of a battle gallantly and fairly fought. Tank commanders, especially of the Prussian upper class persuasion, were the noblest of the fighting breed, and no one was nobler and more gallant in battle than Hasso von Manteuffel. Nazis and other criminals, whom know-nothings confuse with anyone German, did not lead men into battle; they stayed behind and murdered the innocent. I'll take noble German tank commanders as fighters over anyone, and that includes the great George Patton's Third Army. But back to the present. And yet another gallant defeat, this time in cricket.

It was Badminton village vs the Marquess of Worcester's team, the latter a strange group consisting of two Greeks, a Persian, Mark Shand with his elephant (non-playing), a poker player named Machine, the English Lothario and Hemingway fan Ben Elliot, Lord John (the music man) Somerset, John Parry . . . you get the picture. We batted first and did a Rommel. (Strong start, weak finish.) Shariah Bachtiar and Mark Shand had half centuries each, although Ben Elliot was the first one to score – the night before, that is. Despite a Thermopylae-like speech, before we took the field, by Bunter, our Führer, my English teammates fielded as if they were Belgians facing the Wehrmacht. (I dislocated my thumb and have bruises all over from throwing my aging body around, but to no avail.) Down we went like good sports, which is more than you can say about those ghastly oiks who have been cheering for Tim and Greg as if their opponents were mass murderers. My God, whatever happened to good sportsmanship in tennis, particularly at Wimbledon?

Badminton is a hell of a place, and there was a wonderful party for the young the night before the cricket. But like two years ago at Highgrove, I am not at liberty to write about who was there and what went on, except to say the hacks would sell their backsides to a Transylvanian anthropoid ape if only they could have had access for even a minute. Mind you, it's been a hell of a lot of fun since I landed in Blighty three weeks ago. The only regret was missing Johnny Gold's seventieth birthday bash due to injury to the brain cells from alcohol. I heard that Roger Moore, although unaware that he was expected to speak, showed himself a real trooper and came up with a gem of a speech. The next night, having recovered completely, I went to an intimate little dinner at Lord and Lady Black's for . . . sixty! It was the closest thing to a Noël Coward evening, with the best cabaret the poor little Greek boy has ever seen. Good things come in pairs, they say, and at my benevolent proprietor's humble little home I ran into David Furnish, accompanying Liz Hurley.

Last year I had libelled David because I had believed a story that appeared in the *Big Bagel Times*. He could have but did not sue or demand an apology. I gave him a wholehearted one that night, and graciously he not only accepted it, he also sent me a nice present the next day. See, good things happen when one is nice, and from now on I swear I'll be nice to everyone except British oiks, all politicians, all Hollywood types, most intellectuals, all race hustlers, all phony left-wingers, all *Guardian* women and *Guardian* readers . . . oh, furgedaboudit.

Earthly Power

Saturday, 17 August 2002
Gstaad

An article in the *Herald Tribune* announces that the UK's upper crust
has made way for CEOs and celebrities. 'It's not so much your family
that matters; it's what you've achieved, and how much money you've
got.' Well, we are in the middle of the silly season, and what the writer
had to say wasn't any sillier than what the rest of the ghastly purveyors
of trivia and salaciousness bombard us with week in and week out.
But leave it to an American journalist writing for the *Washington Post*
to discover in the year 2002 that the aristocracy isn't what it used to be
in the tight little island that's Britain. A television broadcaster, Joan
Bakewell, whoever she may be, blamed the aristos' demise on the fact
that they've been reduced to selling tickets for tours of their gardens.
Charles Spencer, brother of Princess Diana, was singled out as the
perfect example. The passage I liked best stated that traditional class
divisions still influence basic elements of daily life – 'language, diet,
schools, even the news business'. Hooray for you, T. R. Reid (the
writer); scoops like yours should get you a Pulitzer in no time.

Do the upper classes have a different diet? Judging by, say,
Alexander Hesketh and his brother the 'captain', I guess they do.
Or Sir David Llewellyn, for that matter. Dirty Dai is now so big he
passes for Robert Maxwell at times. But then one looks at the
lower classes, say Peter McKay, who writes in the *Daily Mail* under
the pseudonym of Ephraim Hardcastle, and he, too, resembles the
Heskeths, in girth only, that is. McKay is a strange chap. He is very

amiable in person, but vicious as hell on paper. He loathes Charles Moore and the Telegraph group. He calls Charles Lord Snooty. But Charles is nothing of the sort. He is naturally reticent and a born gentleman, nothing more. To McKay's working-class jaundiced eye, he's a snob, as are the rest of those who work for Lord Black. What T. R. Reid failed to mention in his less than eye-opening piece was the jealousy and envy that go hand in hand when those of the lower classes write about their betters.

Mind you, I've always been against the very human inclination to condescend, but there are times when one has to look down one's nose on certain of God's creations. For example, Jack Straw. This piece of low-life tried to humiliate General Pinochet, the saviour of Chile, but all he managed to do was to bring the general back into the news for a while, spend a lot of tax-payers' money, and then eat humble-pie. To those of us who know better, Pinochet was, is and will always remain a great man. Just as Straw will always be a low-life coward who has not lifted a finger to help the white Rhodesians, but has instead kissed the black arse of the murdering Robert Mugabe. If ever snobbery came in handy, it's in the case of Straw. Tony Blair ditto. The man is pathetic, almost on the level of Bill Clinton, except for the hair.

Britain is now a joke, with the worst health service, the worst transport system and the worst state schools in Europe, yet after five full years in power Blair is blaming the Tories and the thickest people of Europe nod their approval. A person's chances of being mugged in London and other major British cities are six times higher than in the Big Bagel; only in England is defence of person or property regarded as an anti-social act, with the victim likely to be treated with more severity than the assailant. But the moment Blair returns from his holidays, he will stand up in some forum, spout the same tired old bullshit, and the people will cheer. Just as those Chileans who disappeared got their just deserts for trying to impose a Marxist dictatorship, so do the Brits who fall for Blair's lies deserve what they get. In Britain's welfare state, crimes against property are not taken seriously. Ergo no house is safe, except for those who can afford twenty-four-hour guards, many of whom funnel moolah to the ruling Labour wallet-lifters.

Personally, I feel sorry for those who pay their high taxes and get nothing in return. But I'm afraid Blair and his gang of lunch-bucket pilferers are in for the long haul. He's obviously made a deal with Murdoch, and he's got the rest of the scummiest media in Europe eating out of his trough. T. R. Reid should be writing about the demise of the English as a race, not about the expiration of aristocratic influence. It is obvious that the spread of proletarian brutalism as personified by the grotesque Prescott has engendered snobbery even in an egalitarian soul such as that of the poor little Greek boy. Thank God that I live in Switzerland and my doctor in America.

The Ultimate Challenge

Saturday, 24 August 2002
Gstaad

Bismarck famously said that the Balkans were not worth the bones of a single Pomeranian grenadier. Nor is Iraq. We had Saddam cold back in 1991 but stopped the war a day too early. With good reason. The ghastly Saudis, the treacherous Turks and the shitty Iranians were not keen on a separate Kurdistan, ergo Saddam was given a pass by Bush senior. Now we're back to square one – this time, however, with Sharon calling the tune. Talk about massive overload. Uncle Sam seems to be everywhere, from Colombia to the Philippines, the Middle East, Pakistan, Afghanistan, India, North Korea, you name it, Sammy's involved.

I'm off to America for the launch of *The American Conservative*, the national fortnightly out of Washington DC edited by Pat Buchanan and myself, with Scott McConnell doing the heavy lifting. Why a new conservative fortnightly? Why not, is my answer.

Basically it's armchair warriors such as William Kristol, John Podhoretz and Mark Steyn, to name just a few, who gave Pat, Scott and me the idea to start a mag. There are many such heroes in America right now, all ready to fight, as long, of course, as others are doing the fighting. Mind you, they're not the first. It's always been like this. *The American Conservative* will have a few things to say about these gentlemen war heroes, but not until the end of September, when the second greatest magazine in the English-speaking world will debut.

In the meantime, while I sun myself in Gstaad, but still on the subject of war, one Laurence Rees, a bald BBC hack, stands out as a perfect example of what I was talking about previously. While reviewing a new book on the kamikazes, the bald BBC hack (the tabloid his review appeared in ran a picture of him, that's why I know he's bald and he wears glasses to boot) denounces the myth of the kamikazes and proclaims that 'the historical reality this book omits is that in Japan's sick, ultra-conformist wartime society, it took far greater courage to speak out and resist becoming a kamikaze pilot than it took to volunteer.' What a crock, typical BBC peacenik bullshit, and then some. In the *Sunday Telegraph*, Saul David, reviewing the same book, shows the difference between bullshit lefty artists like the bald one with glasses and real historians. According to David the difference between Western and Japanese philosophy is that the former tells a person how to live, whereas the latter tells them how to die. Hear, hear!

It might sound contradictory, but what armchair war heroes like Kristol and Podhoretz and bald BBC hacks with glasses have in common is a disdain for manly death. The armchair ones see death as unimportant, a necessary evil, like DDT-ing mosquitoes. The BBC hack views death as macho posturing, a sham. Both, of course, are full of shit. Death, and the way a man faces it, is the ultimate challenge. The Greeks, the Romans, the German knights and the Japanese Samurai revelled in it. A soldier's death is the greatest honour, and, yes, I do know that 'dulce et decorum est pro patria mori' is now considered passé by Guardian types who pee sitting down. Japanese soldiers believed that if they fell in the field of honour they would become *kami*, or gods. When 150,000 Brits surrendered to 55,000 Japanese without firing a shot, Anglos became a laughing stock to the Japanese. Soldiers who surrendered were seen as cowards. And rightly so. The BBC hack describes the kamikaze poems written before the final mission as pathetic. He would, wouldn't he? Bespectacled bald hacks do not understand warrior sentimentality. They cry at science fiction movies when the robot's batteries run dry, but not when young men go willingly to their death. BBC hack bad. Kamikaze pilot good.

I have always loved the Japs, starting with Yukio Mishima. The grotesque FDR forced the imperial army to attack Pearl Harbor by denying the land of the rising sun oil. It is as simple as that. The rest is bullshit. Japan was willing to compromise but FDR kept raising the stakes. And who the hell was FDR to tell Hirohito to get out of Manchuria? We fire-bombed Tokyo, incinerated Hiroshima and Nagasaki, and have now perpetrated the ultimate crime against the little yellow people; we have turned them from warriors into consumers. Still, they say nothing. Samurai and martial-spirited Japanese good. American bullies, BBC hacks and Guardian types bad.

Eat the Right Cake

Saturday, 5 October 2002

Washington DC

I have only one thing to add to the John Major-as-a-stud saga. He should be ashamed all right, but for his choice of woman, not for having screwed around. I've said it before and I'll say it again. They can have their cake, and eat it too, as long as they eat the right cake. This Edwina slag was bound to spill the beans. What was Major thinking? A self-publicist, a low life and ugly as hell to boot, is a lethal cocktail made for the tabloids. They say that you can judge a man by the women he's had. If true, Major comes out even worse as a person than he was as a prime minister. I've done some pretty dumb things in my life – who hasn't? – but no girl has gone to Murdoch's filthy tabloids with the Taki story because I don't screw, drink or dope with Edwina Currie-types. And this also applies to poor Jeffrey Archer. If he had not trusted a Judas, he'd be sitting pretty right now. Let's face it. Archer did nothing wrong. He stuffed a hooker – so what? And when the tabloids got hold of it, he said he hadn't. Again, so what? Why is it that journalists can lie and misrepresent themselves with impunity, but when somebody gets caught doing what they do regularly, they're sent down and the key thrown away.

Being sent to a tough prison and solitary for having 'broken' the rules in lunching with an old colleague? This is the stuff of stealing a piece of bread in *Les Misérables*. You English should be ashamed of yourselves, but your lives are so miserable you don't even know what shame is. There's so much hate, jealousy and envy in England. I'm very, very happy to be in the Bagel among some of the crudest people on earth. Not that journalists are much better over here. During a press conference held in the National Press Club here in the nation's capital, all that the Fourth Estate geniuses could come up with was what could Pat Buchanan, who believes in family values, and yours truly, who loves wine and women, possibly have in common. I am not a whinger by nature, but I thought it rather unfair. My coke bust of eighteen years ago was mentioned in every article that appeared, and the *New York Times*, the *Washington Post*, the *Washington Times*, *UPI* and the rest had the story on the front pages of their style sections. In fact, they made me feel like Giovanni, in the old joke: Giovanni is sitting on a park bench looking extremely depressed. When asked why, he points at the library across the way and says, 'You see that library? I paid for it. You see that hospital down the road? I paid for it to be built. And that school next door? I had it built. But once, only once, I sucked a cock. So everyone calls me Giovanni the cocksucker.'

Robert Kennedy Jr – now a public figure – was caught red handed when smacked out, got no time in jail, and ever since it's never mentioned. A guy called Eric Breindel was caught buying heroin, did no time and it became a non-story once he made it big with Murdoch. In fact he was given a state funeral by the Australian dirtmonger, with Rudi Giuliani and Governor Pataki attending. Bob Evans, the Hollywood hustler, was caught with close to three kilos of coke, never did a day in jail, and when I mentioned it once in this here column, it was as if I had betrayed my mother to the Gestapo. Alas, the poor little Greek boy does not enjoy this kind of impunity. Could it possibly have anything to do with inherited wealth and right-wing politics? A little bird whispers 'yes' in my ear.

And it gets worse. There I was, following a drunken dinner to celebrate the first issue of the American Conservative, on a leafy Georgetown street with a beautiful Southern belle. I was trying to kiss her and things looked hunky-dory for a while.

Then she gasped. 'Oh my God,' she said, looking over my shoulder, 'that's my church.' She ran down the street. 'But Jesus loved young lovers,' I yelled after her, but it was too late. She had disappeared into the night. So I sat on a bench like Giovanni feeling awfully depressed, but not for long. A Hungarian countess came driving by and . . .

Norman's Wisdom

Saturday, 2 November 2002
Provincetown, Mass

One of the pleasures of owning and being involved on the editorial side of a magazine is the people you meet in the course of business. Norman Mailer, the heavyweight champion of American letters, is an old friend, so my executive and managing editors and I flew up to Boston and then drove to Provincetown to interview the great man for our next cover story. Until the interview I had seen Norman only in social situations, with lots of women interfering whenever he and I tried to solve the problems of the world. This time it was all business, four hours of it, and once it was finished I swore to myself that I would never again waste time chasing pussy and getting drunk with fools. Provincetown, incidentally, is a beautiful and historic town by the sea, but the day we were there was during *Women's Week*, which meant that thousands of lesbians were walking around holding hands and smooching in public. (Now, if any of you entertain aesthetically erotic dreams of two women together – which I have all my life – fuggedaboutit. Never have I seen such dumpy, ugly dykes.)

The impending war with Iraq was the main topic. Unlike fearless Samurai such as William Kristol, who itch to send others to fight but who have never served a day (God forbid), Mailer has seen lotsa action, and against real fighters, the Japanese during the Second World War. He categorised conservatives as either flag wavers or value conservatives. The former want power, and are willing to start wars in order to get it; the latter believe in true family values, honour, religion, patriotism and so on. (Hear, hear!) On religion Norman was perfect. Islam's main point is egalitarianism, but no one has betrayed Islam more than the leaders of the Muslim world, where only the poor are equal and where everyone is poor (except the leaders, that is). Christianity's strong point is compassion, but according to Norman we have not only been extremely insensitive to others, we haven't exactly been very compassionate of late. Judaism's strength is reason, and here Norman got quite angry. But I'll let this one go, no use getting him and myself in trouble just as Sharon is ready to take over the world. (Or at least the West Bank.)

Making money with money is immoral, according to the all-knowing one. He reminded me of Hilaire Belloc, and his favourite target, the money-shufflers. 'What about inherited moolah?' I asked. 'That's your problem, but you didn't go out to make money with yours . . .' I sure didn't. He nevertheless plans to leave money to his large brood, which has to be good news for my friend Michael, his son, and producer of the greatest film ever about to be made, *Nothing to Declare*, written by you-know-who. Norman believes in capitalists who create enterprises which bring benefits to others, including oneself. Again, hear, hear!

Talking about the root of all envy, there's been a great change in

America, just as there has been in Britain. The man in the grey flannel suit has been replaced by the imperial CEO, the latter going from $1.3 million per year compensation – 39 times the pay of an average worker around 1970 – to $37 million per annum during the late Nineties, more than 1,000 times the pay of the average Joe. Now there's something very wrong with these figures. Public companies are being run by people unconcerned with right versus wrong. Top execs were cashing in stocks even as their companies were tanking. The 'little people' were left holding the bag. This is a new phenomenon which began during the go-go Eighties. Before that, top executives behaved more like public-spirited bureaucrats than Gordon Gekkos. Management ruthlessly rewarding itself has to be the numero uno danger to free enterprise.

Needless to say, the reason the Gordon Gekkos got away with what they have is very simple. They were the ones who appointed the members of their corporate boards, the very people who determined which executive got what. And there's another thing: the disappearance of the Protestant establishment. For two hundred years the Protestant establishment with its certain puritan culture occupied the top jobs in business, government and politics in America. Around the 1960s that establishment was suddenly gone without a fight, without even a whimper. It was Kennedy, Johnson, Clinton, Gekko time. You know the rest.

The one thing I regret was not following up a remark of Norman's about his old man. 'He was charming and funny, but not there . . . ' He then gave us a smile, the one that misdirects fools towards self-pity, but in reality is the secret handshake of a very exclusive club – those whom absent fathers have made stronger.

Beauty and Bloodlines

Saturday, 7 December 2002

New York

Suzy, the society columnist of the bygone era when gossip columnists covered real society — unlike today's lot, who publish names given to them by publicists listing who attended which store opening – called it a union of beauty and bloodlines, an exquisite ceremony, the best of New York, Connecticut and international society. Although I do not possess Suzy's talent to panegyrise the rich and the chic, I must admit it was just as she described it, but more, much more. Suzy went home early, I was the last to leave; ergo my advantage. There is always a moment of truth during a party.

It arrives just as the booze, the late hour, the heady music and the sex drive fuse, creating a magical juncture that remains in the subconscious for years to come. I felt such a moment of truth throughout the Herrera ball, most likely the last great one I'll be attending in my lifetime. (I say this because – at least here in the Bagel – the barbarians are now inside the gates, the old guard having gone the way of Napoleon's, with the nouveau riche and vulgar being the ones giving the parties.)

The occasion was the marriage of Patricia Herrera and Gerrit Lansing Jr., two young people blessed with looks and charm, and not a small amount of the root of all envy. I'll start with the parents. Reinaldo Herrera is one of my oldest and closest friends, scion of an old and noble Spanish-Venezuelan family whose seat in Caracas is the oldest continuously inhabited house in the Western Hemisphere.

Built in 1590 by his ancestor, La Vega is perhaps a white elephant in today's egalitarian times, but proof that powerful people back then knew not only how to spend, but also how to live graciously and in the best of taste. Not that you'd know it meeting Reinaldo. Like a fool, he renounced his title of Marquis of Torre Casa, proclaiming that the times in his country are not conducive to handles. I say the opposite. Now's the time to stick it to the vulgar ones, and having a real title today is as important as not having one was, say, in Italy circa the Thirties, when so many had phony ones.

Be that as it may, his wife, Carolina, is the greatest of designers, a unique beauty whose designs combine the elegance of Valentino, the tradition of Balenciaga, and the flair of Oscar de la Renta; and this, coming from someone who knows as much about fashion as Tony Blair's father-in-law knows about manners, is really saying something. All it takes is a bit of common sense. For example, I look at a beautiful girl dressed in Stella McCartney, and I want to puke. Ditto for those other Brit queens, like McQueen, who humiliate women by wrapping them in freak costumes. Carolina's managed to transmit her innate grace and class into the clothes she designs, and women are the better for it. But back to the party.

The night before, the Lansings threw a bash at Indochine where I found myself seated on the right of Mrs Lansing. She's from an old Philadelphia family, with the kind of friendliness and warmth that very old money provides. In fact, she and her husband reminded me of people I used to know during the Fifties, very few of whom are still around. Gerrit Lansing descends from Robert Livingston, one of the most important political families in colonial America. Needless to say, it was a great start to a great weekend of festivities. Who was there? Well, it'll be easier to say who wasn't. For starters, no hacks, no celebrities, no drag queens, no chic drug dealers. The Herrera ball was white tie, in a tent by Robert Isbell which turned the outdoor space of the Cooper Union into an eighteenth-century garden room. Pilasters covered in camellia leaves, a wonderful band playing both old and modern, and two hundred young people tripping the light fantastic – now that's what I call a great party. I watched my young son doing the rounds, girls looking at him the way girls tend to look at someone who is extremely good-looking but doesn't know it, and I felt happy and proud, despite the fact I was not part of the main action.

Carolina had placed me next to her, so I took it easy on the booze. Up to a point, that is. The mix was perfect, 3–1, three youngsters to one oldie, like a good martini. The bride and groom were just perfect, none of that *Four Weddings and a Funeral* stuff – no freaks, no uglies, no slobs. My best moment was when I spotted a certain Miss P, and asked my daughter whether she knew her. 'She's a coke-head, a drunk and a whore, daddy,' said my little girl looking decidedly angry. It was the best news I had since the fall of France in 1940. Alas, it was not to be. Miss P disappeared into the night while I was dancing with the mother of my children. Oh well, another time perhaps. Nothing like a triple-threat woman to wake up these old bones.

Women Trouble

Saturday, 28 December 2002

Cherie Blair's lies brought back memories. Of Evita Peron, the bottle-blonde hooker that became Argentina's first 'lady' while her crook husband robbed the country blind in the name of the *decamisados*. (Of course they were shirtless, their chief had stolen the whole kit and caboodle.) Nowadays, people seem to forget what a terrible, terrible man Peron was, and what a poisonous, envious whore was Evita. All Argentina's troubles can be traced back to Bonnie and Clyde Peron, and the socialist measures they imposed on that once rich and wonderful country. When Eva Peron took her last European tour, it was rumoured that Ari Onassis had given her one when she stopped over in Monte Carlo. Onassis did like famous names, and bedded lots of them, but never la Peron. How do I know? I asked his closest friend, Kostas Gratsos, two or three years after the golden Greek had died in 1975. 'Not even close,' was the answer. 'He knew her back in Argentina, but he stayed away. She had the habit of putting the bite on one, and in the millions.'

Juan Peron was such a liar and natural demagogue, the idiotic Argies brought him back to power in the mid-Seventies after twenty years in Spanish exile. (Franco should have suicided him, but was too decent a man to do it.) As if that wasn't enough, after the old boy croaked, the Argies actually allowed his second whore wife, Isabellita, to run the place for a while. Alas, Peronism is still around, and that's why Argentina – once among the top three richest nations – is now on a par with Bulgaria.

Not that I'm calling Cherie Blair a whore. Anything but. She couldn't be one even if she wanted to; not good-looking enough. No, where Cherie reminds me of Eva is in her politics (much, much more to the Left than she's been given credit for), her meddling in policy à la third-world dictatorships, and her ability to play the little wife when it suits her. Most people today have been influenced by Evita, the Lloyd Webber play, which whitewashed the bitch once and for all. Yet, if people refused to read the lefty and Murdoch rags, they would see that Cherie and Evita are one, except for the sex for hire, that is. Both are tough as hell, both are meddlers and very ambitious, both are terrific liars, both took the easy way up, via their hubbies.

Mind you, Hillary Clinton is the same, except, again, for the whore part; she, too, could not make a living from the world's oldest profession because of ugly looks and terrible ankles. In all fairness la Clinton did win election to the US Senate, but even that was a bit tainted. She had great exposure as the long-suffering wife of the greatest liar ever to inhabit the White House, and her natural constituency is Noo Yawk, a place full of Hispanics, blacks, homo-sexuals, cross-dressers, and people on welfare. Last but not least, Rudy Giuliani, who would have kicked her butt, got cancer you know where, so she was home free. Still, she won fair and square, even with people who can hardly speak a word of English voting overwhelmingly for her.

And somebody else comes to mind. Libel laws prohibit me from telling the whole truth, but Mimi Papandreou, not so long ago Greece's first 'lady', is Evita's clone, except for much bigger tits. Andreas Papandreou was the biggest crook among his socialist ministers still in power, most of whom are crooks. On a salary of around £30,000 per annum he left real estate worth many millions, and I'm not counting the millions he paid his American wife Margaret for the divorce.

Mimi now lives in great comfort and luxury, although the socialists in government shun her. For the life of me, I don't understand it. Just because the poor girl shoved her big tits in an old man's face while up in the air – she was an airline stewardess – and he got all hard, divorced his wife, stole the country blind and built her a palace – two palaces, in fact – is no reason to be embarrassed by her. Unlike Greece's ministers, she didn't steal the money; she earned it the old-fashioned way. Big Tits, however, does not remind me of Cherie. Big Tits was ambitious, and the moment she got Ali Babandreou she began firing orders left and right. It was obvious that she was a goner the moment Ali Baba went to hell. Cherie is smarmier and far more intelligent. Cherie and Hillary, Evita and Mimi, two of a kind, and two of a kind; all four, however, liars par excellence who have dragged and will drag their countries into socialist sleaze given half the chance.

Have a very happy New Year, keep reading *The Speccie*, and don't wish any of these women on your worst enemy.

2003

Bleak Omen

Saturday, 4 January 2003
Gstaad

What a way to start the new year. Back in jail. Yes, I've done it again, but this time only for an hour. It was the Radziwill wine that did me in, having dined with the Polish prince and his Greek princess prior to my arrest. I guess my sixty-six-year-old liver ain't what it used to be. No sooner had I downed a bottle of an awfully good red than I was sloshed and needed some action. 'Hush' is the newest 'in' place in Gstaad, owned and operated by Jeffrey Moore, son of Roger, and the place was jumping with nubile things. In fact I was by far the oldest person there, but was soon shamed to a hasty migration by my daughter. Normally I would have walked to the Palace, but that particular night I happened to be driving my brand new yellow Mini, so unwisely I decided to motor up the hill, literally a two minute drive. I never made it. What I did was reverse into a large tree rather hard, demolishing the rear of the Mini, never mind the poor tree. I am not a lawyer, but, literally speaking, this will be a hard one to prove. Drunken driving, after all, means going from point A to point B under the influence. In my case I went from point A to point minus A, all three yards.

Having inspected the damage, I left the car against the tree and walked to the Palace. I told Andrea the concierge what had happened, asked him to take care of it in the morning, and went down to the GreenGo nightclub for some more fun and games. At around five I decided to call it a night and walked home. Just as I was getting into my warm bed, my daughter informed me that I had two visitors: a man and a woman, both police officers with guns in their holsters. Although confused as to why they were there, I nevertheless asked them to join me for a nightcap. Both refused. 'Have you had anything to drink?' was the first question. 'Of course I have, do you think I always talk this way?' 'You must come with us. You left the scene of an accident without informing the authorities,' or words to that effect. In view of the fact that no one else was involved except for the Mini and the tree, I begged to differ with the fuzz. Worse, while trying to charm the female cop, I made a romantic suggestion to her. Well, I never! Off we went to the hospital for a blood test and to the station which – predictably – had been shut tight since ten the previous evening. When I pointed this out, the two Sherlocks scratched their heads and drove me back to Palataki, where a welcoming committee was up in arms. Oh yes, I almost forgot. As I was being escorted from my house, I took a bust of Il Duce with me. Mussolini is hardly my hero, but as his image is being revised in Italy, I thought it might help. When asked who else was in the car with me, and whether I was the driver, I pointed at Il Duce and put the blame on him. Well, I never, yet again.

If this was an omen, 2003 looks bleak. There's absolutely no snow, the place is crawling with rich nobodies, and the Goths are at the gates. Mind you, it could be worse. For example, I wouldn't want to be in George Soros's shoes, found guilty in France on charges of insider trading. Or I could be questing for the America's Cup down under, and, after spending hundreds of millions, be facing charges of stealing design secrets – as Microsoft co-founder Paul Allen and the cell phone entrepreneur Craig McCaw are. Incidentally, sportsmanship and fair play were once part of the America's Cup rules. Try and tell that to a vulgarian like Larry Ellison, leader of the Oracle BMW syndicate. Ellison once said, 'Whatever I want, I get;

that's the beauty of being worth 26 billion.' (I assume that does not include sportsmanship and fair play.)

Personally, although a great Kiwi fan, I am rooting for the Alinghi group, headed by Ernesto Bertarelli, Switzerland's richest man, and heir to a Swiss pharmaceutical fortune. Bertarelli has just joined the Gstaad Yacht Club, whose board of admissions is headed by yours truly. Two summers ago, he came on board the Leander to visit Gianni Agnelli, and he could not have been nicer. He's married to a pretty young Brit, and has just built a humongous chalet in Gstaad. He has nothing in common with people like Allen, McCaw and Ellison except for the billions. If he wins, and he's second favourite after the reigning champion and defender New Zealand, the 64 dollar question is where he'll choose to defend. For those of you unfamiliar with Swiss banks, Switzerland is landlocked. (If the Hungarians could have an admiral, Horthy, for their big chief, why can't the Swiss defend the Cup on a glacier?)

Be that as it may. If I end up in the clink for making a pass at a woman policeman, you'll be hearing from me next week from Chillon.

Funerals and Friends

Saturday, 1 February 2003
Gstaad

I finally did not go to Gianni Agnelli's funeral. When I say finally, I mean I was on my way, but then I began to think. Gianni died early Friday morning, the funeral was on Sunday. There was no time for people to be invited. But Gianni was a public person – to use an overused cliché, he was the uncrowned king of Italy. Which means every politician, civil servant, important person – you know the type – would naturally be expected to attend. I was just a close friend of forty-five years, nothing more. What convinced me was Paul Johnson's column in these here pages about Roy Jenkins: 'I shall miss him, especially his presence at memorial services, which he attended assiduously, whether or not he knew the dear departed, provided that he was eminent enough.'

Well, there was no one more eminent than l'avvocato, but I'm no Roy Jenkins. I have no honorary degrees, no literary awards, no glittering prizes. (Just a lot of rusting trophies to remind me of my arthritis.) Mind you, the Agnellis knew that, so they had it organised in a jiffy. A whole hotel had been booked for family and friends, but I still got cold feet. Another life-long friend of Gianni's, Gunter Sachs, rang me early on Friday. 'Let's take a plane on Sunday morning and fly right back . . . ' I know that Gianni adored Gunter, whom he had known even longer than yours truly. The trouble is both Gunter and I had a funny feeling about attending. I suspect in both our cases – we are both past the point of no return at sixty-five – we felt intrusive. Reflected glory and all that. You're either a very close friend, or you're not. Gunter always was, and I like to think ditto, where I'm concerned. But this was a state occasion, and we were, after all, just friends.

And another thing. In view of my age, I don't handle funerals as well as I used to. When the trumpeteer plays *la ultima saluta*, I lose it. What clinched it was that Turin airport was shut down early, as were all the streets leading to the cathedral, so our dilemma was solved. Anyway, I said what I had to say when Dominic Lawson – as always, an early bird – rang me and asked me to write about l'avvocato for the *Sunday Telegraph* one week before the great man died. I did not like my piece. Gianni was too much a man of parts for someone of my literary abilities to zero in on at one sitting. I wanted to be lyrical, but only managed it towards the end, when I asked myself whether riches, physical beauty, great style and cultural taste, happiness brings.

All I know is – like in Graham Greene's novel – Agnelli made me. He taught me to be unfailingly polite to those who couldn't answer back, just as my father taught me to take crap from no one, however grand. He showed me what style is all about, not fashionable things but that elusive quality no one is capable of buying, the opposite of pretence. The ability to command attention without soliciting it. Being authentic without making a conscious effort at being so. Agnelli had it all, and I got the message early on, when I was twenty-one, and he was thirty-seven.

Hemingway used to say, '*Il faut d'abord survivre.*' I agree. Survival is somehow important, the trouble being one loses all one's friends. In the last five years I've lost Yanni Zographos, Jimmy Goldsmith, John Aspinall, Charles Benson, and now Gianni Agnelli. One for each year, and in that order. I wonder who's next? Perhaps I should befriend that incompetent buffoon Jack Straw, or that prancing phony, Tony Baloney. But I digress. What am I doing mentioning such malevolent clowns in the same breath as l'avvocato?

I'm off to the Big Bagel and Washington DC where – speaking of phonies and buffoons – the William Kristols of this world have convinced George W. Bush to play the role of Alexander the Great. Heaven help us.

Superior Living

Saturday, 15 February 2003
Paris

'Why do the French have to be so bloody-minded?' asked a *Daily Telegraph* headline last week. Well, sitting in Café Flore, sipping a very good white wine early in the day while waiting for friends to lunch across at Chez Lipp, the answer seems obvious. When the quality of life is as good as it is in France, it tends to make people feel superior. It's also because the Frogs are the most intellectual of races, because they are stylish and charming when they want to be, because Paris is the most beautiful city in the whole wide world, and because they view the British as philistines and the Americans as barbarians. *Zut alors!*

It takes me less than an hour once in Paris to become pro-French, just as it takes me less than an hour once in London to become anti-British. Ergo, why I have moved to neutral Switzerland. Having grown up disliking the French and liking the English, I'd like to keep it that way, but how? In France, prime ministers have been known to cheat on their wives, a good thing, whereas in Cool Britannia the premier cheats by plagiarising a twelve-year-old thesis written by an American student. *Quel con!*

In France the TGV trains are on time and speed along at close to 150 mph; in grubby old England the Eurostar traps people in airless agony ten minutes out of Waterloo. *C'est le bordel!* In Paris even the rain is good. It makes the place feel romantic; in London just more depressing. *Merde!* France has great writers like Michel Deon; England has midgets like Martin Amis. *Pauvre type!* France has St Tropez; England Blackpool. *Zut, flute!*

But back to Café Flore (two pretty girls deep into their books, chain-smoking and sipping endless cups of coffee, now that's what I call a civilised morning) and Chez Lipp.

The reason for the Parisian visit was a sad one: the memorial service for my ex-brother-in-law, Le Marquis François de Caraman, a wonderful friend who died much too young in Guatemala on 11 November. L'eglise Saint-Thomas d'Aquin, between Boulevard Saint-Germain and la rue du Bac, was a perfect setting. François, after all, as I said in my speech, was a Left Bank type of man, sweet, artistic, sensitive and spiritual. He also loved pussy and chased it non-stop all of his life. Bravo! His beautiful daughter and ex-wife were there, as was his father, le Duc de Caraman, looking extremely ducal in black, but with all the pain of his son's death written over his face. Many of François's friends were present, from Peter Bemberg, the Argentinian heir of oligarchs, to Nicola Anouilh, son of the great playwright Jean.

When Peter, Nicola, Vladimir and François were in their late teens, I was about ten years older, and could get them into New Jimmy's, the chicest club of the period. The first time Porfirio Rubirosa set eyes on François, he called him the spitting image of Johnny de Caraman. 'Well,' said someone, 'who do you expect him to look like, the milkman?' 'You'd be surprised how many sons of aristocrats look like the milkman,' answered the wise Rubi.

After the service we walked to Brasserie Lipp, an historic old place full of wonderful memories. The Bembergs were the hosts and we did lotsa drinking and reminiscing. God, those were good days to have fun. We were young, rich and right-wing, quite an accomplishment back then as it was extremely untrendy. Afterwards, I walked from Lipp to the Gare de Lyon, a fifty-minute hike through history. Down rue Bonaparte, right turn on the quai, past l'Odéon, la Conciergerie, cross over the bridge to Quai des Celestins, rue du Fauconnier . . . it's like walking though an outdoor museum. L'Hotel Fieubet, so baroque it baroques you out of your jockstrap. Finally, Place de la Bastille, Austerlitz and on to Lyon. The French name their streets after brainy and artistic types, and victorious battles. Imagine if the Saudis did likewise. You'd need Dr Livingstone and then some to get around.

John Adams called Paris the 'capital of dissipation and nonsense'. Adams was a New Englander who fretted that French culture would pollute the new country called the United States. The French eighteenth-century diplomat, Charles Gravier de Vergennes, opined that republics have no manners. Two hundred and fifty years later America and France are once again shadow boxing. Republics do not have manners, I agree, but the French have hardly polluted America with their culture. And monarchies, too, no longer have manners. Look at Cool Blairtannia. For the moment, I'll take Frogland. Vive la France. Vive Paris. Vive le Café Flore. Vive Chez Lipp. Vive François de Caraman.

Weight Watching

Saturday, 15 March 2003

Gstaad

This Khalid Sheikh Mohammed chappie looks like a porn star, grubby, tubby, hairy and very, very ugly. I'm talking about the alleged mastermind of the attacks on 11 September 2001, who got picked up last week in – as reported by the British press – 'an upper-middle class suburb' of Rawalpindi. (Leave it to the class-obsessed hacks to describe a slum as middle class.) Although in his pictures he poses as much of a threat as a pastry shop, I guess looks are deceiving. What I'd like to know is how anyone could take orders from such a ghastly-looking fellow.

At least Harry Bin Laden is somewhat handsome. I remember him once in White's bar talking about leadership, and how important it was for leaders to inspire with their looks. If memory serves, Nicholas Soames was there and Harry advised him to lose some weight. Harry Laden had a point. Napoleon won quite a lot while he was thin, but piled up loss after loss when he put on the pounds. Wellington was short but stayed lean and hungry. Philip and Alexander never lost and were never fatties, nor were Miltiades, Themistocles and the beautiful Alcibiades. MacArthur and Patton were skinny and good-looking, as was the best tank commander of them all, Hasso von Manteuffel, all five foot three of him. The only winning fatty I can think of is Kutusov, but I'm basing it on the actor who played him in War and Peace.

So much for accuracy. And speaking of this elusive concept for

British hacks, I cringed at a *Sunday Times Magazine* cover story 'about a *Playboy*' seducing Jackie Kennedy. All I can say is what rot, what balls, what bullshit! Written by one John Follain – a cut and paste collection – it is not a hatchet job, far from it; it is, however, completely made up. Even the pictures lie. Gianni Agnelli and his wife were friends of the Kennedys, Gianni was never in his life alone with Jackie – not even for a moment – and, last but not least, Jackie was hardly his type. Gianni was friends with Lee, her sister, and there was nothing there either. Why make it up? I guess to have the sucker that's born every minute buy the rag. But back to Osama Bin (Harry) Laden.

When he was at Rosey, his nickname was Saladin, which was a play on words because of his love for salads. They also called him 'pass' for his propensity to stand offside in front of the opposing goalkeeper and scream 'pass, pass' to his teammates. Harry's football prowess reflects his revolutionary career. Others do the heavy lifting for him. But I imagine Harry has not been playing much football lately, not outdoors, anyway.

Although I'm not the type to kick a man when he's down, I really am off Harry – 9/11 and all that. And I do believe that Khalid Sheikh Mohammed should be tortured into revealing Harry's where-abouts. (But first they should shave him. His hairy back is much too disgusting even for a torturer.) Incidentally, and now for a serious point, Stephen Glover wrote that 'Torture destroys our values'. Of course it does, but for the greater good it can come in handy. He then writes that the nineteenth-century British Empire survived and thrived without torture. Really? If twentieth-century British soldiers tortured Greek-Cypriots, why should I believe that nineteenth-century Brits did not turn the screws on colonials? The ones the Brits should have tortured were the IRA scum, but they treated them with kid gloves instead.

Another close friend of Harry Laden's was Nicky Haslam, who designed and decorated Harry's house both in London and in Kandahar. When Harry, Nicky and I had a drink there long ago, I thought that the place seemed awfully familiar until Nicky admitted that his design was inspired by the film Gunga Din. Well, I don't know who inspired him last week at Lee Radziwill's birthday party in Paris, but his lyrics would have made Noël Coward proud. (He also sounded just like the master.) They say that living well is the best revenge. I can't think of anything better than celebrating the birthday of a lady I was once madly in love with, and seeing all my old French buddies. Everyone is pissed off with the French right now, but what the hell. They have the most beautiful capital on earth, the prettiest girls (yes, you guessed it, I'm in love again, but platonically) and food and wine to die for. On the whole I'd rather be there than in London.

Forked Tongues

Saturday, 19 April 2003
New York

Just as well I never made it down south. For the last three weeks I've been feeling kinda funny, finding blood on my pillow in the morning and having headaches, things I attributed to my Karamazovian hangovers. While waiting to fly to Iran, I decided to go to see a doctor. He took one look inside my head (via an MRI) and told me I had to have an operation right away. The mother of my children flew over and held my hand, the doctor cut out a tumour of sorts, and I'm now home recuperating and happy as a lark. I shall know next week whether this was a bad or good tumour, but – before some Murdoch and *Guardian* hacks break open the champagne – the doc says it's a good one.

This is the good news. The bad is that, because of my illness, I've now become a real hack, able to lie without thinking and with a very straight face. Let me explain. Like most people outside the journalistic or criminal professions, I try not to lie or mislead. But when the telephone rang one day after my operation and a woman on the other end announced she was ringing from the *Daily Mail* to enquire whether I was dying or not, I never missed a beat. 'Never felt better in my life,' I said, or words to that effect. 'Where do they come up with such stuff?' and so on. She was immediately convinced. I will not mention the woman's name. It's a well-known one, and she should be ashamed of herself. How does someone ring a person they've never met and ask such intimate questions? At the end, the female hack did not get her story – who the hell among *Daily Mail* readers gives a damn, anyway? – and I found out I could speak with a forked tongue with the best of them. (Perhaps I should join a Murdoch tabloid.) But talk about being insensitive and intrusive. Hacks, I was once told by Charles Moore, were considered just above thieves in the hierarchy of professions. I wonder if they still hold such an exalted position.

But enough of such a depressing subject. The British tabloids, starting with Murdoch and his minions, have brutalised society with their sensationalism and outright fabrications. The media presents itself as a tribune of the people, but it's nothing of the sort. It is the celebration of crass ignorance, of the puerile and the scatological.

And speaking of crass ignorance, I read in the *Telegraph* that UEFA, the governing body of European football, is trying to kick racism out of football by charging the FA over the English fans who chanted 'I'd rather be a Paki than a Turk' during the match against

Turkey. Well, I'm not so sure. It depends what kind of Turk. When Byron visited Ali Pasha, the magnificent blond Albanian ruler of Greece, in 1824, Ali offered him access to his harem. Ali had 150 young girls, and 150 young boys. 'Go on, take some of the boys,' he told the poet. 'Why do you assume I like boys?' asked Byron. 'Ah, all you Old Etonians like that,' said Ali, getting it right except for the fact that Byron went to Harrow.

Turn me into a Turk like Ali Pasha with 150 young girls (you can give the boys to Peter Mandelson) and I'd much rather be a Turk than a Paki. But put me in bed with Jemima Khan, and I'd much rather be a Paki than a Turk. I would have loved to have been a German officer in Paris at the start of the war, and an American officer in Berlin at the end of it. Think of all the pussy. What I would not have liked is to have been an Italian officer in Greece during the war – we had humiliated them – or an English officer in Singapore. It's all relative.

Rumsfeld and the sofa samurais are gloating over their easy victory against one of history's greatest war machines. In the meantime, looters have sacked Baghdad's antiquities museum, plundering treasures dating from the dawn of civilisation in Mesopotamia. But why should Rummie worry? His idea of culture is the proverbial piano-shaped swimming-pool, so who gives a damn about Meso . . . what'sacallit? As if the poor Arabs don't have enough problems. Just think of it. No Arab government has ever accepted public responsibility for its own shortcomings. No Arab state genuinely respects human rights. No Arab state is a true democracy. Now we've managed to ensure that they've even lost their past, although Rummie told a press conference that he thinks some of the objects might be returned. With a haircut like Rumsfeld's, what do you expect?

Happy Easter to all of you.

Halcyon Days

Saturday, 19 July 2003
St Tropez

My father died on 14 July, 1989, in an obvious if somewhat self-defeating gesture against the two hundred year celebration of the French Revolution. I always think of my dad on the infamous day which is France's national holiday, especially when I'm on the Riviera, a once magical place where he first took me as a boy in 1952. Those were great times. Very few people had boats, and even fewer people among the haves had bad manners. Everyone dressed for dinner, and fast women tried desperately to act like ladies, outside the sack, that is. Life was very cheap if one had dollars, a large suite at the Hotel du Cap costing something like twenty-five bucks per day. Two short Greek men would run around the Sporting casino of Monte Carlo and the summer one in Cannes yelling 'banco!'. They were the golden Greeks, Niarchos and Onassis, and the latter would become majority owner of the Société des Bains de Mer (which owned the casino and the major hotels of Monte Carlo) the next year.

The halcyon days of the Riviera lasted until the Arab invasion of 1975, exactly one year after the oil-price rise following the Yom Kippur war of 1973. Mind you, like Byzantium, the place had reeked of coming disaster for years. Gianni Agnelli had sold his magnificent villa La Leopolda in 1963; Niarchos kept Château de la Croe, but cruised around Greece during the summer; Onassis was driven out of Monte Carlo by Rainier; the Hotel du Cap was sold by its nice owner to a German company; and the real-estate vultures had begun to circle. By the time the newly rich Arabs arrived the only ones they found still holding the fort were pimps, hookers, gangsters, a few old English ladies too tired to flee, lotsa estate agents ready to deal and the world's most disaffected character, poor little me.

The reason for my dissatisfaction was that I could not believe what had taken place right under my nose. Dick Diver's Riviera had transformed into Sammy Glick's playground overnight. People we used to make fun of behind their backs for their vulgarity and anxiety to please their betters — Robert de Balkany, for example, a Hungarian real-estate developer born Robert Zellinger, who married into the Italian royal family, bought a large boat and played a poor man's Niarchos — had suddenly become the Riviera's old guard, a bit like Lilly Safra lording it over London nowadays. Large stink pots clogged up the marinas, prices skyrocketed as if on Viagra, and the developers even dug up the dead in order to build more high-rises. The obvious move was to the Greek islands, but there was a problem there also. After a while one gets bored with Greek Lotharios cruising dirty beaches in search of h-dropping Shirley Valentines. Back to the drawing-board: Gstaad in summer was the answer. For a while, that is. Summer Gstaad means walking, climbing, tennis, karate, music festivals and watching the cows while discussing the human condition with people one's own age.

The healthy life, however, can get awfully tiresome without young things to admire. Back to the drawing-board once again.

Finally, eureka! A sailing boat, a birth in St Tropez, and instant satisfaction. Well, not so instant. The boat is still being built, as my Italian naval architect, a pussy-whipped soul married to an American, has taken his time. Meanwhile, my French crew are working on their tan on full pay by yours truly, the mother of my children is furious with me because I stayed in London partying, my cricket career seems to have hit a snag, and I have returned to my roots on the French Riviera, this time observing from a friend's villa high above how truly disgusting the newly rich have become. And it gets worse.

The Germans and the Italians are not speaking to each other; in fact, my host and I were told in no uncertain terms to choose between wops and krauts, no ifs or buts about it. All this fighting over a few words about the war. Ridiculous. When Marshal Graziani visited Kesselring as the latter was preparing his defence of Italy against the Allied invasion, he was surprised to see the German wearing his red-striped marshal's uniform. Asked why, Kesselring replied, 'In case I am wounded, I do not want the blood to show and the troops to lose heart.' 'Why didn't you tell me,' said Graziani, 'I would have worn my brown breeches.' Be that as it may, Berlusconi is the best man in Europe, and he was right to tell that German oaf where to get off. Berlusconi good, Schulz bad. Rommel, Guderian, von Runstedt, von Manteuffel good, Romano Prodi bad.

Debbie Bismarck and Maya Schoenburg *sehr gut*, Oriana Fallaci very bad. See what I mean? There are good Germans and good Italians whereas the most disgusting person in Europe is a Belgian, Louis Michel, posing as the foreign minister of the most ridiculous of countries. Vive le Quatorze Juillet! A St Tropez!

Family Courage

Saturday, 16 August 2003
Gstaad

I remember it as if it were yesterday. Rodney Solomon, a friend no longer with us, came into the Clermont club all huffy and puffy and dressed in a morning coat, refused an invitation to lunch, and announced that he was off early to the wedding of 'my great friend Sally Curzon to Piers Courage'. The Clermont back then, it was 1966, belonged to John Aspinall, who was known for his friendly abuse of all and sundry. 'Go on with your social climbing, Rodney, and tell that racing driver that real men don't race but gamble . . . ' or words to that effect.

I did not join in. In fact I was quite envious of Rodney, as Sally Curzon was my dream girl, and Piers Courage my idol. The fact that I had never met either of them was immaterial. As it turned out, I never got to meet Piers, but became a good friend of his widow once she married John Aspinall. Piers Courage, an Old Etonian with aristocratic connections and Swinging London life-style, was the first man to drive for Frank Williams in Formula One racing. He was on the verge of becoming a superstar racer when he was killed at the Dutch Grand Prix of 1970. His wife Sally was present. He was twenty-eight years old and the father of two boys. The winner of the race, Austrian Jochen Rindt, broke down in tears at the solemn podium ceremony at the track, and Piers's premature death has remained with us, his fans, ever since.

Thirty-three years later, a wonderfully nostalgic and beautifully written glossy book has been published under the title *Piers Courage, Last of the Gentlemen Racers*. The author is Adam Cooper, a motor sport journalist of impeccable credentials, with a forward by Sir Frank Williams. I cannot say enough without sounding like a flack. It brought back so many painful memories, but also of those wonderful times when racers were not robots, inferior cars could make their way to the front of the grid through the skill and daring of their drivers, and when one wrong move usually ended in horrible, fiery death.

This not being an obituary column, I will not list the countless brave men who died practising their death-defying sport. Just those I was friendly with, starting with Wolfgang von Trips, the handsome German count who was killed in Monza in 1961 while leading the Formula One championship; the Marquis Alfonso de Portago, the Spanish aristo who also was a bobsleigher and a world-class rider, killed in the last Mille Miglia in 1957. And, of course, my good friend Graham Hill, who went down in his plane after his retirement from racing. Jo Bonnier, heir to a great Swedish publishing fortune, died in Le Mans just as he was seriously contemplating retirement – he had threatened it time and again – and last but not least Jochen Rindt, who was crowned world champion posthumously the very same year of Piers's death.

The book poignantly recalls when Sally Courage went to stay with the Rindts in Switzerland after the Dutch disaster – the beautiful Nina Rindt and Sally were very close – says goodbye to Jochen, and suddenly is filled with foreboding, thinking she will never see Jochen again. (She saw his remains.)

Jackie Stewart, three times world champion, was the moving force behind today's safety measures. Jackie was so shocked at the death of his teammate, François Severt, my ex-wife's betrothed at the time of his death, that he decided enough was enough. Jackie, the Rindts,

Bonnier and various others in the motor industry all lived within walking distance of each other above Lake Geneva, which is where I came in. I remember them all with great affection and respect, Sir Jackie being the only survivor.

Great personal courage tinged with tragedy continued to play a role in Piers's and Sally's family. She married John Aspinall, had a son, Bassa, and her two boys, Amos and Jason, were lucky to get a stepfather such as Aspers. Amos, a conservationist, lives in Africa transporting apes and other endangered species away from the wars that have engulfed that tragic continent. He has flirted with death time and again, but one would never know it from meeting him. Jason, who was three when his father died, tried his hand at motor racing, had a couple of very competent seasons in Formula Ford, but, racing being what it is today, he had to give it up in order to earn a living.

In October 1995, driving his bike at 35 mph going west on the Cromwell Road, some foreigner made an illegal turn in front of him to go south. Jason was terribly injured and has been in a wheelchair ever since. Like everyone else in his family, he has been a model of good cheer and, however corny, courage.

Piers was a charming man, full of laughter and talent. He really was the last gentleman racer. His children are true inheritors of his charm and personal courage. Ditto his wonderful wife Sally. Some-one should make a film of this book.

Soldiering is for others

Saturday, 30 August 2003
Gstaad

All Quiet on the Western Front was written in 1929 and became an instant best-seller; in Germany alone more than three million copies were sold within eighteen months. Hollywood made a film of it the following year and it won an Oscar for Best Picture. I read it during the closing days of the Second World War, my great uncle, a German scholar, helping me along. I saw the film in 1949 and never forgot the haunting scene when the hero, Paul Baumer, kills a Frenchman who had randomly jumped into his foxhole in no-man's-land. Baumer bayonets him in the throat, after which he watches the man die slowly, gurgling blood. Overcome by guilt, the German comforts the Frenchman and, after the latter's death, he finds photographs of his loved ones tucked inside his uniform. In other words, the enemy is just like us.

Don McCullin echoed the haunting scenario when he photographed a dead Viet Cong soldier in Hue in 1968, his plundered belongings lying beside him, a picture of his pretty sweetheart facing his dead eyes. I remember the photo only too well. It shook me like no other. The evil, or so we thought, VC also had feelings, and took pictures of their loved ones into combat just like the rest of us. Both the film and Don's photograph were in black and white, adding great dramatic effect.

I've just been given the McCullin book and an Erich Maria Remarque biography by Hilton Tims for my birthday, both books confirming my recent anti-war feelings about old men sending young ones to die. Here's a United States Marine, Roger McGrath, writing in *Chronicles Magazine* (best American monthly by far) about war:

> And who is to do it? Certainly not the neoconservatives. They use such terms as moral clarity and the need to project our power – but it is to be done with someone else's body. A conversation I had with a budding neo-con reveals their version of moral clarity. Who was included when he said 'we'. He looked at me as if I were a bit dense and said, 'We, the United States.' 'Does that mean you?' I asked. 'No,' he replied, 'the guys in the army.'

McGrath goes on to ask the neo-con whether our boys should be put in harm's way for interests that have nothing to do with the defence of the United States. 'Are you willing to do what you call the right thing with your own body?' asks the Marine. 'Those guys are volunteers – they chose to do it. I'm just finishing my degree and have a good job lined up.'

Need I say more? The neo-con is not a soldier and does not plan to become one. Soldiering is for others. In a republic, it is the job of citizens. In an empire, it is imperial forces who do the fighting. Another Marine, Major-General Smedley Butler, twice decorated with the Medal of Honour, making him one of only two Marines in history to win the greatest battlefield decoration twice, had this to say about war: 'War is just a racket . . . I believe in adequate defence of our coastline and nothing else. If a nation comes here, then we'll fight. I wouldn't go to war again as I have done to protect some lousy investment of the bankers. I would only fight for the defence of our homes and for the Bill of Rights.'

Hear, hear! I remember landing in Tel Aviv in 1973. The Yom Kippur war had just begun and I was covering it for a Greek newspaper and *National Review*. I had to file two stories a day from the Golan front where vicious fighting was raging. The Syrians gave a good account of themselves, as did the Egyptians on the Sinai side. But they did not take care of their dead soldiers. Unlike the Israelis who picked up their dead, the Arabs left them to rot in the desert. I saw hundreds of young bodies lying around, and imagined their fat masters back in Damascus and Cairo covered in medals and sipping sweet coffee.

After Hue in 1972, where the expected battle never took place – American air strikes by B-52s caught the invading Giap army in the open (I can still remember the stink of dead human flesh) – and the Yom Kippur war, I decided war was not such a good thing after all. *All Quiet on the Western Front* attests to a common humanity transcending nation, race, and religion. Erich Maria Remarque became a pacifist because he had fought the war in the trenches. The neocons never have and do not plan to, and do not deserve the right to send anyone to die except themselves.

Memories of Things Past

Saturday, 4 October 2003

What was it that Papa said about Paris? That it was a fine place to be quite young in and that it's a necessary part of a man's education, I believe. Also the bit about being like a mistress who does not grow old but has other lovers now. Well, all too true, yet Paris was sun baked and beautiful as ever last week, the dome of Les Invalides glistening in gold, the chestnut leaves holding on for dear life, the cobbled streets empty of traffic and the people in a festive mood that matched my own.

I was in the City of Light to celebrate my friend Jean-Claude Sauer's book of his forty years at *Paris-Match*. It's a beautiful coffee table tome of his photographs of Vietnam, Algeria, Biafra, Yemen and of every conflict since 1963, as well as intimate pics of de Gaulle and every French president since Le Grand Charles. There's fashion and the arts, with some hauntingly intimate pictures of the tragic Papa, the equally tragic Romy Schneider, Catherine Deneuve, La Callas and a naked Brigitte Bardot that would make Peter Mandelson switch in a jiffy. And then there are the bullfights.

Sauer was close to Papa, Ordonez and Dominguin. Their dangerous summer of *mano a mano* comes alive in brilliant colour, as do the divine Charlotte Rampling and Fanny Ardant. It's the contrast in Sauer's pics that makes the book a real gem. He has dedicated it to Jean Prouvost, the founder of *Match*, with acknowledgments to his three wives and – yours truly.

We met forty-five years ago, in a nightclub, of course. He had just returned from Algeria where he was a paratrooper under the great Massu. I was on the tennis circuit. We were Hemingway groupies, loved nightclubs, fast women and faster cars. He went on to become bobsleigh champion of France and to drive in Le Mans. I sort of trailed behind. Then he joined Match as a photographer and I joined *National Review* as a reporter. Our paths crossed in Vietnam and in the Middle East. He's the one who having dragged a famous French playboy to Kuneitra with him during the Yom Kippur war screamed at me to go and get him when the playboy froze in the car during a bombardment. 'If he's killed we'll never be allowed back to New Jimmy's again.'

In forty-five years of friendship we've never had a cross word. His ex-wife Brigitte de Ganay threw a great bash for him after the opening of the exhibition at the La Béraudière gallery featuring his photos, and it was like a class reunion. All the naughty boys of my youth were there, starting with Freddy Cushing, who had flown over from Newport, Rhode Island. Needless to say, we stayed late and bent the elbow quite a lot.

Next night was my turn, as it was the mother of my children's birthday. This time it was even later, ending up at dawn somewhere on the Left Bank. What a city! After the bistro celebrations, I went to a friend's place in Boulevard St Germain for a last drink and looked out over miles of Parisian rooftops. *Bonjour tristesse.* The place is so beautiful it makes one a little triste, especially when under the influence. But I ain't complaining. This has been a hell of a week.

London was as wonderful as Paris, and on my last night there I went to the Speccie's 175th anniversary party at the Four Seasons. As luck would have it, I chatted with Alistair Horne about French mistresses and the great influence they have on their politician menfolk. The historian wished to know why other nationalities do not. That is when I spotted Daisy Prince, someone I would like to make my mistress but am not likely to. (She is far richer than I am.) I met Daisy's mother, Diana, thirty years ago. I asked her to dinner but she said she was on her honeymoon and could not possibly. If memory serves, I told her that hers was a middle-class reaction. She told her bridegroom, Freddy Prince, who laughed out loud and insisted on meeting me. Then it transpired that I was the man going out with Diana's aunt, then in her forties. (I was in my twenties.) The point of the story is that in the brilliant 175th anniversary issue of *The Speccie* (on sale for six weeks and make sure you buy a copy) Daisy's great-aunt is pictured next to the Duke of Windsor, page 129. Does that date me or what, as they say. But at least Daisy came to dinner, which is more than her mother did, but far less than her great-aunt.

French Lessons

Saturday, 11 October 2003

I've had some further thoughts as to the reasons why a mistress enjoys more influence over a French politician than, say, over an Englishman, a question posed to me by the historian Alistair Horne two weeks ago.

For starters, men in France consider a mistress to be a normal part of a male's panoply, whereas in England terms like 'clean living' and 'decent' apply primarily to sexual behaviour. In France, people have always treated sexual conduct as being outside the scope of moral judgment; not so in puritanical Albion. In France, the lighter character of the men leads them to reflect aloud on their projects while aiming to be the master. In other words, he takes his slave into his confidence. Whether the little woman is of the same opinion does not matter. He has taken her into his confidence. They are sharing a secret. (Can you picture John Major taking the self-publicist Edwina Currie into his confidence? It would have been on the front page of the *Daily Mail* the next morning.) Whether the mistress loves the Frenchman is immaterial. She needs him, and he in turn communicates his ideas to her. *C'est tout!*

The Frenchman informs his mistress of his power, and discusses it with her. Can't you see that rather insignificant little man, Paul Reynaud, the last French prime minister before the fall of France in 1940, bragging to La Comtesse de la Porte how he will stop the Hun (with a little help from 'mon cher ami, Winston')? I sure can. Or François Mitterrand, more cerebral, reflecting with his various women friends about matters most frivolous as well as very important?

De Gaulle was among the very few French politicians without a mistress, and it showed. My favourite was Georges Pompidou, a gent as well as a very able man, and someone very discreet. Pompidou loved good food and wines, so he must have adored women. Once, at Paul-Louis Weiller's house, newly married to the prettiest young girl in Paris, Pompidou stepped aside so my wife and I could pass in front of him to the dinner table. 'Après vous, monsieur le Premier Ministre,' said I. 'Non, la jeunesse d'abord,' exclaimed the gallant Georges.

As I recently wrote in these pages, French women have frivolous habits, a taste for luxury, and a host of little passions, all traits which make them perfect mistresses. The exaggerated coquetry can never be reconciled with true love – that is the wife's domain. The mistress, in fact, is more associated with the thoughts of the man than the *cinq à sept* quickies she is usually associated with by the popular press.

Oh, yes, I almost forgot. Mistresses in France do not go public, no matter what price is dangled before them, nor the threats, as in the case of Claude Grudet, my good friend, who is also known as Madame Claude. She refused to dish the dirt on anyone and ended up in jail, ruined, but still she did not spill a single bean.

Is a mistress a necessary part of a politician's stature? Of course it is, or at least it used to be. Mistresses have managed to help their men far more than they've hurt them, but I haven't enough space here to give historical examples. All I know is that I wouldn't mind having Georgina Rylance for a mistress. Alas, I asked her and she turned me down. And for good reasons, too. She is one of our most talented actresses, having trained at Lamda, and with an Oxford degree to boot. She's been in films, on television, and in the theatre, with her last role being in the remake of *Spartacus.*

I took her to dinner with five men following *The Speccie* party last

July, and a well-known young historian turned into a gibbering wreck when she got up and he saw the legs that went with the face. Why has she refused my offer? Easy. She loves acting, but not in the bed. Worse, her father is a judge who might not take kindly to the fact that an old lecher like yours truly has taken his little girl as a mistress. So Georgina and I are just friends, as horrible a term as there is in the English language. But don't count me out yet. In Paris I made a few contacts, and, if things work out, I expect to continue my well-researched reports about why French mistresses are the tops.

Late Night Antics

Saturday, 18th October 2003
Washington, DC

By all accounts *The American Conservative*'s first anniversary party went off without a hitch. My friend Prince Radziwill came over for it, as did Charlie Glass, a very nice thing for both men to do, not to mention Major Chris Meyers, a tough Marine officer who flew from Los Angeles. Well, not to nit-pick, but perhaps there was a slight hitch, something to do with my speech. I don't know why it is, but whenever a situation demands gravitas, a little voice inside me always tells me to do the opposite.

For example, after welcoming everyone to a rooftop restaurant overlooking the Washington Monument and the Mall, for some strange reason I brought up the 'gay small penis support group', and even produced a New York magazine article which had brought the gay small penis support group to my attention. (I don't believe any of our loyal readers are interested, but perhaps some of their foreign friends might be, so here is the group's address: Room 312 in the Lesbian, Gay, Bisexual & Transgender Community Center on 13th Street, New York.) The reason I brought up the tiny organs was that so many neo-cons (or nouveau cons, as the French call them) were missing from my own tiny organ's birthday. I announced that they had sent their regrets but were busy speaking to the gay small penis support group in the Bagel and had rsvp'd their regrets. Oh well, people cannot be in two places at once, and the nouveau cons made it obvious whom they preferred.

Mind you, size does matter, and I'm very happy to report that we had a full house. Although Washington is not known as a party town, some friends and I did our best to upgrade the town's reputation by some late-night roistering. Actually, it was rather pathetic. I ended up with a buddy in the bar of the Willard Hotel, where presidents Grant and Harding used to get up to no good. I ran into a congressman from Indiana sitting with three sweet young things.

The mother of my children was asleep upstairs, which inspired my friend to tell the youngest of the ladies that I was married to an eighty-seven year-old whose father had put a curse on me which said that, until a very young woman decided to marry me, I would have to stay hitched to his eighty-seven year-old daughter. It wasn't the best of pick-up lines – rather pathetic, in fact – but it worked. The twenty-two year-old assistant to the Indiana congressman felt very sorry for me, and said that she would help me lift the curse from my wicked father-in-law. We agreed to meet sometime in the future. My friend who thought up this rubbish has been dining out on it ever since. All I can say is that either we were too drunk and imagined the whole thing, or there are some awfully dumb people in the American system of government.

Not as dumb as the Dutch government, however. For some of you who may have missed it, Prince Johan Friso, Queen Beatrix's middle son and second in line to the throne of the Netherlands, had to give up his right of succession for the woman he loves. Mabel Wisse Smit, the prince's fiancée, is, it seems, the one-time moll of big-time gangster Klaas Bruinsma. The Dutch premier, Jan Peter Balkenende, is furious with the lovebirds because they gave his government and the queen 'incomplete and inaccurate' information regarding the floozy's past. Now I ask you. Do you know many women who would tell a boring queen and a far more boring politician about her screwing around with a thug like Klaas? Of course not, except if they were very, very stupid, on a par with the girl at the Willard Hotel. Mabelgate has cost Prince Johan his chance at the throne but, like the little boy who stuck his little finger in the dyke, the prince has decided to stick with his little girl and to hell with the throne. The Dutch are fools as well as boring. Mabel's past makes for excitement at a very boring court.

Otherwise everything's hunky-dory. I hope to return to London for Tom Stacey's new book, *Tribe*, on 10 November, and for yet another debate about the war at the Oxford Union. This is the good news. The bad is the death of a wonderful man, Max Rayne, whom I knew from when I was first allowed into a casino back in the Fifties. Lord Rayne was as graceful a gambler as he was successful as a businessman. What a pleasure it was to gamble against a gentleman, rather than the slobs we have to put up with nowadays. I'm sure his business competitors felt the same.

Death of a Gentleman

Saturday, 15 November 2003
New York

My father-in-law Peter Schoenburg died last week. He was eighty-eight. I've often written about Peter in the past because I was very proud to be his son-in-law. No, not for the reasons a snob might suspect. In fact the opposite. It was his gentleness, decency and kindness which made Peter the very attractive man he was throughout a long and tumultuous life. His Serene Highness Prince Peter Karl Marie Anton Pius Benedictus Markus Johannes Schoenburg-Hartenstein was born in the Rome embassy of the Austrian-Hungarian Empire in 1915. His father was ambassador to the Holy See. His mother was Princess Sophie Oettingen-Wallerstein. In a book Peter published for the family, he describes his idyllic childhood in the Palazzo Venezia – as the embassy later became – served by close to one hundred staff, and how it all disappeared overnight once the empire collapsed in 1918. (Paying one's bills by post in Vienna was impractical; the stamp was worth more than the amount owed because of inflation.)

The old Prince Schoenburg refused to serve under anyone else but the emperor, who was no more. He retired to Bohemia, which he partly owned, and that is where Peter and his seven brothers and sisters grew up. Cervena Lhota, or Red House, has been described by the *New York Times* as the most beautiful and romantic castle in Europe. It is a thirteenth-century fortress built on a low rocky spur, which became an island after a shallow valley was flooded. After school, Peter served as a cavalry officer, but just before the Anschluss left the country for South America. Both his brothers served with distinction on the Russian front, and both suffered terribly once they fell into Russian hands. One of his sisters, Loremarie, went to ask the Pope for his approval to assassinate Hitler. The Pontiff did not approve; nor did he disapprove, however. This was in 1942. Peter became active on the Amazon frontier as an explorer and surveyor. He married my mother-in-law, Lyna, in Bogota, Colombia, had my future wife, but then the couple divorced. Lyna was beautiful, spoilt and rich, and liked the high life. He did not.

H. L. Mencken, the American thinker, wrote that every decent man is ashamed of the government he lives under. Peter always gave me the impression he was ashamed of the society he lived among. By this I mean the society which had fallen into the hands of unspeakable philistines, vulgarians and publicity hounds. In the current *Vanity Fair*, writing on a different subject, a reporter describes our tabloid culture as 'Unattractive people doing unattractive things in unattractive places.' Hear, hear!

Peter Schoenburg shunned the limelight throughout his life, secure in his own identity, therefore psychologically free to treat everyone he came across as his equal. This trait has always been the sign of true nobility. Snobbery, after all, is nothing but bad manners trying to pass itself off as good taste. Style, on the other hand, cannot be decoded, nor can it be bestowed. True style is not calculated, but intimately connected with sincerity.

In 1951, Peter married a beautiful American aristo, Lee Russell Jones, and had two children, Peter and Victoria. In all the years I've known the family, I never heard an uncivil word pass between any of them. Young Peter went to Yale and has dedicated his life to defending the poor and defenceless in New Mexico. I once told him that here I was writing about locking everyone up, and he, as a public defendant, was trying to keep everyone out of jail. He gave me a rueful smile, to each his own, type of thing. The reason I go on about the Schoenburgs is because through their example I've become a better man. I know, I know, it's corny and all that, but to hell with it. In a world where society is unravelling before us, their moral anchor, compassion for others and civic virtues have been a great example. Especially to my children.

My daughter was Peter's first grandchild, and both she and my son were devastated when they heard of 'Opa's' death. Peter's ashes were buried in a simple cemetery near his property in upstate New York. There was no hymn-singing, no religious spectacle, just lots of tears from the grandchildren. There was a simple procession of mourners, mostly tall, good-looking young people, led by his widow. My daughter read 'Ithaca', the Cavafy poem, one of Opa's favourites, my son read a passage from Opa's memoirs and Victoria's husband, Brian, the grandson of Chico Marx, read out a poem of his own about Opa. Peter's son placed the urn with his ashes gently into the ground and he was gone for ever. But his legacy of *arete*, the Greek word for goodness, lives on with his three children and six grandchildren.

Talk of the Town

Saturday, 22 November 2003

New York

The presidential state visit may be big news in dreary old London, but here in the Bagel it's Paris Hilton's sex videos that are the talk of the town. In fact, we eagerly await the musical. For any of you unfamiliar with the Hilton sex saga, Paris, the twenty-two year-old daughter of Rick and Kathy Hilton – he is the grandson of Conrad, founder of the Hilton chain of hotels – is a publicity hound who makes Tara Palmer-Tomkinson resemble a Buddhist monk.

Paris, like Tara, is not as bad as she sounds. She just misses being pretty, is an airhead par excellence, and the socialite who put the lite in the word social. In other words, a typical club bimbo, except that she carries the name of Hilton. Once upon a time, her great-grand-father's motto was 'Be My Guest'. Paris, alas, has obviously taken this literally. She was filmed in bed with one Rick Solomon – as repulsive a man as I've seen this side of Sumatra – for a good forty-five minutes. (No, I did not buy the tape. It was being shown at a friend's house, and like most porn videos it was sleazy rather than sexy.) In fact, Rick Solomon's publicist informs us that copies of the tape are being distributed to media outlets, talent agencies, PR firms and the like. 'Everyone in Los Angeles has one,' gushed the PR slob.

Well, let's start with the Hilton family. I never met Conrad, the patriarch, but knew Nicky Hilton, first husband of Elizabeth Taylor. Although we fought over Joan Collins during a drunken evening, he wasn't a bad guy. He was good-looking, but a slob. He drank himself to death early on. His brother, Barron, father of Rick Hilton, was more serious, but he, too, left something to be desired where manners and polish were concerned. Rick and Kathy Hilton are straight out of *The Beverly Hillbillies*. They eat hamburgers covered with ketchup washed down with Château Latour, live in a large flat in the Waldorf Astoria which is decorated in early-Eisenhower style, and entertain extremely democratically. By this I mean they have their servants sit down with their guests during meals. ('Yo, Rick, pass down the mustard . . . ')

One thing is for sure, Rick and Kathy are not about to win the Parenting of the Year award. Paris and her younger sister Nicky have been running around with cheesy people since they were fourteen years old. They wore haute couture outfits when kids their age were still donning baseball caps and volleyball uniforms. They became famous for preening almost nude for the cameras at every opportunity, including funerals, so what came next was sort of inevitable.

The Solomon and Hilton tape has outsold *Gone with the Wind* many times over, and the *mauvaises langues* have it that Paris did it for the publicity. I ain't so sure. Tarts kiss and tell, ladies don't. Gents ditto. Sleazeballs not only kiss and tell, they also tape and sell. Mind you, the Paris Hilton–Rick Solomon tape is good news for today's youth. In fact, as reported in the *New York Times*, it might have a seismic effect on the nation's sense of propriety. When a youngster gets caught with his or her pants down, all they have to say is, 'C'mon, Ma, it's not like I taped it.'

And speaking of low blows, a Murdoch rag screams that Barbara Black spent $3 million spiffing up the Hollinger plane. So what? That's how much it costs to spiff up a plane. What the rag did not tell us is how much Murdoch's Chinese wife spent in spiffing up his planes. Murdoch flies around on a company plane just as Conrad

Black does, and Conrad did not stick his sons and the rest of his family on the Hollinger payroll, as the sleaze merchant did on News International. What is grotesque about Britain is that the slimiest of people are giving us lessons in manners and ethics. Prince Charles is as gay as I am, but the poor man has to go on the defensive because the mudslingers paid a drunken buffoon to make all sorts of incredible allegations. I've had my run-ins with Lord Black, but he has always treated me fairly. He built up Hollinger from zero, which is more than the pirates around here have done. They buy and strip. He built. Black is a serious man who has been on the right side on most important issues. That is his real crime. If the Speccie ever comes up for sale, I am a buyer.

Trumped by the Donald

Saturday, 6 December 2003
Palm Beach

When William Paley died aged ninety, fourteen years ago, he was referred to as being middle-aged in the Palm Beach press. Paley would have liked that. He had panache and lots of drive, and he loved women. Going into his tenth decade could not have been much fun. Mind you, he made the best of it. He surrounded himself with women, used his boundless charm until the end, and went to meet his Maker essentially heartless and self-absorbed. There are a lot of middle-aged people in Palm Beach, but none can compare with Paley. Although I had met him many times, I was hardly a friend. But Paley had style, and that's more than I can say for most people nowadays. Palm Beach ditto.

The place had lotsa style back in the Fifties – 'only the very rich and very refined needed to apply – but then came the developers and they developed. The island of Palm Beach, 'a sandy stretch between the ocean and Lake Worth', has retained strict zoning laws and all that, but zoning laws can do nothing about people. Most of the old estates – those of the Youngs, the Firestones, the Munns and the Phippses – have either been broken up or sold to new arrivals. New arrivals tend to have new money and even newer manners. Let's put it this way: there are some very crude people floating about Palm Beach, people whose rich children are some of the dumbest, most vacuous human beings since English football fans were pronounced brain-dead.

Although I was invited by friends to stay, I chose a hotel. I got around on a bicycle, the old-fashioned way. Except for a large Thanksgiving dinner at Terry Kramer's, I stuck close to home and saw only old friends ' the last of the great foreign correspondents, for example. Arnaud de Borchgrave, a teenager by Palm Beach standards at seventy-six, is preparing to leave for Iraq, having just returned from Afghanistan. He and I reminisced about Palm Beach and the glamour that is no more. He told me that the Palm Beach club – restricted to Jewish members only – has 250 members and they in turn own 190 private jets. I think he was joking, but then maybe not. The Gentiles-only clubs have been under siege lately because the Jewish-only clubs have allowed a few Christians in. This is seen as a Trojan Horse situation by the Christians, and they expect a lawsuit any day now. For obvious reasons, I think I'll give this one a miss.

My favourite club story is that of Donald Trump. But before I go on, I have to declare an interest. I have met Donald Trump once in my life, at Lady Black's sixtieth birthday party in New York. I was drunk and he was laughing at my state, but in a very nice manner.

Having said that, Donald Trump can do no wrong in my book. What he lacks in style, he makes up in panache and chutzpah. His use of hyperbole is, for lack of a better word, hyperbolic. He loves and praises his buildings in the same manner that the mother of my children loves and praises my children. When he bought the Mar-a-Lago, the famous Post cereal estate located next to the very exclusive Bath and Tennis Club, he immediately put out the word that the B&T was trying to steal his membership list.

He also built a tunnel which leads his nouveaux barbarians on to the beach adjoining the B&T, driving the latter's members to apoplexy. Actually, it is extremely funny. You have these short-fingered, hairy vulgarian money-bags covered in gold, sunning themselves next to very proper one-piece bathing-costumed ladies whose jaws have been tightly wired since birth, forcing them to look like affronted duchesses at the invasion. Plebeian pride lives. The Donald, in the meantime, is chuckling and raking in the moolah.

Up in wintry New York, the new Time Warner building has gone up in Columbus Circle with enormous pomp and publicity. But wait. The Donald has suddenly taken it all away from them and it didn't cost him a penny. All he did was hang out a sign on the back of his Trump Tower pointing out to the suckers who had paid top dollar at Time Warner that his building was on Central Park, and that theirs was not. As The Donald would say, this is absolutely, totally true. Time Warner advertises an on-the-park address, which is like saying Bulgaria is on the Med. There is the behemoth Trump Tower blocking the way. The Donald's sign was the only thing we read about the TW opening extravaganza. Final score, Donald Trump 2 – Time Warner 0.

Sure, Palm Beach ain't what it used to be, but then what is? But if the nouveaux were all like The Donald, I, for one, would move there.

2004

City of Danger

Saturday, 20 March 2004

I sat down and calculated that if I had continued to live in London I would have died about seven years ago. Sixty is not a bad age to drop off, but I'll take sixty-seven and kicking any time. The problem is not London, it's my friends. I've got too many good ones who live here, and who like to trip the light fantastic, as they say. Take, for example, last week. Jasper Guinness reached the seminal age of fifty, and gave a party to celebrate his maturity. We sure matured – too much, in fact. Put Jasper, Timmy Hanbury, Harry Worcester, John Somerset, Charlie Glass, Robin Birley and yours truly in a room, and one's life span shortens quicker than you can say Iraq. Add a few sweet young things, and the result is the best time I've had since Robert Maxwell went swimming in the Med thirteen years ago.

This was on a Tuesday. The next day, after a lunch to celebrate Jasper's fifty-plus-one day, it was Annabel Goldsmith's book party. I reviewed her book for the Evening Standard, and, as I wrote in its pages, it was an unconventional review to say the least. I had sworn that I wouldn't touch a drop for the duration of the party. The trouble was that it wasn't a conventional book launch. You know the kind. Cheap white plonk, sweaty, literary types jammed into a crappy room, ugly women talking highbrow gibberish. It was the Ritz. There was champagne, beautiful young women and many buddies. I blame my demise on Lord Tebbit. There he was, always with the wonderful Lady Tebbit in her wheelchair (compliments of the brave IRA), and I just had to have the odd drink to keep him company. We discussed sailing boats and he told me a wonderful story about his son falling off one as he ogled some bikini-clad beauty off St Tropez.

After that it was all downhill. Dinner at San Lorenzo with Harry, Timmy and Johnson and a bevy of you know what. Then Tramp, where William Astor was celebrating his birthday, twenty-first I believe (or was it eighteenth?), with about a hundred beauties to help him forget how disgustingly young he is. When that was over, and it wasn't over any time soon, it was Aspinall's and poker with Zac Goldsmith and other pokeristas until dawn. I hope you see my point. London is very dangerous to my health.

Mind you, I'm seriously thinking of moving back, and to hell with a long life. Better one hour of pleasure than a hundred years of solitude. Not that I'm very solitary in Gstaad. Last Saturday was the Taki Cup, as well as the last night before the Palace closed for the season. The Taki Cup involves going up the Wassengrat, the steepest mountain in Gstaad, on snow shoes, or rackets, against the clock. It is excruciatingly hard on one's heart, lungs, legs, but mostly on one's willpower. As everyone who has ever competed in sport knows, the spirit always quits before the body. My record going up is sixty-one minutes, this time it was sixty-seven. A young German managed it in forty-three minutes, which surely is a record. He almost ran straight up. I had to meander, as my heart rate was over 200 for a while. While giving the cup, I recounted how his grandfather had reached Paris in two days back in May 1940, only to be told by an agent that the bulk of the German army was still outside the Belgian border. He hustled back. Everyone believed me.

That evening, although feeling a bit out of sorts, we celebrated yet one more closing of the bar of the Palace. The mother of my children was in St Moritz, so my son and I, plus an assortment of hard workers, enriched the owner in the manner he's gotten very used to (35 Swiss francs for a shot of vodka, 350 Swiss francs for a bottle of champagne, and one thirsty man usually has a couple of bottles of bubbly and, say, ten shots before calling it a night). When Alexandra is in town, she more often than not arrives in curlers (just kidding) at 4 a.m., insults the young virgins I'm entertaining, and drags me back home. Not this time. There's nothing worth celebrating more than freedom, and feeling very free that evening, I managed to overdo it. Never mind, I'll have plenty of rest you know when.

Otherwise, everything is hunky-dory. I'm looking for candidates to share my life on board the new Bushido this summer, and am looking forward to going to the Olympics on my boat with five fellow martial artists. They say that Israeli girls go wild when there's a war on, and, when I covered the Yom Kippur war in 1973, what they said turned out to be correct. In Greece, girls go wild when the Olympic Games take place. What is great is that Greek girls think the Olympics are on every day of the year.

Drivel and Bilge

Saturday, 3 April 2004
New York

My house is being renovated by a team of Chinese men who speak no English and who smoke non-stop. I suppose people do not say good morning in China, or perhaps it's just me they've not taken a shine to. It's a creepy feeling. I walk into my house, or rather they do, I say hello, to be greeted by a silence to make Harold Pinter cringe. But they're hard workers and the house will be 'leady befole election'. (I hope mine, not theirs.)

Needless to say, my Chinese visitors have forced me to eat out, and this has been a revelation. Not that I'm exactly a homebody, but never before have I taken lunches by myself next to American ladies who lunch. And never before have I heard such drivel, such bilge masquerading as talk. American women have never been my favourites, but now it's getting ridiculous. In civilised societies such as ancient Athens and Imperial Japan, women tried to make life a little more pleasant and easier for the breadwinners; only in the United States does the male spend his time pampering and, worse, listening to women. I suppose it all went wrong in 1920, when effete American men gave their womenfolk the vote, a mistake on a par with a White Star so-called unsinkable liner speeding through icebergs in the North Atlantic back in 1912.

In return for their emancipation, American women decided to reform their menfolk by assuming manly traits. This makes for some very ugly scenes at lunch. Women, you see, need to connect through emotional bonding, which was once a key to survival for the weaker sex. Now it causes nothing but trouble as women are caught between the demands of their genes – to be feminine, obedient, married – and a society telling them that they are equal and independent. Mind you, some of these women I've been listening to during lunch would make a Panzer division led by Rommel turn tail and head for the hills. Never have I heard such screeching, never have I witnessed such vulgar displays of materialism, not even in Monte Carlo during the month of August. One of these creatures, making a nasal sound which could stop a car salesman at fifty paces, banged on about having her teeth whitened for close to an hour. I wanted to get up and overturn her table, but then I had no tape recorder. No judge would send me down if he heard what I had to hear.

I suppose that after taming the frontier alongside their menfolk, American women then decided to tame their menfolk. But what about the Jews? There were very few Jews building log churches, shooting Indians and busting up saloons. So I rang my friend Martin Gross, who had the answer. 'Jewish women are as tough as they are because of the Cossacks . . . ' It seems that during the Russian pogroms the Tsar decreed that Cossacks should not attack Jewish women, just the men. So the men stayed home and sent their women out to demonstrate for food. In no time there was a role reversal. Jewish men became effeminate homebodies, and their women turned into ferocious maneaters. Martin's theory makes sense, but, having witnessed some extremely gruesome scenes during my lunches, I wish the Tsar had not issued this particular decree. Just as I wish American women had not tamed the frontier.

In the meantime, *Spin Sisters*, a book about how women of the media sell unhappiness and liberalism to the women of America, is making a big noise in the Bagel. Written by Myrna Blyth, a former editor of a women's magazine, it's right on the money. Women's glossies in America and in copycat Britain are liberal, anti-man and presume that all women think alike. They concentrate on fears about stalkers, breast cancer, hairy parts, you name it. That they promote a victim mentality is unquestionable. They also promote improvement. Improve your posture, they scream, your derrière, your teeth, your hair, your husband, your lover, your pet, your furniture, your clothes – it's enough to make one buy a large shotgun and start shooting glossy women's magazine editors. What no women's magazine ever offers to improve is women's minds. Remember the old joke: what's a Jewish princess's favourite position? Facing Bloomingdale's.

Last week I was in Washington and stayed with my old friend Willy von Raab. His wife Lucy was the proverbial breath of fresh air. She had gone off to compete for the Lavender Cup, in the American Daffodil Society's yearly competition. Lucy won the cup for miniature best daffodil, a feat straight out of Mrs Miniver or State Fair. Now that's what women should be doing. Daffodil competitions, show jumping, having babies, facing Bloomingdale's, being the respite of warriors, but never, ever lunching and screeching about whitening their teeth.

Meeting Ron

Saturday, 1 May 2004
New York

The scene is Tramp, about ten years ago. There's Johnny Gold, the genial host of the second longest-running nightclub in London history; Mark Shand, the English Lothario, writer and elephant rider, as well as the future Queen Camilla's brother; and the poor little Greek boy. Nobody's feeling any pain. Oh yes, there are also a few ladies present, but I shall keep their names out of it, Johnny, Mark and yours truly all being happily married men. In comes Ron Atkinson, escorted to our table by the great maître d', Guido, who announces that 'Meester Atkinson would like to seet with your highnesses . . . '

Guido is Italian and tends to exaggerate. Shand pays absolutely no attention to the latest arrival; in fact he's almost rude. Gold and I stand up, shake hands, and get back to the business at hand. After a while the penny drops – for Mark, that is. 'Are you the Ron Atkinson?' and so on. After a while, the girls lose interest as football talk wins over sex. So what else is new? Mark told me later that he went on partying with Ron until dawn. They're both obviously football crazy. I can see the point of staying up all night waiting for a lady to make up her mind, but to talk about football – no way. That was the first and last time I saw or heard of Ron Atkinson –

no, I do not watch football – until last week. Of course, I feel sorry for the poor bugger.

Atkinson, as every newspaper has gone out of its way to point out, is no racist, yet the punishment has been disproportionate to the crime. One dumb word and thirty years of hard work down the toilet (sorry, loo). Why not bring back hanging and be done with it? Hang everyone who utters a racist word, intentionally or unintentionally, and it would fix the problem once and for all. The fact that more than three quarters of the country would be up for hanging is immaterial. Eighty per cent of the British people do not want Brussels to rule them, yet that is what's going to happen.

The fact that black people use Atkinson's word routinely is immaterial. It is a horrible adjective and insult, but it is also inconsistent. African-Americans use it more than Ku Klux Klaners. Just take a look at one of the funniest films ever, the all-black cast Barbershop, and you'll see what I mean.

Inconsistent is also the only way I can describe what took place in the Bagel last week. Donna Mills is a dreadlocked Manhattan supreme-court judge who was on trial for drink-driving. The arresting officers were both black and had literally to help her out of the car as she was too intoxicated to move. Mills's drinking buddy, another black woman, testified that the judge had been imbibing Scotch whisky steadily for seven and a half hours the night of her arrest. No matter. The judge, who wrecked the Rolls she was driving against three lesser parked cars, insisted her only crime was 'Driving while black'. An all-minority (read black) jury acquitted her in less than an hour. I guess it gives a new meaning to the old adage of being drunk as a judge.

And speaking of being drunk, was that grand old aristocrat Richard Desmond under the influence or what? If the *New York Times* is correct, the porno-scumbag challenged Jeremy Deedes, a gent of the old school, to step outside. Needless to say, one shouldn't sink to Desmond's level, and Deedes did not, but I would have. I'm sixty-seven, Desmond fifty-three: it would have been a fair fight. And, hopefully, my Germanophilia would have taught him a sharp lesson in manners and Germanophobia. Perhaps in future. But I do regret not being on the *Telegraph* board; it would have been interesting.

Otherwise everything is hunky-dory. The sun is shining, the Bagel is great fun, Mayor Bloomberg has killed more small businesses with his smoking ban than I've gotten plastered in my life, and a Rutgers University student newspaper showed a frightened Jewish man suspended on a carnival-style contraption above a burning oven. 'Knock a Jew in the oven!' read the caption. 'Three throws for one dollar.' (A contestant is throwing a ball at the target.) University officials said the school would not cut the funding that the paper receives, citing the First Amendment. Go figure, as they say in Brooklyn.

Manhattan Manners

Saturday, May 14 2004
New York

Thank God for Anna Wintour. For any of you living deep in the shires and unaware of her name, Anna is always referred to by the British tabloids as 'the Queen of New York', despite the fact that she never uses the royal we and has been known to get embarrassed when people from, say, Iowa curtsy to her. She's a good old English girl whose father used to be editor of the *Evening Standard*, and a very good editor to boot. Anna has been the big cheese at *Vogue* (in the Bagel) since always, or so it seems. The Brit tabloids also refer to her as 'nuclear Wintour', for she does not suffer unfashionable fools gladly, especially know-nothing, scruffy tabloid reporters sniffing around for a story. Last week I sat next to her at a dinner given by Robert De Niro and Graydon Carter and asked her about Plum Sykes, the flavour de jour nowadays because of her book about dumb Bagel blondes looking for rich hubbies.

I had read that Sykes had taken up airs – you know the kind: slightly bored, spoilt and turning up her nose at those she sees as her inferiors – and I was planning to give her a drubbing. Not so, said Anna. Mind you, Sykes works at Vogue, but I believed her boss. 'Don't forget, the English hate success,' said Anna, and *Bergdorf Blondes*, la Sykes's opus, has been doing quite well. Where Plum blew it was in an interview with the *Sunday Telegraph*. She was quoted as prattling on about how 'dreadfully inaccurate and unprofessional the English press is'. Absolutely correct, as far as I'm concerned, but a dumb thing to say when trying to sell a book. (Actually, it's something I would say, but then I'm not known for my salesmanship.)

Be that as it may, Sykes only left herself open when she ventured on to literature. American lit, that is. She confused Truman Capote with the great F. Scott Fitzgerald, akin to collating the Wehrmacht with the Kuwaiti army. Never mind. Bergdorf Blondes is no Breakfast at Tiffany's, and it's certainly no Great Gatsby. It's a fun thing to read on the beach, if you like reading fluff rather than looking at girls, that is. What I liked was the way in which English hackettes described Plum Sykes, her opus and her New York world: 'Hers is a Bible for the fabulously wealthy . . . No society soirée is possible without her . . . The social cachet that surrounds her is such that there is scarcely a television talk show in which she does not feature . . . ' and so on.

Actually, it's all balls. Society is dead in the Bagel, murdered by greedy Wall Street and Hollywood types who bought their way into the charity circuit back during the Eighties. The Wasps had beaten an ordered retreat sometime during the Sixties and Vietnam. Out went the Winston Guests and Jock Whitneys, in came the Henry Kravises and Ron Perelmans. Out went style and restraint, in came glitz and conspicuous consumption. Interior decorators became arbiters of taste, and PR hucksters arbiters of civility and manners.

Oh yes, I almost forgot. Out went the Cushing sisters and in came the Hilton ones. Babe Paley never again spoke to Truman Capote once the tiny terror betrayed her and her circle in his thinly disguised novel *Answered Prayers* (unfinished). Paris Hilton would have got her daddy to give Capote a hotel had she been born earlier. Nowadays, young Manhattan women tape themselves while masturbating and simulating oral sex and email the videos to men they find 'hot'. This is what we've come to. It's the Paris Hilton effect, and the girl has become a star because her boyfriend – a gentleman of the old school – had the bright idea to sell the video of the two of them doing what comes naturally. Exhibitionism has replaced every other -ism, including solipsism, in the Bagel.

But then the English tabloids speak of society. Shome society, as old Winnie would have said. When I was growing up – OK, it was very long ago – women bettered themselves by learning the piano or improving their minds. Now a Manhattan broad betters herself through plastic surgery. Femininity and grace have been replaced by women behaving like male louts – to the detriment of both sexes, I might add. Where once upon a time women provided a civilising influence, now they provide the culture of the strip joint. All one has to do is turn on the idiot box and listen to the talk shows. Monosyllabic, moronic, so-called celebrities spout inanities that would drive the Marquis de Sade to Mount Athos for life. It is depressing, but there it is. Modern Manhattan manners. Actually, I'll take those of Madame Claude's any day.

Incidentally, I wrote last time that Geneviève de Galard, the angel of Dien Bien Phu, had lived to a ripe old age. Well, she's still around, and last week President Chirac decorated her and the great cinematographer Pierre Schoendoerffer (La 317ème section), marking the fiftieth anniversary of the battle. My friend Jean Claude Sauer, an old Indo-Chinese hand, informs me that Geneviève is full of beans and has all her marbles. For once, good news.

Oxford Beauty

Saturday, 12 June 2004

The three most beautiful words in the English language are Emma, as in Maurice, Ella, as in Lister, and Stephanie, as in the incredibly beautiful French girl who refused to give me her surname 'because my fazzer reads *Ze Spectator*'. I met the above students at the Oxford Union and I've been heart-drained ever since. What pulse-wearied torment, what despair. These ultimate creations of supreme beauty had me bewitched for most of the evening – and then it got worse.

Jemima Khan appeared with Harry Worcester (an undergraduate asked him if he owned Harry's Bar . . .) and Nicola Formby, and that was too much for me. This is the curse upon those who follow the supreme beauty – that is to say, the beauty that belongs not to ideas and ideals, but to living forms like Emma and Ella, and Stephanie and Jemima. When I paid Emma a compliment and she blushed, it was like a Keatsian ode, an echo of the past which leaves one enchanted.

But enough of this purple prose, although for once I mean it. The motion was 'Is Britain America's poodle?' Defending it were Brian

Eno, Charles Glass and the poor little Greek boy; opposing it, the formidable Nicholas Soames, Lord Parkinson and Nigel Evans, MP. Soames, Evans and Cecil Parkinson are professional speakers, MPs, and know their way round. Soames was self-deprecating, Falstaffian and wonderful. Parkinson was by far the best, making good sense when he argued that long after Bush and Blair have disappeared the special relationship will continue to benefit both nations. Cecil has held high office and knows how the world works. I thought it a slam dunk for them.

Some slam dunk, as they say in Eiraq. Let's face it, Britain's foreign policy for many years has been about as independent as Kazakhstan's was in the days of the Soviet Union. When international law needs to be broken, it is left to the supposedly punctilious Brits to assure the world that the breach of law is only temporary. And, of course, it is very much a master–poodle relationship. While the Brits are expected to do whatever needs to be done to serve American interests, British interests have consistently been given short shrift in DC. It all began with lend-lease. The Americans set out to pressure the British to open their imperial markets, particularly their possessions in the Western hemisphere.

They also made sure that the Brits depleted their gold reserves to pay for the war against Germany. In Martin Gilbert's words, 'It was a very hard bargain, depriving Britain of what was left of her economic power.' The old joke said it all: the Yanks were overpaid, oversexed and over here, and the Brits were underpaid, undersexed and under Eisenhower. The Americans justified their policy of dismembering the British Empire as being necessary for the fight against communism. The truth was that they also wanted Britain's markets.

Under different circumstances, I would have been on the side of Nicholas and Cecil, not with the leftwing views of my buddy Charlie

Glass. The opposition tried to paint our pro-poodle views as being anti-American, which we are not. I went as far as to say that, if England could re-colonise Africa, I would be for it. It can't get worse, can it? But Americans are incapable of running an empire and all you have to do is look at Iraq. They will cut and run as soon as it's looking like they're not.

What I enjoyed most about Oxford was the students and people like Michael Beloff, president of Trinity College, whom I drunkenly addressed all night as Max Beloff, his dad. I did not hear the F-word once, which is a record of sorts. Until I got back to London, that is. And to the best party of the year by far. Jessica de Rothschild was born in 1974, so it was a 1974 party. Much more than that, of course. Jessica is an enchantress and although I don't remember much, the venue and the mood of the guests were perfect. Jemima had given her Penelope dinner at Annabel's before the bash. All the suitors were there, and we dined looking at each other like dummies.

It was a hell of a night, and I was feeling like hell when the D-Day ceremonies began. In fact, I was so fragile, I could hardly watch. Nothing bothers me except thinking of young men who fell in battle. I was happy to see a few German paratroopers of the 6th Para Division taking part, although they should have been allowed to wear their medals. Let's face it, the Allies had an overwhelming advantage in manpower, ships, arms and ammunition. Total air-cover, too. Rommel was caught napping. But if that moron Hitler had listened to Rundstedt and allowed the three hundred Panzers at Calais to roll down, I am convinced the Wehrmacht would have held. Perhaps not. I was very moved by the German headstones, low and dark, like Knights' Crosses, and under one 'Ein Deutscher Soldat' taking the last salute from his comrades sixty years later. As far as I'm concerned, all soldiers, especially the dead, are comrades in arms.

Pole Position

Saturday, 17 July 2004
Gstaad

As everyone who has ever read history knows, Poland is the country most trodden on by bad guys, set as she is at the heart of Europe between two, er, shall we say voracious powers, Germany and Russia. Throughout the centuries bad guys have tried to enslave the Poles, the bravest and most devout Christian people in Europe. They, in turn, did not exactly roll over and play dead *à la* Belgians in the first and second world wars. They rose against the Russkies in 1830, 1863 and 1905; fought the Bolshies in 1920–1; finally rose against the Nazis in 1944 only to be betrayed by the murderous Stalin whose armies just sat across the Vistula outside Warsaw and watched the capital reduced to rubble and hundreds of thousands of courageous Polish fighters killed.

So much for those scummy types who until 1989 believed Uncle Joe to have been a nice sort of person. We, of course, were not much better. We supposedly went to war against Hitler for Poland, but in reality all we did was to declare a state of war against Germany, which was not exactly the same thing as going to war to help the beleaguered Poles. In fact, we did the contrary. The Poles retreated in orderly fashion in the first two weeks of September 1939, hoping that an Anglo–French expeditionary force would come to their aid. Count Potocki, who had resisted the Anglo–French–Polish treaty, knew that this was horsefeathers. Neither the Brits nor the French were capable of helping anyone in 1939, so why sign the treaty? On

17 September someone did come, in the name of the Soviet hordes who attacked from the east. So what did we do? Did we declare war on Stalin? Yes, we did, and if you believe that you also believe that the Russian oligarchs are honest businessmen.

Mind you, if we had, the British trade unions would have overthrown the government. So what did the Poles do in return for the Allied betrayal? Easy. They volunteered en masse, saved England with their airmen during the Battle of Britain in the summer of 1940, and distinguished themselves as the bravest soldiers fighting for the good guys. (Not such good guys in my not so humble opinion.) And the Allies continued to thank them by betraying them in Yalta when Churchill and Roosevelt connived to appease Stalin by ceding Polish territory to him. No people have ever been betrayed as much by so many. Even Napoleon, under the influence of the wonderful Marie Walewska, betrayed Poland, although he had 2,000 Polish lancers come all the way to Spain to break the stubborn Spanish resistance in the Somosierra ridge. (Once the Poles took it, Napoleon bared his head in saluting them, the only time in his career he did so.)

What does all this have to do with 'High Life'? Well, as some readers of this column may have noticed, I am a very big Polish fan and try to praise them whenever the opportunity arises. Sometime last winter I received a letter from the Lady Belhaven and Stenton. Polish-born and active in her country's affairs, she suggested that I have my portrait painted and hung at the Polish Club, 55 Exhibition Road. I agreed, and a very talented Polish artist, Barbara Kaczmarowska Hamilton, finished it in pastel after just three sittings. In return I gave a dinner at the Polish Club for the unveiling. My friend Prince Radziwill, with typical Polish generosity of spirit, flew back from Gstaad for the dinner, as did the mother of my children. (John Radziwill's uncle was the same Count Potocki who was against the shameful treaty.) Barbara Hamilton's portraits are in the De Laszlo style, soft pastel hues, lending her subjects a dream-like quality. I was very happy with my portrait, wrinkles and all. Bravo, Basia.

Given that my own country Greece was, like Poland, second to none in its gallant resistance to both the Nazi and communist tyrannies, I felt extremely honoured by the unveiling. The chairman of the Polish Hearth Club and the Polish Council both pointed out this fact in brief speeches. The Russians have never apologised to the Poles, nor have Britain, France and the United States, for betraying them as cruelly and cynically as they did. Mind you, neither the Americans nor the British have ever apologised or recognised their responsibilities for the murder of millions of innocent women and children via their bombing. At least the Germans have. The sacking of Warsaw was no less a crime than the bombing of Dresden, Tokyo and Munich, except for the fact that our ally Stalin could have prevented it. I am very happy for my likeness to be near that of the great General Sikorski. If there's one person I could have chosen to be near, it certainly would have been him.

A classic Head-turner

Saturday, 31 July 2004
On board S/Y Bushido

I know, I know, it's a bit much, filing from one's yacht — but, what the hell, it's not every day that hacks own boats. One thousand, one hundred square metres of sail, 125ft-long overall, steel hulled and very fast downwind, she is my latest pride and joy, now that I've been shot down at the Oxford Union, that is. Mind you, I began thinking about building a boat only three years ago. All my other ones were hand-me-downs from my old dad. The reason for building from scratch was that classic sailing boats were on the market but at astronomical prices that not even Russian oligarch-crooks could afford. As I love only classic ones, the deal was on. My friend George Nicholson introduced me to Paolo Scanu, the Italian naval architect, who chose Gek-Lift, a Turkish yard in Bodrum, and although way behind schedule it has delivered not only a true classic, but also a rare thing of beauty.

My instructions were very simple. She had to be a head-turner. And she sure is. She has a black hull with gold trim, Bushido (the code of the Samurai) written in subtle gold letters, and the deck is teak and mahogany. With four double cabins, each with bathroom and shower en-suite, she is of fairly heavy displacement – 180 tonnes – but very traditional in appearance. When I first decided to build, I wanted a 90-footer run by three crew. I ended up with a 125-footer and a minimum six crew. She is a ketch and looks like a mini-Creole, the ill-starred magnificent classic yacht owned by Stavros Niarchos and later by the murdered Mauricio Gucci. (The wife had him knocked off and she's at present doing a Taki for life.)

I don't know if impatience is one of the deadly sins, but I sure suffer from it. For example, the idea of waiting a week or two for a girl to make up her mind is totally unacceptable. Even worse is the idea of having to wait to see the finished boat – sheer hell. My remedy was not to go anywhere near where the boat was being built and outfitted (Turkey and France) until the very end. The mother of my children had predicted a disaster all along, but unlike most women she did something about it. She flew to Turkey and changed some very modern cabin designs into probably the most beautiful classic interiors afloat anywhere. Ditto my daughter, who designed the saloon and advised on the materials. Even though I say so myself, these two should go into the business of designing boat interiors. What one sees nowadays is absolute crap – cheap, plastic and garish decoration, with chandeliers and vulgar furniture which at times shame even their ghastly owners.

And speaking of garish people, this year takes the cake. By far. Never have I seen so many uglies on such humongously ugly boats. To my horror, many of them are American, fat-bellied, baseball-capped, trash-talking billionaires with their baseball-capped, water-sipping wives and tarts. Then come a few Russian crooks on giant refrigerator-on-steroids-like gin palaces, followed by shady Arabs crouching in their tents situated just below the winches and above the waterline. Oh, yes, I forgot, there is also a charter by Puff Daddy, the gangsta rapper-cum-multimillionaire who has not only given gangsters a bad name; he also makes the rest of the vulgarians seem to possess plenipotential dignity by comparison.

Luckily, I have good friends and family on board. My son with a beautiful Spanish senorita, Andrea, my daughter with her Greek beau, Lord John Somerset with Rosie Hanbury, and Count Roffredo Gaetani, Italy's greatest seducer, with the exquisite Svetlana, a woman whose looks could launch 10,000 missiles and then some. I have not as yet ventured out to mix with the vulgarians, but now that the mother of my children has left the boat, it won't be long in coming. There is something decidedly fascinating in seeing such horrors, or perhaps it's just that they make one feel superior.

I don't know and probably never will, but one cannot do anything against the punani. For any of you dear readers unfamiliar with the word punani, it is Jamaican argot. A Jamaican percussionist was complaining to Johnson Somerset about his woman. 'I cannot take it any more, she is driving me crazy. I hate that bitch. I'm through. But, Johnson, no matter what I say, there is nothing I can do. She has the punani.' And then hung his head and cried. I agree. They have the punani, and no matter what we do and how big and beautiful a boat we build, they who have the punani have the last word.

Elephant in the Room

Saturday, 14 August 2004

Gstaad

Sorry to bore you, but more about Poles. In all the years I've been writing 'High life', no column of mine has had such a positive response as 'Pole position', of three weeks ago, which is a record for yours truly. Poles in general and Taki in particular are not everyone's favourites, but this time it seems we're suddenly the cat's whiskers. Even here in Gstaad, the Mecca of the nouveaux riches and almost-famous, people have come up to me and thanked me for writing that the Poles are the best and bravest people in Europe. (I thank everyone who has written so kindly, especially Andrej Zatuski, who enclosed his very good book *The Third Estate*.) When Michael Howard recently said on *Desert Island Discs* that his grandmother perished in a Polish concentration camp, he meant a German-run camp in Poland, but his lax language had the opposite effect. Never mind. Howard has his own problems, starting with the EU. As long as he dithers, the Tories will remain irrelevant. Fish or cut bait, as they say in piscatorial circles, but when was the last time a politician gave a straight answer?

Diplomats, Saudi diplomats in particular, are no better. Diplomatic immunity was never intended to shield child molesters, but this is what it's come down to. The Saudi ambassador should hand the alleged molester over to the fuzz and be done with it. If the man is innocent, all well and good. Otherwise he should have the book thrown at him. (There will be more about a European child molester later on; for the moment I am gathering evidence from lawyers.) Like many people, I have Arab friends, but political correctness being what it is, I tremble every time I put pen to paper.

Let's take it from the top: at the 1972 Olympic Games in Munich, several Israeli athletes were massacred. In 1983, 241 American Marines were killed by a suicide bomber. In 1988, Pan-Am Flight 103 was blown up, killing 270 people. In 1993, there was the first bombing of the World Trade Center, and in 2001 it was reduced to rubble, killing more than 3,000. In 1998, US embassies in Kenya and Tanzania were bombed, killing 200 and injuring more than 4,000. All these outrages were perpetrated by Muslims, many of whom had been financed, however indirectly, by Saudi Arabia, which has embraced the Wahhabi doctrine for decades, and continues to support it. Thanks to a conspiracy of silence, most of the world ignores the involvement of the Saudi government in promoting Wahhabism and its hatred of the West. I take second place to no one in my support for the Palestinian struggle, but the Saudi game is becoming a sick joke.

Mind you, most of these attacks were against Uncle Sam, and his reckless and short-sighted Middle East policies. Instead of President Bush calling in the Saudi ambassador to Washington and reading him the riot act, they go shooting together and pose for home movies. Wahhabi-sponsored terrorism will only be destroyed when Western governments develop alternative sources of energy and deprive the Saudis of the moolah to support home-bred fanatics. But don't hold your breath. European intelligence chiefs smile and talk about the elephant in the room that politicians like to ignore: Islamist extremists who become European citizens and hold EU passports. These bums are not only active against us, they are also protected by laws that guarantee their freedom of speech and assembly. Do we wish our destruction or what? Very depressing, I agree, but not half as depressing as the Sudanese genocide. After the Second World War, the world said never again to genocide. But did the words ever carry real weight? In the 1970s as many as two million out of seven million Cambodians were murdered by the homicidal Marxist regime of Pol Pot, but the perpetrators all died – or will die – in their beds after Uncle Sam decided they were a bulwark against the North Vietnamese. Talk about double standards. In the 1990s almost a million people were massacred in Rwanda, while the UN gave chic cocktail parties and was busy ripping up parking tickets issued against brave diplomats. Now Arab militias, supported by Khartoum, are carrying out mass murder against black Africans. The UN is finally doing something. It has decided to accept a few parking tickets issued against brave diplomats. As my father used to say, diplomats are very good at marrying rich women and making polite conversation at cocktail parties, but don't ever expect them actually to do something.

So far, so bad. Next week I'm off to Athens and the Games. Yanna Angelopoulos, who has made this Olympiad possible, has asked me to attend the opening ceremony as her guest. I'll most likely watch it on the telly. At my age seeing the Greek flag moves me to tears. Too many memories of hard-fought contests. But I will be at her dinner, following the opening, and will tell you all about it in future.

Cry from the Grave

Saturday, 18 September 2004

The story so far: on 28 August 1997, Philippine Lambert, aged twenty, known as the most beautiful and enchanting girl of her generation, killed herself leaving many documents and her personal diaries accusing a friend of her family, Vincent Meyer, then in his forties, of sexually abusing her many times when she was aged between twelve and fifteen years old. I have written about this case before, but, because of an altercation which took place in Geneva last month, the Swiss lawyers who handled the case for Philippine's parents have given me sworn affidavits which show the accused used a statute of limitations to beat the rap. Baron Philippe Lambert is the scion of a grand Belgian banking family, and a cousin of the Rothschilds. His wife Marion is known among artistic circles as a patron and collector. Both are close friends of mine, as was Philippine and their son Henri, now studying law here in Britain. Vincent Meyer I have never met. He is the grandson of André Meyer, of Lazard Frères renown.

After the family filed a criminal complaint against Meyer in Geneva, he was indicted for sexual relations with a child, sexual violence and involuntary manslaughter. He was jailed for three months and bail was set at six million Swiss francs, a record. In July 2000, after an investigation lasting three years, the criminal proceedings against Meyer were discontinued. Here's Mick Brown, writing for the *Telegraph Magazine* in 2001: 'While the General Prosecutor acknowledged that the evidence against Meyer constituted "serious charges", they could not be considered because of a five-year statute of limitations.' In other words, Meyer, enormously rich and well-connected, walked free using a ruling which says that a count of harm to the sexual development of a minor cannot be continued after five years have passed. (The manslaughter charge was not pursued by the Lamberts.)

Vincent Meyer is no shrinking violet. His rich and powerful friends came immediately to his rescue. I was bombarded by letters – some from people I know and respect – telling me to lay off. That Meyer could not have done such vile things to a twelve-year-old and so on. But I knew better. Two other mothers had complained to me after my original article about Meyer's creepy habits of paying attention to their below age-of-consent daughters. Fear of publicity prevented the women from coming forward, and I don't blame them. Meyer is president and principal benefactor of the London Philharmonia Orchestra, and a generous donor to other musical venues such as Glyndebourne.

The reason I'm dredging this grotesque story up again – after all, Mick Brown's piece in the *Telegraph* was as close to the truth as it gets – is that last month in Geneva Philippe Lambert, a gent of the very old school, ran into Meyer in the street and attacked him. Lambert is seventy-five, is in bad health and has trouble walking. But a loss such as his makes one forget physical infirmities. Meyer fled, but had his lawyers warn Philippe that he would take action if it happened again. The Lamberts, of course, would like nothing better, as would I. The ruling for Meyer was called a '*nolle prosequi*' order. *Nolle prosequi* gives the right to the accused to appeal against it. Meyer could be discharged of all charges if he did, but has refused to do so. It is obvious why. 'As a consequence, prosecution against Meyer could start again if any circumstances proper to have the nolle prosequi order reconsidered would occur.' Such as a complaint by Meyer against Philippe Lambert taking a poke at him.

I have a simple question. Meyer has gone around stating that he was found innocent and has been acquitted. But the significance of the final ruling was that, although Meyer walked, he was definitely not found innocent. His name was never cleared. Moreover, he did not undertake any legal action, as he could have done, nor did he try to obtain acquittal. So my question is why do good people choose to ignore such facts? Why does even Prince Charles, who should be setting an example of moral standards, have anything to do with him? Is his money so powerful that people are willing to ignore the fact that he molested the most divine little girl for years, and got away with it? All child molesters act in private and always deny any wrongdoings. But Philippine's cry from the grave cannot and should not be denied. Meyer left Geneva, moved to London, remarried and spun a tale of woe. The Lamberts lost their divine daughter and obviously will not forgive and forget. Nor should anyone. Next time you listen to the London Philharmonia, perhaps you will be able to hear Philippine's cries from her early grave.

Sex, Lies and Videotape

Saturday, 2 October 2004

New York

Except for the people, this is a wonderful time of year to be in the Bagel. Summer's blistering heat has gone the way of Britain's Davis Cup hopes – tiny Austria, using natives, has just eliminated big bully Britain, which was using Gurkhas like Rusedski – the days are getting shorter but crisper, and Mother Nature is putting on quite a display of colours. Shades of yellow, red and gold, and orange are the order of the day. Autumn is by far the most colourful time of the year in the Bagel. It also inspires people.

Take, for example, Paris Hilton, the monosyllabic hotel heiress. She has just joined Flaubert, Charles Spencer (Diana's little brother) and Papa Hemingway as an author. The opus is titled *Confessions of an Heiress*, and its style makes it obvious that Paris had Teddy Kennedy take her English high-school exams for her. 'Never be too easy,' she advises; 'play hard to get.' This is excellent advice, reminiscent of that last, wonderful book of Lavrenti Beria, *How to Make People Love You.* Alas, there are threats of a lawsuit. Paris has been videotaped doing what comes naturally, and some bore has brought up truth in advertising and all that.

Mind you, Paris is not alone. Gloria Vanderbilt, too, has joined the ranks of the immortals. (Eat your heart out, Michel Deon.) Gloria has written about her past lovers, who include many stars such as Marlon Brando, Frank Sinatra and Claus von Bülow. *It Seemed Important at the Time* is a better read than Hilton's, not that

I've read either. Gloria is a 1940s creature, baffled by men, incapable of observing anything except a man's celebrity, remembering nothing of those she was intimate with except their press clippings. She is now an old lady, and hers is a sepia-tinged melodrama of a life. Women writing about men whom they've bedded is not as bad as men writing about women, but, still, it is a slight shock to the system of a sixty-eight-year-old.

Which brings me to Christopher Buckley. No, Christo has neither been videotaped with Paris nor has he been one of Gloria's celebrity lovers. What he has in common with the two ladies is that he, also, has just published a novel, but that is where all similarities end. *Florence of Arabia* is brilliant comic fiction by the funniest writer in America. (He must have had a hell of a sense of humour when he was my best man twenty-five years ago.) I won't give the plot away, but just for starters read this: Nazrah is one of the wives of Prince Bawad (read Bandar), ambassador to the United States from Wasabia (read Saudi Arabia). When Bawad is made foreign minister and prepares to return to Wasabia, Nazrah makes a break for freedom and asks her friend Florence, the American deputy assistant secretary of state, to help her get asylum. No go. Nazrah is returned to Wasabia and is put to death. Nothing funny about that – it happens all the time in Saudi – but that is when the fun begins in the novel. Florence does not take it lying down. She resigns her post, hires all sorts of funny characters from past Buckley novels, and starts a women's satellite TV station in nearby Matar (Qatar), a secularised state which Wasabia needs for its ports.

But enough said. The irony is that it's easier done than written. If the people who govern us were not as corrupt as they are, we would have told the Saudis where to get off long ago. Not only have we not, we also allow them to finance terror in return for their safe passage to Europe and America in pursuit of hookers and booze.

Oh, yes, I almost forgot. Christopher Buckley also sets up an Oprah Winfrey show in Matar, which features a Wasabian female freak, a woman who has actually driven a car. Oh well, it ain't about to happen, but Buckley's novel might get people thinking.

If the Americans had any balls, they'd send a Paris Hilton type to Saudi Arabia as ambassador. Or perhaps Gloria Vanderbilt. Fidelity being the last refuge of a faded woman, Gloria would not get into trouble. Let's see what the elections bring and then I will publish my list of women who should be sent to various Arab lands as ambassadors. Starting with Monica Lewinsky.

Double Standards

Saturday, 6 November 2004
New York

Bright Lights, Big City, Jay McInerney's breakthrough opus focusing on New York City yuppies, was published twenty years ago this month, and some of his idioms – such as Bolivian marching powder – have become part of the English language. I read the book much later because at the time of publication I was waiting to pay my debt to society for possession of marching powder, and the last things I wished to read about were things Bolivian. Jay and I have been good friends for a long time, and last week I trudged down to the Odeon, the café where most of the action in the novel takes place, for an anniversary blast given by Sonny Mehta and Gary Fisketjon, two great editors and two very nice human beings. I was not disappointed. The trouble, of course, are the hacks who were not around back then but who demand to know what it was like, Biros and notebook in hand. How can one explain a period in the midst of a fun party with some very pretty girls floating by? As I told one pest who wished to know which of all the nights during the Eighties was the best, 'If one remembers anything, one obviously did not have a very good time.'

Of course it was all a blur – a very pleasant blur, however. The one thing I do remember is telling the beautiful owner of the Odeon, a lady back then married to a friend of mine, that the topless lavatory bowls in her restaurant were redundant, and she wanting to know why. Despite popular belief, there were some innocents in 1984, and she was one of them. It all seems very long ago, and I'm thankful most of us survived. At least the ones I saw at the party.

This is a very good time to be in the Bagel, especially as neither candidate for the presidency bothered to come and tie up traffic. Bagelites rarely vote for a Republican, and, if memory serves, in the past hundred years they've gone for a capital R president only five times, twice for Ike, twice for Reagan, and once for Richard Nixon over McGovern in 1972. New York is about the arts and making money, professions which are all about self-aggrandisement and celebrity and nothing to do with understanding the moods or needs of the rest of the people.

Although the city is buzzing with prosperity, most so-called celebrities act as if they lived in Grozny. They whine and complain about the Patriot Act and the impending midnight knock, forgetting to mention that the knocks they hear are those of their dealers delivering goodies to their doorsteps. 'Outsourcing' is the operative word they go on about, yet most of the fashionable and extremely expensive clothes they wear are made in foreign countries by cheap labour. Ah, what would we do without the double standards of our celebrities? And, as Andy Warhol predicted a quarter of a century ago, everyone now has their fifteen minutes of fame. Including Lizzie Grubman.

For some of you still in the dark about who is in and who is not in in the Bagel, Grubman is the lady who four years ago ran down sixteen people with her SUV as they waited in line outside a nightclub because she had been refused a parking space by some dumb white trash of a parking attendant. Her words, certainly not mine. Grubman served a month in jail and then hit the ground running as a celebrity. Her PR business became a great success and she will now be starring in a new reality show playing herself. So, for any of you celebrity wannabes, all you have to do is run some people down in front of a chic nightclub, do a bit of time, and hey presto. I suppose it's called capitalism, but it could also be called Murdochism, or just plain bad taste.

Never mind. There is always Paris Hilton, who last week got into a brawl with another woman over their seating in a club. It made the papers, which was the reason for the brawl in the first place, which is what New York's all about. Publicity with a capital P. I know la Hilton's ma and pa, and they are true stage parents. When I read about the human Hobbit discovery in a prehistoric cave, I had an idea. If Paris could find someone who resembled the Hobbit, she would make the front pages for sure, but then I realised that Jack Straw would not play along, so I dropped it forthwith. Still, it's a pity. (Straw without his glasses is a real glamour-puss.) Having disparaged the city for the creeps it seems to draw, I must also praise it for what it has become in comparison with what it was. You remember it, the bankrupt, dangerous, graffiti-slathered, mugger-haven of the Seventies and early Eighties. It is now a cleaner, safer, tree-lined metropolis playland inhabited by celebrity wannabes, artsy-fartsy types and billionaire bullies, and I'll take that lot any day, even if some of them make the human hobbit look almost beautiful.

Sexual Imperative

Saturday, 27 November 2004

Back in London for a debate at the Intelligence Squared Forum on the motion that monogamy is bad for the soul. I am arguing against it, as well I should. Had I not wasted my life and time chasing women non-stop, I could have been a contender, a somebody. As the twentieth century's greatest philosopher, Groucho Marx, once said, 'Some people claim that monogamous marriage interferes with romance. There's no doubt about it. Anytime you have a romance, your wife is bound to interfere.'

Kidding aside, marriage does protect against feelings of loneliness. But that's about all. Although I will argue for monogamy, I won't believe a word I say. What I won't dare say is that monogamy should apply only to women. The fairer sex avoids danger far more easily than the brutal sex. Most men, including the poor little Greek boy, crave beautiful women at all times. Ever since I can remember, I have been walking around in a frustrated daze having just seen a beautiful woman. Let's face it, man's sexual imperatives drive everything we do. At least in the case of most of the men I've been close to or admired. Alexander the Great was obviously polygamous, but did not waste his time chasing it. Nor did Napoleon, although his polygamy was annulled by Josephine's fooling around. The moment he became monogamous, down he went. Both Hitler and Churchill were monogamous, whereas Stalin and Mao were not. Does this tell us anything? I doubt it. Talleyrand chased non-stop, whereas Castlereagh did not. Jimmy Goldsmith was like the former, and his best friend, John Aspinall, like the latter. Go figure. Gianni Agnelli was as polygamous as his brother Umberto was not. Ditto in my family. Monogamous men, however, can be terrible bores, especially when they extol the virtues of their wives.

Discretion, of course, is what polygamy is all about. Back in 1956 I began an affair in New York with a Greek ship owner's wife, a French-born beauty. We were immediately discovered and I was dispatched to Paris by my father once her husband had filed for divorce and named me as correspondent. One year later, back in the Bagel, more problems. This time a society lady became pregnant and was demanding marriage. Back to Paris, all expenses paid. (The good news is she was pretending.) In both cases, and throughout the next fifty years, there were all sorts of complications with women. Some claimed to be expecting, others demanded moolah for the time they wasted with me, but not a single woman ever went to the gutter press. Was I lucky? Not at all. I have always chosen to go after a certain type of young woman, the type who would rather die than sing to a gossip columnist. Ergo, I've had a charmed life, including the greatest mother of children that it is possible to have.

I've stepped out with three rather famous film stars, but have never written about them nor – in the case of one who died – added to their biographies. When one so-called biographer came to see me, I denied having ever been intimate, and after he showed me something he had found in her letters which gave me away, I told him she was bragging falsely. (He thought I was the biggest shit he had ever met, and he had met many.) Screw him. Again, it's nobody's business.

Mind you, polygamy can get one into trouble in the afterlife. My greatest hero by far, Don Giovanni, ended up down below as some of you may have heard, but what the hell. He did enjoy himself while on the surface. And now a few words about the virtues of monogamy, words which I have jotted down for the debate: Western art and literature are replete with the passionate declarations of love of one person for one other. Dante and Beatrice, Tristan and Isolde, Romeo and Juliet, Abelard and Heloise, Antony and Cleopatra, Robert and Elizabeth Browning, even Don Quixote and Dulcinea. Devotion to one woman is held to inspire men to rise above their baser natures, to demand sacrifice and courage on behalf of the woman. As the song says in *Guys and Dolls*, 'When you see a guy reach for stars in the sky/ you can bet that he's doing it for some doll.'

Alas, there is no literature celebrating love for the many. This is why I will win the debate tonight, but will go to my grave unknown and unlamented. Well, except by the mother of and her children by me.

2005

That's Rich

Saturday, 1 January 2005
New York

Lest there be some of you that missed it, a lifelong dirty dealer is walking around us free as a bird, and there's nothing any of us who don't flout the law can do about it. Let's start the new year right and not be beastly to Mr Marc Rich. He is the man who was pardoned by Bill Clinton on the last day of the Draft Dodger's presidency. (Rich was indicted on tax-evasion and other crimes but had fled the United States and was living in Switzerland as a very rich fugitive.) When the Clinton pardon came through, all hell broke loose. It was considered too venal, too corrupt, even for the scandal-scarred presidency of Bill Clinton.

Mind you, Rich's ex-wife Denise was very close to Clinton, contributing millions to the Democratic Party and more millions to the Clinton library. A source swears that the fugitive Rich and his ex-wife dangled a multimillion dollar bribe in front of the Clintons and that it will be used for Hillary's presidential effort in 2008. Needless to say, there is no evidence. It is, after all, hearsay and rumour.

While all this was going on, Saddam launched his campaign to woo international support through sweetheart oil deals under the UN Oil For Food programme. Who better qualified to help him beat the sanctions than Marc Rich? The New York Post recently alleged that Marc Rich was up to his neck in beating the sanctions – accusations which Marc Rich has not as yet denied as far as I am aware.

Rich's base is Zug, Switzerland, where he has made himself popular with the denizens by contributing to local charities. Nothing very difficult about that. It is a well-known fact that, when a Swiss is held up at gunpoint and challenged to give up their money or their life, 97 per cent of those challenged need lotsa time to decide. Rich is also popular in St Moritz, where he winters. The only thing I'm grateful for is that he chose St Moritz rather than Gstaad. (I'm afraid he'd be just as popular over here, too.)

If the charges are true, it was elementary. Saddam allocated 4.4 billion barrels of oil to friendly politicians and businessmen to help him beat the sanctions. UN officials were said to have looked the other way. Oil allocations were granted in the form of vouchers, which gave recipients a contract to buy Iraqi oil at a discount and sell it on the open market at a 50 cents a barrel profit. It was like printing money, but safer.

I once had the bad luck to dine next to Denise Rich, the one who did all the negotiations with Clinton. I immediately raised the question – this was long before the current scandal – but she refused to talk about it. 'No politics, no politics,' she kept repeating. Mind you, she could not have been more polite, downright nice, if vulgar. The last time I ran into Denise was in St Tropez last summer. There I was with my young son and his pretty girlfriend, and suddenly Denise pitched up in the company of a Manhattan furrier and a Bagelite socialite, Serena Boardman.

Marc Rich was born Marc Reich in that miserable little country we went to war over, ninety years ago. He fled to America in 1942. He began trading with rogue states and more or less created the 'spot' oil market in which middlemen purchase and resell oil. He made his fortune by dealing with Iran during the hostage crisis. He was, until pardoned, accused of failing to pay $48 million in taxes.

Marc Rich is a lucky little man. About seven or eight years ago the

American Feds were set to snatch him in mid-air while on his way to Spain, the only other country except for good old Helvetia which refused to extradite him to the United States. But someone – and I have strong suspicions who that was, but libel laws prevent me from telling you – warned him off.

Rich has not set foot in America and for good reason: the latest allegations of dealing with Saddam. Nothing, of course, surprises me about Marc Rich. Nor about Bill Clinton. The Clintons were the most dishonest couple ever to occupy the White House, and we would be fools to put them back in the Oval Office. Bill Clinton got to be president of the numero uno country in the world despite all the lies. Marc Rich got to be a multibillionaire despite all the alleged wrongdoings. Someone should write a book about these two and call it Parallel Lives.

Numero Uno

Satruday, 29 January 2005
Gstaad

Sir Roger and Lady Moore braved a snowstorm but made it on time driving from Crans-Montana. Sir Peter Tapsell flew in from Britain, snow or no snow on the runways. The poor little Greek boy had to travel less than a mile, but was the last to get there. While Gstaad was being covered by the thickest snow we've had in years, some fifty lucky souls dined with the finest product of this region, the one and only Ruedy Mullener, the uncrowned King of Gstaad and its environs. The occasion was Ruedy's eightieth birthday, and some enterprising young man should try to bottle him and sell him to

Hollywood. He might be eighty, but he looks fifty, skis as if he were thirty-five, and has the sweet nature, humbleness and wisdom of a ninety-nine year-old. For those of you who have never heard of him, Ruedy taught both Roger Moore and me, as well as countless others, how to ski, walks up and down mountains throughout the summer with Peter Tapsell (keeping the latter's mind clear from the bull he hears daily in the Commons) and has been the numero-uno ski instructor in Gstaad for sixtyodd years. The Mullener family has lived in these parts for some five hundred years, which means they've owned land for five hundred years longer than most of the baboons that have descended here have been giving body language signals.

Oh, yes, I almost forgot. Ruedy was and continues to be a caricature of the ski instructor-cum-seducer. He is fair, always tanned, with bright blue eyes, a winning smile and a very handsome face. About forty-five years ago, while he trained me for the winter Olympics, I noticed that he drew girls around him like the proverbial turd draws flies. I quickly proposed to him a year-round association. He would accompany me everywhere, draw the girls and leave the rest to me. But he let me down terribly. He had met a Scottish beauty by the name of Leslie and revealed to me that he was monogamous. It was a terrible waste and shame, but what can one do with unrelenting monogamous love? Despite my pleas, Ruedy married Leslie and they've been happy and inseparable ever since. (Needless to say, I gave up on him and Sir Roger took over, followed by Sir Peter.)

But last week we all sat down to a wonderful dinner at the Posthotel Rössli, Gstaad's oldest inn, still owned by the family which first welcomed Papa Hemingway when he came to these parts to begin A Farewell to Arms. Hunting horns – very difficult instruments, incidentally – played rousing tunes of mountain scenery, and we washed the carré de veau and rosti down with Fendants, Syrah and champagne. Leslie's and Ruedy's beautiful grandchildren posed with James Bond, his fellow instructors serenaded him, and, despite becoming legless, I managed to make sense in the few words I said about Ruedy. The most gracious speech was Roger Moore's, a gent if ever there was one – and very quick with a pun, too: he responded to someone telling him that she was born two blocks from where Monica Lewinsky was with 'This is hard to swallow . . . ' The evening finished with Ruedy thanking everyone for coming, forgetting to mention that without him Gstaad would not mean what it does to most of us old-timers.

And, speaking of golden oldies, I received a telephone call from the *Daily Mail* the next day asking me whether I was dying. Actually, they put it this way: 'We hear you're not well, and you've been given three years to live . . . ' Well, although the evening before hadn't helped – I continued late into the night after the birthday boy, the mother of my children and the knights had retired – it was news to me. That I had fewer than three years to live, that is. (If the *Mail's* info is correct, I'd better start having some fun.) Oh well, I wonder who sold this particular rumour. It had to be someone who dislikes you, said the princess. Not necessarily. When people think you're dying, they're usually nice to you. It's probably a friend who thinks I've been defending the Germans for much too long, and need people to stop hating me. Why hate someone who's got fewer than three, *n'est-ce pas?*

Take Susan Sontag, for example. She of the great punchlines and clear sentences. (And if you believe that, the Tories will sweep it next May.) Never has death come at a better time for someone who has been conning the *soi-disant* intellectual community for as long as she had. Just as she was about to lose credibility even with the swine that used to defend Stalin's crimes, she drops dead, and bingo – to the Pantheon. She was a posturing fashionista, always trying to jump on the next intellectual trend, but in death she has been turned into an icon by the same clowns who, like her, make up for their lack of serious thought by acting seriously depressed. Imagine if this were to happen to the poor little Greek boy. It would be a fate worse than death.

Ideology of Violence

Saturday, 5 March 2005

In *The American Conservative*, Leon Hadar asks, 'Is it possible that a homeless and failed artist from Vienna, a paranoid gangster from Georgia, and a paedophile and drug addict from Beijing led to the ruin of millions and millions of lives?' Hadar is reviewing a book by William Pfaff which he compares to drinking a good French wine. 'You have to be in the right mood and sip it unhurriedly so as to appreciate the aroma and flavour.' All I can add is that there's nothing like a good French wine.

William Pfaff I have never met and know nothing about. I always read his column in the *International Herald Tribune*, however, because of his nostalgic view of life – one he tries to hide – and because of the disdain he has for those tiny little twerps who have been posing as tough guys these past few years. Namely, America's neo-cons, those sofa samurais who talk big but demand that others do the fighting for them. The book's title is *The Bullet's Song: Romantic Violence and Utopia*. Don't miss it.

How did the creative but sick minds of Stalin, Hitler and Mao manage to turn the twentieth century into the bloodiest ever? Apparently, it wasn't that difficult. The delusions of utopia coupled with the ideology of violence stirred up millions to kill other millions. Pfaff deals with those who carried the sick messages to the masses. Unlike the sofa samurais, these messengers were the real McCoy. They fought on the front lines, boozed, drugged and chased women, and looked like stand-ins for swashbucklers of the silver screen.

A brief parenthesis. One of life's great mysteries, at least to me, is how people who don't look the part manage to get others to follow them. If David Frum or John Podhoretz had yelled 'En Avant' on 18 June 1815, would anyone in their right mind have galloped forward towards the English squares? Of course not. But when the bravest of the brave, Ney, ordered it, they all followed. Don't let me confuse you. Pfaff's book does not include my childish ravings against cowards who send others to fight. On the contrary. It deals with those inside the ring, such brave men as Willi Munzenberg, who seduced a generation of innocents to support the Soviets, including many useful idiots in the West, but who ended up seeing the folly of his ways and was strangled by Stalin's agents in a French forest. Arthur Koestler, who served communism as faithfully as Alastair Campbell serves Blair but turned, like Munzenberg, after seeing the light. T. E. Lawrence, spy, archaeologist, brave leader of the Arab revolt, hero of William Pfaff's. André Malraux, revolutionary, Lawrence of Arabia wannabe, also writer and man of letters. My favourite, Ernst Jünger, great First World War hero, novelist, Second World War hero, anti-Hitler plotter. And Gabrielle D'Annunzio, father of fascism, novelist (Il Fuoco, Il Trionfo della Morte), seducer extraordinaire, duellist and fighter.

Compare these romantic men, with their chivalric assumptions, with such drawing-room Rambos as Frum, the Kristols (*père et fils*) and Podhoretzes (*père et fils*) and laugh yourself silly. Or, better yet, weep. *The Bullet's Song* laments the death of a code of national and personal chivalry – see what I mean about Pfaff's nostalgia? – which reminds me that the great warrior himself, the Draft Dodger, bombed Serbia to smithereens from 15,000 feet in order to ensure a Muslim presence in the Balkans. Now another warrior is about to accomplish a Shia-led Iran–Iraq axis and to hell with the WMD we went to war over. But I digress. Reading the review of Pfaff's book in *The American Conservative* brought back memories. Such as D'Annunzio's early awareness of his greatness. He was born Rapagnetta, but knew by the age of eleven that no one would follow a man called that. So he changed it to D'Annunzio and his parents thought he was playing hooky in school. Such as meeting André Malraux on board my father's sailing boat, and Dad trying to pick up the girl I had sailed in with to the great amusement of the great man. Such as my mother's youngest brother, who was invited by Mussolini himself to visit Rome in 1934, as a twelve-year-old, and who proved himself so brave fighting the Italians and later on the commies. Yes, as Pfaff writes, those brave men demanded the reconstruction of the universe 'through the redeeming power of violence and war' (Hadar's quote), but at least they laid their lives on the line. Like Byron in Messolonghi, Lawrence in Aqaba, D'Annunzio in Fiume, Malraux in Spain, Jünger in the trenches, they dazzled with their intellect as well as with their guts.

Broke and Desperate

Saturday, 26 March 2005

Gstaad

The murder of Edouard Stern, widely reported in the European press but less so in Britain – after all, what's the loss of a ruthless banker or two? – has dominated the 'on dit' among the swells sweltering in this here smart section of the Alps. Yes, I am aware that one should not speak badly of those no longer with us but, in this particular case, exceptions can be made.

Stern was not only ruthless and a terrible bully, he was as close to being a monster as anyone can be and still be free to walk around in polite society. Mind you, no longer. The lady who put four bullets in him was not a friend of mine, but I knew her. Cecile B., as the Swiss media refer to her, is a thirty-six-year-old blonde, not bad looking if one likes that sort of looks. Stern obviously did. She was a dominatrix who specialised in rough sex. She was also an art lover, and painted and sculpted in between rough sex sessions, which made her quite unique – at least in my book.

Stern was the son-in-law of Michel David-Weill, the patrician head of Lazard Frères, and as nice a man as one can run into in the cutthroat world of high finance. Beatrice Stern, the ex-wife, is an attractive young woman and a friend. Like others of her ilk, she has never spoken ill of her ex, nor has she ever acknowledged the double life her ex-husband led. Having screwed a lot of people, Stern had a lot of enemies, and lately had been dealing with the Russians. So I put two and two together and got five. The Russian mafia had dealt with him the only way they know how. Well, not for the first time, I was dead wrong.

Actually, even after Cecile admitted to the crime, I was sure that she was covering up for someone. Stern had many girlfriends, but he was also homosexual. It was widely known that he was a rough trade connoisseur, plus he had kept an undercover boyfriend for years. I figured that he had advertised for rough male sex, and the Russian mafia had sent a good-looking torpedo his way. Much too complicated, my dear Watson. Cecile was caught because she had a key to his Geneva pad, and was filmed by the security cameras as being the last to leave his place after the murder. After two days of interrogation, she spilled the beans.

And now for the nitty-gritty. Why did Cecile kill him? Her lawyers insist it's a *crime passionel*, but the poor little Greek boy doesn't agree. Cecile B. was a very tortured soul, quite mad, but not all bad. She served Stern's sexual whims for years, and he gave her a gift of a million Swiss francs. Not bad, but not that great either. She had been doing his bidding for a long time, had been discreet, and after she left him and went back to her boyfriend he blocked the funds and went after her the way very rich and powerful men go after that kind of woman.

In a Hollywood film she would get off, but Geneva ain't Hollywood. The way I see it, she was broke and desperate. Money, after all, is the last *atout* of a fading woman, and she sure was fading while he was trying to take away her last *atout*. Never very stable, she went to see him and begged him to reconsider. She had a latex suit and a large dildo delivered to her from Australia days before the murder. Stern was found wearing both. I imagine that after sex he still refused to unblock her moolah, and, in the great tradition of Roxy from Chicago fame, she put four bullets in him. End of Stern and end of chalet-prices conversation in Gstaad and its environs.

Mind you, in a perfect world, Cecile B. would be seen as a victim of a ruthless and manipulating bully and would get off. But in a perfect world, people simply do not go around murdering bullies because there are no bullies. I hope Cecile B. does not get the book thrown at her. She has had a horrible life, and, although I do not subscribe to the victim culture, if anyone was a victim, she's it. One thing is for sure. The conspiracy theorists will have a field day.

First-rate Educator

Saturday, 9 July 2005

A note from Jeremy Sykes enclosing an article about a friend of mine who died forty years ago last Tuesday, on 5 July 1965. In his kind letter, Jeremy Sykes assumes that I knew the man who died in his Ferrari returning from a Parisian nightclub so long ago, and he is absolutely spot on. In fact, I was with Porfirio Rubirosa until 3 a.m. in New Jimmy's, the legendary Montparnasse club, and had left only because I had to be on court in Nice the next morning for a tennis tournament. (That's how we trained back then: in nightclubs doing a fast mambo.) Rubi left Jimmy's after 6 a.m., drove through a deserted Paris into the Bois de Boulogne on his way home across the Pont de St-Cloud. As an ex-racing driver – Le Mans, Sebring and a one-off in a Formula 1 – Rubi was going much too fast. He clipped the back of a parked car, and with his steering jammed ran straight into a tree, dying instantaneously. A passing ambulance picked him up but it was too late. As a newspaper wrote the next day, 'Had he been wearing his seat belt nothing would have happened to him. But if he had put on his belt, he would not have been Porfirio Rubirosa.'

What was it about Rubi which still makes people talk about him? Was it the legendary sexual prowess? The charm? The sense of danger whenever he was around? Well, all I can say is definitely all three, but much, much more. Rubi sort of adopted me when I was just twenty. He loved to be around younger people, and I soon joined his polo team. I also moved into his house in the chic suburb of Marnes-la-Coquette, where I proceeded to box with him every morning in the ring he had built inside his grand seventeen room country house, and drive into Paris to work the ponies in the Bagatelle Club, where we played every weekend. We also dropped in on Madame Claude's famous brothel rather regularly, having first dispatched Rubi's wife Odile and whatever girl I was with to go shopping on their own. It was a good life. Not a very spiritual one, mind you, but as Papa Hemingway had said earlier, 'It was a necessary part of a young man's education.'

Rubi was fifty-seven when he died, but the mundane death of a minor diplomat from a tiny country most people had trouble locating caused headlines the world over. Rubi's reputation was such that even newspapers from communist countries included an obituary. The Forties and Fifties were the golden days of international playboys, men who should never be compared with what passes as playboys nowadays. Back then, a playboy had to be first of all a man's man: physically tough and ready to defend his turf, a sportsman and a dandy, as well as one who always treated a woman like a lady, especially those of the world's oldest profession. Rubi's peers were men like Alfonso de Portago, dead at twenty-seven driving a works Ferrari in the Mille Miglia of 1957; Prince Aly Khan, dead in a Lancia sports car aged forty-nine going to a ball – also in the Pont de St-Cloud; Errol Flynn, the greatest swashbuckler of the silver screen, dead at fifty from a heart attack; and others less well-known, like Harry Schell, a Formula 1 driver who also died at the wheel, and Juan Capuro, the best-looking man of his generation and a Rubi clone, dead in his Porsche returning from a party somewhere in Chile.

Rubi was appointed to the Paris embassy of Santo Domingo just before the Second World War by his father-in-law, General Leónidas Trujillo, whose daughter Flor Rubi had seduced earlier. After Flor, Rubi married Doris Duke, the richest girl in the world as the tobacco heiress was known; then, in quick succession, the beautiful French actress Danielle Darieux and the second-richest woman in the world, Barbara Hutton, the original poor little rich girl. That's when I met him. The Hutton marriage lasted only eighty-seven days, but Rubi got an old Dakota airplane, his Cifonelli tailor bill paid, plus some ready cash of about two million. When my father complained to Rubi in El Morocco that he had ruined his son ('My son's idol is a gigolo'), Rubi answered that he was not a gigolo but a Robin Hood, who took from the rich and gave to the poor. Women, that is.

And that he sure did. Rubi's conquests were many: some famous, some less so; some incredibly beautiful, like Ava Gardner, others not so, like hat-check girls and waitresses. Rubi seduced them all and was always very kind to them. His last wife, Odile, became his widow – much too merry for some of us among his close friends, but what's a young woman to do after her man is gone? Grieve forever? Death, of course, did Rubi a favour. Some even said that he may have driven fast on purpose, tempting fate. Not so. But I knew that by 1965 his funds were running out, that some Dominican friends he was counting on had let him down, and, after Trujillo's fall and Kennedy's assassination, his future as a big spender looked grim indeed. Rubi always insisted on going first class, or not at all, so death in fact was merciful. But those who knew him still speak about him with awe, and forty years later I still count myself fortunate to have known him.

Spite and Envy

Saturday, 6 August 2005
On board S/Y Bushido

With plenty of time on my hands to read – television and DVDs are forbidden on board although both are available – I am shocked at the severity, downright viciousness, in fact, of the reviews about my two old friends, Jimmy Goldsmith and John Aspinall, in John Pearson's book *The Gamblers*. You'd think they'd murdered somebody and got away with it, judging not by Pearson's opus, but by those reviewing it. OK, Lucan did murder an innocent, but got away with nothing. I have not read the book, just some criticisms, and the latter tells a lot about some of the reviewers. Let's be open about this. Ugly people are more likely to dislike those born with good looks, just as people who are *mal baisé* tend to be jealous of those whom women find attractive. Just think. Here are two men who went to public school, made their own way in life without a penny from their fathers, had a great time, made hundreds of friends, and left fortunes behind for their children, not to mention breeding and saving thousands of animals in the case of John Aspinall. Oh, yes, I almost forgot, and having lotsa beautiful, very much desired women in the process, as in Jimmy Goldsmith's case.

I ask you, what is wrong with that? So they didn't invent a cure for cancer, but nor have those calling them gruesome, fascist and nasty. Both Jimmy and Aspers did not suffer fools, did not take crap from anyone, especially from those calling themselves journalists, and lived their lives as they saw fit. The answer, of course, is envy. Here's a pretty gruesome-looking chap, with a grotty wife, grotty children and a grotty house. He is assigned to review a book about people he has never met and only knows about from reading the tabloids. He looks around his grotty environment and begins to read about a world which he can never enter. Bingo! Enter the green-eyed monster and then some. In fairness, just because someone doesn't fancy the lifestyle of, say, flamboyant men like my two buddies doesn't necessarily mean they envy them, but human nature being what it is, I'm not about to give them the benefit of the doubt.

As luck would have it, there's also a new book out about another old friend, Porfirio Rubirosa. I recently profiled him in this space, so I won't bore you with more details. Again, I haven't read the book, so I don't know if the writer or the reviewer got his dates wrong, but someone surely did. Yes, it's true, Rubi wasted his life, but did he hurt anyone except for me in the boxing ring? So he hit and ran where women were concerned. So have I all my life, and so have billions of others. And, no, I do not sit up at night worrying that the Commendatore's statue is about to come alive and take me down below. Rubi never spilled the beans about women, nor did Jimmy, Aspers or, I'm glad to say, yours truly. We will extend that privilege to the 'gentlemen' of the press. In the meantime, I will enjoy the memories of many beautiful ladies.

But enough about spite and envy. Let's talk a little about bull—t. As in Tony Blair hailing the late King Fahd's 'great vision and leadership'. Come again? If it weren't for the short-sightedness of Fahd, a big buddy of Aspinall's, incidentally, perhaps Harry Laden – aka Osama bin Laden – would have been content to buy drinks in White's bar instead of blowing people up. (Apparently, both the Duke of Beaufort and Nicholas Soames are in trouble with the club because neither has apologised for sponsoring him as a member.) Blair's latest posturing about terrorism, while he remains committed to supporting the European human rights convention, is as phony as his message to Saudi Arabia. Human rights mean only one thing. They can kill and maim us with impunity, whereas we have to have proof beyond any doubt to try them if and when we catch them. Posturing is what Blair is all about, no ifs or buts about it, and his ministers are even worse than he is. Yet his popularity keeps climbing. Tells us something about modern Britain. And the new Brit.

Mind you, I shouldn't be writing about such low lifes. Here I am anchored off Patmos, the sacred Greek island dominated by the imposing monastery of St John, standing on top of the hill above the harbour. I visited the cave where St John wrote the Book of Revelation. St John the Divine was exiled here from Ephesus in the year AD 95 by the Emperor Domitian for preaching Christianity, and it was on this island that he lived the life of an ascetic and wrote the Apocalypse under the influence of visions. Patmos is a civilised island where civilised people like John Stefanidis and Michael of Greece own houses. Stefanidis's is a jewel of a house, built on a cliff with terraced gardens hanging as in a theatre set. Only a fool like me can be in Patmos and write about the people I've just written about.

Stirling Moss
Saturday, 24 September 2005
St Tropez

The last – and only – time the wonderful Kate Moss was at my house in the Big Bagel was about twelve or thirteen years ago, when my buddy Michael White dropped in with her in tow. 'This is Kate' was the way he introduced her, leaving the rest of us in awe of how a middle-aged man like Michael could still come up with such goodies. She was sweet and pleasant, and no one in the room had the foggiest who she was, until my young daughter came in to say goodnight and was momentarily open-mouthed. 'But that's Kate Moss,' stammered Lolly. 'I didn't know daddy knew her . . . .'

A couple of years or so ago, while gambling at Aspinall's, Kate said hello. 'I came to your house. Do you remember me?' 'How could I ever forget you?' was my obvious reply. Apart from flattering me by remembering, she also brought me luck. I hit an '*onze, noir, impair et manque*' with £100 '*en plein*'. Now poor Kate has the muck-wallowing tabloids after her at their squalidly sanctimonious worst. Role model lets down our youth, they cackle, as if Kate were that ghastly Widdecombe woman or, better yet, a Tony Blair-appointed anti-drugs czar. An utter indifference to embarrassment is a British tabloid trademark, but surely this is much too over the top. Since when is a fashion model a role model for the young? Role models are people like Charles Lindbergh, Dr Salk, Mother Teresa and the Pope, not the beautiful Kate, nor, for that matter, any of the rest of the young men and women who have become famous by using their looks in the celebrity culture we live in today. Why are Kate and Naomi Campbell repeatedly singled out as letting the side down? Beautiful fashion models, as far as I'm concerned, let the side down if they go home to hubby every night and watch TV.

The problem, of course, is not only the tabloids. It's also the scum Kate and Naomi rub elbows with, scum that takes pictures while pretending to use mobile phones and then sells them to the filth-merchants. This role model business is indeed getting out of hand. Celebrities were never supposed to be role models. What kind of role model could Paris Hilton be? Could anyone – except those who wish to film themselves while being shagged in order to get their picture in the papers – look up to her? This tiresome Widdecombe woman wants the fuzz to take action against Kate. Law-abiding people are being mugged and knifed left and right, and this bore wants the cops to go after a pretty little thing who has only turned violent against her septum. Go figure. The implication that the weak and vulnerable will turn to cocaine once a superstar has abused the drug openly without being prosecuted is as valid as implying that because the Prime Minister lies lying is now acceptable in public life and will also be taught in schools.

Actually, it's far worse. The government encourages crime by giving cash incentives to young women to have children out of wedlock, children who grow up without fathers and who indulge in crime when they're old enough to run. Kate made her own way up the greasy pole, pays her taxes, has never asked the state for anything, not even the protection she deserves from the ghastly paparazzi, and here we are going after her, rather than those politicians who got us into the mess we're in. Talk about having the wrong priorities. Stick to going after the real criminals, boys, or if you have to, those vacuous, rigged celebrities with overdeveloped egos, and leave beautiful taxpayers like Kate and Naomi alone.

And speaking of those devoid of talent, beauty and embarrassment glands, St Tropez was mercifully without them this time around. It was like time remembered. The way we were, you name it. No slobs, no Abramoviches, no Paul Allens, no sons of bitches of any kind. No Larry Ellisons. (I will write about this bum next week.) I had the Bismarcks on board, Chantal of Hannover, Nick Scott, Jean-Claude Sauer, and a recovering-from-the-Parker-Bowles-wedding Timmy Hanbury. Needless to say, Timmy did not recover on Bushido. We also ran into the Dean of St Tropez, Rupert Dean, infamously attacked by the gutter press for his astute remarks about miners during the strike of 1984. (Pheasants are bred to be shot, Labradors are bred to retrieve them, miners are bred to go down mines.) What

I'd like to know – and I love miners – is: what is wrong with that remark? Miners traditionally followed their fathers and grandfathers down mines, and were proud to do it. Just as journalists are proud to lie, invade people's privacy under false pretences, file phony expenses and judge those far, far better than themselves.

Did we enjoy ourselves on board? Even if I say so myself, yes, we did; in fact so much so that I have come to the conclusion that Bushido is as lethal for my health as the code of Bushido was once upon a time lethal for the health of Lord Toranaga's enemies.

Spanish Style

Saturday, 8 October 2005
Madrid

This is the sultriest city in Europe and, along with Paris and Rome, the most romantic capital of the old continent. When visiting Madrid there is only one place to stay, the Hotel Ritz, right in the heart of the city, opposite the Prado. There is a bucolic air about the Ritz, with the wide leafy streets that surround it and its beautiful garden restaurants, which hint of romance and the forbidden pleasures of long ago. The past, of course, is what Spain is all about. Charles V had made it the most powerful country in Europe, imbuing his people with pride as well as melancholy, which his chronically depressed mother suffered from. Back then Spain was a closed country. Diplomats would report that hidalgos would sit down to dinner with only a few crusts of bread, but served on a gold dish. The fairy moonlit courts of the Alhambra were eventually succeeded in the public imagination by the sinuous dancers with great flashing black eyes of Merimée's and Bizet's Carmen fame. Spain, however, always remained mysterious, proud and melancholy, until the death of Franco, that is.

Until then, Madrid was the living symbol of the divorce of old Spain from the new. I remember the first time I visited Andalucia in 1957, the legends of the smugglers and brigands etched in the faces of the gypsies. There was not a single high-rise anywhere, just extreme poverty and extreme pride, real Hemingway stuff. And then I went to my first bullfight. El Litri was the star, if memory serves. I got hooked on the drama and the atmosphere quicker than you can say Pete Doherty. The great Papa never apologised for bullfighting. He wrote that it was not a sport, but a tragedy, symbolising the struggle between man and the beasts. As usual he was right. Bullfighting had been going on since AD 1126.

Later on, still during the Fifties, while playing in a tennis tournament, a gypsy bullfighter by the name of Chamaco, asked me to go with him and his entourage to a nightclub to watch flamenco dancing. Chamaco was known to like young men, but there was no way I was going to miss the flamenco in the company of a bullfighter and his court. Real blood-and-sand stuff. The only pass that was made that night was mine, when I was presented to Ava Gardner, a pass that missed by a mile, but that's a different story altogether. (She asked me if I was a *maricón* when I told her I was a tennis player).

I went back twenty years later on a boat, and from afar Malaga looked like a white monster, with cement fangs sprouting all over the once inspiring landscape. I did not return until this year, for Gunilla Bismarck's ball to end all balls. Madrid, of course, is another story. If Castille is the country's soul, Madrid is Spain's ego. Monuments from the Middle Ages are few, with many Baroque and late-Gothic chapels of less architectural importance than the religious buildings of provincial capitals. In fact Madrid is an upstart at the expense of

Toledo and Seville. And yet, Madrid is alive, a lovely, serene city of beautiful turn-of-the-century apartment houses lining its wide boulevards and green parks. And the Madrileños are civilised. There are few traffic jams, people are polite and no one blasts their horns. The city is quiet, as if trying to recapture Spain's mysterious past.

The reason for my visit was the marriage of Leonidas Goulandris to Andrea Herrera, daughter of the Marquis and Marchioness de Viesca de la Sierra. Leonidas I have known long before he was born. I am a childhood friend of his parents, John and Aliki, ergo the reason an oldie like myself was asked to be a witness. And what a wedding it turned out to be. In fact, it will stand as a template to good taste for years to come. The Herrera house is situated one hour by car west of Madrid, a house, incidentally, built by the same man who put up another little edifice known as the Escorial. If Philip II's colossal monastery is worthy to be called the eighth marvel of the world, the Marquis's house matches it in beauty and simplicity.

Early Saturday morning, after a riotous greeting party in Madrid the night before, we arrived at El Santo and took our places. We were around four hundred, with fifty of us inside the chapel, built at the same time as the house. The chapel was very simple, with white walls adorned with Baroque gilded mirrors and beautiful paintings of the Crucifixion. It led out to the lawn, where the couple took their vows in a Catholic and Greek Orthodox ceremony as beautiful as it was short. The rest sat outdoors, as ingenious a plan as I've seen in the years I've been attending weddings of friends.

Then came the good part. We lunched in a beautiful but simple tent in the grounds, and after a solitary speech – mine – we began to dance. The father of the bride, Juan, is a Spanish version of Errol Flynn, in looks, that is, and the mother, Christina, a true enchantress. (Sitting at my table there was also a loyal *Spectator* reader in Don Juan de Areilza, who pulled my leg non-stop.) The beauty of an early start is that by five in the afternoon, one feels as free and relaxed as if it were 5 a.m., which is the time I come into my own. After fourteen hours of dancing, a little sleep and then a grand but relaxed lunch in the garden of the Ritz, the most memorable of weekends ended, one I shall not see again any time soon, I'm afraid.

Roman Holiday

Saturday, 22 October 2005

Another bride, another groom, another sunny honeymoon, another season, another reason, for making whoopee . . . Like the song by Sammy Kahn, we made whoopee in Rome last weekend, the excuse being – yes, you guessed it – a wedding. Il Principe Boncompagni Ludovisi and his former wife Benedetta, born Barberini Colonna, married off their boy Bante to Delphina Lapham, daughter of two very old friends of mine, Lewis and Joan Lapham. Lou – as I call him because, although he's posh, he has always fought for the underdog – was the star witness for the defence of the recent lawsuit by Roman Polanski against *Vanity Fair*. Which VF of course lost because it took place in the UK. As Graydon Carter wrote afterwards, it was hard to see how one could injure the reputation of a man who had pleaded guilty to statutory rape, had fled the country in which the outrage had taken place, and was now seeking damages for a story which mistakenly had him propositioning a woman at Elaine's before the funeral of his murdered wife. Had I known about the case, I could have been of some assistance, but it's just as well to let bygones be bygones.

The winter after the tragedy of Sharon Tate's torture and murder, Polanski arrived for the first time in Gstaad. Despite not having many friends there, he was nevertheless made to feel welcome everywhere because of what he had gone through. It didn't last. Within a month he was banned from the Eagle over a dalliance with a young girl, and then he and I had a falling out. It was nothing important, kid stuff really, but he did get Bruce Lee to fly all the way over from Hollywood to straighten me out. (Lee and I ended up being friends and training together. All this was written in these here pages twenty-eight years ago.)

Actually, I wish Polanski well, especially now that he has rehabilitated Fagin with the great Ronald Harwood. Roman has always been a difficult character, and his problem was that, after the Tate murder, he thought the world owed him. Which it did, but it doesn't always work that way. He never paid the price for what he did in California long ago, choosing to live in Europe instead, which may be the smartest thing he ever did. But back to the wedding.

The new Princess Boncompagni is a childhood friend of my daughter, and we will soon be related. My young son is also getting hitched, to the beautiful granddaughter of another grand Roman family, the Borgheses, so we will be back in Rome sometime next year for yet another wedding. This one will be tricky. It's easy watching other young people get married, but, when it comes to one's own, I no longer trust myself. So now the Taki brood has moved from Austrian nobles to Romans, a bit like Alaric the Visigoth, who in AD 410 moved to Rome and sacked the place.

The Palazzo Boncompagni is smack in the middle of Rome, with enormous gardens, Tiepolo and Caravaggio ceilings – the works. It's grand, it's impressive and it's full of history. And another thing. Its genteel shabbiness is the perfect antidote to some of the expensive crap one sees nowadays flaunted in architectural glossies. I sat with the Radziwills and Laphams, and then moved to the Juventus table, where the real fun was. As they say, when in doubt, go to the table where the young are, and you can't really go wrong.

Rome, of course, has to be the most beautiful city on earth, but it is plagued by tourists. In the middle of October the place was full of sandal-wearing gawkers and fat people in shorts, but what the hell, no one's perfect, not even the Eternal City. In a strange way Rome is rather provincial, a place where no one works too hard or too much, a good place to retire to. It never became the embodiment of Western civilisation the way the Greek world did, but then it didn't do too badly either. Of course, I love its aristocratic decadence most of all, along with the baths, amphitheatres, forums, palaces and the sweet life in general. In fact, I've often wondered how we Greeks, had we not imploded, would have handled the coming of our Lord Jesus. Greeks have always believed that God's part in human life is not active but passive. The sinner is brought to destruction by hubris, in other words his own doing. Jesus's teachings would not have disturbed them as it did the Romans. It was a Greek, after all, not a Jew, who first proclaimed that the name of moral evil is not envy but sin.

But enough of such talk. If you really want a cheap laugh, read about Jack Straw touring Alabama with Condi Rice trying to lift Bush's poll ratings. If one asked the first 100,000 Alabamans in the telephone book who Jack Straw was, I'll bet my last greenback no more than ten would know. *Pensa ci*, or go figure, as they used to say in Roma.

The Right Woman

Saturday, 5 November 2005

Unlike Peregrine Worsthorne, I thought the Duff Cooper diaries were interesting and terrific, and also made me envious as hell. Oh, to have lived back then. People sure had fun. I particularly liked the part where Duff puts down a certain party as boring because of the presence of spivs. Well, lucky old Duff. If he were around nowadays, he'd be writing about some sponsored event where among the spivs he might run into a gent of sorts.

Of course, one could have fun back then, because the barbarians were still outside the gates. No journalists, no people in trade, no cheap celebrities, no It girls, no New Labour. One thing I have not understood is the complaint from some reviewers about Duff Cooper's infidelities. He stayed married until the end, didn't he? And his wife adored him to the end, didn't she? And some men have stronger sex drives than others, don't they? We can't all be expected to be Harold Macmillans, get cuckolded and go to the Beefsteak and talk with the chaps. Plus another thing. Women, real women, that is, adore womanisers, and Don Giovanni wasn't written by Beaumarchais because he was a cad and a seducer, but because he was adored by women. *Punto basta.*

I think it was Sir Peregrine who wrote that Duff's infidelities caused Diana to take drugs. What bullshit. She was taking morphia, as she called it, long before she married, with her girlfriends in order to have fun. I've only been administered morphine after being under the knife. But I get no thrill from morphine. Cocaine is another

199

matter, and I think – perhaps my memory is playing tricks on me – that I took some coke with Lady Diana Cooper back in the early Eighties. It was at 86 Eaton Square and Nicky Haslam had introduced me to her. She was not all there. In fact, I think she mistook me for Talleyrand and offered me a snort. And I believe I took it. But I could be mistaken. Only the great Nicky Haslam knows for sure.

But back to womanising. I find it extraordinary that people nowadays condemn men for it. Some asshole attacked General Patton for chasing women non-stop – he did take time to wage war, too. Having just read the biography of the wonderful Diana Mosley, I see that Sir Oswald is attacked time and again by Anne de Courcy for the success he had with the fairer sex. But, unlike the rest of them, Oswald Mosley never had to wear the horns of shame. Both his wives stayed totally faithful to him, and, in the case of his first wife, so did her sister while the going was good. Ditto Diana Cooper. Great swordsmen like Mosley fascinate women and are adored by them. Let poor old George Melly have an open marriage. That's his choice. He's bohemian. Some of us are not. Neither Cooper nor Sir Oswald would have put up with it, and what pisses people off is that they never had to. Show me a faithful woman and I'll show you a great man. Plus one has lotsa fun doing it to others while it's not being done to him. All one has to do to belong to that special club is to choose the right woman. She has to be upper class, beautiful, and she has to love you madly. The rest comes naturally. As Diana Cooper told her son John Julius when he asked her if his father's infidelities bothered her, 'Oh, they were the flowers, I knew I was the tree.'

Princess Alexandra Schoenburg couldn't put it better. The other reason I loved the diaries was that towards the end I read about people I met once I got to Paris in 1957. Gaston Palewski needs no introduction. As randy as Duff and Oswald, he invited me to the Elysée in June of 1967 because he had his eye on my first wife,

Cristina de Caraman, who had a vague idea who he might be. The lunch was grand, he tried to play footsie, she told him to lay off, and I commiserated with him afterwards. 'These young people are unaware of the old customs, monsieur . . . ' type of thing. The other person I read about in the Cooper diaries was Marie-Laure de Noailles, the grand hostess and keeper of the most important intellectual salon of Paris. According to Duff, Marie-Laure had had a bad war and was laying low. By bad war he meant Marie-Laure had given her charms away to some very good-looking Wehrmacht officers and the Frogs were pissed off. Again, I beg to differ. How could it possibly be wrong to have bedded good-looking Wehrmacht officers? It sure beats bedding some slob American soldier who might even go off with the Fabergés. France and le maréchal Pétain had signed a peace treaty with Germany. Prussian officers were known for their looks and culture. Marie-Laure was hot-blooded. Good for Marie-Laure. Anyway, she got away with it, and by the time I was taken to her salon, she was long over the hill. But she did make a pass, which flattered me greatly. Read the diaries and see how we used to live, and weep.

Nothing but Trouble

Saturday, 31 December 2005

For the end-of-the-year issue, the joke to end all jokes: a few weeks ago I wrote about my acquaintance from White's Bar, Osama (Harry) bin Laden, and how he had been sold life insurance by another friend, David Metcalfe. Now I hear from the latter that not only did people take it seriously, some earnest souls have even turned their backs on him. When I stopped laughing, I decided perhaps the joke had gone far enough. Let's put it this way. By no stretch of the imagination has David Metcalfe ever met bin Laden – for God's sake, whatever happened to that famous English sense of humour? – and any suggestion that he sold the cave-dweller anything is just too outrageous for words. No wonder advertising works. People will believe anything they see in print, especially when they wish to believe it.

Mind you, Harry Laden is a very generous fellow – just ask the boys in White's – but even he would not go around buying life insurance, especially from a monarchist he's never met like David Metcalfe. What he does do all the time is contact me and drop hints of his whereabouts, in order that I can write about it and confuse the spooks in the CIA who are looking for him. (Tora Bora, White's club, Aspinall's, Annabel's, the Ecuadorian Galapagos Islands, Ecuador, even Langley, Virginia.) The man is very bold, but he also has no shame. He's been nothing but trouble for me, and a woman in Palm Beach, Pauline Pitt, stopped speaking to me because of my friendship with him. Such are the joys of knowing people who are on George W. Bush's hit list. But I must say, Osama did laugh like hell the last time we chatted. I asked him what the difference was between neoconservatives and women? He did not know. The answer is that you can sometimes find women on the battlefield.

Oh well, speaking of Ecuador, Neville Shulman, a good and loyal buddy to the great but ailing Nigel Dempster, has written a fascinating book about his adventures in the jungles and mountains of Ecuador – *Climbing the Equator* – with a foreword by Chris Bonington. As has Michael Ashcroft, written a book, that is, about how dirty the Dirty Digger's doughboys play. Lord Ashcroft sent me a nice note with it because he used a column of mine. For once

I had it right. When *The Times* started to attack him, my shit detector, as Papa Hemingway called his instinct, told me that the Murdoch creeps were trying to destroy a man on orders from New Labour. Back in the good old days, such people were either tarred and feathered, or ended up doing a Taki in Pentonville. Now they receive knighthoods.

Of course, it could be worse. One could have to deal with Bianca Jagger. The Nicaraguan publicity hound has outdone herself recently. Every time I looked at some moronic news programme concerning America, she was out in front of the camera railing against the execution of a thug who murdered four innocent people for two hundred greenbacks a quarter of a century ago. (She didn't get her way.) Murderers have now discovered new ways of escaping responsibility. Such as remorse-promoting and behaviour modification sessions. Self-promoters like Bianca Jagger get on the news by defending these modern ways of escape. Perhaps if there was less bullshit a father and husband like John Monckton might still be alive. La Jagger, who has stuck to her ex-husband's name like superglue, styles herself a Unicef ambassador. This is an insult to hard-working, paying-their-own-way ambassadors like Sir Roger Moore, who tirelessly circles the globe helping starving children.

And now for the very good news. At my advanced age I've become a . . . bookie. Mind you, a top-of-the-line bookie, but a bookie nevertheless. My partners are Teddy, Zac and Ben Goldsmith, James Osborne and two geniuses whom we stole from Ladbrokes. The name of our firm is Fitzdares, and I will offer a very good bottle of champagne to the first reader who guesses why we named the company thus. The reason for becoming a bookie is obvious. There is no bookmaker today who treats his clients like Aspinall's or Annabel's do. We will. We will accept any bet, and only gamblers who have been introduced to us by friends will be able to play. Big firms today are only interested in online poker and fixed guaranteed returns. In other words, they will lay off any big bet and are too chicken to play. We will. Plus we will offer services like no other, from chauffeured limos, to choppers and private planes. For big punters, that is. If we go broke, I can always rely on my *Spectator* salary to feed my children. Although having read the valedictory article by the ex-sainted editor in the Christmas issue, I'm awfully nervous about that, too. See you in the poorhouse, but perhaps not.

2006

Lament for a Learned Friend

Wednesday, 31 May 2006

Athens

On a sad trip to Athens for my friend Yanni Goulandris's funeral. Throughout the years, mostly in these pages, I have always referred to him as Professor Yohannes Goulandris, mind you, mostly to annoy him. Yanni did not think much of the Germans, the reason being he was fifteen when they occupied Greece, and, unlike me at five years of age, did not allow the glamorous uniforms and gallant tales of Teutonic knights to impress him. Yanni was an unusual Greek shipowner. He loved music, literature and art much more than business, and knew more about those three subjects than most professors. Hence his Speccie nickname. Yanni was no stuffed shirt. He loved wine and whisky, beautiful women, and was the first Greek to find those awful hippies of the awful Sixties quite interesting. He was among the first Greeks to have friends outside the shipping community, writers and artists mostly, although he remained close to the Greek community until the end.

He and I went to the same school in Athens, and then he attended Cambridge. He was a friend of my father, and when I came of age – when I hit the Riviera, that is – he took me under his wing. For some strange reason my children were brought up in his house. His wife Aliki, the tobacco heiress, and the mother of my children were very close, so Yanni, Aliki and Alexandra carried the can while I went gallivanting around the world looking for thrills. In other words, I owe him big time, but now it's too late for payback. Yanni and Aliki have a charming country house with a bewitching garden north of Athens, where we would sit until dawn surrounded by jasmine and listen to Wagner, jazz and old Greek songs. He made his own retsina, which was kept in a humongous barrel in the cellar, a barrel which somehow emptied always on the last day of summer. As the end of the season drew near, Yanni would up the ante in order to ensure nothing was left scraping the barrel.

The irony, of course, was that for a German-hater he loved German music. He would go into ecstasy, with a smile on his face and his eyes closed while listening. That is when I would start praising the Wehrmacht ('Come on, Yanni, you gotta admit the professionalism that allowed Germany to fight with astonishing effectiveness against impossible odds, and the obdurate pride that led the officer class to fight until the end . . . '), whereupon he would pull a Jekyll and Hyde. After the liberation, the commies picked him up right away as he was among the haves. Held in a football stadium, and oblivious to his plight, he began playing ping-pong with one of the prisoners and was slapped around rather hard by his captors. He never understood why. He was a very old friend of John Aspinall, of Jimmy Goldsmith, and of the other Yanni, Zographos, who was the first to leave us back in 1997.

His son Leonida had a New Orleans jazz band fly in from Paris, and, after he was lowered into the family tomb, we followed them back to the Grande Bretagne hotel where we drank to his memory. Aliki and Yanni were married for fifty-one years, and I don't think they ever spent more than a day or two apart. My heart goes out to her because she not only loved him madly throughout those fifty-one years, but he was also the only man she ever looked at, if you know what I mean. He leaves three children, Leonida, Atalanta and Alexia-Cassandra.

Losing a friend at my age is normal. But losing a friend who taught one so much makes the loss harder to take. I remember when I first started writing and if I hit a brick wall, which was a daily occurrence, all I had to do was ring Yanni. History, anything to do with music or philosophy, literature, he was my Google – decades before it was invented. The German army aside, the other things which would annoy him were my indiscreet questions about women – he had great success with the fair sex until he got married – and the fact that I always denied having borrowed ten pounds from him during my first Wimbledon. (I had borrowed five.) He insisted it was ten. For close to fifty years we would argue about a fiver, prompting some people to think we were both rather petty.

Oh, yes, and another thing. Back in 1952, in the Blue Bar in Cannes, Yanni spotted Picasso sitting at the next table. He promptly got up, introduced himself and began to give a lecture about modern art. He was for it, and knew a hell of a lot about it, but Picasso wanted to be left in peace and told Yanni so. Until the end of his life, he refused to admit it. 'Not in the least,' he would say. 'The artist and I had a very good conversation, he heard me out and I heard him out . . . ' Funny, I don't exactly remember it that way, but then again, I was young and could have been mistaken, which I wasn't.

So, goodbye, old friend, and as we Greeks say, may the earth which covers you be soft.

A Better Class of Patriot

Wednesday, 28 June 2006

The Fitzdares' party at Annabel's was not quite the kind of shindig I was expecting. After all, Fitzdares is a bespoke bookmaker, and bookies are not known for classy parties, only for classy fleecing of their clients. Not Fitzdares, however; a company I have invested in along with the Goldsmith boys and James Osborne, uncle of the shadow minister. Actually it was like old times. Great food, lotsa good wine, very good company, and then disaster. Fitzdares, alas, decided to go all-out the patriotic way, which other bookies have not. We backed England to win against Sweden and we wuz robbed by that late goal. As an investor, I wish they thought less of England and more of Taki, but what the hell, it's nice to see someone who still cares for the old country who does not have an enormous beer belly, a bald head, and lotsa stupid tattoos all over.

The other thing that bothers me about Fitzdares is how nicely they treat both the winners and losers. If I had my way, only the latter would benefit from private cars and choppers, but then I'm not a businessman. And speaking of business, the poor old Queen should dissociate herself from Corporate Ascot, which is what the once proud racecourse has turned into. What a vulgarity. Whoever is responsible for this should be knighted for turning something old and very English into an airport facility which doubles for drunks, ugly women and some good-looking horses. After all, destroying the old and beautiful gets one a handle nowadays, so why not a knighthood for those who did for Ascot what Bomber Command did for Dresden. I only went once, but I could see the disaster even before I got inside the perimeter.

Who were these people? Traders and corporate types have replaced the old aristos and the wonderful and colourful spivs who used to be as much a part of the place as the horses. Ascot has now surrendered its soul and has turned its back on its

history. In fact, the place has the grandeur of a parking ticket. Too bad, and much too sad, but this is how the modernists, whose imperative is to proletarianise everything, want it.

Mind you, just as one despairs about a gracious way of life one was used to and which no longer exists, a telephone call from Willy Shawcross gives hope. Olga and Willy have many friends, among whom are Lady Solti and the patriotic playwright Ronald Harwood. Back when I was on the tennis circuit, big ones like Emmo and Hoad used to hang out with small-timers like yours truly. And gave tips. Not many noticed. But it's the same in the world of words. The great ones, like Sir Tom Stoppard and Ronald Harwood, are extremely nice with small fry. Why? Easy. They're secure of their talent.

I cannot think of anything I'd like to see more than *Collaboration*, about the relationship between Richard Strauss and his Jewish librettist Stefan Zweig. The playwright told me what a hero Strauss really was, and how he called Zweig a collaborator for killing himself in South America, thus doing what the Nazis would have wished. Although I am not turned on by women of my generation, in the case of Lady Solti I will make an exception. Alas, I didn't race her motor. The Shawcross party was like a good sniff of you know what, without the lousy feeling the next day.

This is supposed to be a social column, and, if it appears shorter than usual, it is the sainted editor who censors it when I try to slip in a political thought or two. But June, after all, is the season, so to hell with politics. Incidentally, if Ronald Harwood does not receive a knighthood, I will personally protest in front of Parliament dressed in a German officer's uniform carrying a sign which says: 'Even the Nazis would have knighted him'. I've often written about this outrage. How can lawyers and greedy businessmen be honoured, and not playwrights?

Incidentally, I met a beautiful girl at Willy's, Catherine Day, who spent nine months in Iraq on her motorcycle of Second World War vintage. She's made a film about that God-forsaken place, but I am convinced she must be a spook. How can a beautiful girl risk her life for a documentary unless she's a spook? 'You're too beautiful to die in Iraq,' was all I said to her. I could have added, ten for the legs, nine for the body, eight for the face, ten for femininity. The fact that I couldn't possess her depressed me to such a degree that I admitted to Lord Hindlip what his nineteen-year-old daughter pulled on me. I asked her for her number, offered eternal love and my boat, and she in turn asked me how many girls in my life I had said the same thing to. I was drunk but I am smart when it comes to such matters. 'Seven,' I said with a straight face. 'In that case, here's my number,' said the divine Sophie. I rang her last Monday. 'Brompton Hospital, can we help you . . . ' Bitch. Anyway, I only loved her because she reminds me of her older sister who is pregnant, not by me, alas, so there.

When Maya Schoenburg pointed out that she is nineteen, I pointed out that I am sixty-nine, and fifty years is a very good difference of age between men and women.

Midsummer Marriage

Wednesday, 12 July 2005

Rome

Frankly, this was not a cool wedding. There were no security guards, no stretch limos, no Liz Hurleys, no cutting-edge genetic technology, not even a same-sex marriage. Not very with it, I know, but there we are. John Taki and Assia got hitched last Saturday in the most magical setting I have ever seen – a Xanadu. 'And there were gardens bright with sinuous rills/Where blossomed many an incense-bearing tree;/And here were forests ancient as the hills,/Enfolding sunny spots of greenery.'

Old Sam Coleridge must have visited Prince Nettuno Borghese's property by the sea, west of Rome, because what Kubla Khan decreed is where my boy got hitched. Assia's father Count Maurizio Baudi di Selve and her mother Maria Grazia never let on what they had in store for us. Maurizio is the scion of the Borghese clan, the oldest princely family of Italy, and he began the celebrations on Friday evening in the Palazzo Borghese, with a small dinner for around 250.

Back in the good old days, Rome was led by princes who built palaces reflecting their power. The present head of the family still lives in an apartment there, sharing the rest of the palazzo with the Circolo della Caccia, Rome's most exclusive gentlemen's club. Liveried staff move silently, evoking a time when nobility led from the front. The place is so grand and so beautiful even I managed to behave. The trick for a successful wedding is to keep it small. Only good friends need be invited. The mother of my children, John Taki and I invited ninety, Assia's family 135. Not a freak among them, no stuffed shirts, no charlatans, just young people full of grace and manners to match their beauty.

Afterwards, on the terrace of the Hassler, we began to blow off steam. I had friends who had flown in from New York, Los Angeles, Athens and three all the way from deepest Mexico. The jet lag helped. At five in the morning, the management declared the bar closed because a few bores upstairs found it hard to sleep. Next day was the big one, so I went to the Borghese Gardens and tried to sweat off some of the booze. After a while I had to sit down next to some fat American tourists who, I think, were complaining about the lack of air-conditioning.

Around five in the afternoon I was driven towards Anzio, where Nettuno lies high above the sea. A long alley lined with hay bales suddenly revealed a beautiful small chapel next to a handsome red house which I mistook for the main one. (It turned out to be the gardener's cottage; some cottage.) Two large semi-circles of armchairs were provided for the guests outside the chapel. The ceremony was conducted by Father Ramsay, a close friend of my family who had flown in from Staten Island, Noo Yawk.

Though I say it myself, never have I seen a better-looking couple. The father of the bride is a tall and very handsome man, some twenty years younger than me, and when he came in with Assia, the Med glistening in the distance behind, the green walls of the surrounding woods, spots of light penetrating, the scene was so moving I almost blubbed. Close but no cigar. John Taki, an incredibly sloppy dresser, was for the first time in his life looking like Beau Brummell. He had spent three months preparing his sartorial triumph. Two violinists played Vivaldi and, after a ceremony conducted in English and Italian by the polyglot Father Ramsay, it was time for . . . yes, the baptism of Taki Tancredi, aged six months. (Leave it to a son of mine to get married in front of his baby son.) My daughter Lolly was his godmother.

The party that followed I will not soon forget. We walked from the chapel to a wood under a canopy of pines where a jazz band played in the pink light of dusk. My friend John Sutin mistook the round tables lined with drink and pizza-makers for the real thing, and had twenty-four slices of freshly made pizza. As it got dark and we were asked to proceed to an open lawn under an eleventh-century tower for dinner, Sutin looked like the proverbial cat that had swallowed you-know-what. Dinner under the stars, topiary transforming the house into a stage set, so many beautiful young girls, it was a bit too much for me. I got completely blotto, gave a good speech, and danced all night to Zulu music, something I don't do that often. The newly-weds left as the sun was rising, on Bushido, anchored off in the distance and gave a long whistle goodbye. I thought I saw some dolphins escorting them away, but obviously my eyes were playing tricks. A long summer day and night had ended but the memories will always linger like echoes of the mind.

Grinding the DC Rumour Mill

Wednesday, 16 August 2006

Broadsides from the pirate captain of the Jet Set

I have received some very complimentary letters about my 22 July column, the one dealing with the plight of a Palestinian female doctor in Gaza. I will not mention the names because they were, after all, private messages. You know who you are and I thank you. And now for the bad news: my Washington spies report that the Israeli invasion of Lebanon was planned on 17 and 18 June of this year, between the former Israeli prime minister Benjamin Netanyahu, Likud Knesset member Natan Sharansky, and US Veep Dick Cheney. Basically, the assault on Lebanon was stage-managed between the government of Israel and the neo-cons in the Bush administration, those nice guys who have given us Afghanistan, Iraq and who now threaten Syria and Iran. Netanyahu and Sharansky laid the groundwork, as they say.

Easy to say, you might say. The internet, which incidentally I don't read, is full of conspiracy theories. And DC's rumour mill is as vibrant as Paris Hilton's sex life. But consider this. Israel looks as if it pre-planned the attack when it denied entry to the West Bank to Palestinians holding US passports. The denial of entry to Palestinian–Americans was a violation of both the Geneva Convention and the Oslo Accords. But the fix was in. Israeli planners, after all, know how to play Palestinian extremists like the proverbial fiddle. Israel's border exercise inside Lebanon immediately following – and the subsequent kidnapping of two Israeli soldiers – provided the pretext for the attack on Gaza and Lebanon. We know the rest.

Netanyahu, who had some interesting things to say to Allister Heath in these here pages last week, was the author of 'Clean Break', a white paper written in 1996 by him and other militant Zionists such as Richard Perle and Douglas Feith. Perle, Michael Ledeen and Netanyahu himself still call the shots on US and Israeli policies. With an American election not too far away, turmoil in the Middle East, and the ensuing 'terrorist' threats, are not exactly vote losers as far as the simpleton in the White House is concerned.

So far so good, as far as Israel is concerned. But what about if one is a poor Lebanese in south Lebanon, or an Iraqi, for that matter? Here's John Podhoretz, a slob of a man whose warlike rhetoric is matched only by his sloppy and unattractive physical appearance. He is writing in Murdoch's New York Post: 'What if the tactical mistake we made in Iraq was that we didn't kill enough Sunnis in the early going to intimidate them? Wasn't the survival of Sunni men between the ages of fifteen and thirty-five the reason there was an insurgency and the basic cause of the sectarian violence now?' Do you see, dear readers, what coarse rhetoric we're up against back in the Land of the Depraved?

Even the civilised John Derbyshire, a Brit, writing in *National Review*, the magazine which gave me my start, wishes 'we had rubbled Iraq' in order to show our enemies we know how to punish them. Does no one remember what our Lord Jesus said about turning the other cheek? As Sam Leith wrote, had we treated September 11 as a criminal outrage, and not gone ahead and rubbled innocent Iraqis, not only would we be holding the moral high ground, I doubt if we would now be unable to carry a shaving kit on to an aeroplane. Violence breeds more violence, something the Israelis have failed to understand in all these years of suppressing and humiliating the Palestinians. You'd think some monkey in DC would have figured this out by now, but no. Not with bloodthirsty slobs like Podhoretz, Bill Kristol, Perle and Ledeen as the organ-grinders. What saddens me is that the often talked about special relationship is a joke. There is no special relationship between America and Britain. There is only one SR, and that's between Israel and the United States, with the former calling the tune. Get used to it, you Brits.

And now for further bad news: as of last Friday I had lived 25,656 days, and the same amount of nights. A friend figured out that I must have been conceived on the 19 November 1935, most likely the second time my sainted mother ever made love, and definitely the last. The mother of my children, in cahoots with the divine Charlotte Goldsmith, made a short film which made me out to be some kind of Ancient Greek hero. Paul Johnson, Norman Mailer, Tom Wolfe, Alexander Chancellor, Charles Glass (who asked me to emerge from the closet), Bill Buckley, Nicky Haslam, the Duke of Beaufort, the sainted arts editor Liz Anderson were some of the contributors to a propaganda film that would have made Dr Goebbels blush with feelings of inadequacy. A beautiful painting of my boat from George Nicholson, a signed-by-Papa first edition of *A Farewell to Arms* from John Rigas, and a hell of a lot of other nice presents softened the blow. I am now considered middle-aged even in Palm Beach, which must be the cruellest blow of all.

Disturbing Legacy

Thursday, 24 August 2006

It's that time of year again, the last week of August, and people are already jockeying in order to cash in a year from now on the tenth anniversary of Diana's death. Tina Brown, a lady who would dumb down Big Brother, was first out of the blocks, her book promising to reveal unheard-of-before secrets. Incidentally, Tina Brown never met Diana and does not know many people who did, but is nevertheless considered a Diana expert. As far as I'm concerned, the only person outside Di's family who is qualified to write about her is Rosa Monckton, Dominic Lawson's wife, who not only was a good friend to the tragic one, she also knew about the charade that was Diana & Dodi.

I, too, am cashing in. I am a contributor to the Larry King book on Diana; Larry King being a very popular TV chat show host based in Washington DC. About fifteen years ago, while on a book tour, I appeared on his programme and let it drop that the Chuck and Diana marriage was practically over. King forgot all about my book – the third bestseller in history after the Bible and *Mein Kampf* – and pumped me non-stop for info. In fact, my segment lasted one whole hour, to the annoyance of some minor celebrities waiting to go on. Mind you, it seems everyone knew about the bad marriage except for 300 million Americans much too busy eating hamburgers, memorising television ads and watching American football.

Never mind. Diana died for a blurry picture, a real insult to a nice but tortured woman who used her fame well. As Bill Deedes correctly said last week, what a disturbing legacy she left behind. The idea that a couple of self-publicists are trying to involve Prince Philip in her death is not only bizarre, it's an outrage which should be prosecuted. Conspiracy theorists in my book are almost as bad as the crimes they purport to be uncovering.

Ironically, I was among the last to speak to her. I had the great Nigel Dempster and the late Charles Benson staying with me in Gstaad. The papers were full of Diana gallivanting around with Dodi Fayed. I told my two buddies it was all a fake, a publicity stunt. Nigel, a real pro, pushed me to ring her. Which I did. 'Hello, stranger,' was her opening line to me. 'This is a professional call,' said the greatest Greek writer since Aristophanes. 'Will you be wearing an abaya soon?' 'Now what do you think?' came her reply. Something in her laugh and voice confirmed that it was all play-acting for the cameras and tabloids.

We all know the rest. On the evening of her death, I was dining with Jeremy Menuhin, son of Yehudi, and Oliver Gilmour. My two houseguests had abandoned me for a grand dinner down the road. The subject of Diana came up and Oliver and I got into an argument. We were at my chalet. I went downstairs, turned on the telly, and got the news. When I told Oliver, he felt so guilty he almost broke down.

Someone said that beauty is death's antithesis. I'm not so sure. Beauty deserves a special place of honour in the world, but the uglies don't like it. Diana proved it. If Helen of Troy's face launched a thousand ships, Diana's launched a million tabloid front pages. The celebrity culture began with Jackie KO, and reached its apotheosis with Diana. Now we have Tara PT, Liz Hurley and Paris Hilton. Heaven help us.

The first time I met Diana was at Harry Worcester's wedding.

Nicky Haslam introduced us and I slurred my words terribly. She mistook it for a speech impediment, took my hand and slowly articulated 't–a–k–e i–t e–a–s–y'. Nicky ruined it by saying that I was just drunk. The second time was when she dispatched Johnson Somerset to bring me to her table at a Jemima Khan do. I was writing 'Atticus' at the time and had suggested she was bonkers. Alas, yet again I was the worse for wear. When I approached, she asked me to sit down but I missed the chair and ended up under the table. She screamed with laughter, looked down and asked me point-blank: 'Do you really think I'm mad?' For once I came back with a good one. 'All I know is that I'm mad about you.'

These are old stories which I've written before in these pages, but what the hell. Finding something original to say about Diana nine years after her death is hard work. Not my speciality. My last story involves young Louis Franck – now a major rock-star in the Ukraine – who arrived at my flat after the dinner I gave in order for Diana to meet a few choice editors. He did not know she was there, sat next to her and asked her whether she was Russian. She said no, and asked him where he was from. 'Gstaad' was the answer, and then he moved on to other things.

Party Time

Thursday, 5 October 2006

The trouble with throwing a party is it only lasts for a few hours. Compared with the time and effort it takes to organise, it seems, well, a waste of time. John Aspinall spent months preparing the extravagances he used to stage at Howletts and Port Lympne, his perfect Palladian structure near Canterbury. At one of his parties, the staircase was festooned with dwarfs, while acrobats and wild animals roamed around the rooms. I remember playing chemmy next to Tina Onassis, or Blandford, as she then was, and a large tiger making an entrance and sniffing the green felt table. Tina fled to the loo. I was too embarrassed to do likewise and called banco instead. I was too nervous to notice whether I won or lost. All Aspers's parties were centred on a theme or one of his heroes, people like Mithridates or the Diadochi or Cuauhtémoc, the last emperor of the Aztecs. The expense and attention to detail at each feast were enormous. I once told him that gamblers were ignorant types, and the name of Mithridates was as likely to be recognised by them as that of Theotokopoulos (El Greco to us art lovers). Never mind. The pleasure was in organising the bash.

My party at Annabel's was nothing of the sort. I flew in an orchestra from New York, one which played only Gershwin, Cole Porter and Rodgers and Hammerstein tunes. Anything after 1956, I don't pay, I told Alex Donner, the true successor to Lester Lanin and leader of the band. The trick, of course, is to have lotsa young people coming in after dinner. And a change of pace. This was provided by Jackson Scott, a fantastic flamenco guitarist whose new band of youngsters kept us dancing until five a.m. Many of the oldies had departed by then. My Greek friends ditto. They thought the party had come to an end as the bands were changing. Just as well. Eighty young people had come in with a vengeance and they needed room to roam. At one point I went to the outside bar and noticed an Italian lady whom I know slightly. She was not invited but I was nevertheless happy to see her. Until she cut me, that is. I almost felt like saying something, but I was too far gone by then. My problem continues to be the same. I drink too much in nervous anticipation, and then become like maple syrup. Too nice by half. I often wonder what it would be like if I turned yobbish and violent, like so many Brits do after having one too many. Perhaps more interesting, I imagine.

The reason for my party was having turned seventy in August. I was very flattered to have Paul Johnson accept, as well as Antony Beevor, both of whom I placed at my table next to the Queen of Greece, while the Duke of Beaufort, who had not visited Annabel's in thirty-five years, sat with the mother of my children and King Constantine. But while I'm at it, and as one who has not spoken to any member of the Birley family, there's been a great injustice perpetrated against my friend Robin Birley, who for obvious reasons did not attend my blast. I will not go into details, but my old friend Mark Birley has done a great injustice to his son Robin. It is too bad because Annabel's resurgence is owed to Robin and his young friends.

Basically I think Mark never liked the fact that Robin was close to Jimmy Goldsmith and Aspinall. My brother goes around saying terrible things about me, and all I did was give him half of what didn't belong to him. I don't mind because he's a bitter old man whereas I am a very happy old man. But a father should never humiliate or fire his son, at least not where I come from.

But to more pleasant revelations. The words used by the first man to step on the moon seem to be in doubt. 'That's one small step for man, one giant leap for mankind,' is the accepted version. Neil Armstrong insists that he meant to say 'one small step for a man . . . ' but what he really said was 'one giant step for Manny Klein'. How do I know? His half-brother, Nigel Armstrong, was my tennis coach and continues to coach the Bismarck children. Who is Manny Klein? He was Neil's roommate at the Airforce Academy. On his wedding night he asked his bride for some oral sex. She refused. Nice Jewish girls don't do that sort of thing. 'Not until a man walks on the moon,' she told him. Hence Neil's remarks. It pays to have well-connected coaches, and it also pays to have a sense of humour like Neil's. But whether Mrs Manny Klein lived up to what she had promised, I am totally ignorant.

Cheap Tricks

Wednesday, 11 October 2006

The telephone rings and a downmarket voice greets me with a cheery hello. 'This is Peter McKay, your old friend,' says the bubbly one. 'We hear that *Vanity Fair* paid for your party.' For any of you unfamiliar with McKay, he is a scandal-purveyor of talent, malice and unparalleled mischief, who writes under the pseudonym of Ephraim Hardcastle in the *Daily Mail.* My first reaction, needless to say, is to wonder why *VF* should pay for my party. And I tell him so. 'No, *VF* did not pay for my party, but Graydon Carter, the editor, and his wife Anna, as well as Dominick Dunne, a *VF* columnist, were invited as they are old and good friends of mine.' McKay obviously read this as an affirmation because the next day he led off with an item which stated that 'the shindig, which lasted until 5 a.m., was planned in consultation with Graydon Carter, editor of *Vanity Fair*, which flew its society writer, Dominick Dunne, to London, berthing him at Claridges, to report exclusively on the bash. Columnist Taki often rebukes vulgarians whose parties feature in celebrity magazines. Did *VF* buy up his birthday bash?'

The mind boggles. The English language provides words only up to a point when one wishes to answer in the negative. If one goes on too long, one tends to protest too much. So, what to do? Hang up is one way, but it will be taken as an affirmation. Make sure gossip merchants do not have one's telephone number is another, but that, too, will be seen as an affirmative answer to their non-posed question. Kill all gossip columnists seems to be the only solution. But then I might have to commit suicide myself.

The trouble with gossip-mongers, especially those working for British papers, is their malice. And their lack of access. When I saw the item which referred to me, the penny dropped. The man who is trying to fill Nigel Dempster's shoes had rung me the night before my bash and offered to send a photographer. I trust the *Daily Mail* as much as I trust Bill Clinton, so I politely but firmly said no. The only photographer allowed in was doing it for *VF* because, as I told him, I trust Graydon Carter. Punto basta, as they say in the land of pasta. The result was, of course, a bitchy item hinting very strongly that I had taken a dive and sold my party out. To gossip-mongers like McKay, it was a normal thing to do.

There is a rich Iraqi woman in London as I write, one Rena Sindi, who has come to London from New York to do just that. Give phoney parties paid for by celebrity magazines and luxury-goods merchants. Gossip columnists don't know the difference between, say, Rena Sindi and Countess Bismarck. They are both called society hostesses by them. It's like calling gangsta rap and Mozart's Don Giovanni one and the same: music. Sindi will come up with Euro-trash and desperate New York socialites and desperate London D-list celebs and ring up the gossips. The opposite applies to the countess. She will ring up her friends and her husband will pick up the bill and *c'est tout.* This is what London society has morphed into nowadays, at least where the gossips are concerned.

A wise man once observed how easy it is to tell a lie, how hard to tell only one. Gossips are known for avoiding hard work so, after their first one, they go on lying with a clear conscience. God bless them. What would we do without their snide comments about people they've never met? As the mother of my children said to me, 'People in glass houses . . . '

Which brings me to Intelligence Squared and the London–Paris festival which took place last weekend at the Royal Geographical Society and turned out a great success. It was a weekend of lively debate with heavyweights like Bernard-Henri Lévy, François Bujon de l'Estang, Dominique Moisi, even Taki, among the contributors. I participated in the 'Better Paris than Washington' debate, arguing for Paris. On my side were the French Ambassador and the gentle and very wise William Pfaff, of the International Herald Tribune. We had Bruce Anderson, Peter Jay and Christopher Hitchens against us. Hitchens was OK, not too insulting, Peter Jay was fat and very pompous as well as boring, and then the Brute went to work on the French. It was not pretty, nor very funny, but certainly insulting. He called them 'cheese-eating surrender monkeys', and because the Brute looks menacing when he speaks — he is, after all, one of Britain's scariest characters, especially if he threatens to undress — my side took it rather badly. 'You don't know the Brute,' I told them.

He once stayed with me in Gstaad twelve years ago. During dinner with Arkie Busson's father, a war hero in Algeria, he talked non-stop about Agincourt. Pascal Busson said nothing. Then the Brute started on the Greeks, and how South Africa barely let them in as whites. I stood up over him, demanded he apologise and retract, otherwise 'I will perform a *mawashi geri* [a round kick] on your fat head', which he immediately did, and then we went back to dinner as if nothing had happened. There were twelve witnesses. The Brute has no shame, but nor does he intend harm, which is more than I can say for gossip-mongers.

2007

Vintage Tony

Wednesday, 10 January 2007

Gstaad

About twenty years or so ago, Tony Lambton, the mother of my children and I drove from Siena to Florence in my brand-new Audi Quattro. Our destination was La Pietra, Sir Harold Acton's Florentine marvel of a villa, where the great man was expecting us for lunch. It was Tony's idea that Acton should meet the Speccie's High life correspondent. While I was putting the Audi through its paces, Tony, sitting in the back, kept repeating in his high-pitched, nasal voice, 'Isn't Taki good-lookinnnnn . . . he's so good-lookinnnnn . . . ' Obviously embarrassed, I begged him to stop but on he went. Once in Florence we stopped at a chemist, for his lordship needed some pills. Alexandra and I waited in the car in air-conditioned comfort. 'Isn't Tony great?' I asked the wife. 'He sure is, but all the time he was saying how good-looking you are he was trying to put his hand up my skirt . . . '

It was pure Tony Lambton. A cheap feel took precedence over friendship, and why not? Anything to shock. I first met him in 1957, at the Agnellis, and I was not yet twenty-one. 'Do you masturbate a lot?' was the first thing he said to me in front of lots of people I hardly knew. I turned red and furious. In a trembling voice which gave me away, I lied that I never did that sort of thing. 'Well, I do,' he said. 'Especially when I go on a long plane trip . . . ' It was the start of a long friendship.

Both the Profumo and Lambton scandals had an irony about

them. The *soi-disant* frigid English male pumping away in a glorious macho way with prostitutes, in Tony's case simultaneously with two of them. Atta boy, Tony. Compare that with the ludicrous Bill Clinton, getting it up with Miss Goodyear Tyre in the Oval Office.

There was a lusty abandon about the Lambton scandal. Only Ted Kennedy could match it, but, unlike in the fat Irishman's case, no one died with Lambton or Profumo. My then young children called him Lorlambton, one word, and he once sold me a house next to his Tuscan property. I literally gave it back to him after one season, asking for nothing in return. The trouble was his mistress. Too hysterical and unpleasant for me. The place was also much too hot in summer. But I will remember Tony with great affection, for his wit, his humour and trouble-stirring, not to mention his ability to be both totally cynical and yet loyal, as in the case of Diana Mosley and countless others. He once told me while lolling around his pool that George Weidenfeld was the hairiest man he had ever seen, and that when a large ape had escaped from a nearby zoo, some carabinieri had mistaken George for the ape and almost shot dead the publisher. I thought it extremely amusing but I didn't believe a word of it. Tony insisted. In fact he was so convincing, I wrote about it in these here pages in August of 1988.

Needless to say, it was totally made up. Lord Weidenfeld, it turns out, has absolutely no hair on his back or on his chest, for that matter, and no ape had escaped from any zoo except the one in Tony's mind. Weidenfeld was not best pleased but he forgave me. Tony was furious with the publisher because he had just come out with a book attacking Diana Mosley, so he got the Greek idiot to write a column ridiculing Lord W. It was vintage Tony, and he also managed to involve two grand ladies – no longer with us – who supposedly ran up to the Italian fuzz and begged for the ape's life to be spared. Although it was *grand guignol*, I fell for it until a solicitor's letter arrived at 56 Doughty Street setting me straight.

As a lady wrote in the *Daily Telegraph*, 'In an age where spin doctors outnumber sheep, and you would not believe Tony Blair if he told you the world was round, it is rather refreshing to hear of an MP who was caught with his pants down and actually admitted it.' Actually, most people don't care if a politician screws around. Most people screw around. I remember how the pompous Robin Day asked Lambton why he needed to use prostitutes as he already had a wife and a mistress. Why not, was the answer, if one still feels like it? Robin Day was a grabbing type, the kind that clasped a girl's thigh while in a taxi, pretending to have fallen over as it swerved. He was shocked, shocked to find out that Tony was double-dealing. But he double-dealt openly, and that's why he was so special, and the Robin Days of this world are not.

Get Carter

Wednesday, 31 January 2007
Gstaad

A London friend has sent me a book whose subject caused a few faint complaints in the beginning but has now escalated to a full-scale furore, Jimmy Carter's *Palestine: Peace Not Apartheid*. Racist and anti-Semitic have been the operative words used by out-raged pundits to describe it, while people such as the Harvard law professor Alan Dershowitz and the director of the Anti-Defamation League Abe Foxman have gone overboard in calling the thirty-ninth

President of the good old USA not only an anti-Semite but a Christian madman and a pawn of the Arabs.

Let's take it from the top. Jimmy Carter has dedicated his life to humanitarian causes and is as anti-Semitic as David Ben-Gurion. He was a weak president but always a man of integrity. His book clearly states that the blame for obstacles to a just peace is shared by Israelis, Palestinian and American leaders. He also states that the Israelis are attempting to gain land illegally in the occupied territories, just as some leaders advocate violence and are refusing to accept Israel's right to exist. So far so good.

What has caused this furious backlash is that Carter also points out that the pro-Israeli lobby in Washington has stifled debate, and that the Israelis are guilty of human rights abuses in Israeli-occupied Palestinian territories. Talk about shooting the messenger. Is there anyone except the usual suspects who can deny that the editorial pages of American newspapers rarely present anything but pro-Israeli viewpoints? Carter could have used another title, as he himself acknowledges, but he stuck to the 'apartheid' word in order to make a point. The apartheid followed by Israel at present, in which Israelis are dominant and Palestinians are deprived of basic human rights, is a milder version of the one used by white South Africans who oppressed blacks.

Most Europeans will welcome Carter's view of what has been going on in the occupied territories since 1967. But not Americans. The Anti-Defamation League has been running ads in major news-papers defaming Carter, and pundits like Michael Kinsley have gone ballistic over the 'loaded word', as he called apartheid. But a forced separation of two people in the same territory with one group dominating the other is apartheid in my book, and to hell with those who will call the poor little Greek boy a racist and an anti-Semite. I've been called these names before, and they have yet to break any of my bones. But Jimmy has been getting worse flak than I ever did. 'Holocaust denier', a 'patron of former concentration-camp killers', a 'Christian madman', a 'man who condones mass murder of Israeli Jews' are some of the grenades lobbed Jimmy's way by the likes of those who would rather shut one up than debate the issues in DC. Namely, the Israeli lobby.

The trouble with Foxman, Dershowitz and their ilk is that they've cried wolf once too often. They doth protest too much over the slightest criticism of a country which has a hell of a lot to be criticised about, and whose most respected newspaper, Haaretz, has long pointed out the brutalities perpetrated on the Palestinians by Zionists of the old school of Begin, Shamir and Netanyahu. Let's face it, a vocal Palestinian viewpoint is nonexistent in America, but Foxman is outraged by any suggestion that this might be the case. 'The reason he [Carter] gives for why he wrote the book is this shameless canard that the Jews control the debate in this country, especially when it comes to the media.' Well, yes, Foxman old boy, that was the point of the book, and that's why you've gone bananas over it. The Jewish lobby in America has stifled debate, and if one refuses to admit it there is no point me banging on about it.

Read the book and make up your own mind, says the Greek sage. Which brings me to the European apartheid practised by our Muslim cousins (distant cousins, I might add), aided and abetted by our own politicians and media. Channel 4's courageous exposure of what extremists preach within the walls of Britain's leading mosques had as much coverage as Taki's win of the Sudan Open in 1959 did. Channel 4 managed to film mad mullahs preaching against Kuffars (that's us) and calling for a holy war against us, yet none of the busybodies who pounce on anything they deem offensive to Muslims have raised a finger. No politician has stood up and demanded the arrest of these hate-mongers, and none of the police seems perturbed in the least. Where are all these watchdogs now that we need them? Don't European Christians have any rights left? Can you imagine the reaction if a Christian church allowed a priest to say such things in, say, Saudi Arabia? Well, not really as there are no churches allowed in Saudi Arabia.

Not to worry. We have David Cameron who will save us once these Scots go back up north. Well, the poor little Greek boy is not going to wait for his rescue. I am Ukip all the way, and hope all the rest of you Kuffars back the only party which might save a little bit of Britain the way we knew her to be.

Russian Invasion

Thursday, 15 February 2007
Gstaad

There's more happy dust to be found indoors around here than powder on the slopes. Last week I drove to the Diableret glacier and skied my legs off trying to catch up. At 3,000 metres – the maximum height the old prop planes used to reach when crossing the Atlantic – and upwards, the white stuff was perfect. (I mean the snow on the ground.) Although I smoke non-filter Camels and drink the heavy stuff, my lungs felt perfect. My feet hurt like hell, however, and I became convinced while skiing that I had gangrene, or something equally disgusting. After two hours I could bear the pain no longer. I stopped and took off my boots. Eureka! They were not mine, but my son's old ones, worn when he was sixteen and at Le Rosey. No wonder I thought I had gangrene. But I had to put them back on and ski down for another twenty minutes non-stop – twenty minutes which felt like five days in the company of Paris Hilton and her distinguished family. Never mind.

The greens are having a ball with the surrounding greenness, and as the temperature rises daily, so do the predictions that Switzerland will soon be rivalling Palm Beach for beachwear in winter. Mind you, many of the ecologically minded folk, at least here in Gstaad, drive Porsche Cayennes, Range Rovers or the disgusting Hummer. And speaking of the unspeakable, the nouveaux Russkies are capped at 10 per cent in Kitzbühel, one of the most *gemütlich* resorts of the alpine persuasion. Bravo, Kitzbühel. I wish the Swiss would do the same, but I won't hold my breath. I know it sounds racist, but billionaire Russian kleptocrats are not as yet classified as victims, so one can let 'em have it.

Courchevel, the French Riviera, even St Moritz have been Dresdened by the Russians, their obnoxious spending and lack of basic manners amounting to a grotesque deformity. Here in Gstaad we live in fear of the coming oligarch invasion. When I say we, I don't mean the locals. Sublimely blind to the disaster of Courchevel, the Bernese would welcome them with open pocketbooks. And why not? They see us as one and the same. Foreigners, with lotsa moolah, flashy cars, pulled women and incapable of yodelling. One of the reasons Sarkozy will be the next French president is that Johnny Hallyday, the Gallic equivalent to Elvis, has moved to Gstaad for a favourable tax deal. Sarkozy has defended him by saying that Johnny has worked hard all his life but the state has taken most of it away. The notion of a French symbol decamping to a Swiss resort has had an incendiary effect on French politics.

It's worse over here. Johnny has applied for a season's membership to the Eagle club. Forty-four years ago to be exact, the rocker and I had a terrific punch-up in the Palace bar. He had come over to sing, and, after the performance, he sent one of his minions to ask my then soon-to-be wife, Cristina, to join his table. She politely declined. The gofer insisted. That's when I said, 'Elle ne danse pas avec le personnel.' You'd think I'd told him his mother was a hooker. All hell broke loose. He went back and reported to the star, and it was October 1917 all over again. Even back then, in 1963, pulling rank was a no-no, but five against one was OK. I lost, but what the hell. Forty-four years later I am not about to blackball anybody, especially an aging rock star who is quite lovable because he looks so awful.

Eagle club aside — next week it celebrates fifty years of existence with non-stop parties, which I will report on to you, as boring as it may sound – my worry is that the country which invented tax shelters for the rich might pull a Marx, and I don't mean Groucho. (A very long time ago, in these here pages, I revealed that I was related to the great Marx by marriage. My wife's sister, Princess Victoria Schoenburg, is married to Harpo Marx's grandson, which makes me Harpo's grandson-in-law. So there.) If we poor little rich are not allowed to do a discreet let's-make-a-deal with the Swiss tax authorities, the result will be worse than the tsunami of two years ago. This time it will involve poor little Greek, Italian, French, German, Belgian, Dutch, Spanish and Scandinavian victims. No one will come to our aid. The hacks will cackle with glee. And the Swiss peasants will finally smile. (Not for long, mind you.)

Here's Henry James on the Swiss: 'The want of humour in the local atmosphere, and the absence, as well, of that aesthetic character which is begotten of a generous view of life . . . ' I should not go on. I've always got along fine with the locals, and I count some of them as good friends, but however hard I try to warn them against being Courcheveled, their answer is always the same: 'Would you refuse to sell your chalet if someone offered you five times what it's worth because he's a Russian?' Alas, so is mine. 'Do you know of any Russian who would offer me five times that for my wife?'

Seduction Rules

Thursday, 8 February 2007

I am seriously thinking of suing Silvio Berlusconi for plagiarising many of my lines. I love Berlusconi, but while he was crooning on board a liner long before he made his billions I was using lines such as 'With you I would go anywhere . . . especially to a desert island . . .' or 'I would follow you anywhere, even to the loo . . . I feel so possessive and jealous . . . ' and other such corny lines. Uncool as they may sound now, believe me they used to work, and sometimes they still do.

All seductions begin with flirting. Flirting is the key which turns the engine on. It is as simple as that. Without flirting, you cannot seduce, and without seduction the race becomes extinct. The British newspapers used the term 'playboy antics' to describe Silvio's badinage with young attractive women. But not everybody who uses chat-up lines is a playboy; otherwise you'd have 50 million Italian playboys and ten million Greek ones. Show me an Italian or a Greek man who doesn't flirt and I'll show you a pervert. Flirting has never ruined a marriage or driven a wife to drink. Coldness does that. Men who flirt usually service their wives regularly, and everyone else they can get hold of. Nothing wrong with that; we Europeans need more people and less immigration.

About two years ago Rachel Johnson rang me and asked me for some tips while researching her novel *Notting Hell*. Basically, how to handle a wife, a mistress and – hopefully – a few girlfriends. I wrote ten basic rules which were originally published by her in an article about her novel. So here, at last, are Taki's ten rules for playing away, straight from the horse's mouth:

(1) Always remind your wife that you love her and will never leave her for anyone else, ever.

2) Always remind your prospective lover that, if she gives in, you will never leave her and that you love her more than your wife.

(3) Always promise marriage. Promising marriage has served me well these last fifty years, although if one is past sixty, one should promise that the last will and testament will look very kindly upon anyone who has had carnal knowledge of the soon-to-be deceased.

(4) Never raise your voice or show anger. Always fake jealousy with both your wife and lover, and especially with your mistress.

(5) Deny, deny, deny. Never admit the slightest indiscretion. Confessions are for amateur adulterers.

(6) Be very generous before and after the affair. Women talk, and word that one is generous gets around quicker than bad news.

(7) Marry a beautiful woman, preferably upper class and sure of herself, and cuckold her with lesser, uglier beings. She won't mind and they will be flattered to cuckold someone superior to them.

(8) Be romantic. Whisper. Write notes to both the wife and the lovers.

(9) Make love to everyone concerned regularly. Well-serviced women do not go looking for trouble.

(10) Always be in a good mood and always make them laugh. Show me a man who makes women laugh, and I'll show you one who gets laid a lot.

Berlusconi first laid eyes on Veronica in 1980. He was a builder and she was a B-movie star. He saw her on stage, was thunderstruck and hey presto. He not only got the girl, but also 35 billion big ones. He also became the longest-serving premier of postwar Italy. Somehow he rubs people up the wrong way – he is very tacky; no jokes, please – but I'm a fan. I've never met him but I like it when he shows off in front of cold Anglo-Saxons, telling them he lost his hair because of making too much love. (He's had implants since.) And I envy him terribly for getting the object of his affection. If only it would happen to the poor little Greek boy. Let me explain.

Three weeks ago I flicked the television on and suddenly my heart began to pump so rapidly I thought I was having a heart attack. The film was *The Dreamers*, a Bertolucci movie which is the sexiest pic ever, and then some. The divine one's name is Eva Green, and in *The Dreamers* she loses her virginity in front of her brother, having driven a young man crazy by undressing completely while dancing to 'La Mer', sung by Charles Trenet. In no time Eva had made me forget Juliette Binoche, Irène Jacob and Isabelle Huppert. Like a crazy man, I began to make inquiries. And found out that two good friends of mine had their cavities filled by her father, a Parisian dentist by the name of Green. Her mother is the actress Marlène Jobert, quite sexy in her youth. Their daughter is surely one of God's greatest creations. Alas, Dr Green has retired and sold his practice, otherwise I'd be on my way to Paris to have everything redone. And my yearning and adoration for her is made more bittersweet because she doesn't know I exist. Oh, yes, I almost forgot one important item in my ten commandments. Persistence. I am not about to give up. Eva is twenty-two and I am seventy. It is the perfect age difference between a man and a woman. I am not favoured to win her, but stranger things have happened.

Manners over Money

The lack of snow drove me to the Engadine valley and the queen of ski resorts, St Moritz. Mind you, the queen is no longer what she once was. At the beginning of the last century, St Moritz was the undisputable numero uno winter spot. European aristocracy flocked there for amusement and sport. Downhill skiing had not as yet been invented, but there was curling, tobogganing and, following the latter, the bob and cresta runs which saw brave young blades risking their necks after a night spent dancing and pursuing the fairer sex.

In between the wars St Moritz reached its zenith. And even after the second world war, it managed to draw the best of what was left of the old aristocracy, combined with the smoothest of the newly rich. No longer. The Russkies have arrived with their bodyguards en masse, and no resort or watering hole can withstand such a battering. The physical side first. Every brand name you have ever heard of now has a boutique in the main streets, and ubiquitous tarts prowl the place the way once upon a time German U-boats prowled the Atlantic. Needless to say, the great hotels and nightspots are now Stalingradised, with goons, their shaven heads glaring under the spotlights, setting the tone. But there is also good news. The old guard, as tradition demands, never surrenders. Adversity, after all, requires ingenuity, and there are three places left which have turned into enclaves for those who believe in manners over money. These three private clubs keep out the rabble and make it possible to rub shoulders with one's own type.

Mind you, the only thing I rubbed shoulders with was the snow. I fell head first in the third gate of a Corviglia club giant slalom, making a fool of myself to the great amusement of Tim Hoare, who between loud guffaws described me as a Messerschmitt shot down by a Spitfire plunging nose down into the English Channel. Some Messerschmitt. I was going slower than a Soviet-era Skoda. Two days later, back in Gstaad, I was given the privilege of being the first runner for the Eagle club's gold cup and 50th anniversary. I wore my lederhosen but was advised at the last minute by Prince Nikolaos of Greece to refrain from wearing my Wehrmacht helmet. (Actually, I followed a friend's sound advice not out of good taste, but fear. If one tumbles at speed the steel could cut one's throat.)

I took off like a speeding bullet and thundered down through the gates, my mind already busy with the speech I was going to give as I received the gold cup. Somewhere towards the end I decided to cut down on the speed as victory was assured. Alas, there was something wrong with my calculations. The only people I had beaten were a couple of old-timers who died natural deaths during the race, three or four girls who had taken up skiing that morning, and a fat Greek gentleman who stopped halfway to eat a souvlaki kebab. Such are the pleasures of old age. The mind is willing but the old body says niet.

I did make it up that night, at the Eagle's fiftieth anniversary ball. The president of the club, Urs Hodler, had kindly asked me to do the commentary for a slideshow called 'The way we were'. I was in my cups, standing on a large stage in front of 550 people, the mike in my hand, but for once I did not make a total fool of myself. My friend John Sutin had prepared me with good one-liners, and Jeffrey Moore had told me to keep my cheap jokes for the end. It worked. No one was offended but not for lack of trying. The English, of course, laughed the loudest at my joke: when an Italian finishes making love he looks at the mirror, flexes his muscles and tells himself, 'Magnifico!' When a Frenchman is through, he tells the lady that she may have captured his body but not his soul. When an Englishman finally manages it he asks, 'Was it good for you too, George?'

I must say it was a very good week. In St Moritz I went to a dinner for Tassilo Bismarck's eighteenth birthday given by his parents at the Dracula club (one of the three enclaves left), and the night before, at Princess Chantal Hanover's flat, Tim Hoare, Nick Scott, Leopold Bismarck and I voted three more members into the world's most exclusive private club, Pug's. We are now seven, the three new ones being Prince Heinrich von Furstenberg, Arki Busson and Prince Pavlos of Greece. Pug's clubhouse is located on my boat Bushido, and in a moment of drunken folly I pledged to leave the boat to Pug's. After my demise, that is. The motion was carried unanimously, Arki Busson already trying to figure out how much the boat would sell for and where to place the assets for maximum return.

As I said, it was a wonderful week, although I was a bit sad to realise that fifty years have gone by since I set foot inside the Eagle as a twenty-year-old, bowed deeply to Lord Warwick, the then president, and was made a life member immediately because of my obsequiousness. A Russian oligarch would have head-butted him and then tried to buy the place.

National Symbols

Wednesday, 4 April 2007
Santa Cruz, Bolivia

Bolivia's ruling party is demanding that Coca-Cola drops the 'coca' from its name to 'dignify' the 'bioenergetic' leaf that provides the main ingredient in cocaine. Before any cokeheads get the wrong idea, this is no laughing matter. 'If we are not permitted to commercialise coca, then why should Coca-Cola be allowed to do it?' said the Bolivian president of the Coca Committee, a party which is part of a nationwide Bolivian group which demands a new constitution based on coca. In other words, let's stop hiding behind our finger and tell it like it is.

For reasons I do not care to go into at this particular moment, I cannot disagree with the Bolivians. In fact, I agree with the Coca party. The Saudis don't knock oil, nor do the Greeks put down olives. The Swiss, needless to say, are never beastly about banks. The Bolivians are good people. They all look the same, are all short, have straight hair, Roman noses, and can work for days without food thanks to the coca leaf. Now they want to put the leaf on their flag. Who are we to say no? And who is Coca-Cola to say that its product is the real thing? (It used to be until 1916.)

As everyone knows, big Yankee companies are terrific bullies. Coca-Cola is a company worth dozens of times more than all of Bolivia, and its product contains a flavoured essence of the coca leaf, but not cocaine. The company insists on keeping the name Coca. I say boo to the bully company. It should be sued for false advertising.

Coca means coca leaf, which means cocaine. This is where the Bolivians come in. 'The state recognises that the coca plant in all its varieties as a natural, economic, renewable strategic and bioenergetic resource is a sacred symbol of Andean Amazonic cultures,' says a government proclamation. (Mind you, the government spokesman who wrote this was obviously a patriot and under the influence of the natural bioenergetic sacred symbol.) And it gets better. A government commission has proposed that the laurel and olive branches which currently adorn the national seal should be changed for branches of the sacred and ancestral coca-leaf plant to symbolise popular culture and social cohesion.

I am quite ignorant about national symbols except for the obvious ones: cheese for France, a stiletto for Italy, a Panzer tank for Germany, electrolysis for Greece, and so on. But if any country deserves the coca leaf as a national symbol, it's Bolivia. Washington, of course, is not best pleased. Since Evo Morales, a leftist but a nice guy who likes to get high, became president, the Bushies are really pissed off. They've already cut off millions of dollars in counternarcotics aid, which means that the Bolivians will grow more and more coca in order to make ends meet. When Condi Rice visited Bolivia quite recently, the hospitable natives gave her a miniature guitar to take back to Gringo land. She refused it rather insultingly when it was pointed out to her by Morales himself that the guitar was lacquered with coca leaves. (Guitarists the world over shed a bitter tear over that one.)

A Bolivian senator, Antonio Peredo, took me aside and told me that the current symbols contained in the seal – olive and laurel in the talons of a condor – are a legacy of Bolivia's colonial past, while the coca leaf corresponds to 'Tahuantinsuyo', referring to the ancient Inca empire. Which means that the Coca-Cola company is using Bolivia's sacred patrimony as a commercial label to induce millions of slobs the world over to drink its product. As a Greek, I fully sympathise with my Inca brethren. Imagine if Donald Trump took the Parthenon as his company's logo? Or Madonna used the Crucifixion to sell her videos? (She has.) Institutionalising the coca leaf will put a stop to its exploitation by the big bad Yankees.

Since he took office last January, Evo Morales has legalised coca plantations and is pushing coca to be declared a medicinal substance. It's medicinal, all right, but it also has terrible side effects. Logorrhoea, for example, i.e., diarrhoea of the vocal chords. If one is unfortunate enough to be cornered by a bore on coke, it can be awfully tiresome. Ironically, the more coca leaves Bolivian peasants chew, the less they talk. This is because of the peasants' inherent dignity. No Hollywood types they: talk to them is cheap. Unlike them, under the influence we northern types chatter away like canaries. Just imagine Tony Blair on coke and head for the hills.

Bores and side effects aside, fairness demands that Coca-Cola acknowledge its debt to the coca leaf and pay Bolivia reparations for having exploited its patrimony. Twenty thousand million greenbacks would be just about right. And here I must declare an interest. A Bolivian politician promised me the nation's highest award if I campaigned for reparations from the Coca-Cola company. I am told the award will get you ten to twenty in any Western country except for Hollywood. So I politely declined, asked to be shown just a tiny sample, and wrote this column.

Trouble at Club

Wednesday,2 May 2007

New York

It's been a hellish week for Pug's Club. A week in which I was unable to lend my good offices against the violent outbreak of disapprobation and impropriety. What has been until today a relatively smooth path to the great and most exclusive club in the world was threatened by a member or members unknown, although there are only seven of us. Let me begin at the start: Pug's was founded by Leopold Bismarck, Nick Scott and myself last summer. The club was named after the main character in Herman Wouk's book *The Winds of War*, who was played by Robert Mitchum in the eight-hour-long mini-series. Pug Henry is a United States naval commander who is a friend of Franklin Roosevelt, known to Adolf Hitler and Hermann Goering, liked by Winston Churchill, and trusted by Joseph Stalin. He is sent on all sorts of diplomatic missions around the world, hobnobs with high Nazis, is toasted by Stalin in a great banquet in the Kremlin, flies over Berlin during an air raid, and takes command of a destroyer in the Pacific, winning the war single-handed.

While watching the film and laughing out loud at how ridiculously easily Pug solves his Herculean assignments, Nick had the idea to call the world's most exclusive club after Mitchum's character. Neckties and buttons were ordered and distributed, Tim Hoare was elected, and then, after some heated arguments, Prince Pavlos of Greece, Prince Heinrich Fürstenberg and Arkie Busson also joined.

So far so good. And that is when the trouble set in. Due to the extreme exclusivity of Pug's, all sorts of social climbers among the rich and famous began to drop heavy hints about joining. Count Bismarck stood firm when Nick Scott tried to sneak one of his relatives in. After a resounding blackball, Nick Scott retaliated by declaring no more Krauts welcome. Pug's club day being the 20 April, there were lunches in Harry's Bar in London and on Harbour Island in the Bahamas attended by all the members except for yours truly, busy in Miami trying to purchase some gold.

The next thing that happened almost ended the brief life of the club. Three names were proposed and posted on the internet. (The clubhouse is located on my boat.) The names were Henry Kravis, an American billionaire and takeover artist, Sir Paul McCartney and – believe it or not – Woody Allen. Complicating matters, and before I had an opportunity to call an emergency meeting, Henry Kissinger was proposed. Now I'm a friend and admirer of Dr Kissinger, and figured it was the German connection – Bismarck and Fürstenberg – that had done the proposing. I contacted both men and they both vigorously denied putting up Henry the K. Paul McCartney's proposal was a no-brainer. That was the work of Nick Scott, whose son is a musician and who, after all, is a Brit. Ditto for Kravis. If that vulgarian was not put up in secret by Arkie Busson, I am Monica Lewinsky.

Actually, I went into shock. How can anyone propose Woody Allen, a man who married his step-daughter after he got caught taking nude pictures of her. Or Paul McCartney, who looks like a woman in drag. Or Kravis, for that matter, a man whose Gadarene greed is legendary among Wall Street types. Is this why we started the club? And, after all, Henry Kissinger did side with the Turks against the Greek colonels.

Things mercifully settled down after a unanimous blackball for all

249

those proposed by members unknown. What angers me is that the only one I absolve from this dastardly plot to ruin the club is Pavlos of Greece. No Greek names appeared, although Pavlos did mention once that he would like Demis Roussos to join us. (Fat chance.) But why is the German contingent denying putting up Kissinger? Or Hoare and Scott refusing to admit they proposed McCartney. After a week's contemplation, I think I have found the culprit. It's Arkie Busson. He has a show business connection with the mother of his children, hence the clowns Allen and McCartney. He is a zillionaire himself, like Kravis. And he'd like Kissinger to write the Arkie Busson saga one day. Eureka! Nick Scott is the executive chairman, so I had him fly up from the Bahamas to explain the atrocities perpetrated during my absence. He swore that it will never happen again, but it is very hard for me to believe him. It was Scott, you see, who made Osama bin Laden (Harry to us old hands) a member of White's, and not David Metcalfe, as I had thought. Although I used to be a friend of old Harry, he has gone a bit over the top these past ten years. Scott should have known better. But he is easily distracted by booze and women, both of which cloud his judgment of people. Mind you, I prefer Harry bin Laden to Paul McCartney, but in today's climate I would certainly blackball Osama, if only in order to safeguard my boat from a cruise missile. White's should beware.

Things are now calmer at Pug's, and my only wish is that they remain so. Yet I live in fear that Busson will mount another coup and try to sneak in some showbusiness type. Uneasy lies the head . . .

Pulling Power

Wednesday, 25 July 2007
On board S/Y Bushido . . .

My closest friend Yanni Zographos, who died eleven years ago, had a system for picking up women with young children in tow. As he passed a mother pushing a pram he would announce to no one in particular, 'Les jolies mamans font des jolies bébés . . . ' Starting in the summer of 1956, my first free year after eleven years in captivity, I put his theory to the test. In the fifty-one ensuing years I can confirm that neither Yanni nor I ever managed to pick up a single woman with that line. Still, we always remained upbeat and confident. Another favourite pick-up line of Yanni's back in the Fifties was to yell 'taxi' while riding in his Bentley convertible in Athens. Greece had about 2,000 cars in total, people were poor and public transport terribly crowded and unreliable. Yanni and I would cruise up and down Zographos – an Athenian area named after his family – offering taxi rides to women; yet again I can confirm that in the forty years leading up to his death neither he nor I ever managed to persuade a single member of the female sex to get into the bloody Bentley.

Hence you can understand my insecurity on arriving in a pick-up paradise like St Tropez and finding hardly any women pushing prams, and traffic jams so humungous that people were abandoning their cars in order to walk to their destination. Mind you, after fifty-one years of being shot down, I've now discovered the pick-up line to end all pick-up lines. But first let me set the scene: I anchored the boat in front of Tahiti Plage and went to lunch at Club 55, where the rich, fat and mostly ugly people congregate. There were about ten of us – Nick Scott, Chantal Hanover, Tim Hoare, Richard Northcott, Bolle and Debbie Bismarck, Sir Bob Geldof and a couple of pretty young things. All sorts of loose and chesty broads were table-hopping trying to catch Saint Bob's eye. That is when I had my brainstorm. 'Hello, again,' I would shout, and the line worked as if by magic. As everyone is more or less always stoned in St Tropez, the word 'again' meant that we had already been properly introduced, and perhaps even been intimate. There were smiles of recognition, however faint, and then a mad rush to sit next to the pop icon. Even later on in the evening, the line stood the test of time. Bob Geldof was amazed. 'He's effing seventy effing years old, and his effing line effing works,' he announced.

Of course, it all ended in tears when the mother of my children arrived and decided I had been burning the candle at both ends. Every morning I'd get up no matter how wrecked the night before, and do tennis drills with the wonderful pro Nigel Armstrong, whom the Bismarcks employ to turn their four boys into future Federers. Their rented villa above Tahiti Plage has a tennis court and pool to cool off in after the drills. Cross-court forehands for five minutes, cross-court backhands for another five. Then the same thing but down the line. After twenty minutes, ten minutes volleying and hitting overheads, and then a tie-break up to twenty-one. Playing hard in the midday sun gets rid of the booze as well as any other impurities one's system has ingested in this Sodom-and-Gomorrah-like place. But I must admit it's great fun. Living on the boat and being able to get off and exercise makes one's day. The nights, needless to say, offer more opportunities for sin than Havana did before Castro. Alas, the place is teeming with Russkies, Ayrabs and Pakistanis, all competing in the Cave des Rois to see who will outspend whom. Opening a magnum of Cristal now costs 50,000 euros, and these slobs have been known to pop them open and then spill them on the floor to the last drop. Worse, people cheer.

Thankfully, I have resisted going to that ghastly place, although the young Bismarcks have been accurately reporting the outrages nightly. The problem is one of my crew, Andrew, who is an Aussie. He told me his parents read the *Guardian* and that they are champagne socialists and would be appalled if they read that the owner of the boat where their son works had taken part in such a shameful orgy.

Given the fact that England is under-water, it does sound a bit rich complaining about the outrages of the super-rich on the Riviera, but such are the joys of an otiose class obsessed with materialism and the root of all envy. Which brings me to Boris and the Tories. The latter are finished, history, curtains, through . . . If they've lost two by-elections after Labour has been in power for ten years, they might as well throw in the towel. Better yet, let Boris run the party. He's the one who has the courage to attack Brown on the penal inheritance tax, crime and immigration and force him to hold a referendum on the European constitution. Cameron's populist policies are a sham, and the by-elections proved it. Those few Brits not employed by the state all want to have their voices heard, but Cameron is listening to the Circe-like sounds of the PR gurus. Cameron should either go to the Lords, Lourdes or come down here and join the rabble. Gordon Brown is going to make mincemeat of him, so a Riviera stay is not such a bad alternative.

Man of Mystery

Wednesday, 29 August 2007

OK. It is early 1964, the Profumo scandal has proved beyond reasonable doubt that English men can also be swingers (and with women, to boot), and my friend Yanni Zographos and I have just had a big win upstairs at Aspinall's and are taking the circular inside staircase that connects Annabel's with the casino. Suddenly two nuns block our way. My first thought is a prurient one. Both nuns are great lookers. Then, out of the blue, one of them begins to undo Yanni's fly and quicker than you can say Monica Lewinsky she services him. I am in my twenties, I am shocked and appalled that a nun would do such a thing, but all sorts of crazy ideas are fogging up my mind. What to do next? Not to worry; Louis, the great maître d' for more than thirty years, starts up the stairs chiding the nuns and tells them the game is up. 'You can keep the money but off you go . . .'

The nuns turned out to be hookers who knew that winners leave the tables and go dancing, whereas losers stay upstairs chasing after their loot. Dressing up as nuns gave them an extra kick. Soon after, I met Mark Birley. He wanted to know whether dressing hookers up as nuns was a particularly Greek perversion, or were we just innocent bystanders? When we told him we were the latter he almost smiled, a wintry kind of snicker which hinted at doubt more than anything. Welcome to England, studied nonchalance and, dare I say it, not a small amount of xenophobia. Yet until George opened (four years ago, I believe), Mark Birley had given strict orders that none of his clubs would charge me annual dues. His only request was that I keep it to myself, as other members would surely have complained. I never found out why. Perhaps it was because of how I wrote about his son Rupert's disappearance in Africa in these here pages. But that was almost twenty years after Annabel's was conceived. If I had to take a guess, it would be because the staff in all his establishments liked me a lot. When I'm drunk I'm a good tipper and back then I was drunk every night. Birley asked me to write the club's story for Annabel's magazine, marking its twentieth anniversary in 1983.

A lot has been written about Mark's style, his daunting good taste and his constant search for perfection. Very little is known about the inner man because he was a typical buttoned-up twentieth-century Englishman, a man who would have preferred to have lived in the seventeenth, but with penicillin. He was greatly admired by American ladies-who-lunch types; they would swoon when his name came up. 'Oh my God, does Mark have taste or what . . .' His sister, Maxime de la Falaise, was married to my wife's uncle, but the only thing Mark ever said to me about the French marquis – a great sportsman and ladies' man – was that the man was French.

When Aspers and Mark fell out over Annabel's affair with Jimmy Goldsmith, the inside staircase was removed – there was also a problem over who owned what in the Kent building, which housed the Clermont and Annabel's – otherwise things remained the same. Those were the glory nights of Annabel's, with Sidney and John tending bar, Louis taking care of the dining area, and Nando, the walking death machine, minding the door. It was back then that I spotted Muhammad Ali and asked him to spar right then and there. Two people expressed surprise, and both of them asked me the same question: 'Do you think you could have taken him?', as dumb a thing to say as is possible. They were Oliver Gilmour and Mark Birley.

And so it went, the annual Hanbury Cup, donated by Timmy after Sidney the barman had given false evidence that 'Mr Hanbury never left the bar throughout the evening, sir,' to the cops who were looking for the man who had hijacked a bus full of Japanese tourists while the driver was relieving himself in Berkeley Square. 'Oi, mi Bus . . . .' (This entailed running one lap around Berkeley Square after 4 a.m.) Throughout all the hijinks Mark would sit inside smoking a large cigar, always with a new girl. Invariably the sweet young things looked frustrated. Mark did not particularly like to talk to the fairer sex. In fact, the word laconic could have been invented for him. The reason he never remarried, I believe, was his selfishness. He liked things his way, and women tend to move ashtrays and redecorate and commit other such crimes. The last two times I saw him was at lunch, once in his house with his son Robin, the other time at Harry's Bar with Robin and David Tang. (Tang told one joke after another, cracking Robin and me up, Mark remaining stiff-lipped and worried about the sugar-cubes.)

The end was particularly sad, at least for me, because of his falling-out with his only surviving son Robin. To me it seems inconceivable to turn against my own son. No matter what he does. But then I'm not English. I believe that Mark Birley did not like the fact that Robin loved John Aspinall and Jimmy Goldsmith, his stepfather. When Robin committed a big *faux pas*, Mark remained unforgiving. It was sad, but then who knows what goes on inside a man's heart. We all know about Mark's taste, few know much about the man himself. Perhaps there was nothing there.

Broken Streak

Wednesday, 10 October 2007

New York

Ain't that a bitch! What else can one say? The way I figure it, it was 357 columns without a miss for the first seven years, then, after a Pentonville break, 1,275 straight until last week. The lawyers broke my streak, but then they would. And in my thirtieth year, too. Well, what the hell, all good things come to an end, but at least only Claus von Bulow rang to inquire whether I had dropped dead. Actually, I ran the offending piece on my website, www.takimag.com, so it did see the light of day, and 100,000 visitors got to read it, so there.

What's interesting is how things have changed in the past thirty years. Libel laws are supposedly not as strict as they used to be, but don't you believe it. For example, I will not mention politically incorrect things one was permitted to write in jest back then. When Liberace died of Aids, I wrote: 'Ashes to ashes, dust to dust, and if you had liked pussy, you'd still be with us.' Charles Moore thought it in very bad taste, but too good to keep out.

I suppose what I miss is the crummiest end of Grub Street. Now it's all sex and celebrities; before there was a great emphasis on the bizarre. Hacks back then invented things. Not about brain-dead people like Britney or Paris, but stories which in their perversity and cruelty might as well have been true. One thing is for sure: the readers were amused. One person who was always in the news was Prince Aly Khan, the father of the present Aga. Aly had a reputation as an indefatigable lover. He went on record saying about the English,

257

and the upper-crust English at that, 'They called me a nigger, and I slept with their wives.' And he certainly did. By the time I got to Fleet Street, Aly was long gone – having died in a car crash crossing Le Pont de Saint-Cloud going to a ball on a May evening – but hacks still asked me about his technique. Was it true he used to plunge his wrists in an ice bucket just before you-know-what? Of course, that was his trick, I'd say. His mystical prolongations went to his grave with him, but they sure made a good story.

Hacks used to be overworked and underpaid but in a strange way they were hipsters, always in front of the curve. The idea of a Tara Palmer-Tomkinson posing as a writer was a no-no. Grub Street had pride. Columnists, and there were far fewer, especially gossip columnists, had an obsessive desire for revenge. They were ready to injure anyone in retaliation for the most ephemeral of slights. After all, when I began in this business there was something called the class system, fodder for those with a column to attack anyone, no matter how powerless, to stick the shiv in.

Ironically, there were gents of the old school who made their living in Grub Street, as I'm sure there still are. Second sons, failed priests, impoverished baronets, even ship-owner heirs. I remember Tina Brown writing about yours truly that 'there are a lot of hacks who would like to be ship-owners, but there are no ship-owners who would like to be hacks'. It was the nicest thing she ever wrote about me, and for once she got it right. My father used to laugh about it. 'Don't you realise that journalists make their living through blackmail?' he used to tell me. Mind you, he was judging by Greek standards of the Fifties and Sixties. I may sound melancholy and slightly ridiculous, but I loved the fact that I had never missed a column in the thirty years I'd been writing it except for the force majeure of staying with the *Queen*.

Never mind. There are worse things, like a back operation I have to have in order to defend my title next year in Brussels. By that time, I hope, there will be a Flanders, and my friend Paul Belien will be foreign minister. Incidentally, another friend by the name of Paul Gottfried, a prof. and a hell of a writer, has just published the definitive book on Conservatism in America. *Making Sense of the American Right*, the subtitle, tells it all. Paul Gottfried is no hack. A man of great dignity and as articulate as they come, he is of the Jewish faith but no Podhoretz he. He argues that modern conservatism's roots are not very deep, and that the neocons have managed to belittle their predecessors on their way to power. I particularly liked a passage where he explains how misleading it is for present conservative leaders to pose as inheritors of Robert Taft in 1950, or Bill Buckley in 1955. It is all a power-grab by people who wish to share power only with those who agree with them and who want to bring American democracy to other societies. I cannot recommend the book enough because, no matter what one's politics are, after reading it one will understand what is really going on over here.

So there you have it. A new start, a new column, a new streak. Who was it that proposed killing all the lawyers? Someone called part two, I believe. Finally, the only other thing I regret about the spike last week is that my buddy Oliver Gilmour did not get to read what I had to say about an old proprietor of ours and a wonderful man, Ian Gilmour.

Mailer and Me

Wednesday, 14 November 2007

New York

Three months before the Americans committed their greatest foreign policy blunder ever, I had gone up to Cape Cod to interview Norman Mailer. Towards the end of his life, Norman called himself a left-conservative, and went as far as to agree that losing one's culture through immigration was not a good thing. But he remained adamant about the evils of American corporations. He blamed them for making America an uglier place to live in since the second world war, a country full of 'fifty-storey high-rise architecture as inspired in form as a Kleenex box, shopping malls encircled by low-level condominiums, superhighways that homogenise our landscapes, and plastic, ubiquitous plastic, there to numb an infant's tactile senses'. He told me he was opposed to the notion of an American empire because of the all-pervasive aesthetic emptiness of the most powerful Americans corporations. 'There are no cathedrals left for the poor, only sixteen-storey urban-renewal housing projects that sit on the soul like jail. Sometimes I am tempted to think that I am not so much a left-conservative as a left-medievalist.'

Being a left-conservative, he told me, is an oxymoron, 'but there are elements in the remains of left-wing philosophy that are worth maintaining'. Such as? I asked him. 'Such as the idea that a very rich man should not make 4,000 times as much in a year as a poor man.' I remember sitting outdoors in the brilliant sunshine with him, and, after he said that, I told him that my father, who employed some

5,000 to 10,000 workers, made sure the disparity was never enormous because that is what breeds not only communism but also hatred for the haves. 'Try telling that to Henry Kravis,' he snorted. We then discussed God. 'If you start to talk about God with the average good liberal, he looks at you as if you are more than a little off. But I do believe there is a Creator who is active in human affairs and is endangered. I also believe there is a Devil who is equally active in our existence and is all too often successful.'

This was back in 2002. In the five years he had left, Mailer wrote *The Spooky Art*, on writing, *The Castle in the Forest*, a novel about Hitler (or the Devil), *The Gospel According to the Son*, a novel about how Jesus discovers his divinity, and the painful and powerful journey that ensues, and finally a book on God which made mincemeat of all those atheists and publicity-seekers whose names will never appear in this column. His ability to write both fiction and non-fiction, essays and journalism, plays and films singled him out as a very brave writer who was not afraid of risk. He wrote about all things important, such as space, politics, war and peace, and sex and feminism.

He was not as good a boxer as his son Michael, but he was very brave inside the ring. He was not afraid of getting hit, and it never entered his mind that Michael might be holding back. In 1998 a great party was given for him at Rockefeller Center to celebrate his 50 years of writing. Muhammad Ali was there and the whole Mailer brood lined up with the champ for a picture. 'Wait a minute, I need a fascist in here,' announced Norman. 'Taki, get your arse up here.' So up I went on the stage and had my picture taken standing between Norman and Ali, aka Cassius Clay, and I suppose it was my greatest moment ever. 'Are you really a fascist?' asked the champ.

I spent the day of Norman's death with his first-born son. Michael is probably my closest friend in the Bagel and he confides in me.

His dad recently told him, 'I couldn't have been the writer I am today and also have been a good father.' Michael understood. When Günter Grass admitted he had volunteered for the SS when very young, Mailer defended him while the rest jeered. 'It was a writer's romantic conceit, seeking experience,' said Norman. He once gave a dinner party for about twenty in honour of Abbie Hoffman, then the number one fugitive from the FBI. He told Michael to sit on the steps outside his house, and if he saw any fuzz to yell 'Geronimo!'.

A few hours after his death we had a boys' lunch with Michael, Chuck Pfeiffer, double silver-star winner in Vietnam, Nick Simunek, Coldstream Guards and producing a movie with Michael (one in which I play a grand master in karate) and yours truly. We got very, very drunk, just Michael and I, as the other two have given it up. Next to us was Liz Smith, the best-known gossip columnist in America. Liz came over and told us a Norman story. During Arianna Stassinopoulos's wedding to oil-billionaire Michael Huffington, Norman got bored with the glitzy people who had packed the church to the rafters. He turned to Liz and asked why the two of them had never gone to bed together. 'Well,' said Liz. 'first of all, we were born the same day of the same year. And, second, I'd rather go to bed with Norris [Mrs Mailer].' Norman shrieked out loud, said Liz, and people turned, wondering what had happened.

I knew both James Jones and Irwin Shaw, tough-guy writers, and Norman now completes the trio up in Heaven.

2008

Good Guys, Bad Guys

Wednesday, 27 February 2008

An interesting week, to say the least. A Carlton Club speech on multiculturalism which didn't quite come off, a kidnapping in Gstaad, a party in London to celebrate David Tang's knighthood, the mugging of John McCain by the man who committed adultery with Emma Gilbey, a great Pug's club lunch at our new premises, and the addition of two more members to the world's most exclusive club. Let's start with the kidnapping, a first for Gstaad.

The American lady who was grabbed outside the Palace hotel in broad daylight is married to a Greek close friend of mine who bought Asprey's last year. He deals in private equity and they were coming to my house for dinner that evening. She was grabbed by three hooded men, bundled into a car fifty yards from the hotel and forced to lie on the floor while it sped away. After fifteen minutes, she was almost thrown out of the speeding car having first surrendered her large diamond ring and assorted baubles. She made her way back with the help of a friendly farmer and spent the best part of the evening being interviewed by the fuzz. Like English cops, the local gendarmes know how to give parking tickets in a jiffy but catching the bad guys is not their specialty. A burnt-out car was found five days later somewhere in the Canton de Vaud, but that's as close as they got to solving the crime.

Personally, I was convinced at first that the perpetrators were Russian oligarchs, who since becoming multibillionaires had missed stealing and the thrill of being chased by cops, but it seems the bad guys spoke French, a language as foreign to oligarchs as the concept of fair play. My friends are now back in the Big Bagel, their Gstaad holiday ruined by the resort's attraction for nouveaux-riches, vulgar celebrity wannabes and criminal elements, all fuelled by local greed which cannot resist a buck, no matter where that buck comes from.

My Carlton Club dinner speech on multiculturalism also ran into trouble. The name of it was Ann Widdecombe. She spoke first and said everything that had to be said, leaving me stranded at the post. There's nothing one can do in such situations – no use repeating what she had just stated and very articulately at that – so I made a few jokes at which no one laughed, stuttered a bit, complimented Ann on having remained a virgin, and sat down to a thunderous silence. Oh well, my friend Sergei Cristo, the organiser, did not think it too bad, but then Sergei thinks Lincoln's visit to the Ford theatre was also a success.

Which brings me to the unsuccessful attempt by the *Bagel Times* to smear John McCain. Bill Keller, the executive editor, must have known that it was a non-story. There was no proof, no witnesses, not even an accuser. Just speculation based on a simple acquaintance. Well, it's not always man meets woman, shakes hands and off to bed they go. McCain is not a rapper or a rock star. Keller, however, is another story altogether. Keller was a married man with two children carrying on with Emma Gilbey, an Englishwoman who had burnt her bridges in London and had moved to Washington. In her own account, which she wrote for the *Telegraph*, Keller came home to his family one day with the news that his girlfriend was expecting and that he would do the right thing. He subsequently divorced his wife and married la Gilbey. Like most *Times* editors and writers, Keller is a hypocrite nonpareil, assuming that McCain must be guilty while desperately trying to sink his chances of becoming president. The fact that Keller got trapped by a bun in the oven must have played a role in deciding to run the non-story. Why should McCain get away with it when I didn't . . .

Never mind. Last week I put all that behind me while I lunched with Christopher Lee, Count Bismarck, Prince Pavlos and Nick Scott at our new premises at the Fox club. Christopher Lee is a delight. He told us wonderful stories about the good old days of film, wore his Pug's club tie with pride, and announced he had put his membership in Who's Who, ignoring other clubs and honours. (Incidentally, where is the knighthood for Christopher, a star for more than fifty years?) The trouble with the lunch (Uma Thurman is our housekeeper, having accepted our offer and lowly salary with alacrity) was that the wine was so good I was a mumbling, dribbling wreck by the time I arrived at Sir David Tang's bash at the Dorchester.

I remember little, except Jemima Khan's sexy leggings and thighs, her ignoring me while flirting with young whippersnapper Dan Macmillan, our very own chief executive's kind warning that I was no longer young (thanks, Andrew, as if I can ever forget it), my making a fool of myself by screaming, 'Why Sir David and not Sir Taki,' the fresh beauty of Rosie Hanbury, Tom Parker Bowles dressed as if he were at Glastonbury, and Debbie Bismarck's legs. After that it was all a blur except for the beauty I met at the Henkels, but by then I had become a bore. (A quick word about my host. I went to his mother's house in Düsseldorf back in 1956. It was during the tennis tournament and the Henkels had laid out the silver in their grand house. The Mexican team pocketed most of it until their captain, a South African, made them return it. Her son is just as generous but there were no Mexicans this time.)

Taki Lives the High Life

Wednesday, 16 April 2008
New York

Their memorials were held five days apart, each in one of Manhattan's most hallowed venues, each one attended by more than 2,000 worshipping fans, both attracting A-list mourners as well as the poor and the humble. William Buckley and Norman Mailer had great send-offs, the former, as a devout Catholic, in St Patrick's Cathedral, on Fifth Avenue, natch; the latter, as a non-practising Jew who called himself an atheist, in Carnegie Hall, where art and imagination have flourished for decades.

As both men had been mentors of mine, their families kindly sent reserved-seat tickets, but it was not to be. Death unites the fallen and abjures snobbery and privilege. Paying homage to the dead means first come first served. One does not tell an old Jewish lady from Brooklyn, or a Catholic for that matter, that they're sitting in one's seat. I was in the next-to-last row in St Patrick's and on the third tier in Carnegie Hall. Never mind. Both the service for Bill and the eulogies for Norman were once-in-a-lifetime occasions. Tom Wolfe, sitting in the last row in the cathedral, whispered that the hymns were out of this world. 'Yet the Muslims have passed us in numbers,' I whispered back, 'and all they listen to are screams.'

Only Kissinger and Bill's son Christopher spoke in St Patrick's, a conservative number for the man who actually invented modern conservatism in America. This was not the case with Norman's eulogists. There were twenty-seven of them, including his nine children, all of them talented and smart, all of them in the arts; plus writers, actors, directors and Muhammad Ali's wife. Never have I been less bored by listening to twenty-seven speakers. In fact, Norman's offspring should take their act to Broadway. Each one spoke on a particular subject about their father, but with one unifying theme: how a man with six wives and nine kids, a drinker, a doper and brawler, managed to weave together a single family unit which works. One of his actor sons, Stephen, swaggered to the podium, cleared his throat in the characteristic style of his father, and growled, 'Carnegie Hall, Carnegie Hall, well, why not?' Christopher Buckley also mentioned the venue. Forty years ago, his father told him that if he were famous by the time he died, he would like to have the service at St Patrick's. 'You've got your wish, dad.' My close buddy, Michael Mailer, talked about boxing, Norman's obsession, and how poignant it was when he, Michael, got too good for Norman and they had their last match.

There were many similarities in what one writer described as a requiem for two heavyweights. Both men ran for mayor, both lost badly, but many of the policies they proposed back in the Sixties were prescient enough to have now become law. Bill brought civility into the raucous Bagel politics, and great wit. Norman brought passion and honesty into politics by mixing with the common folk and defying the distinction between words and deeds. Both became famous at twenty-five years of age, Mailer with *The Naked and the Dead*, Buckley with *God and Man at Yale*. Norman published thirty-odd books, Bill around fifty. Both men were extremely brave in the physical sense. Norman would fight anyone, and he was a good boxer as well as brawler. Bill would go out sailing in a tiny boat in storms which would have kept Horatio Nelson in harbour. I was proud to have been a good friend of both men, who incidentally liked each other very much despite being in extreme opposite political landscapes, and they had many debates and tussles defending their ideologies. Bill's civility and wit will be copied – I hope – by future generations, while Norman's enduring power of imagination in the novel will – again, I hope – get us out of the rut relativists have landed us in.

So, death is now ever present. Bill believed in the afterlife, Norman in reincarnation. Who is right, I dunno. What I do know is that starting with Yanni Zographos, James Hanson, Jimmy Goldsmith, John Aspinall, Alan Clark, Gianni Agnelli, Charles Benson, Nigel Dempster, John Goulandris, I have now lost more friends than most men do in a lifetime outside wartime. What is important for me now is to move toward the door marked exit in a gracious manner, as all my absent friends did. I am, however, in perfect health despite the drinking, and even the back is now healed. Here's to doctors. Having fallen violently down the hatch of my boat while trying to bring in a sail, I displaced my pelvis but was told it was just a bruise by a horse doc in St Tropez. In the Bagel, ditto. One wanted to operate, the other shot me full of cortisone, until two osteopaths, one in Geneva the other in New York, diagnosed it correctly. They shoved – it takes a lot of shoving – the pelvis back in its place and I now feel twenty-one years old. Which means I am no longer Quasimodo-like and can marry *The Speccie*'s deputy editor at last. Perhaps Bill and Norman can come back as bridesmaids for my nuptials. *Vive la jeunesse!*

The Lives of Others

Wednesday, 14 May 2008
New York

From my kitchen window I have watched a little boy grow up to be a man. I live in what Americans, with great economy of expression, refer to as a brownstone, actually a townhouse. It is on 71st Street off Park Avenue. My father bought it for us thirty or so years ago, and both my children refer to it as home. Although both have left, my daughter for Los Angeles and my son for Brooklyn, their rooms still feel lived in, with shoes lying around, old books, bric-à-brac and pictures of their parents looking less worn, to say the least. The house, I am told by neighbourhood historians, used to be a whorehouse, but a very upper-class one. Never a scandal, just a few gentlemen going in and out throughout the days and nights. I tell everyone that I visited it while down from school, but I'm not sure it was this one.

About twenty years ago I moved the kitchen to where my office used to be as the children were driving me nuts while I was busy writing the greatest Greek novel ever. Sitting in the kitchen and staring across the back garden into the lives of others is not my idea of fun, but it beats writing anytime. Which means I spent a lot of time in the kitchen looking into the apartment building across on 72nd Street. That's when I first saw a tiny baby being brought home by his parents, and the nanny that slept next to the crib. My wife and I would look as the baby lay on its back and bicycled, his adoring parents standing over him – and a very good-looking couple they were, too – while he made gurgling sounds and strange noises. The nanny had left after two weeks and the baby's door was always open.

As they say, time flies, and in no time the baby had turned into a little boy and was covering the walls of his room with flags and pictures of various baseball and football players (not girls, at that point). This came about ten years ago, one large Technicolor picture of some blonde I couldn't make out. Most well-to-do boys go to day schools in the Bagel, Noo Yawk parents being incapable of hating their children as the English do and sending them off at six years of age. (I knew my parents loved me madly when I was sent away at ten.) And in no time at all, I saw a young girl come into his room pretending to study with him. I was getting old. This year the room is empty, the boy finally having left home, I suppose to go to university.

I never knew what his name was, or what his father did for a living, and I guess I will never know, but I somehow felt sad that it was all over. Last week, during a short heat wave, a maid came in to hoover. She had a broad Slavic face and was middle-aged. It was the weekend and most people had left for the Hamptons. The maid carefully took off her clothes, folded them neatly in a corner, and proceeded to clean the room in her bra and panties. It was a very funny, New York scene. The flags are still up but the blonde's picture is long gone. The room is quiet and dark. The end of an era.

The great New York writer E. B. White said that the city will bestow the gift of loneliness and the gift of privacy. Very true. When I would occasionally play hooky from school after a sporting meet and go into Times Square, it had not as yet evolved into a gauntlet of drug-dealers and porn parlours that it became until Giuliani. There were cheap movie houses lining 42nd Street, where for twenty-five cents one could escape from the boredom of school and regulations. That was privacy and then some. Today, midtown is a lonely place, clean and safe, Disneyised, a bustling suburban shopping mall full of megastores, the same stuff Americans can find anywhere in the United States. If you gave twenty-five cents to a beggar – the price I paid when young to dream happy dreams – he'd most likely throw it back at you. A mediagenic, illuminated blur of people, cars, lights and moving electric surfaces do not inspire dreams or a feeling of belonging. Advertising carnivals can be very lonely places.

The Upper East Side, of course, has remained unchanged. Some old-timers mention the fact that eight blocks away from where I live Rudolph Valentino lay in state, the trouble being that no one under sixty would know who Valentino was. (No, not the dress designer, someone even more famous . . .) Old dad used to call the great silent screen star Rudolph Vaselino, but always added that the greasy one danced the tango like no other. For those of us raised on movies of the 1930s and 1940s, Central Park West's beautiful beaux arts and art deco apartment towers were the backdrop to our vision of urban glamour. Every time I walk by on my daily constitutional round the park, I look at those buildings and I think I can hear witty badinage, the music of Cole Porter and faintly see Fred Astaire in his white tie and tails. New York is nothing like Paris or London, and certainly it's not El Lay. Driving up a deserted Park Avenue last Saturday night, the place looked the loftiest of cities. Manhattan has expanded skyward because it had nowhere else to go. As the lights begin to go out in the pre-dawn dark I think of these past sixty-odd years I've lived in this place, and all the changes that have taken place. The widening distance between the urban poor and the grossly rich, the diminishment of charm and tone in the city caused by violent immigrants, even the little boy whom I watched grow up from my kitchen window. I wish him well.

Belgrade Bell

Wednesday, 11 June 2008

I never thought I'd see it, a beauty winning a major title, at least not since the Williams sisters and the ghastly Maria Sharapova came on the scene. But there she was last weekend, an olive-skinned enchantress winning the French Open and charming everyone with her femininity and grace. If only Ana Ivanovic did not use the word 'guys' so much, she'd be perfect. But, what the heck, that's the price you pay for mixing with Americans on the circuit.

Will her looks last? Not if she keeps playing they won't, so let's enjoy her while she still has them aged twenty-one. Nothing kills beauty quicker than sweating and battling under the harsh sun. Mind you, most women athletes are dogs to begin with, and that definitely includes tennis players, but there have been a few exceptions. Annabel Croft for one, but she quit early on and just in time. Gabriella Sabatini was another beauty who quit on time, as did Anna Kournikova, Gussie Moran and one Carol Fageros, ranked in the top ten during the Fifties in the States. But they were the exceptions. Most champions are not blessed with looks, which I suppose is fair enough. How would you like to face a Keira Knightley across the net when you look like Martina Navratilova? The Almighty knows what he's doing.

My pet hate is that Sharapova woman. She does not grunt, she screams, and she does it in order to put off her opponents. But such is the Gadarene greed of professional sport that no one dares raise the issue. Her sponsors should replace Miss Bovine, all six foot three of her, with Ana Ivanovic, the Belgrade belle who has bewitched me to the extent that I have not thought of *The Spectator*'s deputy editor since last Saturday.

But on to less serious matters, like this Murray chap. He has a book out about his life, all twenty-one years of it, which is a pretty hard thing to do as he's an illiterate. Andy Murray thinks the English are bad at tennis because they're lazy. In view of the fact that he's never won a grand slam, perhaps he should let others make this point, but, in this world of mammon, one has to be blatant, noisy and controversial, hence the opus.

In my not so humble opinion, the reason English players bring up the rear is an obvious one. They've been sitting on their arses since the Second World War and know how to whinge, not how to win. Just look at those Russian women who are dominating the rankings. Most of them look like Soviet-era factory workers, the same workers who stayed on the job and churned out the goods while under German bombardment. In other words, Russians know how to suffer, and modern-day tennis means suffering for close to three hours per day. Gone, alas, are the days when a Belgian gentleman like Philippe Washer could reach the quarters at Wimbledon three times, and the semis in Paris, while staying out late every night with yours truly chasing you know what. (And, as everyone knows, it's not the sex that wears one out, it's chasing after it.) And just look at the Serbs. While the draft-dodging Clinton was busy bombing a Christian Orthodox country in order to make Kosovo safe for radical Muslims, Ana Ivanovic was reduced to training on a makeshift court that was at the bottom of an empty swimming-pool. I don't think many English tennis players would contemplate going out to hit balls while bombs were raining down, which is the difference between the Serbs and the Anglos.

Murray is wrong. The English players do train hard, but refuse to suffer once the match commences. I know how they feel because although I trained very hard I always thought there was more to life than hitting one more ball across the net than my opponent. In fact, that's why I love judo and karate. Five minutes at most and it's all over. One has to be Sisyphus to win today, which is why even the arguably greatest of them all, Roger Federer, is having a hard time. The old fire is no longer there. It cannot be after a certain amount of time.

Enough said about a silly game which was invented by French courtiers hitting potatoes at each other. It's also football time, and Greece, a tiny nation of ten million schmucks, is defending her European Cup victory of four years ago. You wouldn't know it by reading the British press, of course. Back then it was called a fluke, and perhaps it was, but when was the last time England, Wales, Scotland or Northern Ireland won anything? (I'm being unfair. England did beat San Marino three or four years ago in a famous victory.) If tiny Greece and tinier Portugal – the latter plays the best football in the world, better than Brazil – can win, why can't big old England? I'll tell you why. British footballers are taught to play like thugs, not artists, and their lack of education doesn't help either. One has to develop skills, like controlling the ball and passing it, but the Brits only know how to run like crazy up and down the pitch, tackle very hard, spit a lot, use the F-word and get sent off. Not the same thing as playing smart football. Just as well no British team made it this time. I'd hate to see beautiful Austria and Switzerland invaded by pot-bellied, tattooed yobs, although both the Swiss and the Austrian fuzz know how to handle them. I didn't see any of these lager-swilling swine do their stuff in Moscow because they knew what the Russkies would do to them. Go, Greece, Portugal and Germany.

Best Foot Forward

Wednesday, 17 September 2008

Gstaad

Walking up mountains is not only healthy, it gives a man time to think. In fact, climbing in solitude offers one marvellous inner adventures, with epiphanies being the order of the day. There are no boulders where I climb, just a lot of green, steep hills separated by gorges, with lots of cows to keep me company. About fifteen years ago I tried climbing up steep mountains tied to a rope, but it wasn't for me. I suffer from vertigo and the way down was hell. But I did manage to conquer the steepest overhang of Videmanette, the highest mountain in the region. Never again. The fact that the only thing preventing me from flying off into space was a rope attached to a man above me and two thin steel picks helped make up my mind. Judo, tennis, skiing and karate, yes; overhangs, no.

Still, I occasionally dream that I'm fighting for my life perched on some perilous slope and what a pleasure it always is when I wake up. The pain in one's chest when walking up a mountain is the only thing that bothers me nowadays. The legs can go on forever but the lungs ain't what they used to be. The booze and the smokes do not help, but I get around the lung problem with frequent stops, even a smoke now and then. The few people who walk up mountains around here usually attach all sorts of contraptions to their chests and necks, tiny gadgets to monitor their heartbeat and blood pressure. A bit like having a brain scan between rounds while boxing. A generation ago they would have been laughed off a cliff; today the laugh's on me, or so I'm told.

A week ago, climbing with Charlie Glass under blue skies, fresh mountain breezes and a few puffs of Tiepolo clouds, it was as good as it gets. As we walked, the old wedding cake, the Prisoner of Zenda Palace Hotel got smaller and smaller, and as we plugged on the air got thinner and the legs heavier. Getting to the top is a wonderful feeling, because one did what one set out to do, and also because the torture is over. Mind you, the real torture is on the way down, when the knees take all the weight as well as the beating, instead of the much-abused heart. (Anyway, my ticker is by now immune, what with the way my fiancée – the deputy editor of *The Spectator* – has treated me lately.) We crossed wheat-covered fields, forests with sweeps of meadows and wild flowers, smelled rosemary and cow dung, and then, suddenly, we were in thin air and free from pylons and other modern inventions man uses against nature.

As I said, I like to walk or climb alone, but as I hadn't seen Charlie in a couple of years – he has been busy writing a book about Americans in Paris during the occupation – we shot the breeze all the way up but I didn't do much day-dreaming or thinking. Norman Mailer told me the most tiresome time he ever had was when he had Gore Vidal stay for a week at his house in the Cape. This was recently, after the two contemporaries had seen the finish line ahead and decided to make up. Being with Gore was like being in a ring, said Norman, 'every time I said something he came back, bang, and I had to be on my toes.'

This week I walked up alone under stormy skies, Götterdäm-merung weather. As the skies opened up the adrenaline went haywire. Onwards and upwards under rain and lightning keeps one's thoughts pure. What is this bloody thing all about? Just before I took off that morning, I had read Rod Liddle's interview of John Le Carré in the

Sunday Times. So I thought of David Cornwell – his real name – and how he's probably the only man I have never disagreed with over a single word he's written or uttered.

Back in 1985, in the Big Bagel, I had gone up to West Point to watch the cadets slaughter Yale at football. Needless to say, I had gotten extremely drunk after drinking on the way up the Hudson, during the game and on the way down the Hudson. Afterwards I had gone to dinner at Indochine, a trendy Vietnamese place on Lafayette Street, owned by a friend of mine who had started off as a busboy in Saigon, had left with the Americans, and had worked and saved enough moolah to buy the place. In the men's loo I noticed a tall, curly-haired, good-looking but very inebriated man talking to himself while having a pee. It was Willy Shawcross. He invited me back to his table where a sober David Cornwell waited patiently. As everyone who's ever had a drink too many knows, the epiphany sometimes comes along with the hiccups. 'Did you have a small walk-on part in a recent film?' I asked him. 'Yes,' was the answer, and that was it. But I agree with what he had to say about Salman Rushdie, knowingly offending Muslims for publicity, how appalling it is that we are provoking Russia, how small David Cameron and David Milliband look while playing tough guy, and how ghastly the neo-cons are trying to get us into wars as long (my words) as they and their children never have to carry arms.

Such were my thoughts as lightning and thunder burst all around me, something that would have induced heart attacks for the neo-cons, but they, after all, would never be foolish enough to pursue such non-profit practices as mountain climbing.

Riviera Revels

Back in the summer of 1960, a married Hollywood actress and her friend, a Hollywood wife, came to the south of France and met a randy twenty-three-year-old who showed them around the place. The actress was the sexy Janet Leigh, then married to Tony Curtis, and her beautiful friend was Jean Martin, whose hubby was Dean Martin, while the randy one was the poor little Greek boy. We had a very good time boating around the various beaches during the day, dancing in Monte Carlo in the evening, Monaco being not only Russian and vulgarian-free back then, but also looking like Ruritania-sur-mer rather than Las Vegas-on-the-sea. Both ladies were guests of ambassador Joe Kennedy, whose son Jack would be elected President later that year. Kennedy was a regular visitor to Hotel du Cap d'Antibes throughout the post-war years, and although quite busy on the telephone all day and night – it took hours to get through to America and Joe Kennedy was a very impatient man – he nevertheless found time to scold both blondes for wasting their time with 'that Greek tennis player who I gather is a fascist'.

Janet Leigh died some years ago, but I often see her old flicks and remember that wonderful summer week she and I spent together. Janet Martin and I also stayed in touch, writing to each other for the next twenty-five years, especially after she suffered the greatest tragedy of all, losing her son in an aeroplane accident. (Actually, it was the young man's death that drove Dean Martin to drink himself to death.) I'm bringing all this up because last weekend I drove up to Connecticut and spent the weekend with my old friends Oscar and Annette de la Renta in their grand but cosy as hell house, and, like most people of our age, talked about the good old days and the fun we had before the Gulf Bedouins and the Russian mafia turned billionaires overnight. On Sunday Lee Radziwill came for lunch, Lee being Jackie Kennedy's younger sister, and known as a better looker than her more famous sibling. Lee is now in her mid-seventies and lives in Paris, and she goaded me about the summer of 1960, 'when everyone was so busy working for Jack while you were having threesomes on the Riviera . . . ' 'I was for Nixon, and my room at the Hotel du Cap was so small that there was no space for a threesome,' answered poor little me.

Actually, I had just read a review of the autobiography of Tony Curtis and brought the subject up in order to compare it with that of my friend Roger Moore's. Sir Roger's autobio is a graceful story of an extremely good-looking man whose looks match his discretion. In a typically old-fashioned English manner he downplays his achievements by joking about everything – the way it should be. Self-publicists have a funny way of cutting their own throats, sooner or later, that is. Tony Curtis not only names the women he bedded, he also uses a baseball bat to beat us over the head for Hollywood's anti-Semitism. This is a bit over the top. Doesn't this man know that the reason he didn't win an Oscar for his role in The *Defiant Ones* was not anti-Semitism but David Niven's perfectly brilliant performance as a bogus major in *Separate Tables*.

I had asked his wife what Tony Curtis was like and she had told me he was a 'wonderful man'. Hmm! Loyalty becomes a woman. I think that after fifty years of being a star, one should not name names and certainly not make a charge of anti-Semitism in Hollywood of all places. I suppose that's the difference between Sir Roger and Tony. Both came from modest backgrounds, but Sir Roger only mentions it in order for readers not to think he's trying to pull a Lily Safra or a Mercedes Bass. Tony whines about it, and whingers are bores, as they say in Bora Bora.

And speaking of movies, on Saturday night after a dinner fit for King Farouk, we watched an Indian film that left us unable to sleep. It is called *Water*, and it's part of a trilogy. All I can say is that it's among the best films I have ever seen. The little girl that stars in it, as well as her older female friend, are as beautiful as anything seen on screen, and the acting is superb. Why hadn't I heard of it before? It's been out for three to four years, apparently. I'll tell you why. Because it's beautifully made, wonderfully and sensitively acted, and expertly directed. I believe the director's name is Mehta and if any of you out there like movies, make an effort to see *Water*. It beats politics and it beats Hollywood, which by the time you read this should be celebrating O'bama's victory, the first black Irishman to win the White House. But government does not save people. It gets people into trouble. The Fed's easy money and proclivity to lend to those who can't pay back is the one and only reason why we're in a mess. Prudence and fiscal responsibility are not the kind of policies leftist governments follow. Saving for a rainy day used to be what we conservatives preached. O'bama will give the store away and make things much worse, if that's possible, that is.

Party Lines

Wednesday, 26 November 2008
New York

When I heard about it, my own inchoate feelings were confused. A party for Seif al-Islam Gaddafi, son of Muammar Gaddafi, and the caller was Nat Rothschild, son of Lord Rothschild, a major donor to Jewish causes and Israel. What in Mohammed's name was going on here? Nat Rothschild is no stranger to England thanks to his by now famous letter to *The Times*. He is less well known in America, but his Atticus fund, his G-5, his post-modern house in the West Village and his propensity for beautiful women of the Russian persuasion nevertheless make him a bold-face name.

Nat was quite funny on the telephone. 'Will you promise to be nice to Gaddafi? He's not a bad fellow.' 'Hasn't he got blood on his hands?' said I, trying to sound like a pompous Harvard lecturer. 'I'm sure he does,' said Nat laughing, 'but the girls will be beautiful. Make sure you come, but please be polite.' And I was, when Nat introduced me to a man who – how should I put it – was dressed in black, looked like a chic pimp, bald, shaved head, and quite friendly. 'Are you for Hamas, or Abbas?' was my first question to the man who is in New York offering to invest some of Libya's $100 billion sovereign fund in US companies. He did not hesitate. 'Hamas.' 'Good for you,' said I, 'after all, Hamas did get elected.' My next question went unanswered, as Gaddafi junior walked away and mingled with the bevy of beauties in Nat's futuristic abode. 'How much money is your father giving to the Palestinians?'

He obviously mistook me for an ardent Zionist and chose not to answer.

Oh well, the party was great. I hooked up with my old buddy Christopher Brooks, the painter, who used to be known as 'Looks Brooks' twenty-five years ago in London, when his sister Annabel tripped the light fantastic with Bryan Ferry and 'Looks' was making beautiful music with Lady Liza Campbell. More important is the fact that Nat Rothschild, scion to one of the most famous Jewish dynasties ever, can throw a bash and have one of the sons of an ex-major terrorist – now a reformed character due to . . . er, Uncle Sam's forays in the Middle East – attend and actually mingle with the young and the restless. There were some major Brazilian beauties there, but for some strange reason the poor little Greek boy did not make an impression.

About thirty years ago, in this here space, I suggested that the only way to Middle East peace was through commerce. I had noticed rich Arabs being awfully chummy with Jewish merchants of expensive trinkets, so in my simple-minded way I figured if the Arabs and the Jews could get along while bargaining over gold watches and necklaces in places like Gstaad and St Moritz, not to mention the unspeakable Riviera, why not down in places like Jericho, Jerusalem, even in Gaza?

So now we have a Rothschild and a Gaddafi breaking bread together in the Big Bagel, and although I'm puling a George Osborne, I'm doing it for the sake of Middle East peace. Seif Gaddafi is on a private visit to America, and by the time he was introduced to the greatest Greek writer since Aristophanes, he had already met Secretary of State Condoleezza Rice and many members of Congress. Stranger things have happened. Twenty two years ago Reagan was bombing Tripoli and calling his old man the world's most dangerous terrorist. Now the guy is hanging out with

Nat Rothschild and seeing Condi on the side.

What did I really think of him? Not much, I'm afraid. He had the kind of look about him that says my s*** doesn't smell. His dress was appalling – mod, black, tight and ridiculous – but at least he didn't pitch up a tent in the middle of Nat's house like his old man did in the middle of Paris while Sarko and his wife were genuflecting and kissing his arse. What I think is that Nat Rothschild should be named ambassador plenipotentiary by Her Majesty's Government, as he is obviously very well connected. A problem with Putin? Send Nat. Gaddafi making trouble? Dispatch Nat. Low circulation at *The Times*? Have Nat write a letter. Lack of beautiful girls at some party conference? Have Nat throw a party. You get the picture.

And speaking of parties, I flew over for *The Speccie*'s 180th anniversary, and it was well worth spending more money on a first class round-trip ticket than the moolah *The Spectator* has paid me these last thirty-one years. It was a great idea. The party, that is. And a hell of an ego trip. For once I mingled and saw everyone before getting drunk, shook hands like a politician, spoke at length with Lucia, a young and beautiful reader whose parents have been sub-scribers since forever, and generally did my job. Anthony Osmond-Evans gave me his coffee table book on *The Magic of Monaco,* and asked me to make friends of his members of Pug's Club. I mis-placed my notes with their names, but all pugs are automatically members of the club, so there. (I think it's Mo and Doe.) In fact, I had such a good time meeting long-time readers, I forgot to dance with my betrothed, Mary Wakefield, which she took so badly, she ran out in tears and disappeared into the Royal Hospital Gardens, Chelsea, SW3.

And then I discovered back at our Chairman's place that Rod Liddle is as uxorious as Toby Young, but I'm holding this for next week.

The Rot at the Top

Monday, 29 December 2008

The year 2008 was like herpes, very hard to get rid of; 2009 will be worse, trust me, as Bernie Madoff used to tell the suckers. This one, incidentally, is not over. The greatest scam ever perpetrated will go on and on. Madoff was not alone, and if the crooks in the SEC who turned a blind eye to his Ponzi scheme are ever forced to come clean, some pretty big names will hopefully end up in striped suits sewing buttons. Madoff scammed small investors, billionaires, hedge fund idiots, charities, pension funds and multinational banks. What is incredible is that his fund was repeatedly brought to the attention of the SEC, and every time he was given a clean bill of health. Libel laws prevent me from naming names, but they're out there, being talked about by everyone who can smell a rat after the fact. The SEC never subpoenaed the firm's records but 'relied on information voluntarily produced by the Madoff family . . . ' That's like asking Al Capone if he had anything to do with a massacre that took place on St Valentine's Day, and letting him off the hook once he had denied it. Which, come to think of it, is exactly what happened.

There is something rotten in Wall Street and the rot starts at the top. Greenspan, Rubin, Levitt, the main architects of the financial disaster, are cashing in daily. The evil Madoff is skulking around free in the Bagel, and smirking at the paparazzi even after failing to come up with his $10 million bond. (This was an obvious trick. His stolen billions, I suspect, are safely deposited in offshore accounts to be passed on later to his numerous grandchildren.)

Here's my crystal ball for 2009: the Madoff swindle is the first major scam of the current financial crisis. If history is any guide the first frauds to be discovered are not always the largest. The $50 billion loss could be just a foretaste of what will eventually be exposed.

But how does one expose the perpetrators when they are the ones in charge? I know many of the losers, at least three of the major ones live in Gstaad, and last week I was informed by my bank that I, too, had been granted the right to buy Madoff shares. (Not too many, thank God, but a seven-figure sum all the same.) America seems to have totally lost her way. Wall Street and Washington are much too close for comfort. Robert Rubin was the Draft Dodger's Treasury Secretary and is now heading Citigroup, being bailed out by the tax payer. The present Secretary of the Treasury Hank Paulson, was once the chairman of Goldman. Goldman alumni are sprinkled throughout high levels of government. Greenspan is now head adviser to the Carlyle group, instead of a nut house, where he really belongs. In civilised countries such as those in the Middle East and Africa, Greenspan, Rubin, Paulson, Levitt and their like would have been roasted alive and served as delicacies to convicts. Which makes me want to move down south, except that the snow is very good this year in good old Helvetia.

Yup, old Uncle Sam has turned out to be a fool, after all. He never appreciated the past and has no respect for tradition and his ancestors. He relies on militarism instead of conducting a foreign policy, and his love for unfettered capitalism has him now begging the Chinese for loose change. His love of porn has brutalised him and has destroyed any sensibility he might have had after Holly-wood got through brainwashing him. He never read history but listened to the Fifth columnists, the neo-cons. He dismissed Russian orthodoxy and the mysteries of faith. He laughed out loud at religious ritual, and crudely went around invading countries in order to bring them democracy and freedom. Solzhenitsyn tried to warn him about the dangers of losing one's soul, but Sam dismissed him as a nut.

Woodrow Wilson's imperatives that split up the Habsburg Empire were a major crime committed by a major criminal who used the same words that the Cheney–Bush gang did ninety years later. Uncle Sam should have thrown the bum out as he lay croaking in the White House. Instead, he has followed both his principles and his verbiage. He continues to trust and pay homage to the Saudi gangsters, who in turn pay Lashkar-e-Taiba to murder innocents the world over. His war on terror has been an unmitigated catastrophe. The real Arab victims, the Palestinians, Sam calls terrorists and sends cluster bombs to Israel to ensure the occupiers kill as many Palestinian kids as possible. I could go on and on, but Uncle Sam is a busted flush so I'll lay off.

Otherwise have a very happy new year – it will not be prosperous, that I guarantee – and keep a sharp eye out for anyone who tells you he has discovered a genius money manager. In fact, don't hesitate. Call the fuzz.

2009

Takeover Time

Wednesday, 11 March 2009
Gstaad

I stood outside the hotel lobby watching the snow blanket the parking lot, turning it into an almost pretty sight. I had been playing backgammon inside with a large and rowdy cast of characters, some of whom, like Floki Busson, mother of Arpad, and Leonida Goulandris, are veterans of the great games of the past. Others are of more recent vintage, like John Sutin, who read about the three hundred Spartans long ago and applies their theory of no surrender to the game.

Having watched Sutin accept a double that even Hitler in the closing days would have dropped, I went outside for a breath of air when the caravan arrived. Five long cars filled to the brim with flunkeys born under a bluer sky than that of northern Europe. The problem was that the precious cargo they were guarding and flunkeying for had taken off his shoes. Two on each side of the car were busy putting them back on but they were having trouble. It seems the precious one was asleep and kicking them off the moment they had managed to slip them back on his little tootsies. The doormen, all three Spaniards and very nice, were wearing their blank, Roman Abramovich expressions.

Then, finally, it was time for the little s**t to emerge, and I watched dumbfounded as a 'little s**t' did emerge and was hustled up the stairs and into the lobby. The LS was around twenty years of age, tiny and dark, and dressed badly, like young people dress nowadays, boutique-like, or Prada-lousy. He was accompanied by his enormous entourage up to the sixth floor – which had been taken up in its entirety – and upwards to the penthouse. I immediately made discreet inquiries about who the 'LS' was. He was Saudi and the son of some big shot. And that's when the penny dropped. That's what the first Gulf war was all about. To ensure that little and some not-so-little s**ts from that wonderful country could come to Gstaad, take over whole floors, and flood the lobby with their hangers-on. Bravo, Storming Norman, I thought to myself, for making it possible. Thank God, no members of my family died in that holy cause. But just imagine if some American or British parent who had lost a son in that crusade to make Kuwait and Saudi safe for s**ts had been standing where I was. Just imagine what would have gone through their minds. Not that any parent of the kind I just mentioned could afford Gstaad.

Wars nowadays are fought by the poor in order to make Halliburton stockholders richer. Arms dealers have replaced hedge-fund honchos as the new elite. This is the bad news. The good is that the Russians are not coming to Gstaad after all. They've been trapped back home by the collapsing economy just as surely as Paulus's gallant Sixth Army was back in '43. Not that I'm exactly crying over the news. Revelling in *schadenfreude* is a mug's game, but once in a while, and only in exceptional circumstances, it can be fun. The idea that these brutes with their mega-yachts, private jets, expensive hookers and garish properties in England and the South of France managed to change the way people perceive wealth, is reason enough to smile, however wintry the smile may be. These people were and are simply awful. And those who ran behind them flunkey-like trying to pick up loose change even worse. The port of St Tropez was always full to those of us with classic, beautiful sailboats in order to accommodate nouveaux riche slobs.

Yes, it's *schadenfreude* time in more ways than one. David Campbell, head of Everyman Books, was telling me how his business is up 25 per cent. This is the best news I've had since you know what happened in May 1940 around a place called France. More books being sold and fewer oligarchs around is as good as it gets. Now if we could have another Saddam go down and give some order to those who finance Islamists like Lashkar e-Taiba – the Saudi ruling family – it would get even better. Politics have been in my mind of late, as my friend Stanley Weiss had a chalet full of people who'd rather read than bulls**t. Stanley and I met forty-five years ago. He made a fortune in Mexico prospecting manganese, and, to show you the type of fellow he is, he included the taxi driver who told him where to look while shooting the breeze. I always thought Stanley a big-time CIA man because I don't know if manganese is found in places such as Laos, Vietnam, Brussels, Tehran, London, Beirut, Cairo, even Pyongyang, places he visits rather regularly. He had that wonderful writer couple Jung Chang and Jon Halliday staying, David (Everyman) Campbell and Nick Spencer, the only man over seventy to climb more than 23,000 feet. We had lotsa fun, lots to drink, and some incredible skiing as the white stuff keeps coming down like never before.

Paternal Love

Tuesday, 7 April 2009
New York

'Lock up your daughters! Is the world ready for Taki Jr?' This was the *New York Observer* headline, followed by: 'Meet the only son of the world's naughtiest Greek playboy'. Under any other circumstances, I'd be blushing – who the hell wants to be called a playboy aged seventy-two – but when it comes to JT, or my daughter Lolly, the old boy will welcome anything, and smile about it to boot. The *NY Observer,* a pink weekly, has been around for close to thirty years, and Peter Kaplan, the long-time editor, has done a grand job in a very difficult undertaking. Noo Yawkers have no time to read, and, when they do, their attention span is that of a popinjay. Kaplan has overcome this by wonderful film and book reviews, total coverage of high- and middle-brow culture, as well as trenchant political critique of the mess that is New York politics.

I was a columnist for two years at the salmon-coloured weekly back in the early Nineties, and enjoyed myself tremendously. Writing among liberals is fun. One's voice stands out. Then I made a terrible mistake. I was wooed by the Circe-like voice of Rupert Murdoch, and decamped for the *New York Post,* an extremely readable tabloid whose politics are to the right of Avigdor Lieberman and almost as subtle. The *Post* placed my column among the ads that lonely onanists read, and, although I became a hero of sorts among the wankers, the Taki name for all intents and purposes disappeared from the Big Bagel scene.

Well, now it's back with a vengeance, but it's Taki Jr, or JT, my son and hopefully my heir, who is hogging the headlines. Actually I am grateful to the *NY Observer* for putting him on its two front pages. On the first page there's a very nice picture of him with the clip, 'Meet J.T., Bike Messenger, Artist, Son of Notorious Dad'. All true. In the second front page – an Observer innovation listing the contents – there's a sketch of the boy, and more clips: 'J. T. Theodoracopulos, Son of Taki, Suffers For Both Art, Father . . . Bike Messenger – Artist, 28, Adores Notorious Dad'. What bliss. Then on page sixteen, a full profile of him, and a large picture of the two of us fooling around outside some downtown dump.

Spencer Morgan, the writer, did a grand job, and he's not known for sucking up. His column, 'Men of Manhattan', covers so-called society, but in a quirky, offbeat manner in his choice of people profiled. Most celebrities are toadies to superiors and tyrants to those under them. Morgan picks on free spirits, like my boy. The reason I was happy for the profile to appear is because, as I told the reporter, JT is the only artist I know who shuns publicity when untalented people like Dash Snow – a childhood friend of his – become stars overnight by using masturbation as a theme. Artists need exposure but, because of that, shock jocks like the present nonentities are considered stars by the know-nothings who run the art scene nowadays.

JT has been a hell of a good son. He could have had a Ferrari or a Porsche, but chose a bicycle instead. He could be doing the social rounds, but prefers to live in a dumpy part of Brooklyn, paint and bike forty miles per day in his job as a messenger. His company is called Taki Express; he is the boss and only employee, and his partner is George Szamuely, son of Tibor, a man who should be writing leaders for *The Times*, but is the dispatcher instead. Taki Express is not yet listed on the New York stock exchange, but it should be in view of the mess GM and other so-called great companies have managed.

JT's grand marriage in the summer of 2006, with Countess Assia Baudi di Selve of Rome, lasted only two months. He couldn't keep his you know what in his pants, so Assia and him had a boy, Taki Tancredi, and a girl, Maria, and now live apart. He has been very generous with them, which I suppose is easy to be when one doesn't give a damn about the root of all envy. I remember talking about my boy to an ageing socialite by the name of Serena Doorman, who now sells apartments to the rich. She was appalled that the boy wanted to be an artist, and that I had encouraged him to be one. She was even more appalled that he would be a bike messenger. Mind you, that's how many people think. They worship the cheap, the vulgar and the nouveaux riches and understand nothing about values. Money is all. Not in my book, and I have bought out the Observer this week as any proud dad would.

And speaking of phonies, the fiercest in his denunciations of Wall Street greed was Connecticut senator Chris Dodd. As it turns out he has taken more money from AIG than anyone else in Congress, and has committed other financially dubious transactions to make Jacqui Smith's husband proud to be a porno-watcher. British MPs are a pretty bad lot, but over here they're just as bad but also hypocritical. Listening to Chris Dodd fulminate about greed is like reading a column by Taki about Taki Jr. Self-serving, to say the least, but in my case it's only paternal love. In theirs it's greed.

Drinking with Papa

Fifty-four years ago this month, dizzy with happiness at having been freed from the jail that was boarding school, I ventured down New York's 5th Avenue looking for fun and adventure. I knew a place called 'El Borracho', Spanish for drunkard, where my parents used to dine. The owner was an agreeable Catalan, who had decorated the walls with paper smudged with lipstick. Whenever he'd spot a client who was beautiful, he'd ask her to leave an imprint of her lips on a square piece of paper, which would end up on his walls. This had caught on, and women – everyone wore red lipstick back then – whose lips adorned his walls, were among his best customers.

Now I remember the day as if it were yesterday, in fact much better, as at my advanced age I sometimes do not remember yesterdays. It was three in the afternoon, I was tired from walking up and down 5th, and decided to hit El Borracho, hoping the barman would remember me. I had very little money but, when one's eighteen, things like that hardly register. The place was just off Madison Avenue in the mid-50s. I walked into the dark, cool place, and plonked myself at the bar, trying to act bored and sophisticated. That's when I noticed the man three stools down. My heart skipped a beat, then another and another. It was the greatest man in the world: Ernest Hemingway himself. He was drinking a whiskey sour, or so I was about to find out.

Luckily the barman was friendly, especially after I told him about my parents being regular clients. He then turned and introduced me to my hero. I stood up, went over, bowed deeply, ramrod straight, and for the first time in my life was at a total loss for words. 'Have a drink on me, young man,' said Papa. 'What are you drinking, sir?' I ventured. 'Give the kid a whiskey sour,' boomed Hem.

I will not bang on too much about that afternoon. Papa bought me around four or five drinks, I got completely plastered, talked to him non-stop about Jake Barnes and Lady Brett, and Mike Campbell, and Lieutenant Henry and Katherine and even about Nicole, and Rosemary and Dick, and he took it all in, smiling benignly as I showed off my knowledge of Papa's and F. Scott's novels. I then had a brilliant idea. 'Will you please come up to the Sherry-Netherland so I can reciprocate; I happen to keep an apartment there the year round,' I told him.

This was partly true. My parents kept an apartment at the Sherry the year round, and I could charge drinks in the bar downstairs and, of course, room service. That's when Papa suddenly turned cold. He didn't wish to go to the Sherry-Netherland, only four blocks away, at 59th street and 5th Avenue, and in no uncertain manner let me understand that our two-hour bull-session was over. I thanked him profusely, and staggered home.

My mother was in. The first thing she noticed was that I was drunk. But when I told her who got me drunk she actually smiled, as if she knew who Hemingway was. (Greek upper-class ladies back then were not schooled for fear they might become prostitutes.) When old dad came home he was delighted that 'for once you're not out getting drunk with your bum friends'.

The next day I went to Dunhill Tailors, where my father dressed, and ordered a brown Harris-tweed suit, exactly like the one Papa was wearing on the memorable day. Two or three days later, my dad came home and showed me the New York Post. Papa's picture was on page three, except that it wasn't Papa, but the impostor I had spent the afternoon with at El Borracho. No wonder he turned cold when I had mentioned where I lived. That's where the real Papa parked himself when in town. Crestfallen but wiser, I went back to reading Hemingway, vowing to myself that one day I would meet him and tell him about the impostor. It never happened. Two years later, Papa wrote The Dangerous Summer, about the *mano a mano* between Luis Miguel Dominguin and Antonio Ordóñez, which took place in the summer of 1958. Three years later Hemingway died by his own hand in Idaho. I read about his suicide in Greece, and decided right then and there that writing would be my business from then on.

Twenty years later I was challenged by an Oxford don to debate the point I had made in the pages of *The Spectator*, a challenge I took up and lost hands down.

In the late summer of that year we lived in a house in a village that looked across the river and the plain to the mountain. In the bed of the river there were pebbles and boulders, dry and white in the sun, and the water was clear and swiftly moving and blue in the channels. Troops went by the house and down the road and the dust they raised powdered the leaves of the trees. The trunks of the trees too were dusty and the leaves fell early that year and we saw the troops marching along the road and the dust rising and leaves, stirred by the breeze, falling and the soldiers marching and afterward the road bare and white except for the leaves.

This is what I call writing, wrote I, but the don had other ideas. But what would he know? After all, he never spent an afternoon boozing with the great Papa.

Under Pressure

Wednesday, 10 June 2009
On board S/Y Bushido, off Ibiza

As everyone who has followed the America's Cup fiasco knows, it is now up to international courts to decide who shall defend what and where. The egregious Swiss billionaire Ernesto Bertarelli is the holder, and has been sued by Larry Ellison, an American sick-making, money-grubbing billionaire, whose stink pot, Rising Sun, has to be among the world's ugliest gin palaces.

Hence when word got out that the Pug's Club regatta was to take place off the island of Ibiza last weekend, thousands of Spaniards swelled the beaches in the hope of seeing real sailing boats fight it out at sea, rather than in some dreary courtroom in San Francisco or Geneva. An added attraction was the presence of Count Leopold Bismarck, on board Bushido, who reputedly had announced his intentions to avenge the cowardly sinking of the great battleship and namesake by helping me defeat Tim Hoare's magnificent gaff-rigged Alexa (a boat Adolf Hitler admired but was unable to purchase) and Roger Taylor's Tiger Lily, reputed to be the only schooner in the world whose owner (drummer of Queen) managed to water-ski behind.

Other contestants, like Lord Rayleigh of Milk, recently elected to Pug's, had to withdraw owing to swine fever, his boat having raised the yellow quarantine flag somewhere near Galicia. Two other prominent yachtsmen, both members, George Livanos and Edward Hutley, also failed the criteria, as did Mark Getty's Talitha G, and the great trans-Atlantic record-holder Bob Miller, who was so distressed to miss the race he was hospitalised in New York with nervous exhaustion. Mind you, around 700 people turned out for the trials, which took place off the northern shore of Ibiza, but when news got out that Sir Bob Geldof was crewing for Hoare, and that Roger Taylor was skippering Tiger Lily, thousands of rock and sailing fans descended on the outlying towns of San Miguel and San Antonio, sparking alarm on the already stretched resources of the Guardia Civil. Never mind. The dinner the night before the race on board Bushido was a friendly affair, but beneath the surface nerves were running high. Professor Gimlet, aka Nick Scott, president of Pug's, gave a speech urging the competitors to play by the rules, following rumours of tampering and nautical sabotage. He was roundly booed as Tim Hoare, Roger Taylor and yours truly would never descend to such low-life tricks.

Monday morning's 20-knot breeze and calm sea were perfect for racing. On Bushido we dressed for the race. White trousers, Pug's Club neckties and blue blazers. Debonnaire Bismarck, Chantal Hanover and the mother of my children chose long white linen Indian tunics. But Tiger Lily caught both Alexa and Bushido off-guard, racing off on an upwind beat, never challenged as she completed the windward leeward course in a record-setting two hours. The drama took place between Alexa and Bushido. Tim Hoare, an egregious gambler, steered a ragged path, veering dangerously off-course over rocks. What we didn't know is that he had a retractable keel, passing Bushido on the last leg in a move not attempted since the days of Columbus. Thus ended the first Pug's regatta, the beautiful silver trophy of two pugs awarded to Roger Taylor, followed by an extremely drunken lunch which finished at nine in the evening. Strains of 'Bohemian Rhapsody' could be heard throughout the night as thousands of Ibizans danced and celebrated.

Having announced that I would commit *seppuku* in case of defeat – 'Don't you think that's a bit over the top, sir?' said Captain Paul – I took refuge in the bottle, drinking maniacally until I passed out. Bushido was brave but bad upwind. My crew, starting with Andrew, Nick, Carmella and Ruth, were overconfident, having assured me of victory time and again, and insisting we would win even as we came in third and last. One thing has to be said. Tiger Lily is among the fastest schooners around, and Tim Hoare's seamanship a danger to all. But luck favours the brave, and the location for the defence of the cup now lies with Roger Taylor. If he chooses the Greek islands, Poseidon might throw me a crumb. I badly need it. I am getting sick and tired of coming in third.

Give me Nostalgia

Wednesday, 1 July 2009

Poor Michael Jackson. His last words were: 'Take me to the children's ward.' But it was nice of the jockeys in Santa Anita to wear a black mourning band in honour of a man who rode more three-year-old winners than anyone. Mind you, I thought the great Paul Johnson was the best when I happened to tell him over the telephone of Jackson's untimely death: 'Was he a member of the Beatles?' Er, well no, dear Paul, but he was in the same undignified business.

It has been said that you only ever meet the world once, in childhood. All the rest is memory. Jackson, I suppose, wished to remain a child, although from what I've read, his childhood was ghastly. (I never saw him perform and found him so repellent I avoided looking at his picture.) Vladimir Nabokov, on the other hand, said that the 'kindly mirrors of future times will reflect ordinary objects'. Nostalgia combines both memory and the kindly mirrors of future times. Hence it's my favourite. Give me nostalgia any time any day or night. I'm a sucker for it and always will be. The ghost of Harry Lime, Graham Greene's infamous anti-hero, inspires me to see a drizzle-in-lamp-light Vienna, yet the times I've been to the Austrian capital it's always been sunny and hot. But I saw *The Third Man* when I was twelve years old and Vienna has been dark and drizzly ever since. Ditto the Wehrmacht uniform. I saw it as a child being worn by tall, blond German officers who were billeted in our house in Kolonaki. It has remained in my mind as the perfect military ensemble. And speaking of the Wehrmacht, if I couldn't have been a German officer in Paris 1940, being an expatriate American there would have suited me fine.

My buddy Charlie Glass has written *Americans in Paris: Life and Death Under Nazi Occupation 1940–44*, as good a read as you can find, especially if you like this sort of thing, which I do. Glass does not hint, suggest or preach. He has done his homework and Americans speak for themselves. I am old enough to have had many friends who spent the war years in Paris under German occupation, and now I read what I always knew to be true: for many, Paris 1940 to 1944 was a non-stop party. Another friend, Andrei Navrozov, has already reviewed the book in the pages of *Chronicles*, a political monthly I write a column for, and has raved about it. He mentions an instance where the all-conquering German army showed more tact than many Americans did once inside Germany four years later. A German officer is driven up to the Shakespeare and Company bookshop attracted by a copy of *Finnegans Wake* in the window. The owner, Sylvia Beach, refuses to sell it to him. 'You don't understand that anyhow. You don't know Joyce.' 'But we admire Joyce very much in Germany,' says the gentle officer. He then piles furiously into the military car, surrounded by helmeted troops, and is driven away. He returns in a few days only to be refused again. Glass makes no comment about this. Just the facts. I loved them.

When Patton's Third Army occupied Bavaria, the Yanks went ape, looting a Schoenburg castle. An aunt of the mother of my children went to see the great man and – to her delight – was ushered in immediately. He was courteous and soft-spoken and told her no one would ever loot her property again — 'as long as I'm in command here'. No one did. My father named a ship after General Patton, and a lucky one it was, too, and when I met his son, a one-star general up in Hue in 1972, I told him about it. 'Give my regards to your father,' he said, 'but I don't know why a Greek national did what Uncle Sam should have.' Or words to that effect.

Patton admired the Wehrmacht because of its fighting spirit and gallantry. Antony Beevor's book on D-Day confirms what I've always insisted. No one fought better than the Germans going in and on the way back. Not even the Russkies. And speaking of Germans, something disgraceful took place at Blenheim Palace last Saturday night. It was a beautiful evening, and there were 800 guests for Marina Livanos's wedding to Andreas Martinos. Marina's father, George, I have always referred to as the Rommel of Greek shipowners, a comparison he has repeatedly asked me not to repeat. But I will because Rommel, along with Manteuffel, Rundstedt, Guderian and Kleist, is my favourite field marshal. So there we were, in the garden about to go inside for dinner, the champagne flowing and our spirits very high. That is when my good friend Leopold Bismarck made his entrance accompanied by wild applause. Bismarck smiled and waved back to the wildly cheering throngs. He joined me and others, not realising that behind him were the newlyweds, making their first appearance. When I told Bolle about it he seemed to doubt me. I suppose it's normal for him to be cheered, being a Bismarck and all that. But I didn't see any French people clapping. Anyway, it was a great party in a great English palace and I had the greatest hangover ever the next day.

Final Gallantry

So farewell, then, to probably the best Wimbledon fortnight ever, certainly the sunniest that I can remember. Andy Roddick now joins Gottfried von Cramm and Ken Rosewall as a three-times-losing finalist, coming within a whisker of winning the greatest trophy in tennis, but turning into a tragic hero instead. Still, unlike the elegant German baron and the great Aussie, Andy might still do it, although I wouldn't bet on it. But not to worry, Andy old chap, you've got by far the prettiest wife of all the players, and you exhibited more fight and good sportsmanship than the rest of the field combined. Roddick should be made an honorary member of the All England Club for bringing some decency to the game. Not once did he or Federer sully the great final with Murray-like boorish histrionics and screams for support, nor did their wives emulate that ghastly Murray woman, who spends her time fist-pumping and shouting, her square mouth wide open as if in a dentist's chair.

Yes, I might be bitchin' but it's summertime and the livin' is easy. Sir Tom Stoppard turned seventy-two last week and I ran into him in front of the John Sandoe bookshop. He was about to tell me an interesting story about writers when we were interrupted by fans of his. Never mind. I wanted to talk about Arcadia (which is having a revival at the Duke of York's) and the references to summer heat in the play, as I had written something about what heat does to young people in this space a month or so before. The reason I bring this up is that I once walked down Broadway with Alan Lerner, the lyricist, and not a single person exiting from the Great White Way's theatres noticed him. Tennessee Williams was a non-person in El Morocco, as was Oscar Hammerstein, whose daughter Susan I took there with him. This wouldn't happen in merry old England, or in the land of cheese, I'm sure. Playwrights are recognised and treated with the respect Americans give to billionaire developers.

Mind you, I didn't see any playwrights in the royal box at SW19 last Sunday. I saw great champions of the past: Dr Hank Kissinger and his wife Nancy, and a certain buddy of mine – I shall not reveal his or her sex – who reported to me that Princess Michael of Kent also broke a record during the record-setting fifth and final set. The one she broke was her own, established last year during the final. She managed to eat seventy-nine éclairs after having devoured close to forty-seven small ham and cheese sandwiches. In fact, one of the BBC technicians responsible for recording the speed in mph of the serves wanted to include Marie-Christine's numbers, but was told in no uncertain terms to mind the serves and nothing else. Just as well. Food-devouring record-setting can divert the attention of the crowds, and this would have been unfair to the two gallant finalists.

And speaking of gallantry, I thought Tracy Worcester's film on the plight of factory-farmed pigs was brilliant and brave and should be seen by every government official who has sold out to the EU and factory farming in Eastern European countries. She is, of course, up against it, as are small farms competing against the American giant Smithfield Foods. Not to mention what our innocent porcine friends are going through. Sows are kept in crates in Eastern bloc countries, which then undercut UK farmers, who are obliged to spend more on sows' housing. But governments lie, and they refuse to listen to ordinary people's concerns, and the last thing governments do is listen to some aristocrat concerned with animal welfare. Just look how evasive Cameron is about immigration, and he's not even in power yet. Here's what Thomas Jefferson, my favourite American president, had to say about government, back in the eighteenth century. 'It is the group within society that claims for itself the exclusive right to rule everyone under a special set of laws that permit it to do to others what everyone else is rightly prohibited from doing, namely aggressing against person and property.' Amen.

Otherwise, it's been as grand a time as I've had in years. London's mood has been as sunny as the weather, and the Gilmour and Speccie parties remained true to tradition – no rain. For years Ian and Caroline Gilmour's garden parties, as well as our own, were known for their Greek weather. Sadly Ian and Caroline died within a short time of each other – how often that happens with loving couples – and the garden parties were no more. Last week there was a revival by the Gilmour children and the sun shone like never before. Most cocktail parties are halting places for transients in despair. Not this one. I ran into tens of old friends and old girlfriends, now with grown-up children but no grandchildren, thank God, and it was nostalgia time but without the least amount of sadness. Just recalling wild times, which suits me fine. Forced at last to face the fact that most of my dreams will not come true, I'd rather think of the times when I believed that they would. Now that's what I call positive thinking.

Money Talks

Wednesday, 26 August 2009
Gstaad

What I find quite fascinating is how Americans have a blind spot about their own flaws in the area of human rights, and how they feel they have a duty to lecture other countries on the issue. I am, of course, referring to the outrage over the Libyan deal, an outrage shared by most people who have not sold out to Big Oil. But successive United States governments have never had any qualms in maintaining close relationships with dictatorial regimes the world over, so suddenly why the screams? Didn't the sainted Obama play footsie with Gaddafi in Rome some weeks ago at the G8 summit? And weren't the first people to be flown safely out of the United States following 9/11 Bin Laden's relatives? Who do they think they're kidding?

Let's face it, money comes first where human rights are concerned, and Big Oil money before any other kind. The Americans recently forced Switzerland to reveal their bank secrets to the IRS or else. The Swiss folded quicker than Saddam's Republican Guard. Switzerland is my adopted country and the best place in the world to live. It is a real democracy starting at village level. Yet she threw in the towel when faced with sanctions that Uncle Sam refuses to impose on, say, Israel, for its possession of nuclear weapons and illegal occupation of the West Bank. Both Switzerland and Israel are democracies, but not all democracies are the same in Uncle Sam's eyes. And it gets worse. Last week the Swiss President, Hans-Rudolf

Merz, pulled down his lederhosen and humbly apologised to that arch clown and conman Colonel Gaddafi for the brief detention last year of Hannibal Gaddafi, the clown's son.

Such, however, are the joys of Realpolitik. Hannibal Gaddafi and his wife were arrested after a couple who worked for them managed to escape and report to the Swiss police how they had been beaten and held captive by the Gaddafi pair. After one or two nights in the pokey, the Gaddafis were allowed to leave the country after claiming diplomatic immunity, a joke in itself. Libya threatened an oil embargo against land-locked and oil-less Helvetia. For good measure, the Libyans then arrested a couple of Swiss tourists and held them on trumped-up charges. So the Swiss folded their hand, ate humble pie and the two hostages will soon be home in Switzerland's verdant hills and mountains. But all's not well. At the time, I wrote in these pages that Switzerland should have frozen Libyan accounts, made other arrangements for her oil needs – there is always Russia, not to mention Saudi Arabia, whose moolah is choking Swiss bank coffers – and hold Hannibal Gaddafi and wife for trial. But I'm a fool, a dumbo who believes that there is justice in this world, and that beating up a couple of poor Filipinos has consequences. There are consequences, but only for those without power and wealth. Gaddafi's genius is for mischief-making and for making a mockery out of civilised behaviour. And we, the West, are responsible for letting him do it to us because Big Oil holds a gun to our temple. It also shows the total contempt our elected clowns feel for those of us stupid enough to vote for them. Blair, Brown, Milliband, Straw, Mandelson, Obama . . . I could go on for ever, liars and hypocrites all.

Meanwhile, Bernie Madoff's feeders are back in the news. Some not-so-wise investors are suing the auditors of the feeder funds who made Madoff and his family very rich, and themselves eventually very poor. It's about time. My special bad guy is Andres Piedrahita, the Colombian whose motto, according to the *Wall Street Journal*, was 'As long as I make more money than those investing with me'. I've known Piedrahita for years but he was canny enough not to approach me. He's a loudmouth braggart who still swans around in his yacht and private jet despite the misery of many of his investors.

My particular bone with him has nothing to do with Madoff. Years before he had taken down the Swanee Adam Shaw, son of that wonderful writer Irwin Shaw, a friend of mine and a very brave second world war correspondent. Irwin wrote some of the finest short stories ever, including 'Girls in their Summer Dresses', and good novels like *The Young Lions, Two Weeks in Another Town, Evening in Byzantium,* and *Rich Man, Poor Man.* Irwin had only one son, Adam, who went to school in Gstaad and turned out to be a fine writer as well as a tough guy, like his old man. I have not heard any news about him for years, but it seems he invested his inheritance with Piedrahita, who lost it all. After Piedrahita struck it very rich with Madoff, Adam Shaw should have tracked him down, beaten the crap out of him and demanded restitution. But that's not the way of the world, is it? If he had, he probably would have ended up in jail, which is what this column is all about. Those who most deserve prison are running Western governments and getting fat on oil moolah.

They Also Serve . . .

There is a mordant Eskimo proverb that says a good butler is worth at least three wives. The only trouble being I've never heard of an Eskimo with a butler. Gianni Agnelli had two he couldn't do without: Pasquale, until he reached forty, and then Bruno, until the 'avvocato's' death. I inherited mine from the Agnelli household. His name is Andrew Rolleston, and he is an Aussie – along with the Kiwis, the Poles and the Germans, in my Pantheon of best people. On his first day of service I was having dinner with the mother of my children in Cadogan Square when the telephone rang. 'No, Mr Smith,' I heard Andrew say, 'Mr Taki is dining and he will ring you back.' 'Who the hell is Smith?' I asked him when Alexandra was out of earshot. 'It was a lady – Francesca – and she wants you to call her . . . ' said Andrew. 'We are going to get along magnificently,' said I, and we certainly did.

Andrew packed a suitcase like no other, took care of matters like a Jewish grandmother, and deflected embarrassing situations like a Spartan shield. He was my man Jeeves for ever. My children loved him more than they cared for me. He played football with John-Taki, helped Lolly with her homework, kept the female cooks happy by servicing them well and regularly, and then one day announced that he had made his pile and wanted to return to Melbourne and buy a hotel-restaurant. If Keira Knightley or the deputy editor of the Speccie said this to me, my tears would not be as real as the ones I shed once Andrew told me it was curtains. 'Of course I'll stay until you find a suitable replacement,' said Andrew while I wept and lay in my bed Marguerite Gautier-like.

Then he and my divine secretary, Fiona Garland, conspired to have me murdered by hiring a Scots killer who was posing as a gentleman's gentleman instead of doing hard labour in some jail up north. The killer lasted one week, enough time for Andrew and Fiona to say goodbye after a riotous party thrown by yours truly in their honour. I have never been able to find Andrew's equal – not even close – except when I hired Daniel, a young German, as a cook three years ago. Daniel was not only very attractive, he was also mad about girls, a fact that made the mother of my children rather nervous, but filled me with expectant happiness.

Two summers ago, in Porto Heli, off the Peloponnese, with Alexandra in Gstaad and the children gallivanting somewhere in Europe, Daniel put his magic to work. He picked up four female sailors, two of them quite beautiful, and brought them on board. The evening was a great success until neighbouring boats going off for a morning sail began to hoot their horns as they watched me and my crew dead drunk on deck trying to fondle fellow sailors.

Daniel, too, broke my heart when he decided he wanted to travel and see the world. 'What's there to see?' I told him. 'There's nothing but vulgar oligarchs and semi-criminal sports stars out there.'

And speaking of sports stars, Serena Williams showed her real stuff last week when she physically threatened a lineswoman and used the F-word to emphasise her threat. I've always been wise to the Williamses, the whole clan. They rely on intimidation against players as well as umpires and referees, and are very quick to play the race card. What's even more disgusting than her behaviour is the dishonesty of it all. La Williams knew she had lost the match – the wonderful Kim Clijsters had her cold. So Williams attacked the lineswoman on match point against her to somehow deprive the brave Belgian of a clean victory. Typical Williams. Then she denied doing what she had done, called it no big thing and refused to apologise, while showing her Nike logos throughout, which is appropriate. A good lesson for any black ghetto kid coming up the tennis ladder. Intimidate, insult, cheat, and then lie and lie again. That's Nike, folks, sport's original bad-attitude people. And it shows what professional sport has become. The US Open committee allowed her to play in the finals of the doubles two days later, instead of suspending her for at least two years. But back to butlers.

An English friend of mine, Clive Gibson, told me this apropos my whining about losing staff. A French butler once said to his mistress: Madame la comtesse, we have cleaned and polished the tiles, dusted every room in the château, have polished the furniture, and have Hoovered the Aubussons, as well, of course, as serving all the meals. Now we would like to go to our quarters. La comtesse: *Mais bien sûr, et pendant que vous vous reposez, faites l'argenterie.* (Of course, and while you're resting, polish the silver.)

It is a tough world out there without good help, as Roman Abramovich has just discovered. This bum thought he could climb Kilimanjaro using 150 baggage-handlers, probably carrying him to the top. He didn't reckon with the breathing problem. Good butlers can perform miracles, but breathing for you is not something they excel at. Kilimanjaro 1; Oligarch 0.

Double Standards

Wednesday, 21 October 2009
New York

Something's bothering me about the Polanski business. No, unlike Harvey Weinstein and Bernard-Henri Lévy – not to mention that Mitterrand paedophile – I will not defend Roman's actions with a thirteen-year-old, but I will say that, with friends like his making fools of themselves defending him, it will be a miracle if he gets off with a slap on the wrist. Although this may sound pompous, I doubt if any of his defenders have known Polanski as long as I have – forty years and counting – but let's take it from the top.

What Hugo Rifkind wrote about him and his defenders in these pages on 3 October is spot-on. Hollywood has a lot to answer for, and mixing up global warming, Darfur, HIV and Roman's case is not exactly kosher. I particularly liked what he said about Mel Gibson, who was nearly hounded out of Tinseltown for a drunken anti-Semitic outburst, one for which he has apologised more times than I've had hangovers. 'But Polanski shags an actual child and they love him.' Ironically, the four people who failed to sign the petition for Roman were Woody Allen, Robert Blake, O. J. Simpson and Phil Spector, the last two being in the pokey as I write.

Yes, there are a lot of jokes about Polanski making the rounds, but in the meantime he is having a very bad time in a Swiss jail. Psychologically, that is. Let's face it, it does smell a bit of Inspector Javert, thirty-two years on. I first met Roman when he walked into my bedroom in Gstaad uninvited and insisted on watching me punch and kick a tiny piece of paper hanging from a string. (It was to speed up one's kicks and punches for an upcoming karate tournament.) We began hanging out together after that, and he even flew Bruce Lee over and I trained with him. Yes, we did have a falling-out after the events in Los Angeles, and I did write some mean things about him, but we have made up and only he knows the price he has paid for that one moment – or hour – of madness. Roman now has children, is happily married, and, as his good friend the wonderful Ronnie Harwood has said to me, no child, especially one as talented and as delightful as his boy Elvis, deserves this.

I will not try the line that phonies like Bernard-Henri Lévy have used, that artists are above the law and that then thirteen was the new eighteen. Or that grotesque Whoopi Goldberg's that it wasn't 'rape-rape'. The one I will try is this: what in Heaven's name has happened to compassion? Polanski has been on the run for thirty-two years, has never come close to repeating his crime, and has rehabilitated himself in spades. What kind of society are we that in order to further the political career of an obscure California district attorney we use the full power of two states to punish a man who was born punished. First by the Nazis and then by the Manson gang. No wonder poor Roman feels hard done by.

And speaking of forgiveness, I don't remember Menachem Begin, a ferocious terrorist, ever apologising for murdering ninety-one people when he blew up the King David Hotel in Jerusalem, twenty-eight of whom were British. He didn't even apologise for that while receiving the Nobel Peace Prize. Yet the world forgave and forgot once Israel became a big-time player thanks to Uncle Sam. The cold-blooded murderer Magee is received by those whose parents and families he killed, and he certainly hasn't apologised. The only one who got it right on this was, of course, the magnificent Norman Tebbit, whose wife, the brave Margaret, is living proof that those

Irish animals should rot in jail instead of hanging out with polite society. I don't remember the egregious Ted Kennedy asking for Sirhan Sirhan to be set free after forty-one years in a very tough jail. So where's Catholic and Irish compassion where the Palestinian is concerned?

The world is just one big double standard. So before anyone accuses me of defending child molestation, what about Jeffrey Epstein, a man who was tried and convicted of paying underage women to give him sexual rubdowns, but who served less than thirteen months of a ridiculously soft sentence of eighteen months? Epstein had the following going for him. He is a billionaire, despite the fact that no one knows how he made his pile, as he trained and worked as a maths researcher. Epstein also had letters recommending his character to the judge in Palm Beach from Governor Bill Richardson of New Mexico and Bill Clinton, whom Epstein flew all over the world in his private plane and who is a close friend of his.

So, a crime committed thirty-two years ago and paid for in full as far as I'm concerned by a man who has known more suffering than most of us is to be pursued to the bitter end, whereas Jeffrey Epstein, friend of the powerful and a billionaire, does only twelve months in a country-club jail in Palm Beach. If that's true justice, then the law is an ass – but I always knew that. Why don't we try compassion and forgiveness for a change, but not for truly bad guys, just for poor Roman Polanski.

Backing Zac

Wednesday, 4 November 2009

New York

'Why would he run for Parliament?' screams the headline in the *New York Times*. A subheading lists 'An inherited passion for women, gambling, the environment and politics'. As I start to read, I fear the worst, but as it turns out it could have been a lot worse. Zac Goldsmith's name is big in Britain, less so in America, although in green circles he's an international prince. Although meant rhetorically, it's quite dumb to ask why a person would run for Parliament, as if being rich and normal – liking women – disqualifies one from holding office. In fact, that's what's wrong with politics. The wrong people are in it. If more people like Zac Goldsmith threw their hats into the ring, fewer smiling professional wallet-lifters would be running our lives.

In May 1997, election night, I dined at Lord Black's and immediately after dinner headed for Jimmy Goldsmith's house as the first results began coming in. I had had lunch with Jimmy that day, along with Kate Reardon and the historian Andrew Roberts – not as famous and ubiquitous back then as he is today. Jimmy was in a funny mood, reflective, nostalgic almost. None of us knew that he was dying. He was to ring me a week later with the ghastly news, although he sounded quite chipper: 'I've got quite a scoop for you, old boy . . . '

Sir James, an aide, Zac and Jemima, Robin Birley and myself left for Putney and the election centre where the results would be

317

announced. I was drunk. *The Times* reported that I tried to get the telephone number of a female journalist, as if I had committed the greatest faux pas ever. Jimmy was on stage when David Mellor began to whine about Mexican haciendas and the like. I was standing between Zac and Jemima and lost my temper. Here was Mellor, a man who had kissed more rich people's behinds than I'd had hangovers, playing the money card. I screamed a terrible obscenity – c***-s***** – and some of the crowd picked it up. It was great, if not politics as usual.

Sir James was gracious in defeat and very brave in facing the man in the white suit who came to him a couple of months later. I went to see him in his grand house in France the week before the end. Now his son is running for office and I am sure there are Mellors around to play the hacienda card. The *New York Times* article concentrated on the Zac lifestyle, his love of beautiful women, of gambling and his low esteem of the press. It would, wouldn't it? The only thing the writer left out is the fact that Zac is probably the best-looking man in politics, certainly among the greens. I suppose the reason for that is lookism, as in PC. The Ancient Greeks, however, in their infinite wisdom trusted good looks rather than homely ones, which of course is the way it should be.

That radical, drastic action is required in order to save the planet I am not at all convinced, but what I am certain of is that we are wasting our resources and being held hostage by Middle East kleptocrats, which allies me with the greens. Zac is no eco-dreamer, something the article in question does point out. His support of small-town shops versus shopping centres is wonderful, as is his initiative that discourages the production of energy-wasting plasma TVs. (What in hell is a plasma TV anyway?) David Cameron, another man I'm not at all convinced about, and I'm sure he's losing sleep over it, is lucky to have Zac on board. Forget that the rich are far less likely to steal while in power, just look at the facts. Zac Goldsmith on the one hand, John Prescott on the other. Zac drives a banged-up Prius despite being a multimillionaire. Prescott was driven in two Jags between the grand houses his office afforded him and ended up rich after ten years in power. And as far as their women are concerned, I'll think I'll take Zac's anytime over those of Prescott. Watching a beautiful woman dressing in front of one in the morning makes one want to go out and do good things. Doing it over a desk with an assistant drives one to the pub at best.

Much has been said about Jimmy Goldsmith's triple life, mostly by people who would have relished it if they could have had it. According to Shelley, love withers under constraint. Its very essence is liberty. It is compatible neither with obedience, jealousy, nor fear. 'It is there most pure, perfect and unlimited, where its votaries live in confidence, equality and unreserved.' Bravo, Shelley, you got that right, not that you got other things wrong. The poet also asked how long ought the sexual connection to last. And how dare the law assume it knows better than those involved. How odious an usurpation of the right of private judgment, and so on. Sir James Goldsmith marched to a different drummer, made lotsa moolah on his own, bedded lotsa women and scum-like journalists went after him because they had to face their grubby wives each evening. Now I'd love to see his son in Parliament and minister of the environment. It would make for a less greedy, materialistic and selfish House – after thirteen years of Cool Britannia, what could be better?

Tales From
LITTERDALE

John Morrison

Halsgrove

First published by Halsgrove in 2002

Text copyright © 2002 John Morrison
Illustrations copyright © 2002 Jim Watson
Introduction copyright © 2002 Roly Smith

British Library Cataloguing-in-Publication Data
A CIP record for this title is available from the British Library

ISBN 1 84114 215 8

HALSGROVE
Halsgrove House
Lower Moor Way
Tiverton EX16 6SS
T: 01884 243242
F: 01884 243325
www.halsgrove.com

Printed in Great Britain by
The Cromwell Press, Trowbridge

ACKNOWLEDGEMENT

These articles are adapted from those which first appeared in *Peak &
Pennine* and *Peak District Magazine*, published by Dalesman Ltd.

INTRODUCTION

LITTERDALE DISCOVERED
By Roly Smith

I suppose I should be held responsible for launching John Morrison's hilarious Peakland village of Litterdale on an unsuspecting public. As the founding editor of the monthly magazine *Peak & Pennine*, which was published by Dalesman for two years from June, 1997 (it is now known as *Peak District Magazine*), I was looking for a writer who could raise a smile among our fast-growing army of readers. I knew just how difficult it was to sustain this kind of writing, having contributed a similar light-hearted, satirical column to a leading outdoor magazine for two years myself.

I had come to know John chiefly as an outstanding landscape photographer, especially of his home ground, the Yorkshire Dales. But I also knew John as an acerbic wit, who had written some very funny and successful books about life in a small, South Pennine milltown. These thinly-disguised portraits of his adopted home of Hebden Bridge so upset the local newspapers that any mention of the books was banned from their pages. As John pointed out: "It was the best publicity I could have had."

The first "Tales from Litterdale" column appeared in April 1998, and I'm pleased to say it's still running. Thousands of readers have been enthralled by the antics of Scoop, the editor of the *Litterdale Times*, stabbing one-fingered at his ancient Remington like a demented woodpecker; Mandy, Litterdale's New Age seer and expert in feng shui, the Chinese art of rearranging the furniture, and busy-body Violet, the self-appointed village guardian and eco-warrior. Then there's Norman, the saintly odd-job man and Bob, the tuneless postman. Bill, the village's tourism officer, hopes his new slogan "Lovely Litterdale: where the present meets the past and makes an elegant swallow dive into the future" is sufficiently bland and meaningless to attract visitors in droves.

The reason that these apparently over-the-top characters work under John's skilful treatment is because if you've ever lived in a village, they will remind you of someone. Their brilliance lies in the fact that they are not too outrageous as to be instantly recognisable, because every village, indeed every community, has a Mandy, Voilet, Norman, or Bob.

The real star of these tales, though, is the village itself. I'm reliably informed that Litterdale lies smack in the middle of the Peak District National Park. But don't try to find it on the map. As John points out, the village shares a common border with Fantasia and Never Never Land. But despite being a peaceful backwater, Litterdale has not remained untouched by great events: the millennium, foot and mouth diease, global warming and the exorbitant price of replica football strips.

As Bill once said in one of his deathless slogans, Litterdale is probably closer than you think.

SPRING

There's a price to pay for living somewhere as agreeable as Litterdale. It's one of the Peak's 'honeypot' villages, so we get more than our fair share of visitors. Once we've bade farewell to those long winter days, and seen the little rash of snowdrops appear on the verges of the village green, the more optimistic residents can convince themselves that Spring is finally here.

It's difficult to know why Litterdale is so popular with visitors, rather than any one of a dozen, equally characterful, villages in the Peak District National Park. We wonder which came first: the visitors or the car-park. Certainly, when people find the prospect of ploughing through the pile of Sunday papers just too intimidating, and thoughts turn instead to a day in the country, the cry of 'Let's go to Litterdale' seems to have the alliterative allure that will propel couch potatoes off their sofas and into their cars.

On sunny weekends the traffic snakes sedately towards Litterdale, at the sort of speed that gives our local hedgehogs a better than even chance of getting across the road unsquashed. Visitors are an uncomplaining lot; an hour spent in a traffic jam – with radiators, frazzled parents and fidgety kids all ready to explode – seems to be an essential ingredient of a good day out.

It's one of life's minor mysteries why 'pay & display' car-parks are such an irresistible draw to jaded townies. They want to get away to the country – and Litterdale is surrounded by some of the finest countryside in the White Peak – yet no sooner have they reached a 'pay & display' car-park than their courage fails them. Suddenly they become acutely aware of the umbilical cord that binds them, albeit invisibly, to their cars.

Being a keen walker it's hard for me to understand why so many visitors prefer to mooch around honeypot villages, instead of heading for the hills. The reason, as I was told by a National Park volunteer who leads guided walks, is that a lot of visitors are afraid they'll get lost and not be able to find their way back to their cars. It seems a shame, since escaping the crowds and losing yourself in the landscape is surely one of life's keenest pleasures. And the ability to read an Ordnance Survey map can be learned in a couple of hours by anyone able to decipher the cooking instructions on a four-seasons pizza.

So a lot of visitors will settle, instead, on whatever attractions can be found within 200 yards of the car-park. Perhaps *this* is what makes people descend on Litterdale in such numbers; whatever we've got by way of tourist attractions can be viewed without breaking sweat, or straying far from the comforting presence of the car. So what *have* we got to keep visitors amused (and fractious children quiet) for a couple of hours?

Well, we've got gift shops. A strange concept, gifts; the sort of useless tat you buy for other people, but you wouldn't really thank them for giving to you. There's a sign in one of Litterdale's craft shops inviting visitors to 'meet the craftsmen'. To judge from most of the stock on sale, 'meeting the craftsmen' would presumably entail buying a return air ticket to Taiwan.

Nevertheless, some items are genuinely made in Litterdale. Wonky hand-thrown pottery, for example. The quality control manager of your average Taiwanese sweat-shop would probably have his job on the line if he were to allow such deformed offerings to leave the premises. Even labelling them 'seconds' would invite comment from a Trade Descriptions Officer. The thought occurs: why don't the talentless potters of Litterdale just cut out the middleman, and toss their mis-shapen creations straight into a rubbish skip?

We've got an outdoor shop, called 'Take a Hike'. Perhaps it feels more authentic to buy your fleecy jacket or weather-proof cagoule somewhere rural like Litterdale, instead of in town. All I know is that there are villages where you can't even buy a loaf of bread or a carton of milk any more, but where you'll have no trouble finding a selection of two-man tents or three-season, duck-down sleeping bags.

There was a time – it seems so long ago – when walking was a very simple activity. You'd just slip on something shapeless and warm, and put one foot in front of the other. Now, of course, we scorn such a miserly approach. We're happy to spend folding money to ensure that we look the part. We used to buy a pair of boots or a rucksack; now we buy 'a system'. We used to pull on a mud-coloured windjammer, made from the same low-tech, rain-attracting material from which they make bath sponges. Now we have smart, figure-hugging garments – in this year's tastefully co-ordinated colours, of course – which keep us striding through torrential rain long after the enjoyment has gone... just to see if a £250 cagoule really is as waterproof as the manufacturers suggest.

We used to find a forked stick and whittle it with a pen-knife. It was something to do while waiting in some blighted camp-site for the kettle to boil. The result – after only a few hours of graft, and a couple of bandaged fingers – was a home-made walking-stick. Now we go to an outdoor shop instead and pick up a telescopic pole in lightweight titanium, with three sections and an ergonomic handle. And we spurn something as simple as a penknife, in favour of a Swiss army knife. Isn't it somehow typical of the Swiss that their army should be famous, not for a successful military campaign, but for precision-made cutlery?

You can still buy a Swiss army knife with just a couple of blades, but only a skinflint would be content with that. At 'Take a Hike' the knives recline seductively in a display case. Like the brazen denizens of some red-light district, the pleasures become more exotic with every fiver you're prepared to pay: corkscrew, saw, screwdriver, magnifying glass and that pointy thing that no-one knows what to do with. Towards the top of the range – it's serious 'three-in-a-waterbed' money now – you get a watch, compass, hedge trimmer, arc-welder and full internet connection... plus a smart leather case on wheels to keep it in. You want one. You know you do. But if you have to ask the price, you really can't afford one.

'Fashion on the fells' is what it's all about these days. Having spent years making durable, hard-wearing outdoor clothing in muted colours that wouldn't turn heads or scare wildlife away, the designers and manufacturers are wising up. Now they try to instil a sense of paranoia in ramblers by adding another injunction to the Country Code: You must not be seen walking in last year's colours. The ladies in Litterdale's Tourist Information Centre have a choice expression to describe those couples who arrive in identical – and suspiciously clean – designer walking outfits. 'All the gear and no idea', they say, rather sniffily.

Litterdale has tea-shops, too. Weary from their valiant attempts at Litterdale's own 'Munros' (the aim is to browse around every single craft-shop before acute tannin deprivation sets in), visitors can rest their weary legs and enjoy the restorative effects of tea. Anybody too knackered to lift a cup to parched lips can have it intravenously.

The walls are plastered with pastoral prints, and the place-mats feature hunting scenes; vicarious glimpses of a vanished rural arcadia for those with no intention of feeling anything but Tarmacadam beneath their feet. After a few platefuls of pikelets, tea-cakes, fruit-scones, rum-butter, clotted cream, fancy cakes and – sensibly – some low-calorie cola to wash it all down with, our less adventurous visitors justifiably feel they've enjoyed everything that lovely Litterdale has to offer.

Unseasonably warm spring weather is making Litterdale bloom with flowers. The first swallows are here, recuperating after their long flight north. The trees, still only half in leaf, are full of newly-arrived songbirds. The willow warbler's cadence evokes the summer days to come almost as vividly as the sighting of the first ice cream van. As he hurtles round another blind bend on two wheels, the ice cream man activates his chime. It is Greensleeves, played on what sounds like a Rolf Harris Stylophone and then blasted out at migraine-inducing volume to the blameless folk of Litterdale. And if the ice cream man is on his rounds, a new cricket season can't be far behind.

It's the shortest of strolls down to Litterdale's cricket pitch, where the team has reassembled after the winter sabbatical. The cricket ground is a reclaimed swamp down by the river: the natural habitat only of flannelled fools, vindictive horseflies and a handful of undemanding spectators with time on their hands.

With water so close a lofted shot to leg is the cue for a young lad to leap, with practised ease, into a canoe conveniently tethered at the river-bank. He paddles towards the ball, fishes it out, paddles back, ties up, gets out, hurls the ball arrow-straight into the wicket-keeper's gloves, and settles back into his deck-chair... as if this was an everyday occurrence. Which it is.

It seems a long time since October, when Dennis, our captain, offered his resignation – as he has done at season's end for the last twenty years. Mortified by presiding over lacklustre performances, and sickened by the smell of the horse liniment with which his ageing team members insist on daubing themselves, he vowed then that he'd played his last game for Litterdale.

But winter has wiped away those feelings of failure that smarted so much at the time. Now that Spring is here he's having a change of heart: 'Maybe just one more season,' he convinces himself. Perhaps this year we are finally going to fulfil our obvious cricketing potential, and not continue to be the talent-free embarrassments we've been for as long as anyone can remember. Or perhaps not.

Spring is, after all, a time of optimism, before unrealistic hopes have been sacrificed at the altar of bitter experience.

I love the game. Cricket, unlike just about everything else that life can offer, has never let me down. It has never ended a potentially rewarding relationship with a mendacious platitude like: 'It's not you, it's me… I just need more space'. Cricket has never borrowed money and then neglected to pay it back. Cricket has never made silver-tongued promises that subsequently turned to ashes.

Once you start to think deeply about the game (and it's designed to be slow and boring, for this very purpose) cricket offers some distinctly uncomfortable home truths. *Beyond* the boundary there are many flags, many allegiances, many contradictory codes of conduct. But *inside* that boundary the two teams conform to a single set of rules, without which the the game has no meaning. And, speaking as a life-long Labour supporter, it comes as quite a shock to realise that a team operates best when presided over by a benign dictator like Dennis. These are the kind of thoughts that pop into your mind, unbidden, when you're fielding down at fine leg with only horse-flies for company.

The air is filled with the sounds of the summer game: mostly screams of pain as a hard leather ball ruptures tender, unprotected flesh. Our batsmen do their best to minimise the potential damage, with Neoprene, bandages, extra sweaters, box, thigh guard and forearm protector. One or two brave souls don helmets; brave because the other players' cruel taunts probably hurt more than a glancing blow to the temple.

When a bowler *does* hit a batsman on the head, it's considered sporting to feign concern for his welfare, ask if he's okay, then stride back way beyond his bowling mark and try to bowl the same ball again. Only faster. It's hardly any wonder that the bowlers' habitual complaint is: 'Umpire, the batsman's gone out of shape.'

The league umpires – small, dapper, pipe-smoking men well into their anecdotage – are kept in a shed during the week. Every

Saturday the team captains come and take their pick, slipping the nominal umpiring fee discreetly into the breast pocket of an immaculate blazer.

There's not a lot to choose between one Brylcreemed umpire and another. They all played cricket in their youth and, through the distorting lens of time, are convinced that the players of today aren't fit to lace the boots of the cricketers *they* knew. If the umpires had a motto it would be: 'The older I get, the better I was'.

After the game the team gravitates towards the pub. The landlord of the Fox doesn't bother to disguise his sneer when he asks them how they've done. He can spot a bunch of losers from a thousand paces. But after a few pints of cooking bitter, the players tend to forget just how soundly they've been beaten. The team's performance will, in beery retrospect, be awarded a heroic perspective that was entirely lacking on the pitch. Yes, the unwarranted optimism of third-rate cricketers is surely a lesson to us all.

SUMMER

A recent poll indicates that commuters would rather spend two hours in stationary traffic than even consider giving up their car and using public transport instead. The mere thought of sitting on the top deck of a bus, surrounded by hacking smokers and old folk rabbiting on about the war, fills the average motorist with a nameless dread.

Never mind that another recent survey indicates that London traffic now moves at an average speed of just 12mph: a stately sort of progress that even the Hansom cab drivers of Victorian times would have considered dilatory. Never mind that we are slowly choking to death on our own exhaust fumes. Never mind that from now until Doomsday there will not be a single day when huge stretches of motorway are not partitioned off with traffic cones. No, our love affair with the fickle mistress that is the internal combustion engine shows no sign of waning.

It's good to know that the millions spent by the car manufacturers on advertising their sleek new models are not going to waste. Cars are now inextricably linked with power, virility and sex appeal. You don't have to be Desmond Morris to realise what a bright red Ferrari Testarossa represents in the phallocentric imagination of the average male driver. Which, incidentally, begs the question: just what does a Reliant Robin represent? A prostate gland, perhaps.

Since most new models look like they've just popped out of the same jelly mould, the adverts seem to say: 'To hell with boring facts and figures; since all cars look much the same, let's just indulge our most ludicrous fantasies'. Cars in TV adverts negotiate fire, brimstone, whirlwinds and roads that turn into spitting cobras. Most bizarrely of all, they seem to be the only vehicle on that twisty mountain road. The characters in adland seem to live in a parallel universe where driving is an orgasmic pleasure rather than a wearisome chore.

Nowadays the siren voices of the advertisers are tempting us to buy one of those rugged 4x4 off-road jobs. These tough workhorses seem very popular down here in Litterdale, where a lot of motorists subscribe to the scouts' motto: Be Prepared. They're prepared, at a moment's notice, to gear down, leave the overcrowded roads behind, and tackle the roughest and most inhospitable terrain… such as the speed-bumps in Tesco's car-park.

Owners of 4x4 vehicles can look down – quite literally – on other drivers, and enjoy the kudos of owning a vehicle with the aerodynamic qualities of a house-brick. Those intimidating 'bull-bars' on the front aren't merely decorative. Okay, the chances of running into a bull – or being charged by a rampaging rhino – are pretty slim, even in Litterdale. But pedestrians can get aggressive too. Especially if they've just been knocked over by a 4x4 driver who's preoccupied by taking a call on his mobile phone. And a little old lady, once roused to anger, can do a lot of damage to expensive paintwork with a shopping trolley and a bone-handed umbrella.

Ownership isn't enough, of course; 4x4 owners like their possessions to be reassuringly obsequious too. So when they point the key-fob at their car, it flashes its lights and gives an answering 'beep'. 'I am yours, O powerful one', it seems to be saying, 'what might be your bidding?'

Having done their damnedest to make city life well-nigh intolerable, the car manufacturers are making life in the country equally unpleasant. So the ads for these outsize Tonka toys tend to show them perched on a mountain-top, with a spectacular landscape as a mouth-watering backdrop. My usual response is: 'Wonderful landscape; shame there's some 4x4 lunatic parked smack in the middle of it'.

P.T. Barnum knew his stuff. 'No-one ever went broke by over-estimating the public's intelligence,' he once said, with the cynicism of the born salesman. And what these ads seem to be suggesting is that the countryside is just one big adventure playground for people (oh, all right, *men*...) who have plenty of 'poke' under the bonnet... but not a lot upstairs. Combine the body of a grown man, the recreational tastes of a hyperactive six-year-old and the mental agility of a rocking horse... and you have a potent force when behind a wheel. Dressed in their khaki fatigues they can indulge the kind of fantasies that engage tiny minds when national service is but a distant memory.

Every weekend they'll meet up in Litterdale with like-minded loons, with the aim of churning up as much countryside as possible in the course of an eventful afternoon. They'll transform ancient 'green lanes' into boggy morasses, just for the hell of it. They don't feel they've had a proper day out unless they and their tank-like vehicles are covered in mud.

There's a certain novelty value in seeing a 4x4 streaked with mud, instead of being filled with kiddy-seats, green wellies and a week's worth of bagged-up supermarket shopping. It's just a shame that the cherished landscapes around Litterdale have to take the brunt of the off-roaders' warlike fantasies. Perhaps we could convert one of the limestone quarries into a real assault course for these off-road guys, with a few well-hidden land-mines to improve their driving skills and keep their minds on the job. Just a thought...

✳

Smack in the middle of Litterdale you will find a pair of handsome pubs. The casual visitor may wonder why a village as small as

Litterdale should warrant two such substantial inns. The truth is that the village hasn't always been the peaceful backwater it appears today. Litterdale lies on what once was the London road, and the stage-coaches stopped here to change horses and take on new passengers.

In those far-off days the roads joined town to town, and village to village, like pearls strung along a necklace. It's different today, of course. We can built straighter roads now (and are busy carving up our beautiful landscapes to accommodate them) but they strenuously avoid towns, villages and anywhere else you might want to go. Archaeologists of the future will unearth the remains of our late-twentieth century road network with a mixture of awe and amazement. They'll look back on their ancestors' titanic efforts in building roads that seem merely to link a series of identical eateries and service stations. Twenty years after the demise of the internal combustion engine we'll see the car for what it's always been: an experiment that didn't work.

These two inns continue to stare at each other across the broad street, and across the centuries. The Swan and the Fox share an architectural style, perhaps even the same builder. Small details – such as the heavy stone lintels and the pillars on either side of the entrance doors – announce that these aren't just run-of-the-mill village pubs. The old stable blocks are reminders of why two such inns were built here in the first place. The differences between these establishments only become apparent once you step inside.

The Swan is aptly named. The staff, and the pub itself, seem to float serenely along through still waters. There's a calm, unruffled air that proves happily contagious. Of course, it takes a lot of hard work behind the scenes to make catering appear so effortless. The staff give the impression that they actually enjoy working here, which is quite a novelty in itself. They're mostly young girls, smartly dressed in white blouses and black skirts. Intriguingly, they all seem to fall short, by the tiniest margin, of being absolutely gorgeous. They're wonderfully efficient and a little bit shy.

In the Fox the scene is very different. It's entertaining – in a grim, voyeuristic kind of way – to watch an ill-assorted team of incompetents and malcontents bring the noble art of catering down to the level of a playground squabble. The moment you walk in, you are assailed by prohibitions. Considering that Litterdale lies smack in the middle of some of the White Peak's finest countryside, you wonder immediately about the mental equilibrium of a landlord who erects a notice stating: 'No Walkers'.

He neatly reverses the traditional relationship between landlord and customer, by regaling those drinkers foolish enough to drink at the bar with a seemingly endless litany of complaints and grievances about the iniquities of the landlord's lot. When things are quiet, 'It's hardly worth opening the doors', and then, on those rare occasions when the pub suddenly fills up with thirsty customers, he'll shake his head wearily and confide that, 'They'll all want serving, you know'. The more disreputable locals quite like it; his tirades match their mood, but the uncommitted drinker soon gets the idea that there are an awful lot of other pubs to go to.

The landlord is a man who should never have ventured into the licensed trade. Someone with his welfare at heart (his anger management therapist or, failing that, his accountant) should have warned him that, 'It's a people business', and suggested a career more in keeping with his meagre talents. Some walk of life in which bluntness and an almost limitless antagonism towards his fellow man were no bar to making a living: an angler's bait shop, perhaps, or a key-cutting franchise.

His wife is the sort of woman for whom the description 'mousy' would seem like unwarranted flattery. Her every word and gesture speak of a life filled with disappointment. She spends most of her time drinking ever more generous slugs of sweet sherry and comparing her spouse (unfavourably, on every conceivable count) with her first husband. To discourage diners, she hides the menus. Whenever she's asked, 'Are you cooking tonight?' her response is bafflingly enigmatic: 'I hadn't planned to'. Most people take the hint and sidle towards the door, though every now and again a customer will be hungry enough to persevere in his quest for a square meal. Even then, the florid descriptions (*poisson, pommes frites avec pois mushy*) cannot disguise the unimaginative fare on offer.

Across the road at the Swan a food order initiates a seamlessly orchestrated series of events, culminating with a rosy-cheeked waitress sliding a hearty plateful under your nose. At the Fox, on the other hand, a food order sets off a series of unconnected events which culminate in blind panic. The kitchen staff give convincing impressions of people who have never prepared a meal before. Using the smoke alarm as a food-timer, they fill the pub with the overpowering smell of stale and over-heated cooking fat.

Every lunchtime seems to end the same way: with sounds of crockery smashing against the wall, screams of recrimination, the slamming of doors, the wail of a fire engine's siren, and the cook – an unshaven man with a grubby vest and singed eyebrows – sitting at the bar cradling a double whisky, trying to stop his hands shaking.

If you want to take your mum somewhere quiet for Sunday lunch, or are looking for a pleasant venue where you can try to mollify a financially rapacious ex-wife... then, of course, the Swan fits the bill admirably. But if, like me, you are blessed with the priceless ability to laugh at other people's misfortunes, and enjoy watching the discomfiture of the chronically inept... then I have to admit that, yes, the Fox is the only place in Litterdale to spend 'Unhappy Hour'.

*

It's August in Litterdale: high summer, when the air is still and balmy, and the limestone scars gleam whitely beneath skies of unclouded blue. Swallows, swifts and martins race and scream above the village, seemingly for the sheer joy of scything effortlessly through the air. There's no better time of the year to skive, loaf, dawdle, dally, hang loose, take things easy, stand and stare, shoot the breeze, twiddle our thumbs, kick our heels, and generally let the grass grow under our feet. Here in Litterdale we have learned to enjoy the lexicon of leisure.

The warm weather encourages locals and visitors alike to don the skimpiest of outfits compatible with not being arrested for outraging public decency. We get an enticing glimpse of what life in Litterdale might be like if, thanks to global warming, we were blessed with a Mediterranean climate the whole year round... instead of just these dog-days of summer. Young lads loll around on the village green, trying to look as cool as possible despite the obvious ravages of adolescent acne. Young girls take part in an impromptu festival of belly buttons. Even the older folk, not generally given to excess, get in the mood and leave their thermal vests at home.

This would be a good time to put a house up for sale; prospective buyers would take little persuading that Litterdale might be the ideal place to escape from the rat-race or enjoy a tranquil retirement. The country life – spent dead-heading roses, trimming hedges and quaffing schooners of cream sherry – looks an attractive option to jaded wage-slaves.

But appearances can be deceptive. Townies looking to swap the crime and grime of the city for what they fondly imagine will be a rural idyll, are setting themselves up for disappointment. Men who have earned their money in town tend to see the countryside as a recreational amenity. An extension of the gym and the wine bar, where stressed-out executives can unwind by drinking in a gorgeous view (preferably through the windscreen of a stationary Range Rover) and reciting a restorative mantra of FT100 indices. Blissfully unaware that proper farming represents a lifetime of mindless, back-breaking labour, working from dawn to dusk seven days a week (with maybe a couple of days off each year to attend Smithfield Show or a seminar about bulls' semen), they feel the urge to get back to the land.

Men dream of a less-acquisitive lifestyle in the country, unaware that the competitive flame can't be doused so easily. Having spent their formative years stuck in rush-hour traffic, extending the hand (or, at least, the middle digit) of friendship to their fellow drivers, they find that driving in the country is not as much fun as they thought it would be. It's frustrating to crawl for mile after twisty mile in the slippery wake of a slurry-laden tractor, whose driver regards traffic signals of any kind as entirely optional.

Their wives have time on their hands and a rosy view of country life that stems from knowing nothing whatsoever about it. A diet of glossy lifestyle magazines and shampoo adverts has given them unrealistic, soft-focus visions of traipsing around a herb garden in a Laura Ashley frock, with a basket of meadow flowers hung decorously over one arm. They order what the salesman promised was a 'farmhouse kitchen' – all stripped pine and terracotta tiles – not realising that a genuine farmhouse kitchen is more likely to resemble a charnel house or motorbike mechanic's workshop.

In a doomed attempt to ingratiate themselves with the locals, the newcomers take up country pursuits. The men develop an unhealthy interest in killing small defenceless animals – dispatching them with a Purdey shotgun, pack of hounds or a light, last-minute touch on the power steering. The women attend Women's Institute meetings: draughty evenings in village halls entering Most Exciting Tea-towel Competitions.

It doesn't work, of course; after a few months of attempted integration the newcomers will bow to the inevitable. They'll spend more and more of their leisure hours with other disgruntled exiles from the city. Liquor-fuelled evenings when they can let down their defences and admit that the much-vaunted attractions of country life are just lies and innuendo, propagated shamelessly by estate agents and the editors of those lifestyle magazines. Amongst friends they'll mutter conspiratorially about terse, unfriendly farmers, whose eyebrows meet in the middle and who seem to appear – without warning, their clothes in disarray – from sheep-fold and byre.

Once the newcomers have taken off those rose-tinted spectacles, it can be the devil of a job to find them again. Aspects of country life that once seemed quaint and endearing now merely irritate. Instead of filling their lungs with that clean country air, all they can smell is the gut-wrenching, sinus-clearing stench of slurry. They realise, too late, why the Old Rectory had remained empty for so long before they moved in; the apprentice bell-ringers in the church next door spend every Sunday morning trying, in vain, to orchestrate some rudimentary chime.

For the locals, sunning themselves on a hot summer day, the appearance of a removal van is worth a muted cheer. It means that another defeated couple is packing up their goods, chattels and shattered dreams of country living, and heading back to the leafy blandness of suburbia. Another 'For Sale' sign will appear. Another family will be seduced by the prospect of life in Litterdale. Perhaps they'll have no sense of smell. Perhaps they'll be as deaf as the posts that line our village green. For their sakes, we can only hope so.

✳

AUTUMN

Even to consider spending a sunny bank holiday in Litterdale, you would need to love mankind with an unnatural intensity. The village gets so packed with visitors that whatever they've come to see tends to be hidden by the hordes. Those who run the craft-shops, tea-rooms and pubs rub their hands with undisguised glee, of course; they can sniff money in the air. It mingles with the aroma of factor 15 sun-block and whipped ice cream to create a fragrant pot-pourri of profit. Everybody else in the village regards a bank holiday as a good opportunity to visit uncherished relatives in town or apply that second coat of Artex to the back bedroom ceiling.

The Litterdale Show is a late-summer extravaganza that promises something for everybody and a welcome respite from the workaday routine. The event is known – at least by newcomers to Litterdale, accustomed to rather more sophisticated entertainments – as the 'fête worse than death'. To the show committee it's a Family Fun Day, though you have to think twice about any event that includes the words 'Family' and 'Fun' in the same sentence.

A field just outside Litterdale is transformed, for one day each year, into a rural playground filled with marquees, stalls and show-rings. We used to get the local squire to cut the ribbon and declare the show open, but times are hard for the local aristocracy. He still lives in the Big House, but it's mortgaged up to the hilt. The older villagers may doff their caps to him, but his jacket is suspiciously threadbare. And the squire's customary privileges have all but disappeared; even deflowering virgins is something he can't take for granted these days. Opening Litterdale Show was his last public duty, and now that's gone too. This year the committee has made a break with tradition, and invited a second-string soap actress from daytime TV to do the honours instead.

The show provides an opportunity for the local farmers to get together and monopolise the bar in the beer tent. Once they've been let off the leash for the day, they can put a fair few pints away. When they emerge, blinking at the sudden exposure to the mid-afternoon sunshine, they cast covetous eyes over the brand-new tractors and combines on display. They try to convince themselves how their work-rate would increase if they had heated seats, double-glazed windows and a state-of-the-art in-cab CD system. And some gleaming new paintwork instead of the unprepossessing two-tone colour scheme – rust and primer – that typifies the clapped-out tractors languishing back on the farm.

There's always a motor-cycle dare-devil who risks life and limb by jumping over a line of cars. But the stakes are raised every year. It gets harder and harder to impress a jaded audience weaned on the special effects of blockbuster films. Our fearless rider will attempt the usual stunt… but this time he'll be towing a caravan behind him. He's unnervingly confident, though everybody else knows it can only end in tears.

You can find stalls selling all manner of country clothing. With their one indispensible fashion accessory being baling twine, the farmers don't take much heed. But well-heeled newcomers to Litterdale like to reinforce their country credentials and give their gold credit cards a bit of hammer. They'll try on quilted waistcoats that resemble nothing so much as the insulation lagging around an old-fashioned central-heating boiler. And those ubiquitous waxed jackets, from a rather upmarket stall offering 'Mud-coloured Clothing to the

Gentry'. After they've completed the ensemble with a pair of green wellies, they reckon they really look the part.

The vicar's wife runs the children's pet show. When it comes to picking a winner, it would take the wisdom of Solomon to choose between the rival claims of a guinea pig and a shaggy Shetland pony. So, since they're all God's creatures, every pet gets a prize.

I understand her quandary, because I recall doing the same job a few years back. A young lad arrived with an impenetrable stutter and a sturdy cardboard box clutched to his chest. 'So what have you got in there?' I asked him. 'It's a mu, mu, mu, mmmm... ,' he struggled. 'What's that?' I said, 'a mouse?' He shook his head, sadly, and had another painful stab at the elusive M-word. I could see the afternoon drifting away, so I said, 'Let's have a look, then,' and lifted up a flap. Out of the box, with a lot of noise and a flurry of feathers, flew a magpie. It didn't stick around for the judging. The lad gazed after it, his mouth still opening and closing wordlessly like a goldfish. I don't know whether the first prize penant was sufficient compensation for losing his magpie. The other kids didn't seem to mind, and at least it made me feel a bit better.

Litterdale Show is a bittersweet occasion. It's good to wander round and chat with old friends, but we're all aware that the show marks the end of summer. There's a distinct nip in the air as the guy-ropes are loosened and the tent-pegs are pulled out. Already the swallows are gathering excitedly on the telephone wires. Young lads have swapped bats and stumps for a football, and throw their jackets down on the grass for goal-posts.

Litterdale's cricket team has just one game left to play, and Dennis, the team captain, is hoping to finish the season on a high note. He's preparing the wicket on his own. His team-mates have conveniently forgotten to turn up, as usual, but they'll all be there for the match. He ought to be disgruntled... but he's not. When he's walking behind an elderly Acme mower, with the sun on his back and the sweet scent of new-mown grass in the air, the captain of the Litterdale XI is convinced that he has the ropes of life firmly in his grasp. For a few intoxicating moments he is a truly happy man.

Litterdale, as the tourist brochures never tire of telling us, lies smack in the middle of the White Peak, surrounded by rolling hills that seem to invite you to explore them. Nevertheless, there are many visitors to Litterdale who prove remarkably resistant to the siren voices of the countryside. They like the idea that Litterdale is *in* the countryside – that's why they come – but all that greenery is just something to drive through on the way there and on the way home. They feel more comfortable viewing the countryside through the windscreen of what we used to call a family saloon. If they are assailed by any nasty smells, they can just wind the windows up to create a safe, hermetically-sealed environment: Tupperware on wheels.

But autumn brings other visitors, too. A worked-out limestone quarry a couple of miles from Litterdale is quietly going back to nature. Ten years ago it was a site of noise and industry, with the surrounding countryside lent a surreal, almost moonlit appearance by a powdering of rock-dust. But now the quarry is filled with water and the rocky margins are softened by bullrushes and yellow irises; an unprepossessing eyesore is slowly becoming Litterdale's own little Serengheti. The lake has become a magnet, every spring and autumn, for migrating birds. And in their wake come hordes of bird-watchers.

I can thank my dad for fostering my own interest in bird-watching. As a toddler I used to crawl around the garden, and pick up whatever caught my eye. Birds' feathers were probably the least objectionable of these tiny treasures. Still at that blissful age when parents are all-knowing, I'd ask my dad to identify them. Bless him, he didn't just tell me to go away and stop wasting his time. He'd fold up his newspaper and ascribe a different bird's name to every single feather I brought him. No doubt he mugged up with a bird book; how else would a handful of feathers, collected from a small village garden, have included capercaillie, red kite and bearded tit?

His relaxed attitude to ornithological identification helped to sow the seeds of a lifelong hobby that's brought me enormous pleasure over the intervening years, for no greater cost than a field-guide to British birds and a pair of binoculars. A few friends shared my childhood interest, and our gardens became bird reserves in miniature. We'd see how many species we could log in our own locale, and enter the sightings in our nature diaries. But there are only so many species that can be lured to a garden with half a coconut and a handful of bird-seed. And our knowledge of birds was soon outstripped by the need to spot less common species. It got quite competitive, as we tried to beat each other's tally. One day we nearly came to blows about an over-optimistic sighting of a crested tit which, when not eating peanuts on my chum's bird-table, would otherwise only occur in dense conifer forests in the Scottish Highlands.

These childish spats were soon forgotten. It seemed silly to argue about birds, when we should just be enjoying them. In short, we grew up. But little did we know that this ludicrously competitive aspect is actually the *raison d'être* of a barmy army of adult bird watchers, known as 'twitchers'. These are men (the vast majority are men, at least) who would happily sell their grandmothers into the white slave trade if this might add a new bird to their 'life list'. Like ornithological Casanovas, the thrill is in the chase. No sooner have they ticked off a new species than they're off in search of the next conquest.

They share the characteristics of obsessives everywhere. The most extreme of religious fundamentalists would nod in appreciative recognition of their single-mindedness. Some of our twitchers are just too busy to work. Once their life lists of British birds creep towards a figure of 450, it gets pretty hard to add new 'ticks'. So, armed with pagers and mobile phones, they are ready, at the drop of a woolly hat, to respond to the sighting of some rare bird. Any place, any time. Wilson's pharolope in Shetland? Rough-legged buzzard in the Scilly Isles? No problem; they just sling a sleeping bag into the car and hit the road.

These twitchers have allowed their lives to get seriously out of kilter. The urge to compete is so strong that even bird-watching is not immune. And yet, what's to stop anyone from claiming he has seen a bird when he hasn't? He may search unsuccessfully to spot some tiny warbler that all his birding colleagues have seen, but eventually decide to claim the sighting anyway. Who's to know? This is why birders are such a paranoid bunch; they never know whether other twitchers are as mendacious as they are themselves. But it's a reasonable guess...

The simple, unalloyed pleasures of bird-watching are lost on these loons. It's a neat trick to turn a relaxing pastime into just another stressful rat-race. Their affliction is based on a categorical refusal to look at themselves objectively and think: 'Is this really a suitable thing for a sensible, grown-up man to be doing?'

No matter; the lake at Litterdale is a delightful place for sane bird-watchers (yes, like me...) to while away a few tranquil hours. It teems with wildfowl, especially when the autumn migration is at its height. There's no point in rushing around, ticking off new species, when you can lose yourself in such an animated scene. In any case, there are usually a handful of rarities that turn up each year. And when the twitchers come in their wake – with powerful telescopes on tripods, and eyes ablaze with misplaced passion – it's always fun to irritate them by pointing out, with exaggerated excitement, a commonplace coot or moorhen.

For a lot of visitors to Litterdale – raised on the free-market notion that 'you get what you pay for' – the success of a day out can be reckoned by totting up what they've spent. It's a simple calculation. Their pockets are empty by the time they head for home... *ergo*, they must have had a good time.

There's a love-hate relationship between the visitors and the pub landlords of Litterdale. Visitors bring money into the village, and they're not shy of spending it. Our pub landlords rub their hands together – in an obsequious, Basil Fawlty kind of way – whenever a well-heeled family walks into their establishment. A few moments of mental arithmetic – totting up the cost of five bar-meals, two rounds of drinks and a tip – promises a tidy sum. The children's drinks –

tiny bottles of fizzy pop – are the most profitable line of all. The artificial colourings make small children hyperactive, so that harassed parents will buy them another bottle in the mistaken belief that it will quiet them down. It's a real money-spinner.

By this time of the year, though, visitor numbers have dwindled to a mere trickle. Our pub landlords can stop looking so relentlessly cheerful, which is a relief. But pubs still need customers, and that's a worry. So now is the time to win back the custom of the local farmers, plough-jockeys, hired hands, senior citizens and disaffected youth: the very people who were least welcome during the heady summer months. Into winter storage go the patio furniture, the colourful umbrellas and the over-priced menus with their flowery euphemisms. Back come the pool table, the dart board and the man-sized chip butties. The landlords will have to endure the more robust behaviour of this boisterous clientele... but only until next Easter, when the tourist season will begin again.

Bill, our tourism officer, is doing his best to attract visitors 'out of season', when Litterdale presents a less frenetic face to the world. And this year's theme is walking. Seasoned hikers need little persuading about the pleasures of walking the White Peak. They already come in numbers to enjoy the rolling hills and the secluded limestone dales. But, almost by definition, they tend to be a self-reliant bunch. They come prepared for every eventuality, with haversacks full of waterproofs, maps, blister cream, sandwiches and flasks of tea. They don't mooch around Litterdale, throwing their money around; they look to the hills instead. Within ten minutes of arriving in Litterdale, they are just specks disappearing over the first horizon.

If it's tranquillity you want, then it's easily found on the breezy tops. After a stiff climb you can reward yourself with a panoramic view down to Litterdale – wedged into the valley bottom by the folds of the hills.

For every accomplished hiker, however, there are dozens of people whose walking experience extends no further than a brief expedition down to the corner shop to buy a paper and twenty Bensons. People who have never knowingly crossed a contour line. And it's these very people who are currently being wooed by Bill. It's a tactic fraught with pitfalls, as he is beginning to realise.

They come ill-prepared for a change in the weather, or the ravages of hunger and thirst – assuming, unwisely, that there'll be a take-away over the crest of every hill. All they have is a little brochure about the newly inaugurated Litterdale Way: a splendid ramble that incorporates some of the loveliest countryside around the village. The brochure is Bill's proud handiwork; in theory, at least, it offers an easily-followed route.

So much for theory. A few disgruntled farmers have tossed the waymarking signs over the nearest hedge or – more insidiously – rotated the finger-posts through ninety degrees. The result is a lot of disorientated walkers staring uncomprehendingly at their brochures, holding them first one way and then the other. The only thing they are sure of is that they are hopelessly lost.

This is the moment that panic sets in. The hills that looked so pretty through the windscreen of a speeding car now seem gloomily oppressive. The trees creak and bend alarmingly in the stiffening wind. Storm clouds gather. Grouse take off with heart-stopping suddenness, their call a mocking 'Go back, go back'. Circling curlews look more like vultures, sensing that a meal is in the offing.

Groups of terrified walkers are emptying out their pockets. Some, fearing the worst, are scribbling notes to their loved ones. Others are pooling their meagre resources, wondering how long they would survive on a packet of Jaffa Cakes and a can of Irn Bru. And then someone, cutting through the rising hysteria, wonders, 'Would this be any use?' and produces a mobile phone. *Any use*? It's a godsend…

Litterdale's hill rescue service is manned by a dedicated crew of men who would give Chris Bonnington a run for his money in a Chris Bonnington look-alike contest. In the past they've mustered every few weeks to bring injured walkers down from the tops. But now the hills are full of nincompoops with mobile phones, who seem to regard the rescuers as a convenient extension of room service. They have only the vaguest idea of what constitutes an emergency, which is why the rescue service are taking an increasing number of calls requesting they deliver 'a new pair of boot-laces' or 'some milk for the tea, we forgot to bring any'. The callers don't have a clue where they are; 'If we *knew* where we were, we wouldn't be ringing you, would we?'

It's Bill's turn to get a phone-call – from the leader of the hill rescue service. Since he doesn't drink in the Fox – the more disreputable of the village's two pubs – he's not used to hearing this kind of language. When he's able to get a word in edgeways he makes a solemn promise: there'll be no more brochures inviting ill-equipped townies to explore the lovely landscapes around Litterdale.

WINTER

It's December in Litterdale and the villagers mostly have the place to themselves once more. There's a thin layer of ice on the village duckpond, which gives the mallards the appearance of miniature ice-breakers as they make laboured progress across the water. The kids come to feed them with stale bread, and to send stones skittering across the ice. The air is thin and sharp, carrying their shrill, excited voices far beyond the village. No wonder they're excited; they know Christmas is nearly here.

When visitors *do* come in winter, it's usually over Christmas or New Year, and mostly to get away from their loved ones for a few days. It doesn't matter that the December sun has set by mid-afternoon; they don't come to take long hikes over the hills. A brief stroll down to the Swan, wrapped up like sausage rolls against a cold wind, is a more likely scenario. Stone-flagged floors, log fires, a brandy to swirl lazily around a balloon glass; '*This* is more like it', they think, as they settle back into comfortable wing-back chairs.

What the visitors are looking for is a village Christmas, a Breughel painting brought to life. A bare and brittle landscape peopled with tiny figures, all going about their business. And, amazingly, this is pretty much what Litterdale *does* look like in winter. The colour is drained from the landscape, as photosynthesis shuts down operations till spring, reducing the scene to tone, line and texture; the tracery of dry stone walls in the valley, leafless trees silhouetted against a fretful winter sky, sturdy stone houses built to withstand the worst of Pennine weather.

The farmers are out in the fields – come rain, come shine – doing those boring but essential jobs. Even though nothing is growing, the farmers don't think: 'Hmm, things are a bit quiet on the farm. Maybe I'll take a fortnight off, put my feet up and catch up with some reading.' Hill-farming isn't a job, it's a way of life. It's not something you can put to one side for a few days, like a piece of knitting. Cows need milking twice a day, every day. *They* don't know it's Christmas. Hard, unrewarding work is the farmer's currency; if you were to take that away from them, they'd have nothing.

They don't appreciate being told how lucky they are to be 'in touch with the land and the seasons', especially by city folk on holiday. But if you want to see a red-faced farmer incandescent with fury, just suggest that you're thinking about doing a bit of farming too: a little smallholding, a few animals, maybe some rare breeds of sheep. Yes, what gets the farmers of Litterdale really angry is people who just *play* at being farmers.

We are gearing ourselves up for what we laughingly call the festive season. Ah, Christmas, the time of year when we feel our own shortcomings most acutely. When the gap seems to widen, unbridgeably, between what we wanted to be and what we seem to have become. When we are forced to confront the goodness in the world and the badness that's in *us*.

It's a difficult time of year. No wonder we try to make up for these shortcomings by buying expensive presents for family and friends that seem to have more to go with assuaging guilt than the unalloyed joy of giving. We try to be a little better than we usually think we are. But the odds are stacked against us. 'We only do it for the kids,' we suggest, blithely, as we load up the supermarket trolley with surreal quantities of booze.

Christmas seems to have been going on since mid-October, which means that by the time the celebrations actually arrive, we are heartily sick of tinsel, artificial snow and the CDs of Christmas songs that the landlord of the Swan insists on playing from the moment he opens up to the moment he locks the door, with a heartfelt sigh of relief, at closing time. It's a bizarre notion that anyone sane would want to hear, yet again, Roy Wood's probably certifiable request: I Wish it Could be Christmas Every Day.

But no matter how jaundiced you may feel about Christmas (and I bow to no-one in the depth of my distaste for the cynical spending-spree that it has become), it still retains the power to melt the stoniest of hearts. At some point between the last of the mince pies and the Queen's speech, you will be ambushed by the 'true spirit' of Christmas. It happens every year, and it's always a surprise.

One year it was my young daughter looking up at me with her big, brown, trusting eyes. Understanding the need for secrecy at this time of year, she refused to divulge what she had bought for me – merely saying, bless her, that 'It isn't a comb'.

Another year we had friends to stay over the holiday. On Christmas day morning all our carefully nurtured notions of sexual equality suddenly evaporated. The women seemed to feel a primordial pull towards cooking the mountain of food we'd bought. And the blokes felt an equally primordial desire to let them get on with it. Our half-hearted attempts to help (just standing around, getting in the way, saying 'Is there anything we can do?') had the desired effect. 'Why don't you go for a walk?' the women said, in the tone of voice they generally used when speaking to small children.

So three blokes, well wrapped-up, wandered out into the pale winter sunshine. As a local, reckoning to know my way around, I hadn't bothered to take a map so, predictably enough, by the time we'd traipsed over the hills for a couple of hours, we were hopelessly lost. With the weather worsening we decided to knock on the door of a nearby farmhouse, and ask for help. The only sign of life was the smoke billowing from the chimney. But when the door opened we looked into a huge farmhouse kitchen, where the whole family were busy preparing food. It looked and smelt wonderful.

The farmer was happy to point us on the right track back home... but first we had to sample the hot toddy he was making. After a good walk in the cold, this tasted wonderful, too, especially as whisky seemed to be the main ingredient. 'You'll have another,' the farmer said, more than once. We sat round that kitchen table, increasingly full of Christmas spirit, until the candles and the lights on the tree were pleasantly blurred... and then staggered home to our own Christmas meal in Litterdale.

Christmas is over for another year; we've had the giving of the presents and the exchanging of the receipts. It wasn't just the goose getting fat; the orgy of eating and drinking has left Litterdale folk inert and listless, hoping that the hangovers will have subsided by the time the Visa bills roll in. To cap it all, everything we bought in December is being flogged off at half-price during the January sales. It's adding insult to insolvency; since we're feeling corpulent and broke it's hard to know whether to tighten our belts or loosen them.

We fantasise about healthy food, strict diet regimes and proper exercise (not merely walking the dog down to the Fox for a swift pint and a bag or two of pork scratchings). New Year's resolutions are made optimistically but are invariably broken: a process that's generally over and done with in the course of a long weekend. If the road to hell really is paved with good intentions, then over-indulgent Litterdale folk won't be needing an extra sweater in the next life.

Tempers are fraying in every Litterdale household. The children are frazzled and hyperactive from playing too many violent computer games. The women have run through their repertoire of recipes for left-over turkey. Bird tables all around the village are crowned with turkey carcasses – it's like some macabre ceremony – allowing the blue tits and sparrows to pick the bones clean. The men are queasy and disorientated. The holiday drags on, allowing them time to mull over important questions, like: 'Why did I spend so much money just to give myself liver damage?'

Life's familiar tempo has been disrupted over the holiday; some folk don't even know what day it is. Everyone seems relieved at the prospect of getting back to normal. After so much inactivity, the working week has an unaccustomed appeal. Families can survive pretty well on a diet of five days' work and two days of leisure. When those two days stretch into double figures, even the most harmonious families can get crabby and argumentative.

It has been raining for days. A photographer might enjoy the gilded reflections of street-lamps in puddles, and the way that the cobbles glisten in the side-streets of Litterdale. But everybody else just sees cloudy skies, with spring a very distant prospect indeed. The little river that runs through Litterdale has been transformed into a torrent as it surges swollenly beneath the old packhorse bridge. It looks like winter stew on the boil.

There are half a dozen days each year – mostly in winter – when the air is hypnotically clear. When you can stand on top of one of the hills that cradle the village of Litterdale, and see for miles. When you feel you need only to stretch out a hand to be able to touch the furthest horizon. These are special days, magical days, when you're lucky if you're out walking instead of being stuck in the office or workshop. You can't anticipate them.

At this time of the year you may get two dozen dreary days in a row: days when the sun fails to make even a cameo appearance, and the clouds resolutely refuse to lift. The good folk of Litterdale begin to feel gloomy and twitchy from sunlight deprivation. Then, without warning, we wake up one morning to find that the world has been washed clean in the night. Instead of lowering clouds in standard-issue battleship grey, the sky is a rich, regal and unclouded blue. Those same photographers sniff the air, dust down their cameras, and murmur: 'The light, the light...'

The air is clear and still and seems to resonate with the slightest sound. Metal studs on a pair of working boots produce bright, ringing sounds against the cobbles – like a blacksmith overheard striking his anvil in the next village. The noise of a tractor starting up is so familiar around Litterdale that we hardly notice it any more. But on a morning like this we register every judder of a determinedly unmaintained engine; the squeal of an unoiled hinge – and an involuntary oath – as the cab door shuts on cold, careless fingers; the rasping sound of a farmer clearing his throat and depositing a ball of phlegm onto the frosty grass.

Ragged-winged rooks congregate noisily in wind-tossed trees. They can always find something to bicker about. Few sounds exemplify the bare, raw winter landscape like the rooks' cantankerous croaking. Flocks of twittering winter finches scavange for meagre pickings in the field margins: a loose affiliation of chaffinches, greenfinches, goldfinches and bramblings. It's only in such cold weather that they set aside their differences and band together for survival. A wren calls from the thorny heart of a hawthorn hedge. Fieldfares soar across fields dusted with hoar-frost, far from their Arctic breeding grounds.

Pheasants line up on the verges of the quieter roads. Most birds make themselves scarce whenever a car passes, but pheasants can't be bothered. They have a stoical disposition that stems, no doubt, from being shot at by well-heeled businessmen.   Stoical and despondent; it's hard for pheasants to look on the bright side when they know what fate has in store. The gamekeeper puts food out for them – there's no need to forage – and the pheasants keep eating. There's nothing much else to do, except to get fatter and fatter. If the gamekeeper were to put out roasting dishes they'd probably just climb in, baste themselves and set the oven to regulo five.

So is it any wonder that some of the pheasants feel suicidal? They stand by the side of the road, thinking: 'Shall I? Shan't I?' and then, on a car's approach, they give a world-weary sigh. Their last thought is: 'Sod it...' as they scuttle beneath the wheels.

There's not a lot happening in Litterdale. We're in that briefest of interludes between the end of the January sales and the appearance – in those same shops, a few weeks later – of the Easter Bunny. The village is almost empty. Maybe it's a flag-day. Maybe the neutron bomb's gone off. Maybe it's just half-day closing.

The landscapes depicted on the now-discarded Christmas cards differ from reality in one startling respect: there's snow on the cards, but none in Litterdale. The truth is, of course, that we are more likely to get white *Easters* than white Christmases. And, on the whole, we're pretty stoical about our weather; if we'd demanded to enjoy a Mediterranean-type climate, soaking up the sun amongst the orange groves, then we'd have thought twice about Derbyshire in the first place. It's not that we're particularly enamoured with snow, either, but we'd still be mildly relieved to see some. A proper snowfall, blanketing the landscape, not just wind-blown flurries that come and go in a matter of minutes.

A winter without snow seems contrary to nature. An unrehearsed departure from a familiar script. An unwelcome reminder that there are forces at work over which we have too little control. We listen to the news, and nod sagely as the planet reels from hurricanes, floods and earthquakes. We're aware of what's going on. No snow: global warming. Dry weather: global warming. Wet weather: global warming. Alternating wet and dry weather: global warming. Protracted periods of especially wet... or dry... or changeable weather: yes, that'll be global warming.

The rain and wind lash relentlessly against our homes in Litterdale – lifting roof slates, permeating badly-pointed façades and driving through cracks in rotten window frames. Like the probing jabs of a quick-handed boxer, the rain seeks out the weak spots in our defences. It mocks the half-baked attempts of artless bodgers to make running repairs to their dilapidated homes. Slapdash DIY that seems overly reliant on cardboard, sticky tape and string, with scrunched-up newspaper to staunch the gaps where the wind whistles straight through.

These houses may have been built to withstand the worst of Pennine weather, but it takes only a few years of wilful neglect to make the local odd-job man shake his head, suck his teeth and retrieve a pencil from behind his ear. A few figures scribbled on the back of a cigarette packet are enough to convince cash-strapped villagers that essential repairs will have to be postponed for yet another year.

Bob, Litterdale's postman, is one householder who is tossing and turning through many a sleepless winter night, listening for the tell-tales signs that foretell disaster: the creaking of floorboards, the insistent 'drip, drip, drip' of water from unlagged pipes and the last, asthmatic gasps from a geriatric central heating boiler. In those wee, small hours a man with an overactive imagination can almost hear the conspiratorial conversations of death-watch beetles, as they draw lots to see which vital, load-bearing stanchion they'll chomp through next.

No sooner has Bob fallen into a troubled, fitful sleep than the ringing of the alarm clock makes him sit bolt upright, like a mummy in one of those old black and white horror films. The bell is louder than most folk might choose, but a postman needs something insistent to oust him from a warm bed at five o'clock in the morning. Cath rolls over, with a couple more hours of sleep in mind, taking most of the duvet with her.

It's at times like this that Bob wishes he could number more plumbers and electricians among his acquaintances, and fewer traditional folk singers. Michael Schumacher would feel very much at home in Bob and Cath's house: it's the pits. There are so many jobs that need doing – both inside the house and out – that the prospect overwhelms him. He can't decide where to start, no matter how many hints Cath drops, so he never makes a start at all.

He looks on with a mixture of envy and self-reproach as his neighbours make running repairs to their homes. Bob, too, longs for snow; planting the first footprints of the morning in a fresh snowfall, as he makes his rounds. Snow is so egalitarian. For a few blissful days it makes his unkempt, weed-strewn garden look as good as everyone else's.

It's Sunday morning, so Bob indulges in one of his favourites ploys to counter Household Neglect Frustration: transforming an untidy heap of branches into a neat pile of split logs and a few baskets of kindling. If the boiler's about to blow, best make contingency plans. It's a simple, repetitive, strangely absorbing task, the perfect antidote to life's more baffling complexities. Passers-by don't ask: 'What the hell are you doing *that* for, Bob?' They instinctively understand a man's primeval need to bludgeon inanimate objects into submission. It's self-explanatory. Bob doesn't need an instruction manual, or a telephone help-line, or an over-paid consultant to tell him what to do. He only needs to bend his back to get warmed twice over: first from the chopping, later from the fire.

He weighs the axe in his hands, finding it reassuringly heavy, and runs a cautious thumb along the blade. He spits on his palms (he doesn't know why, it's just part of the ritual), takes a swing and brings the axe down in a wide arc onto a fat log. 'Thwack', his bank manager's balding head is almost severed from his shoulders. 'Thwack', it rolls along the cobblestones and comes to rest in the gutter. With every frenzied blow, Bob runs through a rosta of retribution; with every week that goes by, the list seems to get longer. By the time he gets around to the bloke who short-changed him down at the newsagent, he's gasping for breath, his brow is glistening with sweat and a morning's work is done.

SPRING

C ivic pride is one of those virtues – like politeness and sportsmanship – that we now seem to have abandoned as quaint and old-fashioned. But Norman has an old-fashioned view of things, and he doesn't mind who knows it. With his collarless shirts, waistcoats and mutton-chop whiskers, he even looks like he belongs to another age. Some people may find his behaviour a little baffling but, if pressed on the matter, will offer grudging admiration. To the rest of us he's a saint. Saint Norman of Litterdale.

Norman is a fixer, a handyman, a jack-of-all-trades... and master of quite a few. His neat little house confirms the wisdom of doing those vital jobs a few weeks before they really need to be done. Unlike Bob the postman he doesn't lie awake at night, wondering whether his house will still be standing in the morning. He sleeps the untroubled sleep of a man who is up to speed with his maintenance programme. When a job needs doing, Norman doesn't talk about it... he just does it.

Having given his lawn one last cut, back in autumn, Norman sharpened the blades on his mower, oiled every moving part and covered the machine with a tarpaulin. Now, with spring finally within sight, it only needs a smooth pull on the starter cord to bring his mower purring back to life. While Norman is traversing a front lawn that a Wimbledon groundsman would be proud of, everybody else in Litterdale is dragging rusty mowers out of garden sheds and trying, in vain, to breath life into seized-up engines.

They and their lawn-mowers eventually find their way to Norman's workshop. He lets them down easy. Instead of giving them a lecture of mild reproof (on the theme of 'spoiling the ship for a ha'porth of tar') he'll get their machines purring too. He'll take a fiver in payment, a fraction of what an overhaul would cost in town. He knows it salves his neighbours' consciences. And they may have to wait a few days, since everyone brings him their mowers at exactly the same time. Norman is never tempted to remind his more feckless neighbours just how feckless they are. Or if he does feel the temptation, he never gives into it. He should be smug, but he's not. If he had a halo it would be buffed and polished till it gleamed, but he wouldn't dream of wearing it in public.

Litterdale belongs to Norman. Most people are fiercely proprietorial about their little fiefdoms. When they trim a hedge, they go to the limit of their property… and not an inch further. It just wouldn't occur to them to pop next door and say: 'I'm tidying up my bit of the hedge, shall I do yours while I've got the clippers out?' The result looks ludicrous, of course. But Norman has a stake in the village that has nothing to do with deeds, contracts and boundary walls. When he says: 'It's my village', he isn't merely confirming that he was born here fifty-three years ago and that, with luck, he'll be buried here too. It's his village because he looks after it.

We live in a litigious age when, instead of taking responsibility for ourselves when accidents happen, we immediately look for someone else to blame. If a careless pedestrian trips over a flag-stone and turns an ankle, his first response, as likely as not, will be to sue the council. It's 'their' responsibility. 'They' should do something about it. But the wheels of local bureaucracy are notoriously slow in turning. By the time a council workman turns up, rips up the offending flag-stone and makes an ugly repair with a barrow-load of lumpy pitch, half a dozen more Litterdale folk may be nursing swollen ankles.

Norman takes a pride in his little fiefdom too, and chases any cat away that might even be thinking of 'depositing' on his beautifully manicured front lawn. But his gaze extends far beyond his own garden wall; whenever he spies some little corner of Litterdale that needs sprucing up, he takes action. Instead of dashing off a stroppy letter to the council, he changes into his overalls and sets off with his canvas bag of tools to put matters right. Thanks to Norman's efforts, the flag-stones fit together as snugly as pieces in a jigsaw. The war memorial is free from the droppings of unpatriotic pigeons: not just for Poppy Day, but all year round. We can thank the council for putting up hanging baskets of flowers each year, but it's Norman who actually remembers to water them. The sign that welcomes careful drivers to Litterdale can always be read by day-trippers, because Norman gives it a wipe with a damp cloth every time he passes.

Litterdale is a regular prize-winner in the Best Kept Village Competition. When the time comes for the awards to be handed out, the local councillors are happy to accept the judges' plaudits. The mayor and his cronies ('The chain gang', as Norman calls them, dismissively) need no second bidding to crawl out of the woodwork whenever there's an opportunity to claim credit for someone else's work. They always have a banal soundbite at the ready, and smile their ferocious smiles for the photographer of the *Litterdale Times*. For those who give their time to local politics – freely and without thought of personal gain – these occasions act like an intravenous shot of testosterone.

It's Norman who should be up there on the podium, instead of standing in the crowd and applauding these self-important phonies. But he doesn't mind, and he's not bitter about being passed over, thoughtlessly, when the vote of thanks is given. He's seen councillors come and go over the years and, candidly, he wouldn't give a bucket of warm spit for the lot of them. Norman has a different agenda altogether. He's a free spirit, an independent thinker… almost – whisper it – an anarchist. He won't be standing for office, when the local elections come around again, but he'll be ready this spring with his sharpening stone and oil-can when the first knackered lawn-mower arrives in his workshop.

It's Spring in Litterdale, so a young man's fancy turns, naturally enough, to landscape photography. Well, that's Frank's fancy anyway. His working week is spent juggling figures. He'd taken his old math's teacher's advice to heart, believing that there is, indeed, safety in numbers. It's not a bad job, the money's okay and there's no heavy lifting. But even though accountancy pays the bills, his heart's not really in it. By the middle of each week, the figures are starting to crawl over the pages of his ledgers like foraging ants. By the time Friday rolls around, he's getting cabin fever.

Every few minutes his attention is distracted by the view from the window of his airless office. It's 'four seasons in one day' weather outside, the sort of weather that makes a photographer's shutter finger twitch, like a trigger-happy gunman in a bar full of strangers. One minute the storm clouds gather menacingly, and somebody around Litterdale is getting severely rained on. The next minute the clouds part, magically, and a slim pencil of light sweeps across the landscape, like a prison searchlight in an old James Cagney movie, searching for a farmhouse, or a hilltop or a ribbon of road to illuminate against the gloom. Frank holds a biro up to his cheek and clicks it at the decisive moment that the composition comes together. He can't help it, it's just force of habit.

There's no doubt about it, Frank would rather be a landscape photographer than an accountant. But he has to keep it as a hobby, a weekend passion, and maybe that's for the best. Most people in Litterdale have at least one of his framed photographs displayed on the wall. At Christmas time his friends and relatives have learned to feign appreciative surprise when they are presented with yet another moody landscape print. They've learned that: 'It's beautiful, Frank' is all that's required by way of response, not: 'If you'd just moved a few yards to the left, Frank, you wouldn't have had that telegraph pole in the picture…'

Bob the postman has one of Frank's pictures hanging in his living room. It hides one of the damp patches that have appeared, due to Bob's apparent inability to replace the roof-tiles that were blown away in the winter winds. Bob and Cath finally got married last year.

Not before time, it was said, since they've been living together for years. They've got kids too.

Bob was looking, as usual, to save money. What had seemed like a good idea, when he proposed to Cath, after a few drinks in the Swan, was soon getting out of hand. Bob's wedding suggestion – a perfunctory union down at the Registry Office, followed by a pie and pea supper in the Fox – seemed distinctly at odds with Cath's idea of what a wedding should be. A church ceremony, white dress, garlands of lilies, bridesmaids, a five-tier cake, a reception in a marquee, a sit-down meal, champagne – the works.

Bob tried to compromise, even going so far as to suggest a Seventies disco or a karaoke to follow the pie and pea supper. But a mere man of letters is no match against the combined force of a persistent bride-to-be and her family. One by one his defences fell under the onslaught, and everyone in Litterdale agreed that Bob and Cath's was the wedding of the year. One of the few money-saving ideas that *did* survive the rather one-sided wedding negotiations was the choice of photographer. Encouraged by Frank's interest in photography (and discouraged, in equal measure, by the cost of engaging a professional), Bob asked Frank if he would do the honours. Frank, flattered to be asked, but not thinking too clearly, agreed.

Alarm bells should have rung the moment that Frank set up his camera outside the little church in Litterdale. As affable as he is, Frank is not really a 'people person', and the sight of so many wedding guests, dressed up to the nines, got him flustered. A good wedding photographer should combine the tact of a diplomat with the intransigence of a totalitarian dictator. People need to be told – politely – what to do. Forgetting everything he had read in an all-too-brief perusal of the *A–Z of Wedding Photography*, Frank reverted to what he knew best. He thought the scene might be improved with a few of the coloured filters he always kept in his bag.

Big mistake. Instead of being a warm reminder of happy times, Bob and Cath's wedding album is a perennial reminder of what happens when you hire a landscape photographer to chronicle the best day of your life. The sky in each shot is an other-wordly orange… or magenta… or yellow: any colour except the standard-issue Litterdale grey that we know so well. To look at the pictures you'd guess that a nuclear bomb had exploded on the day of the wedding. Instead of being shown off, proudly, to everyone who calls at the house, the wedding album gathers dust on top of the wardrobe.

Bob and Cath have forgiven Frank (well, Bob has, anyway), though Frank still has nightmares about being chased down a long road by a gang of men in top hats and tuxedos. Now he sticks to what he knows best, getting out and about with his trusty Leica, watching the swathes of light as they drift sensuously over the lovely Litterdale landscape. It's his delight to be out at dawn, when the light is doing wondrous things. The local farmers – and maybe Bob on his rounds – are the only ones who see him tramp along the green lanes and out into open country, with his camera bag and his tripod.

The farmers think he's mad; they only get up at dawn because they have to. Frank, in contrast, does it from choice. On those still mornings when the world looks clean and bright and new, the sheer exhilaration of being out in the countryside far outweighs the hassle of those early starts. Big, bland, blue skies fail to set his pulses racing. What Frank enjoys is extremes of weather; his preferred forecast is 'changeable'. The best pictures seem to come at the meeting of weather systems: just before rain and just after. So Frank doesn't feel he's had a proper day's photography unless he's been soaked to the bone at least twice. Whenever he's sheltering from a sudden squall, or sitting on a rock, waiting for the light to do something 'interesting', Frank feels strangely at peace with the world.

Everyday life in our valley is chronicled in the pages of the *Litterdale Times*, a somnolent publication for which even mediocrity would represent an unfeasible ambition. The editor has developed the unerring knack of elevating the dull and the uneventful into headline stories, and burying anything of genuine significance towards the bottom of page five, next to the small ads. On how many other newspapers, for example, would a story be summarily spiked for being 'too interesting'?

The truth, however, is that there's not much call around here for titillating tit-bits, or raunchy headlines. After all, the people the editor writes about every week are the very same people who read the paper. A no-holds-barred exposé of nefarious goings-on might briefly attract a few new readers. But what's the point, the editor reasons, of upsetting people just to double the sales figures? In any case, if his readers were ever to develop an unhealthy interest in salacious stories, they'd be unlikely to salivate over the paper's more mundane headlines, such as this week's offering: Litterdale Man Dies of Natural Causes.

It's easy to knock a local newspaper for being parochial and dull, but it's part of our lives. I read every issue from cover to cover, and those five or six minutes are the highpoint of my week. A subscription to the *Litterdale Times* makes an ideal present for an uncherished relative, or anyone who has left the area and might want to keep abreast of local affairs. There'll be nothing in the paper to disturb delicate sensibilities and, indeed, nothing to make the recipients regret for an instant their decision to have left Litterdale.

The editor – known as 'Scoop' to one and all – sits in his tiny office, stabbing one-fingered at the keys of his ancient Remington typewriter like a demented woodpecker. Provincial journalism courses through his veins; even his conversation can be measured in column inches. So dedicated is he to his chosen craft that not even a breaking story has ever tempted him outdoors. Scoop slept through the moon landings, dozed fitfully as the Berlin Wall came crashing down, and was taking a well-deserved afternoon nap while bombs rained down on Baghdad.

Most of the paper's regular features are concocted by Scoop himself, though an imaginative selection of by-lines gives the illusion of variety. When he's writing the 'Your Stars' column, he's 'Madder Rose', Litterdale's resident seer and sage. The forecasts consist of bland reassurances and undemanding prophesies: 'You'll be getting an important letter this week'. Nothing to give his readers cause for concern. He's particularly kind to Cancerians, on the basis that it can't be much fun to have a star sign named after a disease.

Each week's editorial homily is handled by Scoop in the urbane, authoritative and even-handed guise of 'William Stroll'. He looks at both sides of the issues that concern the good folk of Litterdale, before coming down firmly on the fence. 'Carmine Lake', Litterdale's lady novelist, reviews new books, giving particular prominence to those of local interest. This is the column that gives Scoop most trouble; once he's met his weekly deadline, the prospect of settling down with a book is a less than enthralling prospect.

Financial news comes from 'Barry Wedge', including the day's mickle/muckle exchange rate and the muck/brass proximity quotient. Reports from the livestock auction are kept as brief as possible. With prices being so bad, there seems little point in making our farmers even gloomier than they are already.

Plain-speaking 'Gary Mullet' talks football, chronicling the peregrinations of our local teams as they end this season (like every other season) thrashing about in the relegation zone of the lower leagues. 'Vendetta Lamour' addresses the more intimate problems of troubled readers. Couples whose libidos seem to have gone into hiding without leaving a forwarding address. Bizarrely, not all the letters are made up by Scoop. Our vicar insists on writing his own weekly musings, otherwise Scoop would probably do that too.

There is always a selection of old photographs in each issue, showing how the village looked when the hay was gathered in by hand and the sight of a motor car trundling by was enough to make Litterdale folk rush outside to see what all the fuss was about. People stand around in these old pictures, gazing impassively at the photographer. They give the distinct impression that they have nothing more important to do. Very much like the Litterdale of today, in fact.

The *Litterdale Times* is celebrating its centenary this year. Launched during the last years of Queen Victoria's reign, the paper first found success as a cure for insomnia. Since then, of course, it has witnessed – and largely ignored – the most momentous events of the twentieth century. Scoop had planned to bring out a special facsimile edition of that very first issue, but abandoned the idea when he realised it looked much the same as what he's publishing today. Even that very first headline had a familiar ring to it: Mafeking Relieved, No Litterdale Residents Involved.

A problem shared... is a ready source of gratuitous gossip, and most of the news that's unfit to print in our local paper is readily disseminated over the garden fence, or over a pint in the pub. We don't buy the *Litterdale Times* to be better informed. We buy it because we live here; it's what Litterdale people do. And we'll carry on buying it as long as Scoop's ample figure continues to fill that editorial chair.

SUMMER

Litterdale is a delightful place to live; there's no doubt about it. It's a delightful place to visit, too, which is why a sunny weekend or Bank Holiday finds the village chock-full of people. Once they've arrived, however, they tend to forget whatever it was they came to see, and settle, instead, for mooching around the gift-shops and tea-rooms until their feet start to ache or their car-park tickets expire.

Our village lies smack in the middle of the Peak District National Park: the first landscape to be so designated, half a century ago. Of course, the wage-slaves of our industrial Northern cities had already been escaping, for generations, to these hills and valleys. They had fresh air to breathe – instead of the stale, choking, dusty atmosphere of the mills. Having endured the cacophony of steam-hammers and weaving looms during the working week, they could indeed become 'free men on Sunday'.

It's a truism, of course, that you can't please all the people, all of the time, and the National Park Authority has its critics. There are farmers in Litterdale, for example, who'll prop up the bar at the Fox and complain, to anyone foolish enough to listen, about how hard it is to scrape a living these days. One man's 'treasured landscape' is, after all, another man's workplace. The planning criteria that deter householders from pebble-dashing their cottages, can also frustrate the farmers' attempts to modernise their farms. Farming is a tough way of life at the best of times… and these, most certainly, are not the best of times. When so many farmers' livelihoods are on the line, even the most well-meaning edict from the National Park can seem like red-tape and petty officialdom.

After a couple of beers, the farmers can get pretty agitated. They can foresee a future when they'll be paid not to farm at all, but merely to hang around, leaning on gates, looking suitably rural and picturesque. Misdirecting lost motorists is fine as a harmless pastime, but it's hardly a career move. The farmers keep being told to diversify. But the thought of running some rural theme park, keeping lambs for the kids to pet, makes the farmers shudder. If that's what the future holds, then they might just as well pack it all in now, sell the farm and spend their declining years sunning themselves on a beach in the Bahamas. But they won't, of course. Farming isn't one of those jobs you do until something better turns up; it's for keeps.

Not only is business bad, but even their standing in the community is volatile. One minute the farmers are unsung heroes, stalwart custodians of the countryside. The next minute they're painted as the villains; swanning around in Range Rovers, grubbing up hedgerows, harassing ramblers, spraying crops with noxious pesticides and banking fat subsidy cheques. Old certainties are crumbling. Where farmers once knew their place in the scheme of things, now they're prey to the vicissitudes of bureaucrats in Brussels. No wonder the farmers of Litterdale are disorientated.

It's not just the farmers who complain about living in a National Park. The landlord of the Fox is never really happy unless he's having a good moan. It pains him that he's not allowed to shoot visitors during what is a depressingly long close season. To hear him talk, you'd imagine that visitors come to Litterdale just to make him miserable. On the one hand he loathes visitors; on the other hand he relies on them for much of his income. In an attempt to reconcile these contradictions, he's unfailingly rude to everyone.

This attitude to visitors (can't live with them... can't live without them) is a perennial feature of life in Litterdale. Now, at the height of summer, when the village is heaving with day-trippers, we yearn for tranquil winter days. Yet every winter, when the village isn't tranquil so much as dead, we miss the sounds of summer – especially the reassuring jingle of the cash-tills. If we had a slogan for visitors, it would be: 'Come to lovely Litterdale... but don't stay too long'.

Whenever we start moaning about the influx of visitors, or become complaisant about the lush countryside on our doorsteps, it's a salutary experience to drive to any of the towns and cities that lie beyond the border of the National Park. Sometimes we need to remind ourselves what can happen when green fields are regarded as nothing more than empty building plots.

There was a time when people used to shop in town. Now they drive twenty miles out to some gaudy shopping mall, conveniently sited in the middle of nowhere. Acre after acre of countryside is being sacrificed to our apparently insatiable appetite for retail therapy. And with such breathtaking speed; once we've bulldozed the landscape into submission, the buildings spring up like a virulent rash. Huge, ugly, cavernous warehouses with all the style and cachet of a biscuit tin, surrounded by a car-park the size of Rutland. We're dazzled by the lights of the marketing juggernaut; by the time we come to our senses there may be nothing left but concrete.

Our motorways bludgeon their way through the landscape like a horde of driver ants, consuming everything in their path. Just so that lorries full of corn-flakes can drive up one carriageway, while other lorries, also full of corn-flakes, can hurtle down the other carriageway. We're mortgaging our countryside just to trim a few minutes off our journey times. It's madness.

It's always a relief to see the millstone by the road that tells us we are back in the Peak. Despite the hassles, despite the planning restrictions, despite the endless stream of visitors... it gladdens the heart to be part of a living landscape. So let's give grateful thanks, and a tip of the cap, to the handful of visionary pioneers who fought

long and hard to create our National Parks, before our precious
landscapes were lost for ever.

✳

We don't have a big problem with crime in Litterdale. It's not some
featureless suburb, where people avoid their neighbours. It's a small
Peakland village, where everybody knows just about everybody else.
Residents can either offer grateful thanks that they live in such a close-
knit community, or complain of being surrounded by gossips and eaves-
droppers. One thing's for sure, it's hard to keep a secret in Litterdale.

On those blessedly rare occasions when we *do* have a robbery, it's
likely to end with a red-faced burglar returning a bin-bag of valuables
with an embarrassed shrug of the shoulders and the offer of a
conciliatory pint. We have our fair share of roughnecks, of course, but
they mostly drink out of harm's way, at the Fox, where the people
most at risk from their lager-fuelled outbursts are each other.

To talk of a 'criminal fraternity' makes it all sound rather cosy: a
friendly freemasonry of light-fingered gentlemen, with members' ties
and special handshakes. But the regulars at the Fox have no need of
funny handshakes; an arm twisted sharply up the back is all that's
needed to engage the attention of a fellow drinker for a few eye-
watering moments.

Whenever there's a shortage of genuine stories to print, the editor of
the *Litterdale Times* compensates by composing an eye-catching
headline. 'Crime Wave in Litterdale' is a favourite standby. It may
tempt a few more people to buy a copy of the paper, though what
constitutes a crime wave in Scoop's overheated imagination might, in
a more urban setting, be called a quiet weekend. Most Litterdale
residents are studiously law-abiding; wearing a loud tie in a built-up
area is about the closest they get to a major felony. They're known as
careful drivers too – especially those whose tax-discs have expired.

Scoop, however, can draw on years of experience in provincial
journalism, and he knows how to make a lot out of little. In a recent

editorial he highlighted a litany of crimes that are threatening to rend asunder the fragile fabric of life in rural Derbyshire. Smuggling contraband sheep-dip, rustling geese, forging tickets for the mobile library, and that's just for starters. Even in a community as law-abiding as Litterdale, crime prevention is a mainstay of local politics. Our local councillors read the *Litterdale Times* too, mainly to see if they are in it. Scoop's hard-hitting exposé made them sit up, take notice and recognise a heaven-sent opportunity to bang their own drum even more loudly than usual. They are not the kind of people who hide their light under a bushel. It would be hard to find a bushel large enough.

The council chamber echoes with impassioned debate. The rattling of sabres in a confined space can make quite a din. If a little knowledge is a dangerous thing, then our elected councillors are a lethal proposition. There is one issue, at least, about which they can all agree, on a pleasantly warm summer day. The motion is carried on an enthusiastic show of hands, and a small sum is requisitioned from the Swanning Around on Official Business budget. The rest of us may wonder why our local councillors would even *want* to wear epaulets. No matter. For a few precious minutes there is concord in the chamber (one size fits all, thankfully), but only until a more contentious item comes to the top of the agenda.

As usual, our latest crime wave is largely a product of Scoop's journalistic hyperbole. The miscreant on this occasion is one of Litterdale's senior citizens. He's been forced into a life of petty crime to fund his spiralling snuff habit. Having to find £1.25 a week, *every* week, has made this old codger susceptible to the siren voices of lawlessness. He was caught, red-handed, demanding money with menaces from a Women's Institute Bring and Buy Sale. 'Come on, punk, make my jam,' he'd snarled, unwisely attempting to go cold turkey after a long-term dependence on Old Mill Number 1. It was totally out of character, an aberration. And, once he'd been sedated with a mug of Horlicks, he made a solemn promise to go straight. Straight back to the old folks' home, in fact. If this is what a crime-wave looks like, then Litterdale's more solid citizens ought to be sleeping soundly in their beds at night.

However, once the councillors have got their teeth into a new idea, they're not easily diverted. Which is why the subject of close-circuit TV cameras is currently engaging the hearts and minds of our elected representatives. It sounds an appealing idea… at first. Install a few strategically-sited cameras, and no drinker leaving the Fox after hours would ever again confuse the doorway of the Post Office for a public convenience. Not without starring in his own home movie anyway. Courting couples would think twice before canoodling shamelessly in the bus shelter. We might even discover the identity of the sneak-thief who's been purloining underwear from unattended washing lines these past few months.

The other point of view is equally plausible, and not everyone is happy to have their every move monitored by Big Brother. Security cameras would arguably create as many problems as they'd solve. If it's to be any use at all, camera evidence has to be continually monitored. Who will be prepared to watch hour after hour of unremarkable video-tape, on the off-chance of catching a burglar eyeing up a window of opportunity? Even the most enthusiastic voyeur would soon get bored. Maybe we could market the footage, in 24-hour chunks, as lost classics from the Andy Warhol school of film-making.

Hoarse from haranguing one another, and eager to get home and find a full-length mirror, our councillors end up fudging the issue. They've gone, predictably, for the placebo option. Litterdale will have fake cameras, constructed from shoe-boxes and toilet rolls, mounted in prominent positions around the village. The cost of materials will be minimal, sticky-back plastic mostly. We live in hope that a battery of counterfeit cameras will deter wrong-doers, especially short-sighted ones.

✳

In the Derbyshire police force, a posting to Litterdale is seen as a step down the career ladder. A punishment for past misdeeds, perhaps, or a tranquil semi-retirement for traumatised coppers who can no longer hack it in the city. In crime-fighting terms, Litterdale is a black hole into which a policeman's ambitions can quickly vanish. No serving police officer has ever volunteered for the Litterdale patch; well, not until Sam.

Five years ago Sam Bickerdyke was just another copper on the beat. Pounding the city streets. Upholding the law. Filling his little black book with registration numbers of stolen cars. Writing notes in that strange, stilted language that policemen everywhere feel obliged to use. He tried to learn the off-duty jargon too, the canteen culture that everyone seemed to be talking about. Sam found the canteen easily enough, but precious little culture. Sam is a nature lover, you see. And a bit of a poet.

A more astute recruitment officer might have realised that Sam was temperamentally unsuited for police work. But Sam's father had been a policeman, and his grandfather, and his great-grandfather too. A stern, unsmiling portrait of a man in uniform had been a constant reminder, throughout Sam's childhood, that policing would be his lot. And, to judge from the expression on the bewhiskered face in that sepia-toned photograph, not a particularly happy one. It would have taken more courage than Sam could muster to be the one to break the link in that dynastic chain. No-one ever asked him what he wanted to be when he grew up. Policing wasn't one of many options presented to him. It was the only one.

It seemed, at first, that Sam might have some of the required attributes to be a good policeman. He was tall. He was perceived (wrongly, as it turned out) to be none too bright. He did as he was told. And, conscious of the weight of family expectations, he always tried his best. Predictably, his best was never good enough. Sam found it hard to walk in his father's footsteps. And in his father's boots too; they were at least one size too big for him. Comparisons are odious, of course, but it became painfully obvious to his superiors that Sam wasn't half the policeman his father had been.

His dad was, in fact, the only person who saw a viable future for Sam; he imagined a speedy promotion to the Serious Crime Squad. The rest of the force, unequipped with rose-coloured spectacles, were thinking more in terms of the *Humorous* Crime Squad. Sam, bless him, actually thought a police informant was someone who would give him a tip for the 2.30 at Kempton. Many a discussion began with the vexed question: 'What shall we do with the lad?' So it was a relief all round when Sam decided to jump before he was pushed. The Litterdale posting came up, Sam applied and, in the absence of any other candidates, got the job.

It was a good move. By remaining in the police force, Sam was doing nothing to disgrace the good name of the Bickerdyke family. And by choosing out-of-the-way Litterdale, he ensured that his shortcomings as a police officer would go more or less unnoticed. He has the police house that overlooks the village green. There's a compact police hatchback in the drive. Five years on, it still looks brand new; Sam doesn't do a lot of mileage. It's got a little flashing light, and a siren, but he would feel too embarrassed to use them.

In the front garden is a notice board warning Litterdale locals about the hazards of Colorado Beetles, the wisdom of checking the credentials of unannounced callers and the need for protective clothing when dipping sheep. It's all good advice, especially about the sheep-dip. Having spent too much time dunking sheep in noxious chemicals, some of our local farmers suffer from migraines and sudden lapses of memory (especially around the time when they should be filling in their tax returns).

There's a bird-table in the garden too, which hints at Sam's most abiding interests. He can still hardly believe that he's getting paid to wander round the village, keeping an eye on things. It's not like work at all. His trouser pockets are full of acorns and conkers. Inside his jacket is a well-thumbed field-guide to mosses and liverworts. In the leather pouch where his walkie-talkie ought to be is a compact pair of binoculars.

He was glad to get rid of the walkie-talkie. It made him feel self-conscious, and the antenna used to jab him in the eye. No-one ever called him up anyway. Unless Litterdale is suddenly overrun by mobsters, or cash-strapped farmers decide to diversify into cannabis cultivation, there is a tacit agreement that Sam should be left to his own devices. Indeed, the only contact with his Chief Inspector is a monthly phone call, merely to check that Sam is alive, well, and keeping Litterdale's crime figures down. This is fine with Sam, and keeps paperwork to a bare minimum.

These days he fills his little black notebook with observations about the birds and animals he sees. And, with the elastic pulled tight, he can press wild flowers flat in a matter of days. Whenever he licks his pencil, to make notes, he gazes wistfully into the distance. There's always a dreamy, faraway look in his eyes. He wants to find the right words to describe the shapes of clouds. Or the bubbling cry of the curlew. Or the way the early morning light picks out the church spire against the still-shadowed hills.

It's high summer in Litterdale. The sky is a deep and unclouded blue, filled with ecstatic swallows, swifts and martins. Sam gazes skywards with a mixture of envy and awe. Whenever he looks at the glories of nature, he feels humble. Mind you, he could look at a box of stale biscuits and feel humble too. That's the truth about Sam, he's just a humble kind of guy.

✸

AUTUMN

The cricketers of Litterdale are coming to terms with another poor season. There'll be no new silverware this year, to brighten up the optimistically large trophy cabinet behind the bar in the Fox. It's hard to cope with failure. It's harder still to fail at all, since the Litterdale and District Cricket League operates an egalitarian 'everyone gets prizes' policy. It means that most teams in the league end up with something tangible at the end of each season.

Talk of 'silverware' rings a little hollow, however, now that the league's trophy budget is being sliced ever more thinly. Instead of lustrous metal, the trophies are cheap and nasty: just plastic sprayed to look like gold. On top of each one is a figure who either bowls or bats, designed by someone ill-acquainted with human anatomy. The batsman looks like he's throwing a stick for a dog; the bowler appears to be dancing a jig. The gold paint soon peels away; after a few weeks the figures appear not merely deformed, but leprous too.

There are trophies for winners, runners-up, best individual performances and most sportsmanlike team. There are commemorative medallions for plucky losers. There's the 'clubman' award which rewards good-hearted guys who, though useless at cricket, bring other talents to the summer game. Like turning out uncomplainingly every weekend, even though they'll bat last (if at all), never get a bowl and field down at third man where the horseflies are. Or mowing the wicket every Friday night. Or shouting 'drinks all round' on a slow night in the pub.

So it's actually quite an achievement for the Litterdale XI to end up with nothing at all. Maybe this feat deserves a trophy too: 'Most Undistinguished Team'. The plastic figure could be seated, head in hands. Something based on Rodin's statue, 'The Thinker'. 'The Plonker', perhaps. On current form, Litterdale could probably keep the trophy in perpetuity.

Dennis, our team captain, is feeling every one of his fifty-five years. It's not easy leading a team of losers through the annual relegation battle. Most weeks of the year – and especially now, at season's end – he thinks about giving up the game altogether. But whenever he thinks about what else he could be doing with his summer weekends – driving to the supermarket, trimming the hedge and spending quality time with his family – he remembers why he took to bat and ball in the first place. Dennis won't need much persuading to carry on leading his lacklustre troops. For one more season, anyway.

The decision won't be his for much longer. On the morning after a particularly hard game, he's just too stiff to roll out of bed. The spirit is willing enough, but the flesh is beginning to weaken. His eyesight isn't what it was either, and he refuses to play in glasses. The price of this vanity is being hit by the ball on a regular basis; this makes his eyes water, so he gets hit even more often. After a long innings his legs look like something out of a Francis Bacon painting: 'Batsman Screaming', perhaps.

Dennis sat in the pub, with the rest of the team, after the penultimate game of the summer, nursing a pint through another pointless session of post-match analysis. They may not shine at cricket, but the members of the Litterdale XI are dab hands at rewriting recent history. To hear them talk, you'd think they'd won the game. Dennis, however, is lost in thought. Time's winged chariot may not be here yet, but he's spotted it coming over the horizon and it's heading his way.

The ageing process starts almost imperceptibly, then picks up speed. As he removes another grey hair from the lapel of his jacket, he mentally lists some of the tell-tale signs. At parties you don't try to chat up the available talent, you just hope you don't get stuck in a low chair. You tune into Radio 2 and find they're playing all your favourite songs. Young people stop being 'us' and start being 'them'.

Your conversations are peppered with meaningless refrains like, 'When I was your age...', 'Of course, that was a lot of money in those days...' and 'You know, perhaps Mary Whitehouse was right after all'. You are tempted by small-ads for sensible trousers in the tabloid papers. You develop an unaccountable interest in golf, gardening and church architecture. You get into the habit of making a milky drink before bedtime. You think twice before buying a five-year diary. Yes, it's disturbing.

There will no doubt come a day when Dennis will spend his Sunday afternoons mooching round a garden centre, but not for a while yet. The problem is that he loves his cricket. Unlike most love affairs, however, his passion becomes more intense as the years slip by. What started out as a mere pastime has developed into a magnificent obsession.

We know all about 'blue collar workers' and 'white collar workers'. But Dennis belongs to a third category, 'open collar workers'. He's an informal dresser, and hates getting dressed up for business meetings. He believes, sensibly enough, that ties restrict the supply of oxygen to the brain. There's only one uniform he enjoys wearing, and that's the one he's wearing today. White flannels, flapping loosely in the breeze, a freshly-ironed cotton shirt and, since there's an autumnal nip in the air, two sweaters. It's the last game of the season, being played under skies of pewter grey, so the broad-brimmed hat is not strictly necessary. Dennis just wouldn't feel dressed without it.

Being next man in, he's following the game closely. One false shot by either of the opening pair, and Dennis will be pulling on his batting gloves. He's got mixed emotions: one part apprehension to two parts exhilaration. The perfect combination. It's possible he may get the same sort of buzz from mowing the lawn or trimming the hedge. Possible... but somehow we doubt it.

Like so many other Peakland communities, Litterdale has had to change with the times. To see how the village looked a hundred years ago, you really ought to catch the exhibition of old photographs that's currently on display in the Tourist Information Centre. Shot during the two decades either side of Queen Victoria's death, these sepia-toned prints offer a beguiling glimpse into a world that, though only three generations away, already seems infinitely and achingly distant.

The pictures were the handiwork of one Archbold Quinlan, local worthy and keen amateur photographer. Though born into a wealthy family, he soon wearied of the pursuits traditionally enjoyed by men of his class, such as riding to hounds, seducing kitchen maids and sending game-birds to meet their maker with his father's shotguns. As he yawned his way through the tedium of interminable country-house parties, he longed to be doing something more useful with his leisure hours.

Photography was an eminently suitable pastime for a man of inherited means, with time hanging heavily on his hands. To be able to capture moments of life, instantly and indelibly, seemed to him utterly magical. Once he had converted part of the hall's old stable block into a darkroom, Quinlan began to train his camera on the immediate surroundings. His family despaired of him; his friends wondered about his sanity. To no avail. He'd found his purpose – his focus, you could say – and nothing would deflect him from it.

It is thanks to energetic and mildly eccentric men like Quinlan that we have such an evocative archive of photographs, showing what life was like before the Great War left the fabric of British life so torn and tattered. He photographed feasts and fairs, high days and holidays, festivals and fêtes. He was there with his camera for Queen Victoria's jubilees, when the village was garlanded with bunting. He caught, on unwieldly glass plates, the mood of heady euphoria when

Mafeking was relieved. Best of all, however, he didn't merely concentrate on the recreations of the idle rich, like some photographic dilettantes of his acquaintance. He focused the bellows of his folding wooden camera, instead, on everyday life in Litterdale.

It's fascinating to see what the village looked like on those days when the flags *weren't* flying: unheralded occasions when sober Litterdale folk were simply going about their business. So let's have a wander around the exhibition, before the prints disappear back into the archive: a collection of cardboard boxes stacked up in the broom cupboard.

Here's a picture of the hardware shop: a crowded emporium that stocked just about everything our great grandparents could possibly need. A handle for a yard brush. A length of chicken wire. Nails and screws sold by the pound. The shopkeeper, wearing a straw hat at a jaunty angle, seems rather pleased with himself. Business looks good. He is happily unaware that, a century later, his establishment would be transformed into a gift shop where tourists browse listlessly for tawdry souvenirs.

A boy and his pig stand in a dusty roadway, both looking towards the camera with studied indifference. Neither of them seem in any great hurry to move. There's no good reason why they should; another dozen years would have passed before the first motor car passed through Litterdale.

Litterdale used to have a village idiot, and here he is: the proud owner of a bewildered expression and an extravagent set of mutton-chop whiskers. Having won the North Derbyshire Village Idiot Competition three years in a row, he got to keep the trophy. Village idiocy is rather out of fashion these days – gone the way of the workhouse and the lunatic asylum. Now, with political correctness to the fore, we have a more humane attitude towards the cerebrally challenged. Yes, Care in the Community, or 'sleeping rough' as it's more accurately known.

The Vicar of Litterdale stands outside the porch of his church. The cut of his frock-coat matches the severity of his countenance. He doesn't look like a man in whom you would confide anything more personal than your collar size. By all accounts he could terrify his congregation with a few home truths delivered from the pulpit – leaving women weeping, men ashen-faced, children traumatised and damp. But, of course, this was a time when religion was a rather more compelling force than it is today. A time when the devil walked among us, and wasn't just your dad dressed up. Before hellfire and damnation had become mere lifestyle options. Before the Ten Commandments had been downgraded to the status of performance charters.

The village blacksmith pays no heed to the photographer. Captured in the process of shoeing a burly carthorse, he has other things on his mind. Like keeping his toes well away from those massive hooves. Anyway, he was unimpressed by photography and other such short-lived fads. He knew that as long as we needed to get from A to B, we would need horses; and as long as we kept horses they would need shoeing. Sadly, he was still repeating this mantra when the first car eventually *did* career through Litterdale – raising dust, frightening livestock and changing the face of transport irrevocably. The blacksmith took early retirement (he didn't have much choice in the matter), and spent his declining years bemoaning the invention of the internal combustion engine.

The smithy, remarkably, has a new lease of life. It was recently saved from dereliction by a college professor who, having taken early retirement, decided to spend his declining years producing hanging baskets and ornate candle-sticks for the tourist trade. Isn't it strange the way things work out?

A vanished way of life is preserved in the aspic of Archbold Quinlan's captivating photographs. They transport us back to what we fondly imagine was a rural arcadia, a pastoral paradise. Not strictly true, of course, but that's the power that sepia-toned photographs can have on our jaded sensibilities at the fag-end of the twentieth century.

Nostalgia is an easy game to play. We can remember, or simply imagine, a Golden Age. Being an essentially meaningless concept, this can be any time in the past: Ancient Greece, the Rennaisance, the Swinging Sixties, a week last Wednesday. It really doesn't matter.

It was a beguiling time, whenever it was. Unicorns roamed the earth, people knew their neighbours, the summers were long and warm, the kids had respect for their elders, working people did a fair day's work for a fair day's pay, and beer was fourpence a pint. They were simpler days, when people knew their place in the scheme of things; we could walk the streets without fear, and pop next door to borrow a cupful of money.

We could leave our front doors unlocked back then, without any bother. We'd keep them open all night. When we went on holiday we'd leave notes for the burglars, telling them the house would be empty for a fortnight. We left explicit instructions about where they could find the valuables; sometimes we'd even go to the trouble of placing a small-ad. in the *Litterdale Times*. But did we ever get burgled? Did we buggery...

There comes a time in life when the world seems to be spinning too quickly on its axis, when the desire to learn new things diminishes along with our eyesight and libidos. And, once we stop learning, the temptation is to take refuge in the past. We bore friends and neighbours with a mantra of memories: farthings, florins, fahrenheit and fuzzy felt. Antirrhinums, antimacassars and avoirdupois. Dubbin and dolly blue. Green Shield stamps, twin-tubs, tiger nuts, spanish, singing cowboys, coltsfoot rock, barley sugar twists, temperance hotels, sarsaparilla, sweet cigarettes (what a great idea *they* were... introducing kids to two lifelong addictions – sugar and nicotine – for the price of one), ginger beer, lemon curd, lead soldiers, penny plain and tuppence coloured.

When logic lets us down, we simplify. Life used to be good, yes it did, but now everything is bad. Childhood memories develop a golden bloom. We were young, untroubled and still had most of our marbles. Unlike now when, if it's quiet, we can actually hear those brain cells popping. It sounds like idle fingers bursting bubble wrap.

Nostalgia can strike anyone, anytime. By any yardstick, Bob's still a young man. Although, if you catch him just after lunch, when he's finished his rounds, you might not think so. He has one of those reclining chairs that, with a casual flick of a lever, transfers a weary postman from a prim, upright sitting position to a relaxed, luxurious sprawl. Within minutes he's asleep and snoring – sporadic twitches in his legs the only clue that savage, untethered dogs are invading his dreams.

By the time the kids get home from school, Bob's up and about again. He knows, from painful experience, that kids and an afternoon nap go together like oil and water. 'Shhh, your dad's asleep,' Cath used to say, as Ben and Sophie burst through the door. But she'd give them a conspiratorial wink too, so the kids would leap onto his chest and pummel him back to consciousness rather quicker than he would have wanted.

The kids are older now. They no longer want to wrestle with dad on the living room floor, more's the pity, or ride on his back like a horse. It doesn't matter what he says to them these days; their only response is to roll their eyes. They head for their rooms, to read magazines, go for a personal best on some shoot-'em-up computer game, or play their music. Loud. Too loud. 'They treat this house like a hotel,' says Bob to Cath. 'It's just the age,' she replies, soothingly. 'They'll get through it. And so will you.' Bob's not so sure.

He claps his hands over his ears. The bass notes from Ben's CD player make his fillings rattle; flakes of plaster fall from the ceiling like an unseasonal flurry of snow. The whole house seems to shake, and not in a good way. Bob takes the stairs two at a time and hammers on his son's bedroom door. 'Turn it down...' 'What?' *'Turn... that... music... down.'* Ben glares, but obliges. 'It's giving me a headache,' says Bob, wearily. 'That,' says Ben, coldly, 'is what it's for.' Teenagers...

'That's not music,' Bob says, 'that's just a noise.' He hears himself talking, but the picture that forms in his mind is of his own dad – balding, embattled, uncomprehending – saying those very same words twenty years earlier, as Bob cranked up the volume on his treasured Dansette record player. It's a shock to the system when a man announces (for the first time in his life, but probably not the last) just how much better things were in the good old days. Bob realises, with a crushing certainty, that he is turning into his dad. And not in a good way.

It may be November but Bob, for one, has a spring in his step. As he hoists the postbag over one shoulder (years of delivering letters have left him a little lop-sided), he sniffs the air. There's a heady mixture: the musty scent of fallen leaves mingling with pungent bonfire smoke. He counts his blessings too. He's got a wife who puts up with his failings and foibles. He's got two bright kids who may deign, one day, to have a two-way conversation with him. In five years' time he'll have paid off the mortgage. Yes, things aren't what they used to be. They're a hell of a lot better…

WINTER

From the vantage point of a Peakland village, the whole world seems to be going barking mad. There's an air of near-hysteria, like a kid who can't wait to open the pile of Christmas presents. There's a mounting sense of pointlessness, too, like one of those crazy farm-dogs that runs around in circles, trying to catch its own tail. Yes, for months we've all been whipped into a frenzy of anticipation about the millennium, and what a good time we're all going to have. But there's only so long you can sustain such a level of breathless hype. And now, as we round the final bend in the last lap of the old millennium, we've crossed the boredom threshold. Here in Litterdale, at least, we've had enough.

The landlords of the Swan and the Fox have been rubbing their hands together, as they plan how to spend all the money they reckon they'll take over New Year. Trade in the old car, perhaps, or take a much-needed break. A proper holiday, not just a day at a brewers' trade show. They're hoping to keep their customers in an amiably spendthrift mood for what is expected to be about seventy-two straight hours of drinking and merrymaking.

The Fox is the village's workaday drinking hole: no airs, no graces, no locks on the toilet door. No dress-code either; most of the customers are men who tuck their shirts into their underpants. The landlord – a large man with a face like a beef tomato – is focusing on the youth market, and will be offering a variety of unsophisticated entertainments. He plans to kick off Millennium Eve with a special trivia quiz. In deference to the pub's customers, who are mostly from the shallow end of the gene pool, the questions will be untaxing. Like: 'Who are *you* looking at?' 'Wanna make something of it?' The prize will be a platter of raw meat – not so much a mixed grill as an autopsy.

The Vinnie Jones lookalike contest, pencilled in for later in the evening, might not prove, in retrospect, to have been the brightest idea the landlord's ever had. The after-midnight car-door slamming competition, held in the car-park, is a regular feature in the pub's social calendar. The customers can be entrusted to sort out the running order for themselves.

The landlord at the Swan has no plans for such plebeian pastimes to usher in the new millennium. This is Litterdale's self-styled 'nice pub for nice people', where a new flavour of crinkle-cut crisp is usually reckoned to be excitement enough for his more upmarket clientele. To mark the millennium, however, the landlord is busy creating a brand new menu. A French menu: well, French in the way that *'Allo 'Allo* is French.

It may look like easy money for the licensees of Litterdale, but there's a fly in the ointment. No, not the bug we've heard so much about. The main problem is getting the staff to work at all on Millennium Eve. They've been whispering in conspiratorial huddles, plucking ever-larger sums of money out of the air, just to hear how good they sound. For this one-off occasion, at least, the workers reckon to have the bosses over a barrel. Only now, after weeks of haggling, have the landlords and their staff reached agreement. Those who turn out on that special day will get five times their usual pay, in return for a moratorium on spitting in the soup until the New Year holiday is well and truly over.

Will the rest of us have any 'mad money' left to spend on Millennium Eve, once Christmas has taken its toll on our credit cards and mental equilibrium? The question has been answered already, as we scan the last page of our calendars. We're busy cancelling those millennium parties. A quiet night in, doing a crossword, has never looked more appealing.

Those prepared to drive into town – and leave their critical faculties at home – will be able to see a Christmas pantomime. Probably starring one of the gladiators (Ferret), a monosyllabic Rugby League star with no neck, the straight man in a now-defunct comedy duo, and an actress who was booted out of some TV soap back in 1987. A mouth-watering prospect, no doubt, though live entertainment can also be found even closer to home.

The Litterdale Strollers, our local amateur dramatic company, have been striving manfully to give us quality theatre. God only knows why they bother; to date we've shown ourselves to be stubbornly resistant to the lure of the classics. Two years ago, for example, the company staged *King Lear*. It was an ambitious production, by all accounts, but not even the overly-realistic eye-gouging scene could fill more than half the seats in the village hall. Living in Pennine Derbyshire we already know what it's like to bring up ungrateful kids in adverse weather conditions.

Last Christmas the Strollers put on a musical, hoping that a medley of undemanding melodies would pull in the punters. *Don't Cry For Me, Arthur Negus* was a heartwarming tale of life, love and laughter at the sharp end of the antiques business. There was a glowing review in the *Litterdale Times*: 'You'll laugh, you'll cry… you'll rifle your granny's attic for items of more than sentimental value.' Word of mouth did the rest; the last night's performance was almost a sell-out.

The Strollers have gone back to the bard for this year's offering too, but this time they've given one of his best-loved plays what they hope will be a crowd-pleasing twist. *All's Well That Tideswell* is a triumphant reworking of Shakespeare's play in a contemporary Peakland setting. We're hoping it will bring Litterdale folk out in droves, and break all box-office records.

❄

The whole millennium scenario has proved less than contagious here in Litterdale. Millennium fever? Millennium torpor, more like. While the travel agents were trying to persuade us to spend the first morning of the new millennium in some sun-kissed holiday paradise, we didn't really care where we'd be... as long as it wasn't a place where we'd have to rely on computers and microchips. So not 30,000 feet up in a doomed jumbo jet, if you please, or hooked up to some crucial life-support machine.

The millennium scenario was strangely familiar; Litterdale's more anxious citizens had replayed it many times in their feverish imaginations... The clock chimes twelve on the last night of the old year. Digital timers click fatefully from 1999 into the uncharted territory that is the year 2000. Computers implode, instantly. Irreplaceable data disappears into the ether, never to be seen again. Household appliances go berserk. Savings and investments evaporate; the FT index drops through the floor; we're reduced to bartering with beads. Within seconds we're back in the Middle Ages, the fabric of society unravelling like a badly-knitted sweater.

That was the worst-case scenario, at least if you listened to the merchants of doom who were prepared, at a price, to rid our computers of those pesky millennium bugs. They presented a Shakespearean vision of global meltdown: sour, stinging winds; plagues of boils; birds singing out of tune; the seasons blending into one, an endless winter. But they *would* say that, wouldn't they?

As unpleasant as these predictions sounded, there was an alternative possibility so terrifying that no-one dared even to consider it. What if *nothing* untoward happened on that fateful day? What if everything was the same as it was before? Just another day. Just another dollar. The familiar routine: five days of meaningless labour, with only beer and telly to ease the pain, followed by a weekend of ploughing listlessly through a pile of Sunday supplements.

What if aeroplanes kept flying, toasters worked perfectly and computers continued to spew out specious nonsense? We'd be feeling rather silly on the morning after those 'what the hell, we're all going to die' millennium parties. Adulterous couples creeping out of lustful beds, red-faced and chastened, to face the music from their respective spouses. Disgruntled employees begging to have their job back, having unwisely told the boss, the week before, exactly where he could stick it. Now *that* was the nightmare scenario...

Scoop, the editor of the *Litterdale Times*, has remained commendably level-headed throughout the past few months, refusing to succumb to millennium madness. Idle 'end of the world' speculation would only have encouraged more readers to cancel their subscriptions, and an ailing newspaper needs all the readers it can muster. He knows that every new year is special, and that the year 2000 will prove no exception. But beyond that it's all just numbers, with no more significance than, say, the mileometer on his elderly Austin Princess ticking over from 99,999 miles – as it did recently – to 100,000.

As a founder member of CLOC (the Central Lane Owner's Club) Scoop prides himself on being a careful driver. He's owned the car from new, and – as he taps the polished walnut-style fascia for luck – he maintains that in all those years it's never had so much as a scratch. That's probably because he cruises myopically along at a stately 30mpm, like minor royalty, with a queue of impatient motorists building up behind. Lost in a flatulent fug, humming along to a Gilbert and Sullivan operetta, he remains blissfully unaware of the strong feelings he inspires in other road-users: apoplectic rage, mostly. It always comes as a surprise to Scoop to see angry drivers overtake – often on blind bends, raising a hail of gravel – their knuckles white from gripping the steering wheel too tightly.

Scoop had been keeping a watchful eye on the mileometer throughout the 99,990s; after all, it's not every day that a car reaches the milestone of six figures. When the great moment finally arrived, he was deep in thought, composing a banner headline for the next issue. When he glanced back at the dashboard he found he'd missed the moment entirely. The clock read 100,003. His first thought was to put the car into reverse, and try to 'lose' a few miles. But what would have been the point? Once these moments have gone, there's no way to bring them back. They have to be seized, not choreographed.

Which explains why the millennium celebrations have largely failed to enthral the good folk of Litterdale. When there's too much anticipation, and not enough substance, we know we're only heading for disappointment. Here in rural Derbyshire we haven't yet lost touch with the changing of the seasons. We have schedules and calendars of our own, jobs around the farm that can't be postponed merely because the people on TV have been getting over-excited. When there is something genuinely worth celebrating, we don't spend the whole year thinking 'Wow, what a night *that's* going to be.' We don't talk about it, we just do it. Yes, once the last of the new year hangovers has subsided, it looks as though life in Litterdale will soon get back to normal.

The days are short and the nights are long over the course of a Litterdale winter. When the sun seems to go down shortly after lunch, we have plenty of time to mull over some of life's knottier questions. Like why is there a 'best by' date on sour cream? Why don't we have a 99p coin? Just think how useful it would be. Why don't film censors get depraved and corrupt? And whatever happened to the Bermuda Triangle? Back in the 1970s ships and planes were going AWOL every other day. And now it's disappeared. Without warning. Weird.

Rain hammers down incessantly on our Peakland village. It beats on the roof-tiles, like the drumming of impatient fingers, and bounces off the roads. Water pulsates over unswept gutters and sluices down unpointed walls, turning stone-flagged yards into slippery skid-pans. Fluorescent green moss grows luxuriantly in dank, forgotten corners, creating tiny ecosystems where pale, sightless creatures wait, with infinite forbearance, to take over the world.

The river that runs beneath the twin arches of the old packhorse bridge is transformed into an angry torrent. Wood, swept down from the hills by flood-water, piles up in a disorderly log-jam against the stone stanchions. Scraps of paper lodge in the branches of overhanging trees, and flutter like Tibetan prayer-flags. Mallards shoot the rapids, spinning like corks in the eddies and whirlpools.

It may be wet, but it's not that cold. Not like Litterdale used to be. Older villagers can remember winters when the village was almost buried beneath stowering snow. Sometimes it drifted so deep that they couldn't open their front doors, and had to climb out of upstairs windows instead.

The last really hard winter we had was fifteen years ago, when the village was cut off for days. Thanks to a bout of panic-buying by our more anxious residents, the village shop soon ran short of fresh food. We had to make do with whatever we could find, which meant a monotonous diet of snack noodles for breakfast, lunch and dinner. We soon came to realise that pouring boiling water into a plastic pot does not, after all, transform a mixture of brick-dust and E-numbers into a tasty and nutritional meal. The only people who got through the experience unscathed were the bachelor farmers. They eat pot snacks from choice, thus enabling them to make washing up a manageable once-a-year chore.

Thanks to global warming, hard winters have probably gone for ever. Heavy snow is uncommon enough nowadays to warrant a headline in the *Litterdale Times*. Some years we just get the lightest of snowfalls that leave the tiled roofs of our little houses looking like they've been dusted with icing sugar.

Most of us are happy to have warmer winters. But not all. Our local undertaker, for example, has time unexpectedly on his hands. A frock-coated vulture, he sits morosely at the bar of the Swan, trying to drown his sorrows. As callous as it may seem to those outside this noble profession, he's worried that the mild winters aren't killing off old people in the accustomed numbers. He'd only gone into the funeral business on the understanding that he'd never be short of work. God knows there aren't too many other perks; none that he'll admit to, anyway.

Business is bad. The old folk of Litterdale seem depressingly sprightly. Spring is almost here, and if we don't get some late snow, or at least a hard frost, he'll be forced to lay off staff. He's only trying to make an honest living, but not everyone shares his idiosyncratic views. He wrote a letter to the paper, suggesting that our senior citizens could give the local economy a much-needed boost simply by turning their central heating down by a few degrees. It didn't seem much to ask, yet he's been getting hate-mail ever since. Someone should take him to one side and tell him to forget that 'two for the price of one' offer, as well, before he upsets the whole village. He's losing his grip; maybe he's been in the funeral business too long.

While most folk in Litterdale can see no further than the next rainy day, Bill, our tourism officer, is already dreaming of long summer days. It's his remit to persuade people to spend some of their leisure hours and spending money in and around the valley. To this end he's putting the finishing touches to a glossy new brochure aimed at getting holiday-makers to think: 'Hmmm, Litterdale, that sounds like the place for me.'

During the winter months, Bill has attended some marketing seminars: confrontational days full of sales stratagems, brand awareness and team-building exercises. After all that positive dynamism, it was quite a relief to get back to the relative peace and quiet of his little office in Litterdale. If Bill has learned anything from these gatherings, it's the need to identify, and then ruthlessly exploit, Litterdale's 'unique selling points'.

Maybe we're biased, but we think the valley has just about everything that makes life worth living. Since the stage-coaches stopped running, Litterdale has become a pleasant little backwater, not really on the way to anywhere. And if the local farmers delight in misdirecting lost motorists, well, let's be charitable and suggest that it's a perk of an increasingly stressful job. But we don't have a spectacular waterfall, or show-caves, or a museum devoted to sculptures made entirely of ear wax. In truth, the attraction of Litterdale is that it isn't so special. It's homely, comfortable and welcoming, the touristic equivalent of a fireside rug and a mug of

Horlicks. Visitors know what they're going to find ('A view, a brew and a loo', as Bill acknowledges in one of his more cynical moments) and they all seem to go home happy. It won't be too long before the first visitors arrive, and our love/hate relationship will begin again.

SPRING

It's Spring in Litterdale and the sap is rising. Young men think of love, or lust, or at least a hot date for Saturday night. Mother Nature is showing the way, by giving us the birds and bees as role models. Okay, bees may be conspicuous by their absence, but the birds, at least, are busy building their nests. Blue tits investigate nooks and crannies. Rooks make running repairs to the same wind-tossed, tree-top nests they've used for years. Jackdaws display either stupidity or the patience of Job, by dropping twigs down chimney pots. Sooner or later one twig will lodge in the flue, and a second and a third, to provide a platform to support a nest (and, for the householder, a hearth full of twigs).

You can almost hear the hum of testosterone, as young lads, wreathed in clouds of cheap cologne, try to impress the local lasses with feats of strength. Yes, love may make the world go round, but it's lust that lubricates the moving parts.

Litterdale's senior citizens, in contrast, have largely come to terms with their waning powers, with no more than a shrug of the shoulders and the occasional twinge of regret on seeing a well-turned ankle. In the lottery of love they've long since cashed in their chips. The flame of passion burns less brightly as the years slip by;

sometimes the pilot light goes out altogether. The old folks look elsewhere for excitement these days: a cup of weak tea, a trip to the garden centre, another punt on some hopeless nag in the 2.30 at Wincarnis.

Norman's at that difficult age, when a man has to prioritise. Should he continue his search for a relationship more meaningful than that between a man and his newsagent? Is it realistic now to hope for the love of a good woman, or should he just bow to the inevitable and settle instead for the companionship of a gerbil?

At three o'clock in the afternoon, on a chilly March day, Litterdale's football team is being cheered onto the muddy pitch by a few loyal fans. So few, indeed, that the team has been informed, over the tannoy, of changes to the crowd. The spectators blow on their hands, for warmth, and rub them together. Older guys test the credulity of the younger fans by recalling the Ice Age ('Now that *was* cold…') when the Arctic weather brought such chaos to the fixture list that the pools panel had to meet for three million Saturdays in a row.

Litterdale Rovers are known in the league – the Vauxhall Cars Beezer Homes Sherpa Van Division (North) – as a sleeping dwarf. The manager – it's just Norman in a camel-hair coat – had to take drastic action to turn the season around. When he swapped the entire squad for two bags of Cheesy Wotsits, footballing pundits reckoned he'd got the best of the bargain.

The new crop of players have mostly been plucked from park football. Still unaccustomed to the luxury of real goalposts they have to be dissuaded from throwing their jackets down on the grass before the start of play. The captain picks his team in traditional fashion ('one potato, two potato…') which is why the scrawny players with glasses warm the substitutes' benches for game after game.

When the sports reporter from the *Litterdale Times* – it's just Scoop in a deerstalker hat – says that the players are 'a good advertisement for the game', he is merely pointing out that they are covered from head to foot in sponsors' logos. Norman is trying to adopt the system of man-to-man marketing that has served Derby County so well. The team's strip is now being sponsored, appropriately enough, by a local knacker's yard. To the question 'How's the team performing?' there's only one answer: 'Offal'. Whenever they get injured, the players are contracted to crawl in front of an advertising hoarding, in case the photographer from the *Litterdale Times* has remembered to put a film in his camera. Yes, the financial situation at the club really is that dire.

Norman likes to use a bit of sports psychology, to boost his players' motivation. Nevertheless, when it comes to getting the required result, no-one's yet come up with a better strategy than locking the players in a small room for twenty minutes and hurling abuse at them. The church bells are chiming three o'clock, so the talking has to stop. Before taking his place on the bench, Norman cups his hands and bellows his final encouragement: 'The grass is green, the paint is fresh… so get out there and bloody play.'

New arrivals in Litterdale always attract attention. Whether we're neighbourly, or just plain nosy, is open to question. No matter, we'll accept any excuse to extend the hand of friendship, and check out the newcomers' taste in soft furnishings.

We were flabbergasted when Primrose Cottage found a buyer. It had been standing empty for years, due to a catalogue of structural defects, and every year that passed only made it less likely to sell. It had been on the market for so long that the 'For Sale' sign had almost disappeared beneath an exuberant growth of ivy. The winter winds had loosened roof-slates; leaf-choked gutters had started to sag like a saddle-backed horse. The front garden, once a colourful profusion of lupins and hollyhocks, had become over-run with weeds.

Primrose Cottage has oodles of what the estate agent calls 'character'. The villagers, with a more prosaic turn of phrase, prefer 'semi-derelict'. You wouldn't touch the place with a six-foot barge-pole… unless you wanted to be the proud owner of a six-foot barge-pole with dry rot. Convinced that there's a mug born every minute, the vendor continued to bide his time. So it seemed like Christmas had come early when Mandy arrived in Litterdale and immediately fell in love with the place. Love is blind, a condition that's not improved by wearing rose-coloured glasses.

Mandy has a trusting nature, and she doesn't like to be on the receiving end of bad news. The surveyor's report made such depressing reading that she threw it straight in the bin. She backed her feminine intuition instead, which proved to be an expensive mistake. As pretty as it is, Primrose Cottage is a black hole of a house; it could suck in as much money as anyone would think of throwing at it, and still be barely habitable. But Mandy had a warm feeling about the house; it had a welcoming aura. All it needed, she reckoned, was a lick of paint, a wind-chime and a few house plants. A recent divorce settlement had left her with money to spend, so she bought the place for cash. Unfortunately, that warm feeling turned out to be nothing more than heartburn.

Mandy and her daughter moved into Primrose Cottage, thus beginning a battle with subsidence and rotting timbers that has continued ever since. It's what can happen when you take decisions based on something as insubstantial as the turn of a tarot card or the juxtaposition of the planets. Mandy, you see, is a new-age believer; she's ransacked the wisdom of the East to assemble a pick-and-mix portfolio of irrationality.

She missed the explicit warnings in the surveyor's report, despite them being flagged up with a fluorescent highlighter pen. Yet she's happy to espouse any old mumbo-jumbo, as long as it's dressed up in Eastern robes. The more unlikely the better. She's a big fan of Feng Shui, the ancient art of creating harmony in our homes. Why bother wrestling with the questions that have taxed mankind for centuries, when all we need to do, apparently, is to rearrange the furniture? Some directives seem obvious. Don't use a powerful Hoover near a long-haired dog. Get rid of those unsightly piles of Feng Shui books that are cluttering up the place. And if none of this stuff works there's always the English version of Feng Shui, which consists of tidying up.

With evangelical conviction, Mandy is trying to introduce some of her new-age ideas to the good folk of Litterdale. Having perused half a dozen *Readers Digest* articles on topics as wide-ranging as reflexology, past-life regression and knitting with dog hair, she feels eminently qualified to enlighten us.

Litterdale is a traditional kind of place, and the new-age phenomenon has largely passed us by. We don't rush to embrace every new fad and fashion, like they do in town. Most of the villagers wouldn't know whether shiatsu was a massage technique or a breed of cat. Some of us are only just coming to terms with decimal currency and pain-free dentistry. It's not that we're necessarily resistant to change. And we're not immune to gullibility either. After all, a recent pyramid-selling scam only faltered when every villager was trying to sell overpriced household detergents to everybody else.

Yes, we'd like to believe in all this new-age claptrap, we really would. It's tempting to believe that our misfortunes might be due to celestial alignments, rather than our own fecklessness. But the fact is that we have a more pragmatic approach to reading the future. We have the weather forecast, of course, and we can learn a lot from perusing the auction prices. In any case, the farmers have a pretty good idea what they'll be doing tomorrow, and the day after, and the day after that... because it'll be much the same as what they did yesterday.

The good folk of Litterdale are baffled when Mandy presses one of her pastel-coloured business cards ('Meaningless affirmations, your place or mine') into their reluctant hands. It's mildly disconcerting to hear about other worlds, distant galaxies and alternative realities, especially from a woman who has difficulties reading a road-map. We'd think twice before making an appointment for a tarot card reading with Mandy, in the same way that we'd think twice before hiring the services of a fingerless carpenter.

Genuine evidence of Mandy's powers of clairvoyance are not easy to find. And, let's face it, we're willing to be convinced. Advance notification of those six lottery numbers would make a convincing start. But Mandy gets crotchety when her powers of foresight are questioned. 'Look, I can just *sense* these things, all right?'

It's good to see the smoke curling lazily from the chimneys of Primrose Cottage once again, and we hope that Mandy will settle to life in the village. We hope, too, that she'll find a few paying customers for her brand of oven-ready platitudes; it looks like she'll be needing the money.

Down at Litterdale's compact cricket ground, Dennis is marshalling his troops for yet another assault on the league title. Following last season's disappointment at collecting the wooden spoon, he has made some dramatic changes to the personnel. Now, having brought in seven new players, he reckons he's only three men short of a half-decent team.

Dennis wants to deliver his traditional pre-game pep-talk, so the team has convened in the pavilion. That's what we call it, though it's actually just a shabby pile of breeze-blocks and chipboard, with all the architectural allure of an allotment shed. It's been put together, over the years, in piecemeal fashion – sprouting another lean-to annexe whenever we needed somewhere to keep the mower, make tea, or site a rudimentary toilet. If we carried on building in this way, we'd soon have a shanty town.

The roller stays outside, padlocked to a tree. If anyone wants to go to the trouble of stealing it, they're very welcome. It's big, heavy and almost seized up with rust. We're sick of the sight of it. We've pushed the damned thing up and down the pitch for years, to no apparent effect. Despite our best efforts, the wicket is as unpredictable as ever. Batsmen don't know whether the next ball will whistle past their ears or shoot along the ground. Batting can be an excruciating business.

Dennis crosses his legs gingerly as he thinks back to when he acquired his first cricket protector. He was just a lad, glad to be getting a game or two for the team, but embarrassed to be stuffing a folded-up copy of the *Daily Mirror* down his trousers before he went in to bat. He paid a visit to the sports shop in town, but became flustered on finding a woman behind the counter. Tongue-tied and red-faced, Dennis gesticulated towards a display cabinet with one hand, and proffered a clammy palmful of small change with the other. He left, hurriedly, with the cheapest cricket box in the shop. It proved to be a false economy; the few pennies he saved almost cost him his manhood.

It was shaped like half an avocado pear (the box, that is, not his manhood) and was moulded in pink plastic. The viciously sharp, unpadded edges should have made Dennis think twice before parting with his pocket money. However, it wasn't until he faced some seriously fast bowling that the box's deficiencies became painfully apparent. A direct hit with a cricket ball had the same effect on Dennis's groin (I'll put it as delicately as I can) that a pastry-cutter has when pushed into freshly-kneaded dough. Forty years on, the memory can still bring tears to his eyes and a flush to his cheeks.

There's a poisonous atmosphere in the cricket pavilion today: a heady pot-pourri of sweat, fungus, unwashed socks, cheap deodorant, horse liniment, athletes foot lotion, talcum powder, mildew, hand-rolled tobacco and unrestrained flatulence. It's gloomy too; the grubby windows are shrouded with spiders' webs, where the trussed-up corpses of unwary flies are marinating gently. A prawn salad sandwich, thoughtlessly abandoned under a bench last September, is giving off a pale phosphorescent glow. Scientists seeking the perfect conditions for the propagation of virulent bacteria need look no further than Litterdale's premier sporting facility.

The cricket hut is essentially a masculine environment. Women, even those blessed with strong constitutions, would no sooner cross the threshold on match days than wear jam in their hair. In any case the wives and girlfriends of the Litterdale XI have better things to do with their leisure hours than watch a bunch of overweight men chase a red ball around a field.

It was different in the old days. There used to be an inexhaustible supply of good-hearted women in the village who'd be only too happy to make sandwiches, bake scones and mash the tea. To compensate for the inevitable bruises, visiting teams knew there would always be a good spread whenever they came to Litterdale. Nowadays, alas, the players have to do everything themselves. It means that 'tea' is nothing more than a catering pack of salt and vinegar crisps and a few debilitating cans of industrial-strength lager.

No matter; the sun is shining today on Litterdale's cricket ground, and the players are easing themselves into the new season with a strict regime of isometric inertia. The only member of the team who loosens up before a game is our wicket-keeper; he's the only one with muscles. As he straps neoprene supports around creaking elbows and knees, he appears to be built out of spare parts from a breaker's yard.

While the rest of the team sit around drinking beer and cadging roll-ups, he performs inelegant and painful-looking callisthenics. Consequently he is the only one who ever gets injured before the game: a regular litany of sprains and pulls, requiring yet more liniment and support garments. It's a downward spiral of exercise, injury and visits to the surgical supplies shop that will end, to no one's great surprise, with him falling to bits altogether.

The smell of new-mown grass has the same effect on club cricketers as a boat of steaming gravy has on the Bisto Kids. It makes us close our eyes, adopt angelic expressions and sniff the air. You only need to look at the paunches on display to realise that the members of the Litterdale XI still have an appetite for the game. Or maybe just an appetite. The first swallows are here, so we know that summer can't be far behind. Following Dennis's inspirational team-talk the players take to the field with confidence: a confidence that lasts right up to the moment that the umpire says 'Play' and a new season gets underway.

SUMMER

Everyone has their favourite time of the year, and in a straw poll there would be plenty of votes for autumnal tints, an old-fashioned Christmas and the candyfloss colours of springtime blossom. But early summer would get my vote. A warm, balmy June day is, I would suggest, about as good as the English climate gets. The Litterdale landscape looks serene. The first five months of the year are just dress rehearsals for this; yes, June is the finished article.

The more irritating members of the insect world have yet to muster in numbers. And even the grumpiest of our senior citizens won't begin to complain about the heat for another fortnight. It will be at least a month before the greens in the landscape lose their vivid intensity. Two months before the hay is gathered in, and the Peakland scene is redrawn in desiccated sepia tones. For now, though, we walk around in shirt-sleeves, enjoying the sunshine and the cottage gardens bursting with flowers.

Bill is reviewing all his strategies for attracting visitors to the area. As slogans go, 'Come to Litterdale, You'll Like It' is beginning to look a little lame. He sucks the end of his pencil, in search of inspiration, and stares at the ceiling. He's looking for the holy grail of tourism: a slogan so meaningless and enigmatic that it will attract visitors in droves. Suddenly the light bulb above his head comes on and Bill scribbles furiously on the back of an envelope, before settling back in his revolving chair to admire his handiwork. 'Lovely Litterdale, where the present meets the past and makes an elegant swallow dive into the future.' Yes, it's a masterpiece.

In an effort to pad out this year's tourist brochure, Bill looked for any literary connections that Litterdale may have had. But, drawing a blank, he had to kick-start the new campaign with a harmless white lie. Charles Dickens stayed in Litterdale – that's what the brochure says – and he may have written some of his novels here. An intriguing thought, of course, but still only that… a thought. In truth, Charles Dickens came to this little backwater just the once, and merely for a discreet consultation about an embarrassing rash.

That might have marked the end of Bill's career as a teller of tall tales. Except that he's just received a fax from his boss, congratulating him on his skills at unearthing previously unknown facts about Litterdale, and ending up with 'Can we please have some more?' A march of two thousand miles begins with but a single step, so people say. And Bill is taking his first tentative steps down the perfumed path that leads to the eternal bonfire. The trouble with a little white lie is where it leads you.

This is why, on a sunny day in June, Bill is ensconced in Litterdale's lending library, leafing through the books in the 'local history' section. If anything of importance ever happened in the village, he has yet to find any tangible evidence of it. At this rate, he'll have to harness all his powers of imagination, and next year's tourism brochure will be filed under 'fiction'.

The landlord of the Swan rubs his hands together expectantly when he sees carloads of day-trippers descending on the village. He grits his teeth and forces a smile as his pub fills up with noisy kids. Knowing what the mark-up is on a small glass of lemonade, he's prepared to put up with the inconvenience. At the Fox, on the other hand, children aren't welcome until they're tall enough to stand at the bar and buy a round like everybody else. And the only concession to the tourist trade, here at Litterdale's less salubrious alehouse, is a lacklustre campaign to bring back spittoons.

Across the village green, at Primrose Cottage, Mandy is trying to tap into the lucrative bed and breakfast market. Since Litterdale folk seem disinclined to pay for astrological forecasts, she needs the extra money to do repairs on her tumbledown house. It's a heap, frankly; you could double its value simply by screwing a satellite dish to the wall. So Mandy is offering what she calls 'self-centred accommodation', aimed at people so narcissistic that they won't notice the squalor in which she lives. In addition to basic bed and breakfast, she's throwing in a free tarot-card reading.

Primrose Cottage appears in the new accommodation guide, but only as the village's sole representative in the hastily concocted 'cheap and cheerful' section. And Bill couldn't, in all honesty, award the place any stars for service or amenities. Telling bare-faced lies about Litterdale is one thing, but he can't recommend Primrose Cottage to any visitors who aren't up to date with their rabies shots.

Mandy spends so much time meditating that mundane chores remain undone, sometimes for weeks. Meditating is what she calls it, anyway, though to most Litterdale folk it looks more like sitting around, doing nothing. What kind of meditation includes daytime TV? Housework is not Mandy's forté (even her laugh is infectious), and visitors are wise to sniff the milk before they pour it on their organic muesli.

The first thing that guests are likely to see, as they walk inside the house, is an over-laden cat-litter tray. Sensible visitors understand immediately that they've made a big mistake, offer some excuse and make their escape. After five minutes at Mandy's, fresh air never smelled so good. The turmoil even extends beyond her front door. Litterdale's accommodation guide suggests that the garden of Primrose Cottage looks a picture. Sadly, it's a picture by Hieronymous Bosch.

✳

It's July in Litterdale. High summer when, according to that hoary old joke, thousands come here for the solitude. At times this pretty Peakland village can seem unbearably overcrowded. Despite all the best efforts of the National Park Authority to get them to use public transport, visitors are reluctant to leave their cars at home. Inspired, perhaps, by the name of our village, they load up their cars with litter, and leave it here as a souvenir of their visit. Yes, they like to make their presence felt – with the squeal of balding tyres on hot Tarmac and the relentless boom, boom, boom of in-car stereo systems, cranked up to migraine-inducing volume. If they were subjected to this kind of noise during working hours, their shop stewards would be clamouring for compensation.

It seems a little strange to us that so many townies come to Litterdale, ostensibly to escape the noise, clutter and pollution of our northern cities, only to bring their own noise, clutter and pollution with them. But even on the sunniest of summer weekends, when Litterdale is throbbing with visitors, it's easy to escape the crowds. As locals are well aware (and the more discerning visitors, too), the noise quells to an unobtrusive murmur within ten minutes of lacing up the walking boots and taking any of the delightful green lanes that radiate away from the village.

Some people, sadly, find the countryside unnerving. They feel more comfortable with unresponsive concrete beneath their feet. They prefer the regimented rows of streets and houses in an A-Z street atlas to the sinuous curves of the contour lines on an Ordnance Survey map (which, in any case, they can neither read nor fold). The thought of going without such aspects of city life as lottery tickets and southern fried chicken, even for half a day, seems to fill them with a nameless dread. Worst of all, they are convinced they will get hopelessly lost. Yes, landscapes that beckon seasoned walkers can hold a multitude of terrors for townies.

Midsummer is the ideal time to show these benighted souls that the Peakland landscape can be invitingly benign. The grassy slopes and dry stone walls create ever-changing patterns of light and colour that never fail to fascinate. Even when walkers crest a hill, the breeze that brushes their faces is as warm as a kiss. Bare trees aren't being bent by savage winter winds. Blizzards are unlikely. In short, there's little to disturb the most timid of walkers.

The rivers around Litterdale meander unhurriedly through ancient valleys of limestone crags, screes and moss-covered rocks. No wonder Izaak Walton was so enchanted by their clear waters. Sulphur-yellow wagtails chase each other along the water-margins. Dippers slide effortlessly beneath the surface. Startled moorhens skitter into the reeds. Dragonflies flash by: vivid blurs of electric greens and blues. The air is still and soporific. Stand on an old packhorse bridge. Feel the warmth and texture of weathered stone beneath your palms. Gaze down into the water. Watch the waterweed waving, hypnotically, like manes of hair, and trout basking lazily in the shallows. Let your problems melt away; there'll be time enough to deal with them once you get home. Slip into the silence, with the same ease as the dipper, leaving barely a ripple.

There are many kinds of silence. There's the embarrassed silence you get at breakfast in a seaside boarding house, which only makes the tinkling of tea-cups seem deafening by comparison. There's the blissful silence when a car alarm finally drains the battery and whines to a merciful stop. There's the brooding silence at the heart of a marriage when love has died. But best of all are those moments when the chatter of the mind abates, when memories, ambitions and everyday worries evaporate like puddles on a hot pavement, and, however briefly, you are blessed with stillness.

It gets ever harder to hear the silence through the crackle and static of everyday life. We rush through the working week as though it were a race, hardly daring to stop, look and listen, in case – gulp – we discover we've wasted our best years doing something monumentally pointless, like being an estate agent. Then we fill our weekends with so many activities, that leisure, too, begins to resemble work. It seems we're upset by silence. Even when they're not playing Musak, supermarkets routinely broadcast 'white noise': a low hum, like the noise a fridge makes, that puts us into a relaxed, more spendthrift mood.

But the silence in the countryside isn't just an absence of noise. The sweet song of the skylark and the bubbling cry of the curlew are just two of the sounds that don't disrupt the stillness. In contrast, there are quieter sounds that *do*: radios, mobile phones, even the insistent beeping of digital watches – dividing up the hours into convenient chunks for those who believe that most mendacious of equations, that time is money.

Many people spend their free time playing shoot-'em-up computer games, or watching furiously paced films featuring men in dirty vests outrunning fireballs. These people will probably watch more senseless violence in the course of an hour than you'd witness in the taproom of the Fox over, oh, an entire Bank Holiday weekend. And here in Litterdale we can go for weeks without experiencing anything more cataclysmic than a chip-pan fire in the pub's kitchen. People who are over-stimulated, like children who quaff too many fizzy drinks, need bigger and bigger doses of eye-popping sensation. They are unlikely to respond to the quiet lure of the countryside, where excitements are subtle rather than blatant. Where you can stand on a hilltop and gaze across the patchwork of fields to the village you call home.

Can something this beautiful really be the result of a chaotic accident? Just the chance collision of particles all those eons ago? The 'big bang' that movie directors seem so determined to replicate on film. Looking at Litterdale, spread out in the valley like a picnic arranged on a cloth of green gingham, it's not hard to believe that there is, after all, a celestial hand on the tiller.

✳

It's August in Litterdale. We are in the middle of the school holidays when, with weeks still to go before the autumn term begins, parents are already running out of things to keep their kids amused. 'I'm bored' is an oft-heard cry from children whose first act, on waking up to a sunny summer's day, is to switch on the TV for an hour or two of mindless cartoons.

It's not easy being a parent, of course. There's a conspiracy of silence surrounding the whole business. After all, if young couples knew the whole truth about parenting, the human race would die out within a few generations. Some of them imagine that the most painful part of parenting will be stepping on a Lego brick with bare feet. In which case, they'll get a nasty surprise. That's why the process of conceiving babies is designed to be such fun. We are seduced into thinking that child-rearing will, in its own way, be equally rewarding. Our children will be tiny versions of ourselves, we imagine, to whom we can impart all our skills and wisdom. But those few minutes of fun come at a fearful price, as parenting takes its toll, and prove beyond all doubt that God does indeed have a sense of humour.

It's not so easy being a kid either. Men and women can behave pretty irrationally once they become parents. It begins with something just mildly hypocritical like telling their kids to 'Do as I say, not as I do', but it gets weirder. Parents warn children about the dangers of playing with matches. Then, every autumn, explosives are openly on sale in every sweet shop.

Kids receive dire warnings about talking to strangers. Then, during December, they're encouraged to sit on the knee of a portly man with a red suit, a false beard and halitosis who, almost by definition, is unemployable for the rest of the year. And why do parents wait until they go shopping in order to to smack their kids? 'I'll give you something to bawl about,' they yell at their inconsolable offspring, when it's pretty obvious the kids have something to bawl about already. Yes, it all goes to show that parents are the very people who shouldn't be allowed to have children.

Kids from the suburbs are cosetted: driven to school every morning, and driven home again every afternoon. Then they're kept indoors, because danger lurks outside. But children are at less risk from the bogey-men that haunt their parents' nightmares than they are from the parents themselves. Sad, but true.

Litterdale, in contrast, is a grand place to bring up kids. There's space to kick a football around, without fear of breaking a window. If they want to set up their cricket stumps on the village green, there's no officious park-keeper to chase them away. Whenever they want a bike-ride, there are miles of green lanes to explore. Instead of being confined to a rusty swing in some back-yard, the youngsters of Litterdale have access to what is, effectively, the biggest back garden that any kid could want.

Children need a safe and secure home-life, of course they do, but they need adventure too. And not just the mind-numbing violence of the latest computer games. So it gladdens the heart to see a posse of kids heading off on their bikes, with a rucksack full of sandwiches and bottles of pop. It takes me straight back to my own childhood in Litterdale, when the summers stretched out luxuriantly, like an endless red carpet.

For a year or two I was quite happy grubbing about in the garden: getting dirty, seeing what worms tasted like. Regular kid stuff, but tame. My first attempt at running away from home, for example, was stymied by not being allowed to cross the road on my own. Life became more adventurous once I'd joined a gang. Living in a small Peakland village, we took our inspiration from Enid Blyton's Famous Five rather than the street gangs of the Lower East Side of Los Angeles. So we comprised a particularly unfearsome bunch of desperados. But what we lacked in weaponry, we made up for in resourcefulness.

We built dens in the woods: artless clumps of brushwood to the casual observer, but impregnable fortresses to us. We were prepared, at any moment, to be attacked by wholly imaginary foes: difficult adversaries to defend against. We rooted out crime, even where there was none, and investigated all kinds of suspicious happenings. We found a car parked up in a remote lane, with its windows steamed up. We heard screams, but that was only *after* we'd peered in. We found a man digging in the woods. Assuming, naturally enough, that he was burying a body in a shallow grave, we shadowed his every move. The alternative scenario – that he was just collecting bags of leaf-mould for his garden – seemed far-fetched.

Our gang became quorate, in a strict Enid Blyton sense, by the addition of Kim, a playful Labrador. Though enthusiastic, she didn't seem to understand the role we had earmarked for her, which was to initiate all kinds of new adventures. As loyal fans of *Lassie* and *Rin Tin Tin* on TV, we knew just how much fun a dog could be. So whenever Kim wagged her tail we were ready to say those immortal words: 'Look, I think Kim's trying to tell us something. She seems to want us to follow her down to the old barn.'

Ignoring what she really wanted – a tummy-rub, or a tin of butcher's tripe, we would all troop after her. Not to buried treasure, alas. Not to the scene of some unspeakable crime which we, and not some bungling policemen, would have managed to solve. Not to the old quarry where we might have saved from certain death some hapless rambler who was hanging by his fingertips from the edge of a a precipice. No, Kim would generally lead us to a dead sheep, quietly putrefying in the corner of a field. 'Good dog,' we'd say, not wanting to hurt her feelings, but not thinking too clearly either. Which taught Kim one thing only: that we wanted her to find more dead sheep Ah, yes, happy days.

✳

AUTUMN

With summer coming to an end, the Litterdale Show is here again. It may seem strange that something as old-fashioned as a village show has managed to survive into the twenty-first century. But it has, and that's something to be grateful for. We're not averse to change; we just like to handle it at our own pace, little by little. No sudden upheavals, if you please. So in the main tent we can still admire the displays of fruit, vegetables and home-made produce. The competition categories remain reassuringly traditional; so it's 'three English apples', 'six broad beans' and 'pot of home-made lemon curd' rather than 'three mobile phones' or 'six website portals'.

The children of Litterdale still exhibit woven samplers, and examples of their neatest handwriting. Their models are made, in best *Blue Peter* style, out of toilet rolls, washing-up bottles and sticky-back plastic. We still have the 'guess the weight of the cake' competition, though this year it nearly had to be cancelled when a goat ate the cake. It took a sudden and triumphant leap of imagination to change the name of the competition to 'guess the weight of the goat'.

When we see the marquees going up in Potter's Field, we feel a sense of community and continuity that stretches back as far as anyone can remember. Yes, to rub shoulders with the crowds on show day is to reaffirm some of the fundamental values of village life. And a wander around Litterdale Show offers intriguing hints about the way that country life is heading.

Many people find their way to Fred's stall by smell alone. His roast pork sandwiches are world famous. World famous around Litterdale, anyway. But this year he's giving concerned carnivores a chance to salve their consciences, by offering 'conservation grade' meat. His customers will feel better, apparently, knowing that the animals they eat have enjoyed meaningful lives.

Each 'conservation grade' cut of meat carries a label, giving a brief history of each pig's life, pet-name (if any) and those endearing characteristics that had marked it out from the common herd. The 'conservation grade' charter promises that the animal will never have been spoken to in a gruff or threatening manner, and will have enjoyed a close physical relationship with the partner of its choice.

The end, when it came, is vouchsafed to have been both quick and painless: a lethal injection administered to the soothing strain of Mantovani strings. Deceased animals are given a short, non-denominational funeral service, before ending up on Fred's barbecue spit. It's a good idea, of course it is. But has anyone polled Fred's pigs about what they might want? Option a: enjoy a long, happy life and die of old age. Or option b: end up in a hot roast pork and stuffing sandwich on show day. Just a thought...

Livestock of a rather more animated kind is paraded around the show ring. The farmers may take a professional interest in the proceedings; for the rest of us, however, one sheep looks very much like another. And this year, bizarrely, it seems we've been proved right. The judges have decided not to award any rosettes at all for sheep, on the basis that most of the entrants appear to have been cloned. We're not too impressed with cloning, if truth be told. Let's face facts: if the scientists were really so clever, they'd be busy cloning animals that fetch rather better prices at auction. Or thoroughbred race-horses. We don't need any more sheep; in the current economic climate the farmers can hardly give them away.

Stalls that used to sell undemonstrative walking clothes – scratchy socks, corduroy trousers and anoraks made of old-fashioned water-absorbent fabrics – are going upmarket. Smooth-talking salesmen are persuading people who never walk in anything heavier than a light drizzle to fork out £200 for a cagoule that not merely keeps torrential rain out but 'breathes' too. For that sort of money I'd want a jacket that could do more than breathe; I'd want it to talk and perform card tricks too. But that's just me.

One stall is devoted to the contentious delights of rural pursuits: 'field sports' to those who follow the hounds, 'blood sports' to those who take a more sanguine view. You can buy picturesque place-mats – featuring hunt sabateurs being hounded over hill and dale – and sign the petition. *'We, the undersigned, wish to maintain our traditional right to hunt foxes. If these animals weren't hunted, the delicate ecological balance would be upset. We are conservationists. We love foxes. And the way we express our love for these fascinating animals is by hunting them down and killing them.'* My own opinion, for what it's worth, is that we should stop hunting foxes and start hunting football hooligans instead. Imagine, two social problems solved at one stroke.

The farmers are taking a more than casual interest in a stall selling perfumes their wives keep wanting for Christmas, but are just too expensive in the shops. They now realise, from bitter experience, that a set of matching saucepans, even ones with floral patterns, do not constitute a proper Christmas present. All the famous names are here, at prices that seem too good to be true. Calvin Klone, now that sounds familiar. 'The perfect gift', as the stallholder points out, with the predictable caveat: 'It's almost authentic.'

The high street banks like to make an appearance on show day if only to remind villagers what a high street bank actually looks like. But memories fade; did banks always have a wheel at each corner? The next generation of Litterdale folk will grow up thinking that banks are like Fred's roast pork stall: only open for business on show day. We'll be back to stuffing money under the mattress. We're all going to be banking on the internet, apparently. But online banking just isn't an option for the more Luddite residents of Litterdale, who are still unsure how to programme a video recorder.

For years the country was the holy grail for over-stressed city dwellers. As they gazed out of their airless offices, over streets choked with cars and robotic commuters, they dreamed of a simpler life, an escape from the rat race. A cottage with roses round the door. Maypole dancing on the green. Warm beer. Village cricket. Rosy-cheeked yokels, in touch with nature and the seasons. All the things that John Major once rhapsodised about. As the paperwork piled up, many an office drone was pacified by this sort of bucolic reverie.

As fantasies went, they were harmless enough, like the thought of sharing a Jacuzzi with the new girl from accounts. And as long as they remained fantasies, all was well. But every now and again some frustrated pen-pusher would make it over the razor wire and, with family in tow, relocate to a place like Litterdale. Typically, it would take just a few weeks to realise the magnitude of their mistake. Life in Litterdale can be rich and rewarding, it's true, but only for people with realistic expectations. Those who know the country only from the pages of glossy magazines are heading for disappointment.

Here in Litterdale we've seen these families come, and we've seen them go. Their fantasies having burst like soap bubbles, they put their houses up for sale, take a loss on their investment, and scurry back to the city. They are left with traumatic memories and a handful of bitter tales with which to enliven their dinner parties. 'Country life?' they'll say, with a shudder of remembrance. 'It was a nightmare.'

Occasionally, the incomers are made of sterner stuff. Violet springs to mind. Having taken early retirement, she decided to move to Litterdale and shake us up a bit. Having been the headmistress of a posh girls' school, she was accustomed to getting her own way. Worse, Violet addressed everyone in Litterdale as though they too were naughty schoolgirls. When a large woman with a braying voice ordered us to 'Tuck your shirt in', or 'Stop slouching', the memories of our own schooldays, however distant, came flooding back. In a manner that would make Ivan Pavlov smile in recognition, we jumped to attention, instantly.

Impervious to criticism, and unassailed by doubt, Violet devoted her retirement years to the thankless task of saving us from ourselves, by pointing out our many shortcomings. At a time of life when many people would be glad to slow down a bit, she seemed to be blessed, or cursed, with boundless energy. Having given our village a long, hard look, she decided we could all do a great deal better. Aspects of everyday life in Litterdale that hadn't changed for generations came under her harsh scrutiny.

To our knowledge, no-one had ever complained about the church bells before. In truth, they sound more percussive than melodic since the bell-tower was struck by lightning, but they do their job of rounding up the faithful on the day of rest. In recent years, with congregations declining, the bells reminded forgetful cooks to put the joint in the oven. Now that most people don't go to church – or sit down to Sunday lunch, for that matter – the bells remain as an inoffensive anachronism. You get used to them; after a few years you hardly notice them at all. Yet Violet was moved to pen a letter to the *Litterdale Times*. She complained that the bells brought on her migraine and suggested, in the strongest possible terms, that they be silenced.

Grateful that he didn't have to write all the letters himself, Scoop printed her missive in full – which only encouraged her to vent her spleen on a regular basis. From Violet's pen came a steady stream of purple prose, griping about the way we live in Litterdale.

Despite her house being called, tellingly, The Old Schoolhouse, Violet grumbled about the lack of amenities in the village. The irony was entirely lost on her. She complained that Litterdale's local shops were closing, even though she only ever went in for a newspaper and the occasional carton of milk. She would drive twenty miles to an out-of-town hypermarket, for her weekly shop, and twenty miles back. The few pounds she saved on her grocery bill were spent instead on petrol. And then she'd moan about being held up by a herd of udder-heavy cows, as they dawdled along narrow roads on their way to the milking parlour. The lack of public transport in rural areas irked her, even though she would never dream of catching a bus herself.

Once she'd pointed an accusing finger at our local farmers, we knew we were heading for a showdown. What got Violet's goat was the mess they made. Piles of muck all over the place. Old tractors abandoned to rain, rust and brambles. Dry stone walls repaired artlessly with rubble. Violet wanted the farmers to tidy up after themselves, so that the countryside resembled more closely the suburbia with which she was more familiar. She didn't like the way the countryside smelled, either, and accused her neighbours of dumping loads of sinus-clearing slurry upwind of her new conservatory.

The farmers of Litterdale don't like being told what to do at the best of times. And these most certainly are not the best of times. It's bad enough when some gormless official, armed with a clipboard, a GCSE in sociology and a sense of his own importance, starts sniffing around the farmyard. But being chastised by an uppity incomer was the last straw. Farmers may be slow to show their emotions, but once roused to anger they can work up quite a head of steam.

No-one knows exactly what happened next. Or, if they do, they're not telling. All we know for certain is that Violet was too traumatised to put pen to paper ever again. We tried to reassure her that *everyone's* house gets fire-bombed from time to time. But maybe we didn't sound convincing enough.

It's November, the month when the members of the Litterdale and District Natural History Society traditionally hold their annual general meeting. Essentially a rather staid occasion, the proceedings are sometimes enlivened by a slide show about dung beetles, or the presentation of a paper about the flora of Derbyshire's railway sidings.

The officials are re-elected routinely on a show of hands; being on the committee of the society is generally regarded as a job for life. The secretary reads the minutes of the last meeting. If, through error or a sense of mischief, he were to read the minutes of, say, the AGM of 1950, it's unlikely that anyone would notice. The treasurer presents accounts that, like Mr Micawber's oft-quoted advice to David Copperfield, are a model of fiscal probity. No treasurer has ever decamped with the contents of the society's bank account, to start a new life in Buenos Aires. In short, an AGM holds few surprises; there's nothing to keep the more elderly members awake beyond the first few items on the agenda.

But there's an air of urgency surrounding this year's AGM. Despite being in existence for more than a century, and having survived two world wars, the society is in crisis. Important decisions need to be taken, decisions that will affect all the members. But will enough of them turn out on a Monday evening in November to make a quorum? This is the society's problem, in a nutshell. It's ironic that apathy may succeed where the Luftwaffe's bombs failed. Having brought the plight of so many endangered species to our attention, the society itself is now in danger of extinction.

Yes, the Litterdale and District Natural History Society has reached this landmark year in a poor state of health. The members are dying off in such numbers that the monthly meetings are more like wakes. And the youngsters just aren't interested in keeping the tradition going. Spending evenings in a dusty room, surrounded by badly-stuffed animals, listening to some Charles Darwin look-alike droning on about the sex life of the water flea, is not a big attraction, frankly, to anyone under retirement age.

There are plenty of young people interested in the environment, of course, but they tend to find bigger, more exciting causes to espouse. Dolphins caught in trawlermen's nets. Ancient woodlands bulldozed to make more accursed motorways. The ozone layer now so full of holes, apparently, that it resembles a threadbare cardigan. And who can resist those sad-eyed Pandas, as they chew their bamboo shoots and tug at the strings of our hearts and purses? No wonder the young folk find it more exciting to dig tunnels, build tree-houses and unfurl protest banners, than to mount a lacklustre campaign to save Litterdale's last clump of some rare lichen.

It's hard to enthuse about endangered species we'd never even heard of until Death beckoned them, with his long, bony finger, towards the eternity of extinction. You can't miss what you never knew you had. I'm sorry, but it's true. For any animal that, like the Dodo, has the twin misfortune to be both rare and unattractive, the future looks bleak indeed.

With so many environmental crises around the world, it's easy to overlook what's happening on our own doorsteps. There's a bittersweet moment, every autumn, when we realise it will be six months before we see another swallow, or hear again the whitethroat's scratchy summer song. But that's all it is, a moment. We confidently expect the summer visitors to return next April. The first swallow to arrive in Litterdale, after its long flight north, is a sight that never fails to lift the spirits. It happens every year, bang on schedule; we don't lie awake at nights worrying about it.

Here in Litterdale we've tended to take our common birds for granted. But the truth is that a lot of our common birds aren't quite as common as they used to be. They haven't disappeared overnight, of course. It's been a gradual process – so gradual, in fact, that we hardly noticed it was happening.

It's easy to rhapsodise about how much better things were a generation ago. With the aid of rose-coloured glass, we reminisce about what we fondly imagine were more contented times. The summers were warmer, children showed respect for their elders and the fields were full of birds. That last memory, at least, is undeniably true. No-one needed to point out the lapwings that performed their aerobatics in the fields, like demented black and white butterflies.

They were everywhere you looked. No-one made a fuss about the skylarks that provided the melodic soundtrack to our summer months. You could find them whenever you wanted.

Spotted flycatchers performed somersaults, in search of their insect food. Yellowhammers sang from the tops of hedges, their plumage the colour of butter toffee. Linnets and redpolls twittered prettily in the trees like free-range canaries. Song thrushes smashed snail shells on their anvil stones; a neat trick, but hardly worth stopping to watch when you could see them do the same thing tomorrow.

Year by year, the picture has changed. Now you can walk out into the fields around Litterdale and not see a lapwing at all. And if you do see one, it's something worth mentioning when you get back home. Whenever you hear a song thrush singing now, you stop and listen, idly wondering when you last heard that first, fine, careless rapture.

It's not a disaster. Not yet, anyway. But it's a wake-up call to challenge our complacency. If we continue to destroy the birds' habitat by grubbing up hedgerows and cutting down copses, the wildlife will dwindle. It's a problem that needs to be addressed, before our songbirds go the way of the dinosaurs at the Litterdale and District Natural History Society.

WINTER

The hills are closing in around Litterdale, as the year comes to an end and winter begins to take our little valley in its icy grip. And what a funny old year it's been, a year with three naughts in it. We won't see its like, not for another thousand years, anyhow. By now, though, the novelty has worn off, like the gilt on all the cricketing trophies the village XI has failed again to win this year. Millennium year may have started with a bang, but now we can barely muster a whimper.

We can see, in hindsight, that the millennium was something that only made sense in anticipation. The moment the clock ticked over from New Year's Eve into New Year's Day, the event was effectively over. Once the fireworks had lit up the sky, and the hangovers had subsided, the other 364 days of the year were always likely to be a bit of a letdown. We've all had fun knocking the Millennium Dome, of course, and we've seen that wobbly Millennium Bridge hastily rebranded as a white-knuckle ride. But the celebrations left us with an empty feeling. As so often happens when we get into party mood, we seem to have spent an awful lot of money without having a great deal to show for it.

Even the Millennium Green initiative failed to fire our imaginations. Litterdale has had a village green for generations, but our local councillors didn't want to pass up all the lovely lottery lolly that was sluicing around. So our lottery grant was spent, instead, on erecting a plastic fence around the village green, and a smart new sign that says 'No dogs'. There was no money left in the pot, alas, to teach the dogs to read, which means that villagers still have to watch where they put their feet. The local dogs don't care about the lottery, or prohibitive signs, or our millennium. Since they live seven years to our one, the canine population probably celebrated their millennium while Roman foot-soldiers were plodding around rural Derbyshire, wondering what they'd done wrong to get such a dreary posting.

Millennium madness has achieved the seemingly impossible, making us all look forward to Christmas. The shops are full of festive fare (as they have been since late October). The newsagent's window is a patchwork of little notices, as villagers try to make some pin-money from unwanted belongings by appealing, perhaps optimistically, to the festive spirit. 'Transmission for 1979 Ford Capri: ideal Christmas present'. 'Two tons of dressed paving stones: ideal Christmas present'. Inside, there's a new selection of Christmas cards, their wording designed to reflect our ambivalent attitude to the festivities: 'Though I'm appalled by the tawdry commercialism of Christmas, I would nevertheless like to wish you the compliments of the season'.

Our vicar, too, is in two minds about Christmas. His church will be full, for the midnight Christmas service at least, and he offers up a little prayer of thanks for that. But he won't recognise most of the people who gaze up at the pulpit, their faces flushed with Christmas fervour, or alcohol, or guilt at not having been to church since this time last year. At least he understands the cathartic effect the midnight service can have on even the most self-regarding of his flock.

Whole families walk arm-in-arm, coats buttoned up against the cold, through streets bedecked with fairy lights, to the warm and welcoming sanctuary of our little greystone church. Up way past their bedtime, the children are wide-eyed with wonder; even their parents feel the magic. The unaccustomed surroundings, the flickering candlelight, the deep shadows, the beautiful carols; yes, even in these secular times the primitive power of Christian faith and fellowship still casts a spell. For the good folk of Litterdale, the midnight service acts as a timely jolt to the system, a potent antidote against cynicism and world-weariness.

By the church door is a traditional nativity scene, assembled by the school-children: a heartwarming tableau of familiar figures that tells the Christmas story. The Virgin Mary watches tenderly over baby Jesus in his wooden crib. Joseph is protective, paternal, yet a bit dumbfounded by events he doesn't yet understand. The three kings form an orderly queue, bearing their gifts of gold, frankincense and myrrh. The entourage is completed by donkeys, gazing over their stall, and what looks suspiciously like a My Little Pony.

Men are notoriously bad at Christmas shopping, leaving it till the very last minute. Christmas Eve is no time to start thinking about what to buy for our loved ones. Once Litterdale's shops have closed up for the holiday, the only place that will stay open over Christmas is the 24-hour petrol station on the by-pass. Which is why there are children in Litterdale who'll wake up on Christmas morning to find their stockings stuffed with furry dice, tubs of Swarfega and five-litre cans of high-performance engine oil. Yes, Christmas is the time of year when we try to be a little better than we usually think we are. But the odds are stacked against us.

Most men would rather have a boil lanced than be dragged kicking and screaming around the shops. And they can't always be left at home, alone, with all those bottles of cream sherry lying temptingly around the place. So this year we have a bold new initiative, to stop them becoming bored and fractious. For the days running up to Christmas, Litterdale's village hall is being turned into a crèche for men. Here, in a safe and supervised play area, surrounded by girly magazines, socket sets and a selection of power tools, men can safely be left for an hour or two while their partners get on with the shopping. If it stops some of those family tiffs over the festive season, we can make it an annual fixture.

The weather is a staple of casual conversation in Litterdale. This isn't town, where people pass on the street without a word or a nod. In a village, with everyone knowing each other, a chance meeting demands a response. But we still don't have all day to stand around and gossip. So what's needed is a simple, formulaic exchange that allows us to inquire briefly about one another's welfare, and then move on.

So the reply to the question 'How are things?' is 'Fine, thanks', or 'Mustn't grumble', or 'This cold snap's playing havoc with my arthritis'. The question is rhetorical; the shorter the answer, the better. There's no need for a long list of seasonal ailments. So a glaringly obvious remark about the weather is a better way to achieve conversational closure.

But, my, how things have changed. Just when we thought we'd got Mother Nature under control, like a dog walking to heel, she starts fighting back. And not just with a nip on the ankle, either; we're getting a comprehensive savaging. From the vantage point of a small Peakland village, we watch, with a mixture of awe and astonishment, as our weather takes an apocalyptic turn.

We used to tune into the weather forecast if we were planning a day out, and the farmers would pay particular attention at hay time. But the weather never dominated our lives in the way it does today. Now we huddle round the radio, like folk used to do in the war, to hear news from the front. We listen intently to the forecasts, even though a lot of them seem like guesswork. After all, isn't 'A 50% chance of rain' just a fancy way of saying 'We haven't the foggiest'? We get no answer to the question that's on everyone's lips: do we need to take an umbrella?

The prophets of doom talk about climate change. Here in rural Derbyshire we were surprised to have a climate at all; we thought we just had weather. But even the experts can't agree about what the future holds. A few years back, after a spate of especially cold winters, the climatologists insisted we were heading towards another Ice Age. That chilly prognosis has been conveniently forgotten; now it's global warming that's all the rage.

Maybe the experts have got it right this time, and Derbyshire will one day enjoy a Mediterranean-type climate. We'll all take a siesta after lunch, and vineyards will blanket the landscape where sheep once grazed. We'll be able to drink a toast to a balmier future with a glass or two of Chateau Litterdale. Or maybe not. After all, the weather round here doesn't seem to be getting milder; it's going to hell in a handbasket.

We used to have rain; now we have storms. We used to have wind; now, bizarrely, we have twisters and tornadoes. We used to have dry spells; now we have droughts that empty reservoirs and transform green lawns into tawny tundra. If there's a pattern to our weather, then we haven't detected it. All bets are off. Anything can happen now. Anytime. It's bewildering.

Over the years, the weather has been kind to Old Ted. Long retired, he props up the bar at the Swan, regaling our more gullible visitors with tall tales of weird weather phenomena culled from memory, his overactive imagination and the pages of *Old Moore's Almanac*. He remembers a traveller who, lost during a particularly savage blizzard one night, hitched his horse to a post. Next morning, when the the snow had melted, he found his horse hanging from the church steeple. Incredible... Whirlwinds would regularly pick up chicken coops, barns – even houses – and deposit them in some other village, miles away from Litterdale, without a scratch. Amazing... If the visitors offer to buy Ted a drink ('I'll have a pint of the strong stuff. And a whisky chaser. And one of those panatella cigars. Cheers'), where's the harm in that?

Now, though, we get weird weather all the time, and Ted's stories don't draw the crowds like they once did. Visitors steal his thunder with experiences of their own: 'What a coincidence. The very same thing happened to us. Just half an hour ago.' Ted now cuts a forlorn figure, harassing visitors with irrelevant observations. If he says 'Aren't these fine buttocks for an old man?' one more time, the landlord will have him barred.

The River Litter used to go about its business with a minimum of fuss. This unassuming little watercourse meandered through the village and flowed beneath the twin arches of the old packhorse bridge, before making unhurried progress down to the sea. It was so familiar that, as long as it behaved itself, we hardly noticed it all all.

Now, though, our river is on the boil. We've been getting as much rain in a single day as we'd normally expect in a fortnight, with water issuing, like some Biblical miracle, from pipes and culverts and holes in stone walls. The swollen river surged intemperately past the bridge, the water the colour of stewed tea. With the fields waterlogged, and the rain incessant, there was nowhere for all that water to go. Something had to give.

When the River Litter finally burst its banks, the floodwater took the line of least resistance, straight through Ted's house while he slept, blissfully unaware, upstairs. He was traumatised on coming down next morning to find muddy brown furniture floating around his sitting room. Looking on the bright side, it's the first time that the soft furnishings in Riverside Cottage have been colour-coordinated. But Ted saw red when his Council Tax went up on the basis that he now had an indoor pool. Where, pray, is the justice in that?

Here we are, in the heart of a Litterdale winter. Memories of last summer faded long ago, and the prospect of summer 2001 seems achingly distant. The recent floods have left everyone feeling a bit twitchy. Those of us who waded disconsolately through their homes, knee-deep in muddy water, will never look at rain in quite the same way again.

We used to enjoy the percussion of raindrops on the outhouse roof. It was vaguely comforting, especially when we were snug and warm inside our little cottages. But not any more. Now it sounds like the beating of war drums, as the Zulus laid siege to Rourkes Drift. It's disturbing.

We used to pull the curtains every evening, and bolt our doors, secure in the knowledge that we'd locked out most of life's unpleasantness. We could sleep soundly in our beds, untroubled by thoughts of intruders. That's the point of living in a village, isn't it? It certainly isn't the nightlife. But, as we've discovered, there's not a lot we can do to keep floodwater out. The sandbags may look business-like, but they're pretty ineffectual, like the pills that Dr Harris hands out to the most persistent malingerers who fill up his waiting room. Yes, an Englishman's home is supposed to be his castle, but right now it feels as though we're living in the moat.

Whenever the village darkens beneath an armada of storm-clouds, and the River Litter threatens once again to burst its banks, a little group of cagoule-clad villagers convenes in silence on the old packhorse bridge. They glare balefully down into the swollen river – it looks like Brown Windsor soup on the boil – hoping to bring down the water level by will-power alone.

What have we done to deserve all this rain? Have we made the gods angry? If so, what will the next affliction be? Well, if Bob the postman is anything to go by, it could be a plague of boils. This isn't something he's keen to talk about, even to Dr Harris. *Especially* to Dr Harris. But there's a lot of legwork involved in a rural round. After delivering letters to everyone in the village, and all the outlying farms as well, all Bob wants is to sit down, put his feet up and read the *Litterdale Times*. For the last few days, though, even this simple pleasure has been denied him.

Left to his own devices, Bob would probably just suffer in silence. That's a man's attitude to illness in a nutshell: if you ignore it, maybe it will go away of its own accord. It's the same attitude that Bob has adopted with all the vehicles he's ever owned, which is why he's never managed to sell any car for more than half what he paid for it. Due to his parsimonious use of engine oil (always a false economy, as Cath keeps reminding him), Bob didn't make a penny when he got rid of his last motor. Worse, he had to pay the guy from the breaker's yard in town to tow it away.

Once Cath had found out what was troubling Bob, by a process akin to reading braille, she packed him off to see the doctor. Bob went, with a show of reluctance. He knew that Cath was right (as she keeps reminding him) but felt obliged to put up a fight for the sake of appearances. His immediate fears were unfounded, thankfully, the waiting room being so full that he had to stand.

At this time of year there are plenty of people in Litterdale who are happy to spend quality time in a friendly, germ-laden environment. Old biddies, mostly. What's the point in cranking the central heating up at home, when the doctor's waiting room is so warm and welcoming? There are dog-eared magazines to read, full of recipes and knitting patterns. There's a tank full of goldfish, more entertaining than the daytime TV they'd be watching if they were at home. Apart from *Countdown*, of course, and that nice Richard Whiteley. There used to be a machine that dispensed hot coffee until Dr Harris twigged why he was dealing with an outbreak of scalded lips and fingers. Yes, if these hypochondriacs aren't ill when they arrive at the surgery, they've usually managed to pick up a sniffle, or better, by the time they leave.

Dr Harris can only spare about five minutes per patient, before writing a prescription for some harmless, sugar-coated placebo. But the other patients have no such constraints upon their time, and are happy to sit around, discussing their ailments and recommending home-grown remedies. Who would have guessed that a hot-water bottle filled with Lemsip could have such a pleasantly analgesic effect?

This is what a lot of doctors seem to have forgotten. Older people want someone to listen to them, to take their problems seriously. They want a doctor who will lean back in his swivel chair, press his fingertips together and give his undivided attention to an elderly lady whose main complaint (apart from her aching joints) is that her children and grandchildren don't come to see her as often as they should. They say that time is a great healer. And a few minutes of a doctor's time, plus a little uncritical empathy, often do more good than a handful of pills. After taking a cocktail of tranquillisers, some of his patients can forget their own names.

And what happened to Bob? Well, Dr Harris gave him a tube of ointment, and an inflatable cushion that looked like an outsized doughnut. He'll have to apply the ointment himself (as Cath keeps reminding him), but the prognosis looks good. In a couple of weeks he'll be as right as... well, as right as rain.

SPRING

When he moved to Litterdale, Mark fulfilled two lifetime ambitions at once. He was able to give up his hated desk job and swap town for country. He found the pace of village life to his liking. Through his conservatory window he could watch mallard ducks sail past; slowly in summer when the river was placid, faster in winter when it was swollen with melt-water from the hills.

Emboldened by banking his severance pay, Mark took over the lease on an empty shop in the village. He lined the walls with shelves, from floor to ceiling, and filled them with second-hand books. The name of the shop almost chose itself: BookMark.

He credited his mother with fostering his love of books. 'Read, Mark, and inwardly digest,' she had said, ambiguously, as he sat on her lap all those years ago. Throughout his childhood Mark took her words to heart. When his friends were outside, kicking a football around, he would have his head in a book.

A few years later those same lads would be down at the disco, having rendered themselves irresistible to the opposite sex by drenching themselves with that great smell of Brut. Mark seldom joined them; unless he'd had a couple of beers he was far too shy to dance. And by the time he'd summoned up enough Dutch courage to brave the dance-floor, he'd generally lost what little coordination he possessed. Instead of being a white-suited John Travolta in *Saturday Night Fever*, Mark looked like a man with ants in his pants trying to send a message in semaphore.

Having read more lyric poetry than was good for a growing lad, he harboured unrealistic expectations about love and romance. While his peers were releasing toxic levels of testosterone, Mark would sublimate his restless libido by taking long walks in the countryside. He wandered lonely as a cloud o'er hill and dale. Overly influenced by Pre-Raphaelite paintings, he nurtured the vain hope of surprising a young maiden bathing in the dappled sunlight of a woodland pool. It never happened, of course. If he did surprise anyone, it was more likely to be a courting couple in a car or someone dumping builders' rubble in a much-loved beauty spot.

Real life failed, predictably, to live up to what Mark read in his beloved books. It was no contest; books never let him down like people did.

Many years later, Mark heralded his entry into the retail trade with a muted fanfair. He concocted a press release in rhyming couplets: a novel approach which failed to impress the editor of the *Litterdale Times*, who buried the news item between the obituary column and the court reports. Nevertheless, the opening party at BookMark was well attended; it's not every day that Litterdale folk get to sup cheap white wine and eat warm sausage rolls at someone else's expense. Everyone went away with a complimentary bookmark and a pleasantly light-headed feeling. One or two people even bought a book.

That initial euphoria was short-lived, however, and the shop would never be as busy again. It bothered Mark at first. Some days he would hardly see a soul, and the amount in the till at the end of the day would largely depend on how big a float he'd put in that morning. He'd buttonhole his customers with tales of how poor business was proving to be, though this willingness to stand and chat was arguably one of the reasons why BookMark was, after all the bills had been paid, barely breaking even.

Mark responded to this retailing crisis in the only way he knew how, by ignoring it altogether. He redoubled his efforts to read his way out of trouble. Lost in a book, he would be startled out of his reverie whenever customers walked in. After a while he came to regard them as unwelcome intrusions. They reminded him of his shortcomings as a bookseller. His body language betrayed these feelings; what had once been a welcoming smile was now a glare. He had a ready answer to those who wondered why he read books all day. How could he recommend titles to his customers if he hadn't first read them himself?

Most people weren't actually customers at all. If the weather was bad, they'd come in out of the rain, stand next to Mark's two-bar electric fire and feign interest in whichever book was closest to hand. Other folk treated the place like a public library. They'd browse for an hour or more, then ask Mark for some book he obviously wouldn't have in stock. Feigning disappointment when he said he hadn't, they would sidle out of the door.

Trade is particularly bad at this time of year. The locals are still ploughing through the books they were bought for Christmas, and visitors don't start to appear in numbers until the Easter bank holiday.

As Mark's accountant reminds him every year, with a sigh, there isn't really enough local trade to keep a bookshop in business. Not in a place the size of Litterdale. And anyone casting a coldly objective eye over the accounts would say the same. The figures just don't add up. To make even a meagre living, Mark has to keep his little shop open till late in the evening. The lights are still burning brightly hours after the other shops have closed up for the day.

Mark loses track of time. Sometimes his head nods lower and lower, until it comes to rest against a pillow of yellowed pages. And, this being March, he dreams of golden daffodils. Hosts and hosts of them, waving in the breeze.

Gardening used to be a congenial way for people to occupy their declining years. If their doctor had told them to avoid over-excitement, they could potter around the herbaceous borders, with a trug over one arm, pruning branches and pulling up weeds. It was a cheap hobby too. There was no need to rifle the petty cash tin for anything more exotic than a new dibber or a packet of lawn seed.

But those days are gone. Gardening is the flavour of the month these days, especially when that month happens to be April. We've all seen those programmes on TV in which an unassuming, but perfectly servicable, back-yard is given an elaborate makeover. The rusting bikes and old mattresses are thrown out, a JCB moves in and two dozen labourers roll up their sleeves. The result: a brand-new garden that will make the neighbours purse their lips with envy.

A short stroll around the village in the pale sunshine of a spring day reveals that, under the influence of TV, Litterdale folk have been splashing out. Mandy, the village's self-appointed seer and sage, has designed her garden using tried and tested Feng Shui principles. Noting, cryptically, that 'Less is more', she's gone for the minimalist approach. She has created what she calls a zen garden; it consists of half a dozen rocks artfully positioned in carefully raked gravel. To Mandy it represents a life of spiritual simplicity. To everyone else, alas, it looks unnervingly like a huge cat-litter tray.

An accountant by trade, Frank is a landscape photographer by inclination. So it's appropriate that he's busy developing his garden. 'It'll look a picture when I've finished,' he enthuses, optimistically, as he takes another trip down to the garden centre. He returns with his trailer piled high with decking: what we used to know, more prosaically, as 'wood'. It's thanks to people like Frank that the man who owns the garden centre is making plans to sell the place, take early retirement and move to the Bahamas.

Scoop used to be known as the Jersey Royal of couch potatoes. Once he got settled on the sofa, after a hard day's work on the paper, only an earthquake would shift him. Or maybe the rustle of a crisp packet. Never known for his gardening prowess, Scoop adopted a simple scorched-earth policy to tackle any weed that had the temerity to show its face between the crazy paving. A flame-thrower was the only gardening tool he owned; it was the only one he needed.

It was watching Alan Titchmarsh and Charlie Dimmock desport themselves on TV that gave Scoop a taste for gracious outdoor living. Barbecues, waterfalls, brick paving, raised beds, wattle screens, trellises, summer houses, pergolas; he quickly embraced the whole ludicrous lexicon of instant gardening.

Scoop's a man who knows a thing or two about deadlines. He has no time for old-fashioned ideas like putting seeds in the ground and watching them grow. He wants a new garden and he wants it *now*. Having watched the gardening programmes, Scoop knows how long it takes to create the kind of garden you see in the Sunday supplements. It takes half an hour.

Violet, our local busy-body, treats her garden like she treats everything and everybody else in Litterdale. As an ex-headmistress, she's used to getting her own way. The lines on her lawn are as straight as the creases in a sailor's trousers. If she tells her lupins to stop slouching and stand up straight, that's exactly what they'll do. Weeds don't stand a chance in her garden. Violet has no need of a flame-thrower; she just has to gives the weeds a withering look.

Despite being flooded out over the winter, Old Ted has decided to go with the flow this year, and create a water feature in his cottage garden. This is in marked contrast to Bob the postman who, thanks to a leaky roof, already has a water feature making slow but inexorable progress down his back bedroom wall. The sound of water bubbling cheerfully over pebbles is supposed to make us feel relaxed and at peace with the world. Yet the same noise, when heard indoors on a rainy night, has the same effect on a terrified householder as listening to termites having lunch.

Bob is convinced that his garden is against him too. He stands at the back door, hurling abuse at his blameless garden plants. 'I've had it up to here with gardening,' he shouts, 'you're on your own now.'

He's vowed never again to lift a spade, or dig up another weed. That's until wife Cath tells him to. Their garden is becoming a sublime profusion. To Bob it's a self-sufficient ecosystem; to his neighbours it's a constant source of irritation.

'What are weeds anyway?' Bob asks, rhetorically, before providing the answer himself. 'They're just plants growing where people don't want them. The best way to get rid of them is just to reclassify them as flowers. I'm hoping for a good crop of dandelions this years. And if I do I'll make some wine.'

Bill, our tourism officer, lives next to the village green. It's one of the prettiest cottages in Litterdale; there are even roses round the door. The garden will provide colourful displays of native flowers throughout spring and summer. Of traditional design, Bill's garden has taken years of hard slog to bring it to this peak of floral perfection. That's hard slog, if you please, not just another trip to the garden centre with a credit card and a shopping list of pointless frippery. Bill knows the truth: when it comes to creating a cottage garden, there's no short cut. Gardening is not a destination, as the TV tosh seems to suggest, it's a journey.

We hardly know what to think of farmers these days. Their standing in the community rises and falls like an overheated stock market. But Les's place in the affections of Litterdale folk is not something that causes him too many sleepless nights. If he thought life was a popularity contest, he'd try harder to remember that there hasn't actually been a spittoon in the tap-room of the Fox since 1974. These days he's got too many other things on his mind. Les farms a hundred unproductive acres up on Heartbreak Hill, you see, and was quietly going broke even before foot and mouth swept across the country like one of the plagues of old Egypt.

Hill farmers are an endangered species. In twenty years' time we'll we wondering not why hill farming declined so quickly, but how come it lasted so long. 'Things just can't get any worse,' Les was saying this time last year, as sheep prices plummeted to the point where it wasn't worth the price of the petrol to take them to auction. But things can *always* get worse, as Les and the other farmers around Litterdale now understand only too well. As the old saying goes: when one door closes, another one slams in your face.

Les is a throwback to another age. He wears a suit – albeit a scruffy one, the kind that scarecrows wear – come rain or shine, and a hat pulled down tight over his ears. He lives alone. There never seemed to be enough time to get around to marriage. In any case, he only ever had one chat-up line: 'Would you like to come back to my place and do a little light dusting?' Predictably, most young women of marriageable age came to the conclusion that, no, they probably wouldn't.

To visit his resolutely grubby farmhouse is like going back fifty years. In fact it's almost exactly like going back fifty years; the headline on the yellowed newspaper that doubles as a table-cloth suggests that time has stood still since coronation year. Left to his own devices, Les has minimised his household chores. What's the point of washing up, he reasons; you're only going to have to do it all over again next month. There's a silvery bloom of dust over everything, but there comes a time when, as long as you don't disturb it by carelessly flicking a duster round, it doesn't get any thicker.

His day begins early. Les puts the TV on while he slurps his tea from a chipped mug. The farming programmes used to be worthy but dull: livestock prices, the weather forecast and maybe a film about what to wear when dipping sheep. But those days are gone, and the news from the country now seems like a never-ending catalogue of disasters. This may account for the unexpected appeal of 'You've Been Farmed', a cheap and cheerful montage of video clips. Red-faced farmers are laughing themselves silly at these amusing and possibly unrehearsed vignettes of country life. Accidents with hay balers, children falling into middens, and cross-species sexual encounters hilariously interrupted by a disgruntled farmhand with a camcorder. Les laughs too, but these days it's a laughter that's tinged with hysteria.

His working day ends late. He responds to every new farming crisis by working longer and harder. But if a man can't make a half decent living by working ten hours a day, is he really going to turn things around by working *twelve*? It doesn't really make any sense, but farming is in his blood. He doesn't know anything else. Everyone seems to have an opinion these days about what farmers should be doing. Convert a barn into a guest house, run a petting zoo, sell premium foods over the internet. But Les wouldn't know a website from a hole in the ground. And overnight guests would soon regret not booking into somewhere more salubrious… like the Bates Motel.

He is, in every sense, the last of the line. At one time he regretted not having a son to take over the farm. But not any more. If Les, with years of experience behind him, can't make ends meet, what chance would a greenhorn have?

It seems almost inconceivable that the countryside is changing so dramatically. But, in truth, it's always changed. A hundred and fifty years ago, many voices were raised in protest when the Peakland landscape was enclosed with dry stone walls. Now we would be equally strident in their defence if we heard they were to be knocked down. When the railway came to the Peak, those same voices complained about the viaducts being built to span the steep-sided dales. Now we're slapping preservation orders on them.

Les will carry on farming until he himself is planted in good Peakland earth. After that, who knows? What will become of his ramshackle farmhouse, up on Heartbreak Hill? Dale Head Farm could be transformed into a handsome holiday home for a commodities broker from Sheffield. With a few additions of no architectural merit it could be the clubhouse of yet another golf course. If it stays a farm, I'll eat my hat. If it stays a farm and turns a profit, I'll eat Les's hat too!

SUMMER

The holiday season is well underway. More visitors are coming to Litterdale than we had any right to expect just a few short weeks ago. Thank goodness. The summer won't be a total write-off after all, though everyone who has a teashop or a guest house will be happy just to get through the rest of the year and still have a business to run.

The landlord of the Fox used to treat visitors like vermin, during the summer months at least. And if any of them took umbrage, they were welcome to take their custom elsewhere. He wasn't bothered; there were always plenty more tourists around to fleece. But this summer is different, and one side-effect of the foot and mouth epidemic has been to make everyone a little more courteous to the visitors who *do* come. There is an unaccustomed air of civility in Litterdale's alehouse; it makes the locals nervous.

The downside is that visitors think it's a buyers' market. Just because the village is going through a bit of a bad patch, some of them are treating Litterdale like a Moroccan souk. The landlord of the Fox is doing his best to be agreeable, but the next customer who tries to haggle over the price of a pint and a packet of pork scratchings will find himself spreadeagled in the road, with a boot-print on his arse.

The Litterdale and District Agricultural Show is the summer's major casualty. It's the first time since the Second World War that the tents won't be going up on Potter's Field. Bill, our tourism officer, had to bite the bullet and make some difficult decisions. With so many events being cancelled, he opted to pulp thousands of glossy tourism brochures. In their place is a hastily concocted list of alternative attractions and diversions that will hopefully serve the dual purpose of opening the visitors' wallets, while keeping them well away from farms, footpaths and livestock. To pad out the schedules, even the most mundane events are listed: car-boot sales, blood donor sessions, a visit from a peripatetic chiropodist. Difficult times require desperate remedies.

Bill has been as even-handed as possible in his recommendations. He mentions the Swan, for example, as the best place to enjoy a leisurely lunch. Even the Fox gets an abbreviated mention, along with some much-needed advice: 'On no account speak to the locals unless spoken to, and never, ever complain about the beer.'

A craft fayre each weekend is proving quite a draw, though God knows why. The word 'fayre' should be warning enough. But as soon as they arrive in Litterdale, the visitors seem to leave their critical faculties in the pay & display car-park, along with their family saloons. Why else would they part with folding money for most of the tat on sale in the village hall? Log cabins made from lollipop sticks. Hand-made cards. Wishy-washy watercolours of well-loved Peakland landmarks.

Let's be straight on the matter. Most crafts are hobbies – excellent therapy, no doubt, for idle hands and troubled souls – but not businesses. These crafts-people ought to be told, 'think twice before putting your deformed offerings on sale, and, if they're log cabins made from lollipop sticks, don't even bother to think once.'

With so many paths and green lanes still out of bounds, Bill has created a set of self-guided walks that stick resolutely to Tarmac. Starting, sensibly enough, from the car-park, the Litterdale Trail visits most of the village's landmarks. The village green (the 'Keep off the

Grass' sign has been mothballed till things get back to normal). The duckpond ('It attracts many species of ducks. Mallards mostly'). The cricket pitch ('The scene of many epic performances. Mostly by the opposition'). The office of the *Litterdale Times* (interesting, no doubt, to those who want to watch a large man in a swivel chair eating cake). The River Litter (you can see how far the floodwaters rose during the winter; the high water mark extended well above the knee of Old Ted's gardening trousers, which he hasn't got round to washing yet).

There's one group of visitors that needs no invitation from the likes of Bill. And here they are, enjoying the ambience of a warm summer Sunday. The village green is transformed into an impromptu display of classic motor-bikes. And, a few yards away, lounging on the benches outside the Fox, is an impromptu display of classic motor-bikers. Yes, lock up your daughters, the Hell's Angels are here...

To hear some of the villagers talk, in hushed whispers, you'd think we'd been invaded by aliens. The bikers' reputation goes before them. But that's all it is, a reputation. Respectable parents shield their children's eyes as they walk past, which merely lends the bikers an unwarranted air of mystery and menace. But these superannuated outlaws are, in truth, about as menacing as a troupe of boy scouts. There's no need to lock up your daughters. Maybe just keep granny indoors.

These guys may try to look fierce, but they're not looking for a fight any more. It's too risky at their age; some of their blood groups have been discontinued. They're at that difficult time of life: too old to cut up their own food, yet still too young to be Radio 2 disc jockeys. They loll around on a summer's day, squinting into the sun, and talking about, well, bikes mostly. Good British bikes that sound like an artillery barrage, and drip oil all over the road. None of your Japanese rubbish.

And when the day is done they'll gun those bikes all the way home, through narrow Peakland lanes. They'll make a few old ladies jump. Then it'll be mugs of Horlicks, a few shortbread biscuits and an early night. Yes, their hell-raising days are over, they're the Mild Bunch.

It's high summer in Litterdale. The election provided us with some harmless entertainment, though there's a limit to the excitement that can be generated by a one-horse race. Since there was no space on the ballot paper to vote for 'Democracy', 'Fascist Junta', 'Banana Republic' or 'Enlightened Dictatorship', the only choice was between one load of identikit politicians and another. Or, for those who were bored with politics altogether, there was always the Green Party.

Down here in rural Derbyshire, we're used to straight talking. Some of those politicians may reckon to be big shots up in London, but that doesn't give them the right to swan around Litterdale as though they owned the place. Especially since we won't be seeing any of them for another four years. They'll promise the earth, if that's what it takes to win our votes, but you'll find they've got their fingers crossed behind their backs. We're impressed by deeds, not words. We'll listen, with one hand cupped around an ear, to whatever a politician has to say, but we'll make sure to keep the other hand on our wallet.

Once the polling booths were dismantled, and the ballots counted, village folk were in general agreement: whoever you voted for, it's the Government that got in. The only thing that's changed is that this lot don't have the luxury that all new administrations have, to blame everything on the last lot. We could have voted for the Natural Law Party (with the obvious fiscal advantages of yogic flying) without the even tenor of village life being greatly upset. Even if it was a little green man from the Planet Zob waving from the steps of Number Ten, the cows would still need milking twice a day. And considering the state of our bus service, yogic flying sounds a rather more convenient way of getting around.

It's true that most people in the village own cars. But that just makes life increasingly difficult for those that don't. Yes, once we've sold our soul to the infernal combustion engine, it's the devil of a job to get it back. The bus company reacts to every plea for a better service by cancelling yet another bus. There isn't much point asking anyone when the next bus is due; even the woman on the telephone helpline can offer nothing more than a hollow laugh.

Mandy, the village's seer and sage, owns one of those half-timbered Morris Travellers. It looks like Anne Hathaway's Cottage on wheels. She parks it all around the village, the exact location dependent on sound Feng Shui principles. It's always there when she gets back; only a short-sighted thief of unsound mind would think to try the door handle.

Mandy claims all kinds of special insights, based on the interpretation of signs, portents and premonitions. Of genuine powers there appears to be more hint than evidence; just a meaningful tap on the nose here, a knowing smile there. If you press her on the matter, and wonder what she really can foresee, she'll say, with that little smile and one raised eyebrow: 'Well, I knew you were going to say *that*.'

Her faith in intangible forces extends to her car. It's knackered, basically. When the second-hand car salesman in town saw her coming, he rubbed his hand together; he knew his monthly sales bonus was in the bag. He, too, has special insights; he can spot a soft touch a mile away. Mandy's body language, her aura if you will, seemed to be suggesting: 'I've had my frontal lobes removed and I've got a Barclaycard.'

There was a Morris badge on the back of the car, but a Toyota badge on the front. There's just no pride in the spot-welding craft these days. The salesman told Mandy it was a special edition, but because she wanted it so much, she could have it at the same low, low price as the regular model. That was the clincher.

It's the ideal car for people who, like Mandy, don't really approve of cars. Since she voted for the Green Party at the election, she'd like to do without a car at all. But, as she points out, how else can she take all her empties to the bottle bank? The flaw in this argument seems to have passed her by.

Everybody's car breaks down occasionally, but Mandy's is the only one in the village that actually breaks down in tears. The trouble is that she doesn't know why it goes, and she doesn't know why it stops. It seems to run on the motive power of pleas and prayers. Instead of filling up with petrol she tries, through the power of thought alone, to persuade the needle on the petrol gauge to creep out of the red. It means she misses a lot of appointments, sometimes by a matter of days.

Whenever the car splutters to a halt – a regular occurrence – she knows exactly what to do. She opens the bonnet and gives the engine a long hard stare, hoping to shame it back to life. If that doesn't work, she resorts to desperate measures and cleans out the ash-trays. That represents the limit of her mechanical knowledge; the next step is to ring a mechanic or (if the problem's with the bodywork) a carpenter. Everybody else in Litterdale is keeping their fingers crossed, hoping the car will hold together long enough for her to drive it to the breaker's yard.

✳

There's a regular bus service from Litterdale into town. That, at least, is the impression you get if you stand at the bus-stop and read the timetable. There's no need to hurry; whatever time you arrive, you'll have ages to wait before a bus comes. There are children in Litterdale who have managed to reach school age without encountering one. 'What's that big red thing, dad?' 'It's a bus, lad. Take a good long look; it may be the last one you see round here.'

The Litterdale route, though scenic, does not feature strongly in the bus company's strategy for the future. By reducing the number of buses to a bare minimum, and running them at inconvenient times, the company hopes to prove the route is uneconomic. Then they can do what they've wanted to do for years: shut it down altogether and drive yet another nail into the coffin of rural transport.

An integrated transport system is a mythical sort of beast, like the phoenix, the roc and the unicorn: something we've all heard about, but few of us have seen. Okay, we can catch a bus into town, do some shopping, and catch a bus back home to Litterdale. We'd just like to be able to do it in a single day.

A week on the Litterdale run is viewed, by the bus drivers, as a punishment. But if they want to get their regular routes back, they'll have to follow the bus driver's manual to the letter. This requires them to accelerate as fast as possible from every stop, then braking equally hard at the next one, thus making the journey as uncomfortable as possible for their passengers. With a glance in the mirror and a well-timed tap-dancing routine on the gas pedal and the brake, they can transfer an old lady and her shopping trolley from one end of the bus to the other in less time than it takes to say 'Hold tight at the back'. It's moments like these that make the bus driver's life worthwhile.

There's a lot of information that the bus timetable fails to mention. Such as how long your journey might take. Don't be lulled into any false sense of security by the idea that the bus is just going into town. Imagine your're going on an African safari, and pack accordingly. At the very least, you should take some provisions for the outward trip. If you're attacked by crazed pensioners, suffering from hunger and acute tannin deprivation, you may be able to appease them with some cheese and pickle sandwiches and a flask of weak tea. It's August, remember, so wear a scarf or cravat as a face mask; it will help to keep out the dust and the flies and the suffocating smell of lavendar water.

Some of the bus drivers have such a poor sense of direction that they have to stop periodically and ask the passengers which way to go. And it's not unknown for the drivers to organise a whip-round to fill the tank up, when they've run out of petrol. By the time the bus rolls into Litterdale once again, having covered half the county, most of the passengers will be delirious. No wonder the Litterdale run has been re-classified as a white-knuckle ride.

Bus useage is a sure indicator of social standing, winnowing the wheat from the chaff. Those of us who go by bus generally have no other option. Without a car, we're at the mercy of those mendacious bus timetables. Those of us who don't travel by bus would rather undergo abdominal surgery with a rusty machete than be forced to wait around at the bus stop by the village pond. Petrol would have to to be £100 a litre before we'd give up the sheer convenience of sitting in a traffic jam with hundreds of other stationary cars, drumming impatient fingers on the leatherette dashboard.

A pity, really. It can be quite fun to bounce around the country lanes in a bus, at least for those blessed with strong constitutions. But we look at buses in much the same way as our great-grandparents looked at the workhouse: in fear and dread that one day we too might be reduced to this final humiliation. Yes, if a businessman with a briefcase were to get on a bus, he might just as well wear a badge on his lapel that read 'I've got the sack, they've taken my company car back and I'm on my way to the Job Club. Kill me now; it would be a blessing.'

The social niceties of bus travel don't end there. Do you sit next to someone you've been chatting to in the bus queue? To do so might seem a little forward, while not to do so might be seen as stand-offish. You're sitting next to someone on a crowded bus which almost empties at one stop. Should you now move to a new seat, and risk offending your neighbour, or stay where you are? We need a manual of our own, 'Debrett's Guide to Bus Etiquette' perhaps, to help us mind our manners.

Last week, a bus was involved in a minor accident in Litterdale. A jaywalking duck was the culprit, apparently, though the duck's opinions on the matter were not sought. The driver was on his way back to the depot, so his bus was empty, thank goodness. By the time the police had arrived, though, the bus was packed with groaning pensioners. Who, in all honesty, can point the finger of recrimination at our senior citizens for spotting such a heaven-sent opportunity? After all, it's not every day they get the chance to leap aboard a bus, feign injury and put in a claim for compensation. If the ruse works, maybe they'll be able to afford a little runabout, and not be forced to queue for buses any more.

✳

AUTUMN

A lot of visitors think our village takes its name from all the rubbish they leave behind. They're not aware that the source is actually the River Litter, one of Derbyshire's less celebrated watercourses. Their confusion is understandable; by this time of year, after another busy summer, Litterdale is looking a bit of a tip.

The water in the duck pond is almost hidden beneath a floating raft of crisp packets and empty cans – through which the ducks make laboured progress. The lightest breeze sends paper and cartons skittering along the cobbles; the take-away tumbleweed of a throw-away society. The war memorial is crowned incongruously with a traffic cone. The rubbish bins are overflowing with the unwanted souvenirs of a day out in Litterdale. Encouraged by this squalor, and too idle to drive to the council rubbish tip, someone has tipped a lorry-load of rubble in the lay-by.

After a prolonged dry spell, the river is as low as anyone can remember. The water has a grey, lifeless look. It doesn't really flow; it oozes. With a sharp knife, you could cut it into slices. If you see a fish jump, it's probably just trying to catch its breath. The only thing our fishermen are likely to catch is impetigo. You wouldn't throw a match in; the river might just go up in flames. Yes, as summer is coming to an end, the River Litter is not looking (or smelling) its best.

A condensed history of the last century could be read from the artefacts that are turning up in the mud and the silt. By searching immediately down-river from the old packhorse bridge, the kids are turning up old stone ginger beer crocks, and those old glass bottles with the marbles in the neck. Throughout the ages, men have stood on bridges, bottle in hand, wondering why life has dealt them such unplayable cards. Having finished the beer that has been the cause of this morose introspection (and not, as they had imagined, the cure), men have taken a small satisfaction in hurling the bottle into the river, before staggering back home to their beds.

The Litter is giving up its other secrets too: rusty old bikes and bedsteads, milk-crates and mattresses. A wonky-wheeled supermarket trolley is wedged in the mud, even though the nearest supermarket is more than ten miles away. One mystery, at least, has been solved. It's many years now since Bob the postman decided to extend his repertoire of skills beyond cracking his knuckles and wiggling his ears. He could have taken up Scrabble or marquetry; it was just a shame that he went into town and bought a trombone instead.

Every day, after he'd finished his rural round, Bob would pucker up and practise his scales. Sometimes he'd even make a stab at producing a recognisable tune. Unfortunately, Bob has Van Gogh's ear for music, and his discordant expeditions into the hinterlands of modern music shattered many a peaceful afternoon. Litterdale is a small village and Bob's caterwauling seemed to permeate every home. Even double glazing offered little respite from his atonal tootlings. Yet no-one seemed able to find a tactful way of telling Bob to put the proverbial sock in it. Nobody wanted to upset the man who delivered the mail.

One day the trombone was there in the closet where Bob kept it. The next day it had gone. Bob searched the house from top to bottom. It was nowhere to be seen, of course. Polite enquiries around the village were met with a wall of silence. There were many people under suspicion, music lovers mostly. Bob thought his trombone was lost for ever... until last week, when he saw something gold glinting in the pale September sunshine as he carried the last of his letters across the bridge. He retrieved the instrument with a stick, and put it in his mailbag.

Bob was amazed that his trombone had turned up after all these years. Bob's wife, Cath, was amazed too; she thought she'd long since seen the last of the accursed thing. 'You know,' he said, flexing the mud-caked slide, 'with a bit of work it could be as good as new.' It wasn't until later, when he was idly watching *Crimewatch* on TV, that Bob wondered who had stolen the trombone in the first place. 'Maybe there'll still be some fingerprints on it. I could let the police have a look.' 'I don't think so,' said Cath. 'While you were watching TV I gave it a quick rub-down with a damp cloth. I'm sorry.'

Seeing our river in such a state has shamed us all into action. How can we scold the kids for tossing their sweetie wrappers on the pavement, when the evidence of more adult indiscretion is here for all to see? Showing a unity of purpose not seen in the village since the war – when pots, pans and park railings were dispatched, to be melted down and made into Spitfires – we had a big clean-up at the weekend. Able-bodied villagers congregated at the bridge after lunch on Sunday, dressed for salvaging duties – which ranged from wellies, fishermen's waders and kids in their swimming trunks and costumes.

Over a long, hot afternoon we hauled that rubbish out. It was sobering to see just how much junk there was; we filled a rubbish skip right up to the brim. Let's hope that people will have a little more pride in the village, and think twice before using the river so thoughtlessly.

To thank everyone for their efforts, the landlord at the Fox put on a barbeque. Bob was going to use the occasion to announce that his trombone had miraculously turned up again. Maybe play a few tunes. 'Best not,' said Cath, 'everyone's had such a good day. Why spoil it?'

Here in Litterdale there's a distinct nip in the air. The nights are beginning to draw in. The horse-chestnut tree on the village green has yielded up a bumper crop of conkers. Despite the competing attractions of TV and computer games, it's somehow reassuring that the village kids still compete against each other with conkers threaded on strings.

They stand on the green, hurling sticks into the upper branches. The conkers they can't reach always look bigger and better than the ones that are lying on the ground. The kids pounce on the spiky shells, opening them up with impatient fingers to reveal the smooth, silky, lustrous perfection of the fruit within. The gloss soon fades, of course, giving our children a valuable lesson about disappointment and loss and good things not lasting for ever, a lesson which their adult lives will probably confirm.

This venerable old tree has stood here for centuries. If only it could talk. Imagine all the events it must have witnessed over the years. How many relationships have blossomed beneath its spreading branches; how many people have relaxed in its shade? Mind you, if the tree *did* start to talk, it would probably just mean I'd neglected to take my medication again.

This is a busy time for Norman, Litterdale's resident handyman; almost as busy as spring, summer and winter, in fact. When something around the village needs doing, Norman doesn't wait for someone else to spring into action. He knows, from past experience, that he could be waiting till Doomsday. So once October is here Norman can be found on the village green, raking the fallen leaves into a big pile to burn. When pungent smoke is rising from wet leaves, with Norman in close attendance, we are left in no doubt: Autumn has rolled round once again.

Norman's an adaptable sort of fellow; he could turn his hand to just about anything. But the same can't be said for the hill-farmers of Litterdale. They work all hours, in all weathers. They're persistent, even bloody-minded. They respond to everyday crises phlegmatically. They know all there is to know about sheep and dairy cattle and how to patch up a broken-down wall. The trouble is that they're so busy working that they seldom have time to think about the future of farming. On the rare occasions that they do, it fills them with a nameless dread. So there's every incentive just to carry on as they are and let tomorrow take care of itself.

Hill farmers are being told, in no uncertain terms, to be more imaginitive. This may be feasible for some of the younger folk, but it's not so easy for an old stick-in-the-mud like Les. Any kind of change is anathema to Les, whether it's a penny on a pint in the pub, or some new bureaucratic inanity designed to make farming even more difficult today than it was yesterday. But he's never been one to turn easy money down. So when a bloke from Bakewell waved a wad of notes under his nose, in the tap-room of the Fox, Les was in the mood to listen. It seemed like a good deal: some tax-free beer money just for the use of one of his fields for a day. That's why signs went up all around Litterdale, directing Sunday morning traffic into a car boot sale.

Les had heard about car boot sales, though he'd never quite understood why car boots – rather than spare tires, say, or wing-mirrors – should be the focus of so much attention. When he wandered down into his bottom field, to see what all the fuss was about, he was gobsmacked to find it transformed into a Moroccan bazaar. Displayed artlessly on makeshift stalls was just the kind of junk that was lying around his own unlovely home: chipped coronation mugs, dodgy videos, old biscuit tins, novelty ashtrays, rusty tools, that elusive third LP by Bucks Fizz and Polaroid cameras for which they stopped making films in 1974. The only difference was that all this junk had price tags.

There was even a stall selling home-made chutneys and conserves. This was yet another surprise for Les, who'd assumed that 'money for jam' was nothing more than a colourful turn of phrase. He wandered around the stalls, shaking his head. He'd long suspected that the world was going mad, and here was solid proof.

It wasn't so long ago that people went to church on a Sunday morning. They looked to the man in the pulpit for guidance and reassurance. But the habit's been broken, and it will take more than gimmicks like Hymn Number Bingo to bring the congregations back to fill the empty pews. Nevertheless, they find there's a big hole in their lives where blind, unquestioning faith used to be. So they go car-booting instead, to rummage through other people's cast-offs and maybe pick up a bargain. This is a kind of faith too, as the money-lenders no doubt said to Jesus before he chased them out of the temple.

Here, in the bargain basement of budget retailing, there's plenty of stuff to keep the browsers busy. 'Antiques of tomorrow', as the stallholders say: what used to be described, more prosaically, as 'rubbish'. Those who have suffered the misfortune of having their car radio stolen may find a replacement on one of the stalls. They may even find the one that was taken in the first place. This is half the attraction of car boot sales: an opportunity for boringly law-abiding citizens to become Arthur Daly for a few hours, and to rediscover the lost art of haggling over stolen goods.

A sign on an elderly Hoover reads 'Genuine reason for sale'. The stallholder tries to reassure a punter that it's in good working order. 'I'll be here next week,' he lies, 'if you have any trouble with it.' ('It's a genuine reason for sale, all right,' the stallholder whispers conspiratorially to Les, in passing. 'It's knackered.')

It's that time of year again, when Litterdale folk get together to watch the fireworks. Yes, the annual general meeting of the Litterdale and District Pool League, now in progress in the back bar of the Fox, can be a combustible affair. It should be just a matter of minutes to rubber-stamp a simple agenda, but something happens to even the most taciturn participants whenever they preface a sentence with the words 'Mr Chairman'. It brings out the bar-room lawyer in all of them; they become pedantic and argumentative. No point of order seems too insignificant to warrant a motion, a seconder, maybe a counter-motion, followed, eventually, by a show of hands. Only for someone to find fault with the small print, rephrase the motion in a slightly different way, and go through the whole charade once again.

After a few beers the pool team representatives are giddy with power, even though it's only the power to keep everyone in the Fox up way past their bedtimes, debating points of order that have no meaning beyond these walls (and precious little inside them either). They start dissecting aspects of this simple and diverting pub game that they'd largely taken for granted. Like Rule 34(a), never a contentious directive. Until now.

Notions of sportsmanlike conduct are notoriously difficult to pin down. Players whose parting shot to a victorious opponent is along the lines of 'I'll have you outside, you cheating bastard' are unlikely to be reined in by a minor rule change. But it's eventually agreed, after heated debate, that beating an opponent to death with the butt end of a pool cue is an action that runs contrary to the spirit of the game, and that a penalty of two free shots will be awarded. A second such offence will forfeit the frame. Harsh, perhaps, but fair; we've seen far too much of this kind of thing lately.

Hands are raised, excitedly, to instigate some new motion, and are hurriedly taken down again, as the chairman seeks nominations for the posts of secretary and treasurer. Doing some real work (behind the scenes, throughout the year: a thankless task) doesn't have quite the same appeal as shooting their mouths off at a meeting, so the pool players of Litterdale find this a convenient moment to slope off to the bar.

The start of the indoor games league is a bittersweet occasion. Summer is long gone, and winter stretches out ahead like a long and dreary road. Hibernation seems a very attractive proposition. Who wouldn't settle for curling up under a duvet till spring? Visitor numbers have declined to a trickle, walkers mostly, and we have the village to ourselves once more.

The landlord of the Fox is in conciliatory mood, hoping to attract the locals back through the doors. So out goes the over-priced tourist menu, and in comes good, wholesome, unpretentious fare. Pies, stews, dumplings, chips; maybe a side order of lard or suet. It's comfort food, solid chloresterol to send a man away with a lead weight in his stomach and a light feeling in his head. There's rumoured to be an Egon Ronay inspector buried under the car-park, but don't let the landlord hear you say so.

Games night in the Fox is a convivial affair, giving even the laziest villagers the chance to display their prowess at darts and dominoes, pool and whist. Old Ted, for example, even finds crown green bowling too strenuous. His idea of exercise is to hide the TV channel changer. Yet he turns out for the darts and dominoes team come rain or shine. The only time in recent memory that he missed a games night was during last year's flood. And that was only because he couldn't get the outboard motor started. That's how keen he is.

The fire is banked up, and the ale flows freely. The landlord surveys his grubby little empire with grim satisfaction, as he waves a duster over the scotch eggs. Hygiene is not a high priority at the Fox. A regime of benign neglect gives the place an earthy charm. He listens to the random percussion of dominoes being laid – with knocking noises, like a friendly ghost, whenever a player can't go – and a triumphal flourish as the last tile goes down. Dominoes: our weekly reaffirmation that life could be worse.

Darts, on the other hand, is a more hazardous affair. You wonder who first had the idea of recreating indoors the noble sport of archery. Dispensing with bows, bringing the arrows down to a size that can be gripped between thumb and forefinger and – what imagination! – encouraging the participants to drink beer at the same time. In a sane world, darts players would be isolated in a padded room, where the only people at risk of injury would be each other. Throwing sharpened missiles in a crowded, smoky bar seems like a recipe for disaster. In any other context, the building would soon be surrounded by armed police, shouting terse instructions through loudhailers.

Across the road, the upstairs room at the Swan is transformed. It's amazing what dim lighting and a few Chianti bottles filled with candles can do. Once a month the room becomes the Litterdale Folk

Club, where adenoidal social workers routinely murder ancient songs of lust and revenge. Looking on the bright side, though, it means the pub doesn't actually need to apply for a music licence.

'Hi, I'm Kevin,' says Kevin, 'I'd like to start the evening off with a song about whaling.' He runs the Litterdale Folk Club only because he'd never get a singing spot, on merit, at any other club. When he fluffs verse 12 of his 15-verse ballad, his attempt to start again from the very beginning is drowned out by a desperate rush for the door.

WINTER

Violet is Litterdale's resident busybody, the self-elected expert on just about everything she thinks we ought to know. She's the living proof that dog owners grow to look like their pets. Once she gets her teeth into some new idea, she's just like her little Yorkshire terrier: tenacious, single-minded and impossible to shake off. She was walking her dog one day in autumn, engaging the mutt in animated, though one-sided, conversation. As she passed the old quarry she noticed, to her horror, that someone had thoughtlessly dumped a lorry-load of rubbish into it. What a cheek!

Somebody had to spring into action. As usual, Violet put herself up as the one and only candidate and voted herself into the job. Since then she's been waging a one-woman campaign against the despoilers of our landscape. Yes, Violet's become an eco-warrior. Or maybe that should be eco-*worrier*. She worries about global warming. She worries about acid rain. She worries about the hole in the ozone layer. Most of all, she worries us.

Don't get me wrong; our poor, battered, beleaguered world needs all the help it can get. Those who wantonly despoil it must be made to mend their ways. If God really has given us custody of the planet, then we should be expecting a knock on the door any day now from a team of celestial social workers. Our lame and shame-faced excuses – 'I don't know, maybe the earth slipped and fell, these things happen' – will fool nobody. Look after the planet? Most of us find it hard enough to look after a *goldfish*.

No, what bothers the good folk of Litterdale is being lectured to by an overbearing woman, in the tone of voice normally used to reprimand a naughty child. Perhaps we should be giving Violet a pat on the back for being so concerned, so single-minded and so incontrovertibly right. There's a fine line, though, between doing the right thing and being a complete pain in the neck, and it's a line she oversteps rather too often. She's got something to say about every subject under the sun. And, unlike our depleted stocks of fossil fuels, Violet's opinions seem infinitely sustainable.

She should relax now and again, and maybe let someone else have a turn at carrying the planet. But there's no room for complacency, she insists, while we face the threat of global warming. Low-lying Peakland towns could be lost beneath the flood-water. Litterdale itself could become a coastal resort blessed with a Mediterranean-type climate, where trees laden with citrus fruit would add welcome splashes of colour to the limestone landscape. Problem? What problem?

Violet's ideas are irreproachable, her logic beyond question. And it's pointless to argue with a woman who puts the welfare of the planet at the top of her priorities. If she tells you to don your wellies, wade out into the river and pick up all the old bicyles and bedsteads, the easiest option is just to do it. There's no point suggesting you were were just on your way to the Fox for a leisurely pint. 'Pint? Pint? How can you even *think* about such things at a time like this?' she'll suggest tartly. It's always a time like this, of course. Your pint will have to wait.

But the strain of being ideologically correct – all day, every day, with just an hour off for lunch – is beginning to tell. Her lofty ideals make her susceptible to altitude sickness. And some of her recent stunts, though well-meaning, have backfired badly. When she bought a fur coat for the winter, the saleswoman ensured her it was made of recycled fur. The fur was indeed recycled, it used to be a silver fox. There were red faces all round after that.

Violet has been picketing the local abbatoir, where fat porkers are dispatched on a daily basis to meet their maker. It's humane, of course, to give pigs the opportunity to die with dignity, though Violet's suggestion of leaving a flask of whisky and a pearl-handled revolver in each animal's stall is greeted with snorts of derision by the slaughtermen.

She liberated the trout from the tank in a restaurant, and decanted them into the river. It seemed a good idea at the time; how was Violet supposed to to have known they were *sea*-trout? Being summonsed for polluting the River Litter with dead fish won her no plaudits from the local Friends of the Earth group. They voted her off the committee. Now she's just an associate member, a *Friend* of a Friend of the Earth.

Litterdale's village green looks splendid. Every year about this time, for as long as most of us can remember, Norman has hauled out the boxes of fairy lights from under the stage in the village hall.

He chunters away to himself as he drapes the lights between the branches of the trees. He shouldn't still be doing this. Not on his own. Not at his age. Not with his angina. And definitely not balanced precariously on a rickety step-ladder. Once he's finished, though, villagers come out to admire his handiwork. Norman switches on the lights with a flourish, and gets a small ripple of applause. Those who have marvelled at Blackpool illuminations may find the lights of Litterdale a little short on spectacle. But they give the village a homely air, and this is all we really want.

Our mood is thoughtful, a little sombre. This is a time for quiet reflection, for gathering the family around us. Even those well-heeled villagers who normally spend Christmas abroad – soaking up the sunshine while the rest of us shiver – have decided to stay in Litterdale this year. We've re-ordered our priorities; counting our blessings, not just bemoaning our fates. Even the usual platitudes sound different. Seldom have the words 'Peace on earth and goodwill to men' been said with more conviction.

Les has a traditional view of Christmas. He loathes it. From his familiar soap-box, propping up the bar at the Swan, he bends the ear of anyone who lingers a nano-second too long about the shortcomings of the festive season. Les moans about Christmas from the moment the first tinsel-wrapped stock appears in the shops, all the way through to Twelfth Night when the decorations that haven't already fallen down are taken down. Les is spared this tiresome chore because he never puts any decorations up in the first place. Dale Head Farm is as uncompromisingly spartan at Christmas as it is during the rest of the year.

He moans about the escalating cost of Christmas, even though it's years since he last bought anyone a present. In a good year, his Christmas dinner might consist of a packet of 'Turkey & Stuffing' flavoured crisps, washed down with a few cans of industrial-strength lager. In a bad year he may not bother with the crisps. And the only reason Les doesn't moan during Christmas dinner is because he eats it on his own.

There seemed no reason why this Christmas would break this long-established pattern, so Les was mystified to find himself inundated by invitations. Bob and Cath, moved by pictures of refugees on TV, decided that charity should begin at home. They didn't want to see Les on his own at Christmas. He was welcome to join them for roast turkey and all the trimmings, as long as he promised to keep his boots on. Violet, too, was all affability. Once she had locked away the silverware, she suggested Les might like to pop round, after milking the cows, for a schooner of sherry and a few mince pies. Mandy wondered if Les would like to share a salad and a glass or two of home-made parsnip wine. This latter option held little appeal. 'Salad isn't food,' Les confided to the landlord at the Swan. 'Salad's what food *eats*.'

Disorientated by all this unexpected attention, he accepted a last-minute invitation from Old Ted to bag sileage and heckle the Queen's speech on TV. This, as the pub regulars were surprised to hear on Boxing Day, was the best Christmas that Les could remember.

It's a shame that it takes world conflict to make us all a bit more considerate towards each other. But Steve, our vicar, is not complaining. He never thought he'd live to see what's happening at St Breville's. While there's little of architectural interest about the undistinguished greystone building, it still merits a few lines in the tourist brochure. Mostly for the hand-knitted hassocks, the handiwork of the WI. They feature local landscapes, Biblical scenes and in one case (maybe someone wasn't briefed too well) the grinning face of Micky Mouse. We appreciate that's not enough to entice afficionados of fine old churches. But, hey, if there's another church in Derbyshire dedicated to St Breville, the patron saint of toasted snacks, then we've not heard about it.

Things were different in years gone by. Everyone used to go to church on Sunday morning or, if they didn't, they made sure to have a good excuse at the ready for when the vicar called. So, like a gourmet who loosens his trouser belt notch by notch, the church expanded over four centuries, to keep pace with the ever-increasing population of Litterdale. Sharp-eyed visitors can spot the joins in the masonry where an aisle was widened or a tiny chapel added. The last major building work took place in 1875, the result of a bequest by a wealthy local man who felt the need to atone for some of his sharper business practices. In an unhappy coincidence this was the same year that congregations began the long, slow decline that has continued ever since.

By the time Steve moved into the vicarage, congregations had become embarrassingly small. Scattered worshippers looked lost in the ranks of pews. The thin, reedy voices of Steve's elderly parishioners almost disappeared in all that space, echoing feintly up into the vaulted ceiling.

In a manoeuvre that lovers of parlour games would recognise as musical chairs, Steve took a row of pews out every year and moved those that remained ever closer to the lectern. The empty spaces were filled with screens, on which children's paintings were displayed. Almost by sleight of hand, Steve created a church within a church, to reflect what the village of Litterdale has become. And now, as he surveys his congregation with quiet satisfaction, he knows his work has paid off. Who would have believed it? For the first time in a long time, and not just for the midnight mass on Christmas Eve, people are coming to church again. In a decade of tending his Litterdale flock, Steve has never known the church so busy.

Perhaps some people feel there's a big empty hole in their lives. A hole that can't be filled by a racy sports car, a new shade of lip-gloss or the short-lived satisfaction of giving their credit card some serious hammer. Perhaps they feel anxious and disorientated, as old certainties don't seem quite so certain any more. Perhaps they've weighed their lives in the balance, and come up short. Whatever. All Steve knows is that if things carry on like this, he'll have to put some of those pews back.

Regular attendance is a steep learning curve for some of the less experienced parishioners. Steve has to explain that, no, the absence of White Christmas in the hymnal is not merely due to a printing error. And the numbers on the hymn board have nothing to do with rollover week on the National Lottery. No matter. As he stands in the pulpit, gazing down at the sea of expectant faces, Steve gives a short and silent prayer of thanks.

Litterdale dozes fitfully through another Peakland winter. We don't get many visitors at this time of year, but look what they're missing. The village green, rimed with frost, sparkles in the pale sunshine. Smoke snakes lazily upwards from cottage chimneys, and hangs in the valley. The cottages that surround the green look ancient, organic and elemental. It's a timeless scene, painted in muted greys and browns. The archetypal English village, as long as you ignore the TV aerials. If Litterdale were made of skin and bone, muscle and sinew, rather than stone and slate, you might say the village was hibernating. You'd have to listen carefully to find a pulse. Of vital signs there are few, on a Sunday morning in February: just a single line of footprints across the frosty grass.

A portly figure is hunched over a tripod, wrapped up warm against the cold that turns his breath into mist. It's Frank, Litterdale's resident photographer, busy twiddling the knobs on his brand new camera. He's wearing the sort of down-filled jacket that makes him look as pneumatic as the Michelin Man. The ear flaps on his hat give him the half-witted look of an elderly Labrador; the fingerless gloves look like hand-me-downs from Fagin.

The camera was a Christmas present to himself. It joins the extensive collection of cameras and lenses that he already owns. Since a lot of those lenses wouldn't fit his new purchase, he went out and bought a new range of lenses too. Wide-angle, telephoto and a monster that looks like an anti-tank bazooka, which could take a characterful head-and-shoulders portrait of an ant at a thousand paces. And, since you shouldn't put new wine into old bottles, Frank splashed out on a smart new camera bag as well. This is what can happen when a man pulls in a good salary but has no family to put a brake on his immoderate spending habits.

Frank doesn't see himself as spendthrift, of course, just enthusiastic. He thinks his enthusiasm is about photography, though it's actually the cameras themselves that get him excited. By the time the credit card bills roll in, there's always some fancy new machine that will take better pictures than the camera he bought last month. He just can't resist the allure of matt-black hardware, that's all.

His pride and joy this month is a Cartax 796, with a power-drive. By keeping his finger on the shutter, he could run through an entire film in twelve seconds. For reasons known only to Frank, he sees this as highly desirable. Yet all he's done since Christmas is to take the camera out of the bag, and run his fingers over those sinuous curves. Today is the first time he's actually put a film in.

The camera boasts a baffling array of buttons and programmes and back-lit displays. It takes him months to get to know the idiosyncracies of a new camera, especially since the instruction manuals are mostly translated from the original Japanese by someone for whom English is not his first language. Thankfully, the 796b will hit the market any day now – with a laser viewfinder, or speech recognition, or some other dubious feature that will make him go weak at the knees with desire.

Frank would be happy to show off the new machine to anyone who happened to be up and about. But the good folk of Litterdale have already peered out of their windows and seen the frost on the ground. And, more to the point, they've seen Frank pootling around on the green. These are two good reasons to stay in, bank up the fire and find some odd jobs to do around the house.

There will be Sunday papers to read, when they finally arrive. The paperboy, Bob and Cath's lad, Ben, used to finish his Sunday paper round by the time most folks in Litterdale were enjoying their first cup of tea of the day. But the papers seem to expand every week, with some new lifestyle supplement, and the poor lad's legs are beginning to buckle under the weight.

If he's not careful, he'll end up with as many vague and undiagnosed ailments as his dad. Bob has committed a long list of symptoms to memory, in case anyone asks how his feeling. Which nobody does. Somebody with a wicked sense of humour bought Bob a medical encyclopaedia for Christmas. By the time he'd read a couple of chapters, Bob identified with all manner of conditions from Beri-Beri to Dutch Elm Disease. The only illness that sounded too far-fetched was the one that everyone agrees he's got: an acute case of hypochondria.

Sunday is a day of rest for a postman, which gives Bob the opportunity to discover a few more symptoms. He stands in front of the bathroom mirror. It's not a pretty sight. He sticks out his tongue, then puts it back again quickly. He gazes at his reflection and sees how he'll look in twenty years' time. His chin is stubbly – but instead of looking rugged and manly, he just looks like old-man Steptoe. Bob feels brittle; one false move and a bone could snap. He's got an irritable bowel, a grumbling appendix, a murmuring heart; yes, even his internal organs are telling him he's not a well man.

And now, to cap it all, he's come down with flu. It's one of those gender-related illnesses (women get colds, men get flu), so he's not getting much sympathy at home. Cath told him to stop moaning, or go and see the doctor. Dr Harris didn't have much time for him either, and told him to take a powder. And when Bob asked the chemist to make something up for him, the chemist said there were fairies at the bottom of his garden. Bob can do without that kind of sarcasm from a man who sells suppositaries for a living.

SPRING

It's March. The more optimistic villagers may be able to convince themselves that Spring is here. Realists, on the other hand, know that Winter still has a few tricks to play.

Rain and meltwater have left the ground saturated. Farmers are walking sodden fields and, in consequence, filling Dr Harris's waiting room with pungent agricultural odours and bad cases of trenchfoot. Les is up on Heartbreak Hill, putting a new sheepdog through its paces. His language is the most colourful aspect of a scene that seems to have been re-tinted from a more limited paint chart, mostly in Pennine Drizzle and Sleet Grey. If the darkest hour is just before dawn, then the gloomiest time of year seems to be just before Spring erupts with new life and colour and birdsong.

Les whistles, waves his stick, and calls the dog by name. But he's frustrated, and the name Les calls the hapless dog isn't the one that's engraved on its collar. So the dog becomes confused, and the sheep scatter in all directions. Les has heard about Dolly the sheep, and wishes all his sheep were cloned. Then they might all run in the same direction. They would all look the same too, but Les wouldn't find this a problem.

Les has an unsentimental view of his animals. There's no point getting too chummy with any beast whose last port of call will be the abattoir. In the Biblical parable the sheep that was lost was worth more than the other ninety nine. That rings a little hollow in the Derbyshire Dales of today, since all sheep, whether lost or found, are worth about the same: bugger all.

Every year, at lambing time, there are always a few sickly lambs that need special attention. Les will hoist them over his shoulder, the very image of the Good Shepherd, and take them back to Dale Head Farm. Though he will sit up half the night, feeding them milk from a baby's bottle, the ones that survive will soon be back in the fields again, fending for themselves.

The new sheepdog will find its place at the farm, but that place is outdoors. Les would no sooner have a dog inside the house than invite a pack of rats to come in and make themselves at home. Working dogs belong in the yard, chained up and lying doggo until a group of unsuspecting ramblers walk through the farmyard. That's the moment the dogs leap out, barking insanely, their chains pulled as taut as a ship's hawser. Let's face it, scaring hikers half to death is one of the few perks of a demanding job.

Two months ago the villagers were singing the same tune: a mournful ballad about the perils of self-indulgence and the urgent need for self-improvement through the rigours of self-denial. Fat, flabby and listless after the big Christmas blow-out, and cash-strapped from rushing round the January sales, they vowed to make changes in their lives. Their new year's resolutions ranged from the pragmatic ('I will never, ever, drink after-shave again') to the hopelessly unrealistic ('I will go jogging every morning').

Everyone relishes an opportunity to be a little bit better than they usually think they are. But hangovers subside, eventually, and it's exhausting just watching those fitness videos. By the time that March comes around, most of these resolutions have been forgotten – consigned to the cupboard under the stairs along with the dumb-bells and the fondue sets.

Bob the postman is bucking the trend. He lit up a slim panatella on New Year's Eve, and declared it would be his last. He wasn't going to cut down; it was 'cold turkey' or nothing. And, amazingly, he hasn't touched the evil weed since then. Cath is supportive, but keeps a watching brief. Bob's not known for the strength of his convictions, so this display of will-power is particularly impressive.

He started smoking at about the age of fifteen, because it seemed to be an integral part of growing up. Like millions of other deluded adolescents, Bob thought that smoking would add a little glamour to his mundane existence. But all he did was to welcome into his life one of the most perniciously addictive drugs known to mankind. His dad had issued dire warnings about the dangers of smoking and drinking. Unfortunately he had a Capstan Full Strength in one hand, as he spoke, and a tumbler of single malt whisky in the other, which rather negated the effect of his fatherly advice. This, too, seemed to be a part of growing up: attaining a level of hypocrisy to match your parents.

Giving up is never easy, and Bob's had a few bad moments. He has to stay away from the pub, where the plumes of cigarette smoke are as beguilingly hypnotic as the swaying of a snake charmer's cobra. At moments of stress he still reaches, automatically, into his jacket pocket for a packet that isn't there. The low point was aiming a kick at the cat, in a display of nicotine-related petulance.

Slowly but surely the cravings are subsiding. From being a twenty-a-day man, he has joined the ranks of smug ex-smokers. And, let's face it, people don't come much smugger than that. Bob embraces abstinence with evangelical fervour, always ready to stop and talk to people about how much better he's feeling. His clothes don't reek of cigarette smoke every morning, and he doesn't wheeze any more as he makes his morning round.

Best of all, as he enthuses to Cath, he can really taste his food now. This is something Cath knows already; for the past two months she's been adding fresh basil to the spaghetti sauce, turmeric to her curries and cloves to the apple pies. It's her secret contribution to Bob's titanic effort in helping to give that cold turkey a bit of spice.

Bill, Litterdale's tourism officer, is feeling rather pleased with himself. And why shouldn't he? A two-day brainstorming session (with Bill and his staff holed up, at the council's expense, in a rather splendid four-star hotel) has produced a host of new visitor initiatives. After so many months of misery, in an area of the country that relies so much on tourism and animal husbandry, it's vital that the rural economy gets a shot in the arm.

The session was a great success, with all local tourism initiatives now coming under one umbrella, 'Tourism 2002'. Everyone agreed that this name was catchy and up-to-date. The icing on the cake (Black Forest gateau, incidentally, and 'rather good') was an exciting new slogan. 'Litterdale, it's probably closer than you think.' Bill rewarded himself with a liqueur coffee for dreaming that up. The other candidate – 'Litterdale, Derbyshire's Best-Kept Secret' – appeared to contain a subliminal criticism of the tourism department, and was voted down, five to four, after second helpings from the sweet trolley. Yes, however much that brainstorming shindig cost, it was money well spent.

Tourism 2002 is exceeding expectations. A record number of tourist brochures have been dispatched, each and every one a triumph of anodyne banality, and bookings are well up on last year. We wait for the visitors to come, our fingers poised over the cash-tills like typists waiting for dictation.

The sign that greeted motorists – 'Litterdale welcomes careful drivers' – was taken down last year. After all, even the most accident-prone drivers have cash to spend, and the pubs, cafés and guest-houses of Litterdale didn't want to miss out on their share. If the National Association of Reckless Drivers (and Affiliated Operatives in the Bus and Taxi Businesses) had wanted to hold their AGM and dinner dance in Litterdale, all we would have said was, 'When and where?' Yes, that's how bad things were round here. Norman, bless him, has put the sign up again, and given it a quick, rust-inhibiting wipe with his oily rag. Everyone hopes that summer will be a belter; some of the businesses around Litterdale couldn't survive two disastrous summers in a row.

There are one or two people in the neighbourhood – no names, no packdrill – who believe their front gardens aren't complete without a burning mattress and a clapped-out car propped up on house-bricks. Bill doesn't share their aesthetic, of course; a tourism officer has to lead the way in keeping Litterdale looking its best. So Bill's cottage garden, overlooking the village green, will bloom in colourful profusion this year, as it does every year.

Spring has finally arrived in Litterdale. People we haven't clapped eyes on since last October are crawling out of the woodwork, pale and blinking after another long winter of sunlight deprivation. If winter is like being hermetically sealed inside a Tupperware container, spring is like an unseen hand prising the lid off.

There are sights to cheer the most jaded souls. Colour is returning to the landscape, like the blush to a maiden's cheek. The grass is greening up. The trees around the old packhorse bridge are laden down with blossom; from a distance it looks like freshly-popped popcorn. The scene is softened, for a few days at least, by these candy-floss colours of spring. It's like being in a particularly sentimental Walt Disney cartoon; you half expect a flock of bluebirds to land on your shoulder and trill in three-part harmony.

The trees are filling with songbirds, their little chests puffed out with springtime fervour. What they are actually singing about is anyone's guess. We like to imagine it's a heartfelt paean of love, from a cock bird to his mate, as she puts the finishing touches to her nest. Or maybe it's something rather more prosaic, like 'This is my tree… piss off'. Who knows for sure?

The spring sunshine penetrates the darkest, cobweb-strewn corners of our homes – revealing what havoc has been wreaked by another winter of household neglect. Squalor shames us into action, leaving us with difficult choices: should we clean the cooker or just move house? We wave feather dusters around, without much enthusiasm, succeeding only in whipping up the dust in thick clouds. Over recent months a deep layer of dust has helped to lag pipes, stop draughts and impart a silvery bloom to the furniture. But now the dust seems to dance in the rays of light. It's Disney dust.

The harsh spring light makes a searching examination of our lives too, with rather more clarity than we either need or want. We feel a strong urge to shake ourselves out of our lethargy. And, with our failings and foibles mercilessly exposed, this is a good opportunity to take stock. New Year is no time to make life-changing resolutions; the time for self-improvement is *now*.

This is the time to get fit, to keep those promises to walk down to the paper shop instead of just taking the car. Pessimists can watch the blossom blowing away in the first stiff breeze. Optimists, on the other hand, can give their boots a coat of dubbin, pack a rucksac with sandwiches and Kendal Mint Cake, take a deep breath of good country air and set out to enjoy a Peakland ramble in the sweet springtime air.

That's what Bill's going to do this weekend. Mind you, he's already planning another departmental get-together; maybe a long weekend just after Christmas, somewhere a little closer to Alton Towers, to dream up another snappy name for the unseemly clamour to claim the tourism pound. 'Tourism 2003' is an early favourite, but let's not be too hasty.

Like swallows but bigger – and with wallets – the visitors are back. With each weekend that passes, the car-park gets busier. Purposeful walkers lace up their boots and, keeping their wallets tightly closed, head for the hills. Others – the moochers, the grockles, the rubbernecks – need a little more entertaining. As long as that's a pub lunch, or shopping for nick-nacks, then we can oblige. Litterdale isn't Disneyland, but we're still happy to take day-trippers for a ride.

What about the visitors who want a bed for the night and a hearty breakfast next morning? Mandy, Littledale's New Age representative, opened her doors to guests a couple of years ago. With mixed success, it must be said. The sign in the front garden of Primrose Cottage promised 'Bed and Breakfast', whetting the appetites of passers-by with such luxuries as 'flush toilets', 'wall-to-wall carpeting' and 'hot and cold running water in every room'. Primrose Cottage had been 'Officially vermin-free since 1999', not a claim that every house in Litterdale could match. Despite these proud boasts, visitors weren't exactly beating a path to Primrose Cottage.

When Mandy bought the place, it was a picturesque ruin. The wind whistled through the cracks in the window frames, like Larry Adler tuning up. She 'cured' the leaky roof by the simple ruse of not venturing into the loft any more, and masked the more malodorous smells with incense. There was a greasy, grey-green Galapagos beneath the bathtub, where plants that shunned light could quietly thrive. She coped with the grime and neglect in the only way she knew how, by using dimmer lightbulbs. By the time she was down to 4-watt bulbs, she was bumping into the furniture.

When it all got too much Mandy would sit cross-legged, wherever she could find an uncluttered area of floor, and resort to a tried and tested mantra. 'I am happy, fulfilled and brimming with self-confidence,' she would drone, morosely. 'I know my own worth and I have well-defined goals. I have much to offer the world, and my well-rounded personality will attract luck, money and love. I see only positive things happening to me in future.'

Primrose Cottage was a loose rung on the property ladder. The only way she would ever be able to sell the place was by dismantling it and auctioning off the bricks as individual lots. In desperation she bought a new self-help book. After a brief perusal of *How to Attract Money into your Life*, she did as the author suggested, and visualised coins of many denominations pouring out of a golden cornucopia and into her cupped hands. The results exceeded the wildest expectations of everyone except Mandy. After a decent interval of six months, a distant cousin died, leaving Mandy a tidy sum in her will. Sceptics may mock such credulity, but the cheque went into Mandy's bank account, not theirs. Perhaps these books really do work, after all.

Mandy adopted a two-pronged strategy for renovating Primrose Cottage. She's a firm believer in Feng Shui, the venerable Chinese art of stating the blatantly obvious. By harnessing these principles to the proven power of ready cash, Mandy hoped to breathe new life into the house.

With the help of a local builder who knew which side his bread was buttered, she put the kitchen where the bathroom was, converted the box-room into an en-suite bathroom, raised the roof by two feet and created three more bedrooms. She had the house sand-blasted but, intriguingly, only on the inside. A plan to move the entire house three feet to the south ('to get the morning sun') was abandoned, but only with the greatest reluctance.

The work is nearly finished. The last item on the agenda is to have the overflowing rubbish skip taken away. An eyesore it may be, but how on earth did we manage before the humble rubbish skip was invented? Belying its humble appearance, a skip is actually a sophisticated recycling system – proving that one man's rubbish is, indeed, another man's treasure. When we hire a skip we are, albeit unwittingly, inviting our neighbours to indulge in a traditional, two-part ritual. It happens all over the country, and it goes like this.

Step one: wait until the attention of the skip-hirer has been momentarily distracted. In the few seconds it takes to tie a shoe-lace, or rummage through a handbag for the car-keys, there is just enough time for doors to open and for neighbours, laden down with unwanted possessions, to tip-toe purposefully towards the skip. When the skip-hirer turns around to look at the skip again, he does a deadpan double-take of the kind that a white-faced Buster Keaton all but patented. The last door is closing, noiselessly, and the skip (*his* skip) is filled to overflowing with other people's detritus.

Step two: this is conducted at a more leisurely pace. Over the next couple of days, the neighbours give the contents of the skip a cursory examination as they walk past, followed, under cover of darkness, by furtive forays to liberate perfectly serviceable stuff that others have so casually thrown away. There's wood to burn. And a chair: a perfectly fine chair that will look as good as new after a lick of paint. And that old radio; it probably only needs fresh batteries. And so it continues. By day three the skip will be almost empty once again, allowing the hirer to fill it with his, or in this case, her own junk. Job's a good 'un…

Even the most sceptical villager is impressed by Mandy's efforts. After all the upheavals Primrose Cottage is looking good. Here's an object lesson in how to transform a sow's ear into the proverbial silk purse. She will be opening her doors to guests any day now. We hope things go well, and that the days of food poisoning and private prosecutions will be nothing more than distant memories.

SUMMER

We spent a small fortune, a couple of years ago, on what we were reliably informed was a solar-powered sundial. It seemed an appropriate way to commemorate the Millennium. It was only when we'd put it into position on the village green that some bright spark said that every sundial is solar powered. Yes, we'd been had. And every time we saw the accursed thing, it just served to remind us how silly we'd been. So we took it down. In any case, why would anyone want to remember the Millennium? It's been and gone. Good riddance, we say.

We should have learned our lesson by now. Nevertheless, a lot of villagers were keen for Litterdale to mark the Queen's Golden Jubilee with something more tangible than a monumental hangover. But with the coffers empty after the sundial shambles, we needed to raise more money. The traditional method, here in Litterdale, is to rattle a collecting tin under the noses of drinkers while they're enjoying a pint in either the Swan or the Fox.

The well-heeled patrons of the Swan will dip their hands in their pockets if a tin is rattled loud and long enough. But it's a strange irony that the rougher the pub, the more money the regulars seem to raise for charity. And few pubs in the Litterdale area are rougher that the Fox. It's the sort of pub where bogus MOT certificates can be had for the price of a pint. And if you win more than 50p on the fruit machine, the biggest problem is getting out alive. But when it comes to charity, you only have to mention children or animals to have big men with broken noses getting dewy-eyed and sentimental.

They'll peel fivers from suspiciously thick wads of notes, eased out of back pockets. They'll erect piles of pennies on the bar. They'll organise all kinds of events – often involving feats of brute strength or dressing up in women's clothing. So when the landlord suggested a duck race, to raise money for the jubilee fund, the idea went down well. Even after the disappointment of learning that no real ducks were involved, the regulars were keen to roll up their sleeves and muck in.

They bought 3000 yellow plastic ducks from a place that sold yellow plastic ducks in bulk; it's amazing what you can find in the *Yellow Pages*. Every duck had a different number painted on its bottom, and visitors and locals alike were encouraged to 'buy' one. Sales were bouyant, thanks to the terrific prizes donated by local businesses. First prize: A luxury weekend, all expenses paid, at Primrose Cottage Guest House. Second prize: A free session with a visiting chiropodist. Third prize: Dinner for two at the Fox (pudding not included). By the time the great day had arrived, all the ducks were spoken for. So far, so good.

The River Litter is a watercourse of many moods: a mere trickle in high summer, a roaring torrent after winter rain. Sometimes it misbehaves – like last year when it sluiced through our homes. But mostly it goes quietly about its business.

On the day of the Duck Race, crowds lined both sides of the river in eager anticipation. A net was stretched taut between the stanchions of the old packhorse bridge, the finishing line, to catch the ducks. Two hundred yards out of town, upstream where the main road crosses the river, a tipper truck full of ducks was backed over the parapet. On an agreed signal, 3000 yellow ducks slid from the back of the truck and hit the water simultaneously.

The event, as a genuine race, was over there and then. The breeze, though light, was still stronger than the river's sluggish current.

Three thousand yellow ducks massed together, like the Zulus at Rourke's Drift. But instead of rushing pell-mell downstream, the ducks closed ranks and sullenly refused to move. When the breeze quickened it merely pushed ducks to the water margins, where they got stuck in the reeds.

After half an hour, a few dozen ducks had floated as far as the weir where, years ago, water was diverted towards the waterwheel of the old mill. But instead of taking the plunge, the ducks floated around in ever-decreasing circles. After an hour of surreal inaction, the crowd began to get restless. Little kids, blessed with the attention spans of particularly inattentive goldfish, were demanding chips and ice cream. People started to throw stones. Stewards waded into the water and tried to hurry the ducks along. Men fell over and got drenched; people laughed; words were exchanged. The ducks remained mockingly uncooperative.

A few ducks eventually arrived at the finishing line, but only because they'd been thrown there. 'It's a fix,' shouted those onlookers who hadn't already drifted away. What a shambles.

The *Litterdale Times* subsequently printed this statement from a Duck Race spokesman, who asked to remain anonymous. 'It is difficult to know what to say about the shameful events of last weekend. We are stunned. The entire duck-racing community is stunned. We have witnessed many sporting disasters in recent times. The abortive Grand National of 1993. Mike Tyson chewing Evander Holyfield's ear off. Derek Pringle. But these are as nothing compared to Saturday's debacle. The river level was unseasonably low, making the going firmer than we (or the ducks) would have liked. Some people in the crowd suggested the ducks weren't trying, though it was probably their boos and catcalls that disorientated the ducks and made them swim around in circles. No-one comes out of this fiasco with much dignity. There will be a steward's enquiry. Heads will roll. Thank you.'

Beneath this terse statement was a display advert: 'Almost 3000 plastic ducks for sale. Nearly new. No sensible offer refused.'

The winning duck, incidentally, was number 475, bought by the landlord of the Fox. He has decided not to take up his prize, but to raffle it at a later date. In the meantime he has decided to take a short holiday, and will not be available for further comment about the Duck Race, or anything else for that matter.

✹

The village is a magnet on sunny weekends; people come from miles around to celebrate the fact that the banks are shut. Two kinds of motorists feel drawn to explore the narrow, twisty lanes around Litterdale. There are those who want to pootle around at a stately 20mph ('Oh look, dear, a cow. And there, if I'm not mistaken, is another one.' 'More tea, dear?' 'I don't mind if I do'), and those who see the Peakland hills as a race-track, their very own Indianapolis 500. The prospect of these motorists sharing the same stretch of road is not one to savour. It's a convincing argument for Litterdale folk to stay home, draw the curtains and watch a re-run of *The Italian Job* on TV. Compared to the mayhem on our country roads, those Mini drivers look like paragons of courtesy.

For some unfathomable reason, Litterdale fills up with the sort of vehicles we only ever see in summer. Ancient VW vans announce their arrival with heart-stopping backfires, palls of diesel smoke and unlikely slogans ('Kathmandu or Bust', 'Just one Careful Owner') painted on the side. They give Litterdale the attractive look of a car-breaker's yard.

Visitors park up their beach buggies, soft-tops and natty little sports cars around the village green, so that everyone has the opportunity to admire them. Having shelled out a small fortune for new, in-car stereo systems, the proud owners naturally want to turn up the volume, crank up the bass, and hear what it sounds like. And where better to conduct this aural experiment than a tranquil Peakland village? As anyone living within five miles of Litterdale is painfully aware, it sounds like a man armed with a leg of lamb trying to break out of an IKEA wardrobe.

Last month's disastrous Duck Race left a lot of people with red faces. Not the ducks themselves, of course, which maintained their air of jaundiced inscrutability throughout the proceedings, and the stewards' enquiry that followed. A lot of people, particularly those whose ducks had failed to finish the course, wanted the winners dope-tested. The race organisers refused, mostly due to a sudden outbreak of common sense. We've moved on, thank goodness, and visitors to Litterdale this summer are enjoying a wide choice of family events.

The Green Weekend has been and gone. It was a great success, by all accounts. Even folk living in rural Derbyshire are glad to be reminded, on a sunny weekend, that the world is going to hell in a handbasket. Shopkeepers and café proprietors appreciated the extra business, even those who'd happily vote for nuclear power and badger baiting.

Local pressure groups had stalls on the green, offering good advice. Why pay exhorbitant heating bills, the crowds were asked, when they could harness the power of the sun? And, yes, solar power might seem to make sense in a place like Litterdale, what with its sunny winters and balmy summers. But the truth is rather different. We've got to face up to the fact, no matter how unpalatable it may be, that solar power is just not as sustainable as these eco-warriors suggest. If you leave your solar powered torch on charge by mistake, the next day will be cloudy and dull. Just coincidence? I don't think so.

Wave power is being touted as the Next Big Thing. Poppycock. If we start sucking the energy out of the waves, the seven oceans of the world will soon be as flat as millponds. It stands to reason. And it's been estimated, by people with too much time on their hands, that the methane produced by cattle would meet most of the world's energy needs. All we need is a way to collect it. Yes, if we listened to these well-meaning folk, the earth would be not only a better place, but flat too.

We were told that the Men of the Trees would make an appearance over the Green Weekend. But they had to cancel (a bad experience with a blackthorn, apparently). Their place was taken by Theresa

Green, 'a well-known arboreal activist' according to her business card. She gave a short, heartfelt address, asking us all to think twice about felling trees. 'Would we cut trees down so blithely if we could hear them screaming?' she asked. Well, we might, if they screamed all night and kept us awake.

Of course, once you advertise a Green Weekend, you tend to attract the lunatic fringe too. A 'Honk if You Love Peace and Quiet' campaign had a mixed reception. And the 'Put the Landfill Site Where the Poor People Live' petition is yet to reap rewards. But give it time.

Let's be straight. 'Looking after the planet for future generations' makes a useful, if meaningless, slogan. But, as Old Ted points out, we'd be more concerned about saving the planet if these self-appointed 'greens' could answer this one simple question: 'What on earth have those future generations ever done for *us*?'

Never mind. It's the height of Summer. Foot and mouth is a distant memory (and let's hope it stays that way). Visitors still come to Litterdale; however much we moan about them, we'd be moaning a whole lot more if they decided to stay away.

✳

Life is a gamble; from the cradle to the grave. Even in a quiet, well-ordered community such as Litterdale, danger stalks the unwary. As Old Ted knows only too well, you can be perched on a bar stool one minute, exchanging pleasantries with the landlord of the Swan, and a moment later you can be choking on a honey roasted peanut that went down the wrong way. An immovable object lodged in the windpipe isn't something you can write to an agony aunt about. It concentrates the mind, wonderfully, like having a pistol pointed at your head. Time is of the essence. Yes, if Dr Harris and his wife hadn't been enjoying an all-you-can-eat Sunday lunch in the carvery, Old Ted might have become just one more statistic in the annals of snack-related injuries.

If you'd asked Ted about the Heimlich Manoeuvre up to that point, he'd have guessed it was a Second World War stratagem aimed at opening up the Russian front. But, red-faced, bug-eyed and gesticulating wildly, he was in no position to argue as the doctor, moving remarkably quickly for a big man, sized up the situation. Dr Harris approached Ted from behind and took him in a huge bear hug; it looked like he was lifting a sack of potatoes. With no time for social niceties, the doctor drove his clenched fists, with irresistible force, into Ted's solar plexus. The peanut was expelled with such velocity that it ricocheted off two walls, before embedding itself harmlessly in a bowl of guacamole. Old Ted was so grateful that he allowed the doctor to buy him a drink.

Life's a gamble all right, though we're not too good at reckoning the odds. We'll happily spend a quid or two on the lottery, even though the odds of winning the jackpot are a distant 14,000,000 to one. 'It could be us,' we tell ourselves, with the optimism of the doomed. Yet when we hear similar odds against a nuclear meltdown at Sellafield, we dismiss the idea as 'impossible'. It's flawed thinking like this that provides the bookies in town with a good living. There probably isn't a punter alive prepared to admit that he loses more money on the horses than he wins. So the bookies drive Jaguars, and maybe trade up to a newer model every couple of years, while their customers stand around waiting for the bus to come.

We don't have any bookmakers in Litterdale, so a man with money burning a hole in his pocket tends to gravitate towards the Fox, where the landlord combines his strenuous duties as a waterer of beer and purveyor of pork scratchings with the role of bookie's runner. There's racing on the telly every Saturday afternoon, and an open phone line to the bookies in town. The landlord has mounted the TV high on the wall. The regulars have to crane their necks to watch the 2.30 from Kempton, which helps to makes the beer go down quicker.

With the curtains pulled tight, to keep out the August sunshine, the Fox even feels like a bookies. The regulars scrutinise the racing pages, running stubby fingers down the columns of figures. It's like being an accountant, but doing it for fun. They know all about the runners and the riders, the favourites and the form. They all seem to have inside information (from the horse's mouth, perhaps?). With all these hot tips and dead certs being shared – conspiratorially, like playground secrets – it's hard to know why these guys don't win more often.

Actually, it's losing that they enjoy. They wouldn't admit it, of course, but it's true. Winning would create all sorts of problems: how to hide the money from their wives, for example, and how to avoid standing a celebratory round at the bar. Losing, in contrast, is a male bonding ritual that creates a warm feeling of comradeship. Everyone's in the same boat. Skint.

Anyone who reckons that men don't talk about their feelings should listen to a punter whose horse was way out in front ('twelve to one, it was... *twelve to one!*'), only for the nag to fall, inexplicably, at the very last fence. It's easier to blame life's disappointments on duff horses and useless jockeys than to confront their own shortcomings. If it costs a quid or two each week, isn't that better than just frittering their money away?

Anyone who doubts that life is, indeed, a lottery should try cycling. Those who take to two wheels know all there is to know about white-knuckle rides. Nobody gives way to cyclists, or 'organ donors' as they're known down at the A & E Department. Even when they take refuge in bus-lanes, they have to share them with taxis and buses: the cyclists' natural predators. A nasty accident is never more than a heartbeat away.

Cycling is an 'all or nothing' kind of deal these days. You can't just go for a bike ride any more; you have to buy into the whole cycling lifestyle. If you wear something sensible – a tweed jacket, perhaps, and a hat with ear-flaps – you'll be shunned by other cyclists. But if you wear what *they* wear (a helmet that looks like a pound of over-ripe bananas and figure-hugging Lycra in a variety of day-glo colours, embellished with a stripe of mud all the way up the back) you'll be openly mocked by everybody else. Prat or pariah, it's not an easy choice to make.

No wonder cyclists like to get out of town, and head for quiet Peakland lanes. Litterdale is a magnet for Lycra louts. Especially at this time of year, when sunny weekends encourage them to pedal out here, sit in a café where the tables and chairs are bolted to the floor, drink strong tea out of chipped mugs, and discuss the pressing matters of the day. No, just kidding, they talk about bikes. Of course.

✹